Unruly

qui a non la uictoire pour la uictoire
que dieu out donnee a lui et a son fil.
Et comment les englox trairent mon
seigneur loois quit il fu passez en engleterre

lez la cite de senliz qui a non la uictou
re de lordre saint uictor de paris. en
memoire et en remembrance de si gi
uictoire comme dieu leur out donnee
poi de iours passerent aprez que

Unruly

A History of England's Kings and Queens

DAVID MITCHELL

MICHAEL  JOSEPH

MICHAEL JOSEPH

UK | USA | Canada | Ireland | Australia
India | New Zealand | South Africa

Michael Joseph is part of the Penguin Random House group of companies
whose addresses can be found at global.penguinrandomhouse.com.

First published 2023
001

Copyright © David Mitchell, 2023

The moral right of the author has been asserted

Set in 13.25/16pt Garamond MT Std
Typeset by Jouve (UK), Milton Keynes
Printed and bound in Great Britain by Clays Ltd, Elcograf S.p.A.

The authorized representative in the EEA is Penguin Random House Ireland,
Morrison Chambers, 32 Nassau Street, Dublin D02 YH68

A CIP catalogue record for this book is available from the British Library

HARDBACK ISBN: 978–1–405–95317–7
TRADE PAPERBACK ISBN: 978–1–405–95318–4

To Victoria and Barbara

List of Rulers

NOTABLE ANGLO-SAXON KINGS

Aethelberht of Kent *c.*590–616
Aethelfrith of Bernicia *c.*592–616
Raedwald of East Anglia *c.*599–*c.*625
Edwin of Northumbria *c.*616–633
Eanfrith of Bernicia 633–634
Oswald of Northumbria *c.*634–*c.*642
Penda of Mercia *c.*626–*c.*655
Oswiu of Northumbria *c.*655–670
Ecgfrith of Northumbria 670–685
Caedwalla of Wessex *c.*685–*c.*688
Aethelbald of Mercia 716–757
Ceolwulf of Northumbria 729–737
Offa of Mercia 757–796
Coenwulf of Mercia 796–821
Egbert of Wessex 827–839
Aethelwulf of Wessex 839–858
Edmund of East Anglia 856–869
Aethelbald of Wessex 858–860
Aethelberht of Wessex 860–866
Aethelred of Wessex 866–871
Alfred the Great 871–899
Edward the Elder 899–924

THE FIRST KINGS OF ENGLAND

Athelstan 924–939
Edmund 939–946
Eadred 946–955
Eadwig 955–959
Edgar the Peaceful 959–975
Edward the Martyr 975–978
Aethelred the Unready 978–1013, 1014–1016
Sweyn Forkbeard 1013–1014
Edmund Ironside 1016–1016
Cnut the Great 1016–1035

Harold Harefoot 1035–1040
Harthacnut 1040–1042
Edward the Confessor 1042–1066
Harold Godwinson 1066–1066

NORMAN KINGS

William I 1066–1087
William II 1087–1100
Henry I 1100–1135
Stephen 1135–1154

PLANTAGENET KINGS

Henry II 1154–1189
Richard I 1189–1199
John 1199–1216
Henry III 1216–1272
Edward I 1272–1307
Edward II 1307–1327
Edward III 1327–1377
Richard II 1377–1399

HOUSE OF LANCASTER

Henry IV 1399–1413
Henry V 1413–1422
Henry VI 1422–1461, 1470–1471

HOUSE OF YORK

Edward IV 1461–1470, 1471–1483
Edward V 1483–1483
Richard III 1483–1485

HOUSE OF TUDOR

Henry VII 1485–1509
Henry VIII 1509–1547
Edward VI 1547–1553
Lady Jane Grey 1553–1553
Mary I 1553–1558
Elizabeth I 1558–1603

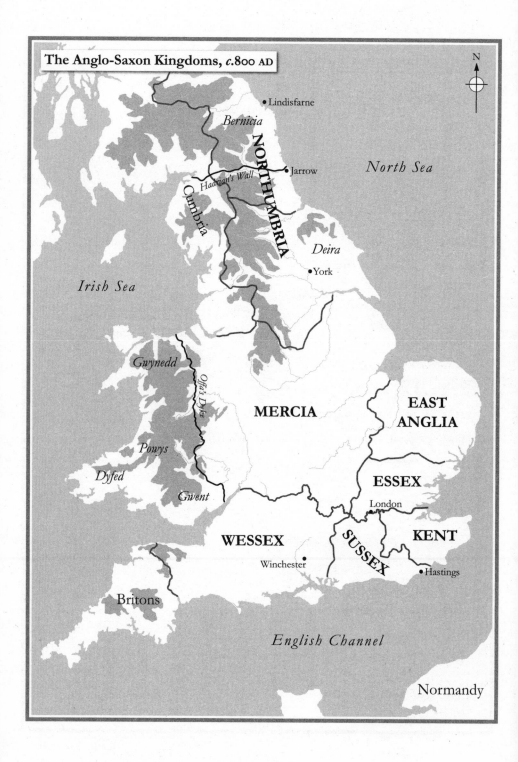

The Anglo-Saxon Kingdoms, *c.*800 AD

N

• Lindisfarne

Bernicia

NORTHUMBRIA

• Jarrow

North Sea

Hadrian's Wall

Cumbria

Deira

• York

Irish Sea

Gwynedd

Offa's Dyke

MERCIA

**EAST
ANGLIA**

Powys

Dyfed

ESSEX

Gwent

London •

WESSEX

SUSSEX

KENT

Winchester •

• Hastings

Britons

English Channel

Normandy

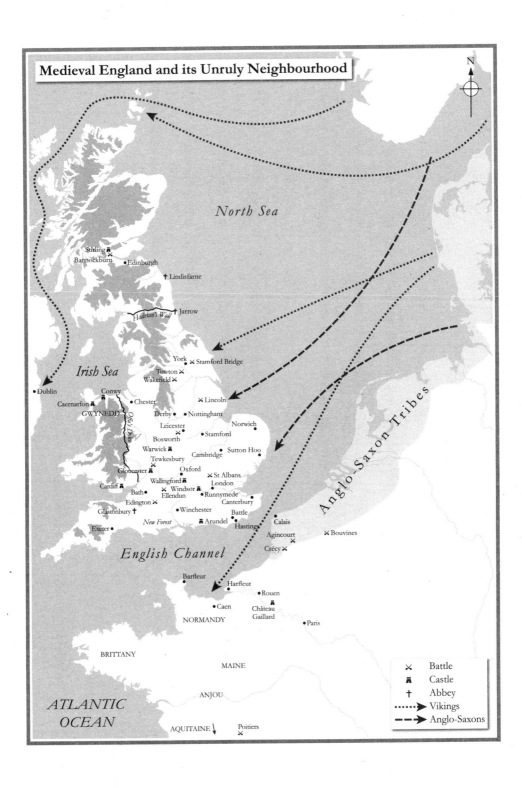

Medieval England and its Unruly Neighbourhood

N

North Sea

Stirling
Bannockburn
Edinburgh
† Lindisfarne
Hadrian's Wall † Jarrow

Irish Sea

York ✗ Stamford Bridge
Towton ✗
Wakefield ✗

• Dublin

Conwy ✗ Lincoln
Caernarfon • Chester
GWYNEDD Derby • Nottingham Norwich
Leicester • Stamford
Bosworth Sutton Hoo
Warwick Cambridge
Tewkesbury
Gloucester Oxford ✗ St Albans
Wallingford London
Cardiff Windsor • Runnymede
Bath ✗ Ellendun Canterbury
Edington ✗ • Winchester
Glastonbury † • Battle
New Forest Arundel Hastings • Calais
Exeter • Agincourt ✗ Bouvines
Crécy ✗

Anglo-Saxon Tribes

English Channel

Barfleur
Harfleur
• Rouen
• Caen Château
Gaillard
NORMANDY • Paris

BRITTANY

MAINE

ANJOU

ATLANTIC
OCEAN

AQUITAINE ↓ Poitiers
✗

✗	Battle
🏰	Castle
†	Abbey
••••••►	Vikings
━ ━►	Anglo-Saxons

House of Wessex (or Cerdic)

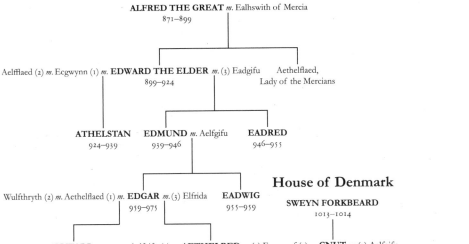

ALFRED THE GREAT *m.* Ealhswith of Mercia
871–899

Aelfflaed (2) *m.* Ecgwynn (1) *m.* **EDWARD THE ELDER** *m.* (3) Eadgifu   Aethelflaed,
899–924   Lady of the Mercians

ATHELSTAN   **EDMUND** *m.* Aelfgifu   **EADRED**
924–939   939–946   946–955

House of Denmark

Wulfthryth (2) *m.* Aethelflaed (1) *m.* **EDGAR** *m.* (3) Elfrida   **EADWIG**
959–975   955–959

SWEYN FORKBEARD
1013–1014

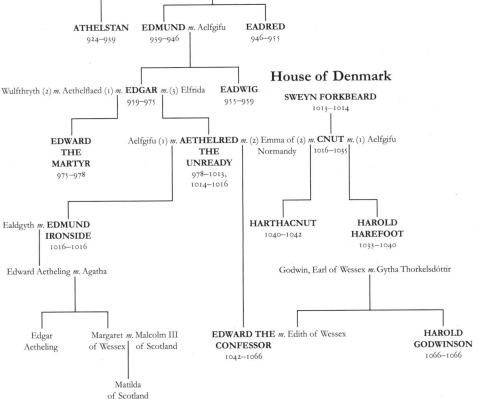

**EDWARD
THE
MARTYR**
975–978

Aelfgifu (1) *m.* **AETHELRED** *m.* (2) Emma of (2) *m.* **CNUT** *m.* (1) Aelfgifu
**THE
UNREADY**
978–1013,
1014–1016
Normandy   1016–1035

Ealdgyth *m.* **EDMUND
IRONSIDE**
1016–1016

HARTHACNUT
1040–1042

**HAROLD
HAREFOOT**
1035–1040

Edward Aetheling *m.* Agatha

Godwin, Earl of Wessex *m.* Gytha Thorkelsdóttir

Edgar
Aetheling

Margaret *m.* Malcolm III
of Wessex | of Scotland

EDWARD THE *m.* Edith of Wessex
CONFESSOR
1042–1066

**HAROLD
GODWINSON**
1066–1066

Matilda
of Scotland

House of Normandy

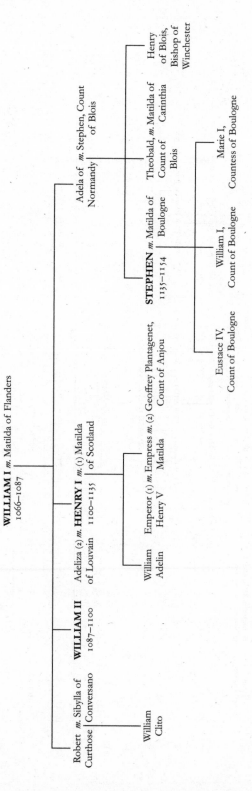

House of Plantagenet

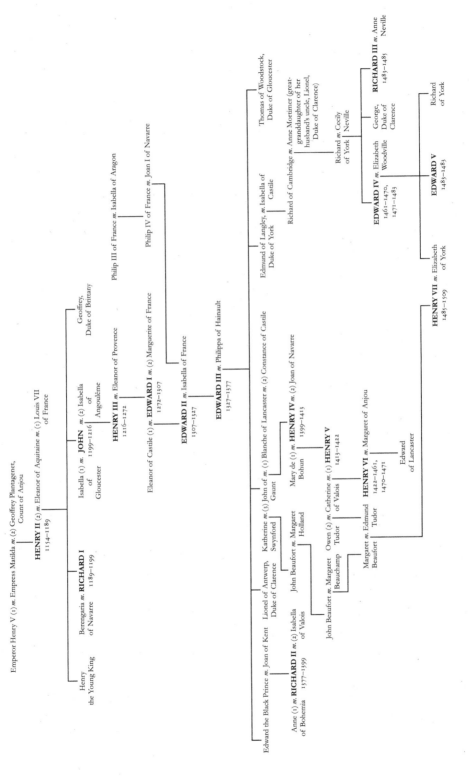

House of Tudor

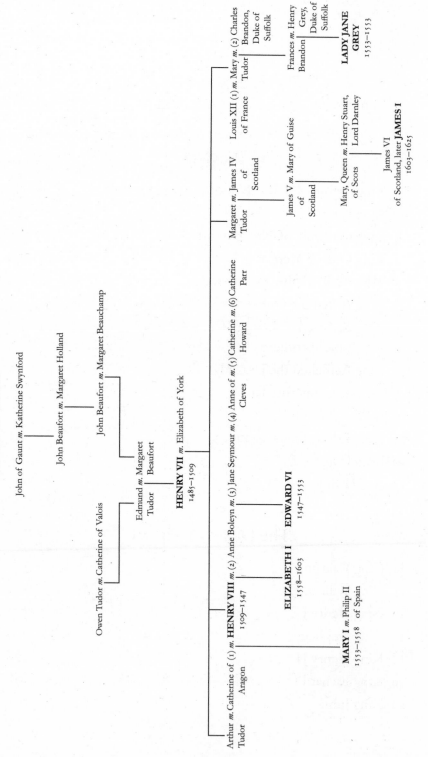

John of Gaunt *m.* Katherine Swynford

John Beaufort *m.* Margaret Holland

John Beaufort *m.* Margaret Beauchamp

Owen Tudor *m.* Catherine of Valois

Edmund *m.* Margaret
Tudor   Beaufort

HENRY VII *m.* Elizabeth of York
1485–1509

Arthur *m.* Catherine of (1) *m.* **HENRY VIII** *m.* (2) Anne Boleyn *m.* (3) Jane Seymour *m.* (4) Anne of *m.* (5) Catherine *m.* (6) Catherine
Tudor   Aragon   1509–1547   Cleves   Howard   Parr

MARY I *m.* Philip II
1553–1558   of Spain

ELIZABETH I
1558–1603

EDWARD VI
1547–1553

Margaret *m.* James IV
Tudor   of
                 Scotland

James V *m.* Mary of Guise
         of
         Scotland

Mary, Queen *m.* Henry Stuart,
of Scots   Lord Darnley

James VI
of Scotland, later **JAMES I**
1603–1625

Louis XII (1) *m.* Mary *m.* (2) Charles
of France   Tudor   Brandon,
                               Duke of
                               Suffolk

Frances *m.* Henry
Brandon   Grey,
             Duke of
             Suffolk

**LADY JANE
GREY**
1553–1553

Contents

CONTENTS

PART THREE

Here Comes the Reign Again

PART FOUR

Everything's Coming Up Roses

Introduction

There was a moment in 1940, the bleakest year of the Second World War with the Wehrmacht carrying all before it, when Winston Churchill made the French government a curious offer. He suggested a merger of the British and French states. He said we could be one country for the duration of the war – the flames of our dual sovereignties would be kept alight in one state – and then, Hitler having been defeated, we could demerge and carry on.

This sort of thing is typical of Churchill. It's a big, quirky idea and he was a big believer in ideas. He had a lot of them and he was drawn to other people who had them. Most of us probably think we're believers in ideas too, but we're deluding ourselves. Believing in ideas is one of those attributes like libido or skill at driving a car that most people reckon they possess in above-average quantities – but that's mathematically impossible.

Admit it: ideas can be annoying and frightening and threatening and most of us slightly shudder whenever someone has one. The internet was an idea. So were self-service tills in supermarkets and privatizing water companies and stuffed crusts. Ideas aren't all lovely vaccines – they can be a right pain. We all like some ideas that have already been had – normal pizza, dishwashers, freedom of speech – but we don't put much faith in those that are yet to emerge. We generally think that a problem is what it is, and needs to be addressed in one of the established ways that have been handed down for addressing it. And we're usually right. When a pipe has burst, you need a plumber not a glittering-eyed futurologist saying,

'What if we could construct a world where we didn't *need* water . . . ?'

Churchill was different. He'd give that proponent of water obsolescence a fair hearing and a modest research budget. On Churchill's watch, Britain was a great power becoming increasingly strapped for resources. For Russia or America, the solution could always be more troops or more money. Britain, on the other hand, was on the look-out for deft ways of keeping up geopolitical appearances, and a clever new idea always held out that hope.

Hence, during the First World War, in the face of the Western Front's murderous deadlock, Churchill championed the idea of attacking Turkey. I think this was actually quite a sensible plan. The knackered old Ottoman Empire was a far feebler military opponent than Germany, or even Austria-Hungary. Sadly, however, the resultant Gallipoli campaign of 1915 was a fiasco that left Allied dead lying thickly along the Aegean coastline like a macabre khaki pastiche of holiday-making customs to come. It was more a screw-up of execution than of conception, but it nevertheless shows that thinking outside boxes can sometimes result in thousands of young men getting buried in them.

By 1940, several loop-the-loops later in Churchill's roller-coaster career, he was hoping this new idea would somehow prevent the surrender of France even if it were to be militarily defeated. If 'two become one', as the Spice Girls put it (in a song that weirdly turns out not to be about the proposed Anglo-French merger at all but just about having sex), then both Britain *and* France would have to be defeated before either of them could be. That was what Churchill reckoned.

The French turned down the offer. Perhaps it felt like a proposed British takeover. That might not have appealed to them at a time when resisting a German takeover was their focus. My suspicion is, though, that they simply didn't see the point of it. They had no sense that their nationhood was dependent on the mere continuity of political organs. They'd had three monarchies, two empires and three republics in the previous 150 years – they've had two more republics since. They knew that the state can be crushed and occupied and yet the country, the nation, some sense of a thing that is France, will continue to exist.

The English feel differently about themselves. Vera Lynn may have sung 'There'll always be an England', but she can't have been certain or it wouldn't have been worth claiming. Just as when someone promises 'You'll be all right!', the implication of jeopardy is clear. But what was actually threatening England, as in the geographical entity, the densely populated section of a small island? Nothing. The song was released in 1939, so predates any fears of nuclear Armageddon, and our current concerns about the climate and rising sea levels were decades in the future. Physically, Lynn must have known, England was bound to endure, the ravages of the Blitz notwithstanding. England might be made to suffer pain and indignity, many of its people might die, but of course it would remain, just like the sea and the sky.

So when Lynn or Churchill referred to England, they weren't just thinking about the place and its people. Their 'England' was a different sort of thing from a Frenchman's 'France'. To the French, Churchill's idea was nonsensical. The notion that the structure of a state, a constitution, could be a more effective vessel for Frenchness than the vast land of France was absurd. German soldiers might march all over it, but that didn't make it Germany – it would remain, whatever happened to it, France.

To Lynn and Churchill, England's existence was inextricably linked to the continuity of its institutions. And, at this point, it has to be said, when a British statesman said 'England', he often meant 'Britain'. The near eclipse of the ancient kingdom of Scotland in the British establishment's sense of national continuity is another thing that might have made the French hesitate before agreeing to Churchill's merger. The UK, the establishment assumption would have been, was primarily England. And England was predominantly not its fields, valleys, lakes, poetry, music, cuisine or folk art, but the pillars of its constitution: its empire, its church, its ancient noble families, its parliament and, first and foremost, its monarchy. For England to always be, those things must always be too.

Monarchy is what England has instead of a sense of identity. The very continuity of English government – the rule of kings morphing into the flawed parliamentary democracy of today – has resulted in our sense of nationhood, patriotism and even culture getting entwined with an institution that, practically speaking, now does little more than provide figureheads.

This has become clearer in the last few years. Britain has been feeling pretty low about itself. Fear, anger and poverty have been on the rise. The only events that have allowed us to pause, even briefly, in the constant mutual recrimination that the situation has aroused have been the Queen's Platinum Jubilee, then her death and funeral, and then the coronation of a new king.

These were the occasions that brought us together and, albeit with varying levels of irony and cynicism, allowed us to celebrate our existence. We seem to need the trappings of monarchical continuity in order to reflect contentedly upon ourselves, just as we need alcohol in order to socialize. The English have more to fear from republicanism than most – we risk losing our skimpy sense of self.

It seems subtly different with Scotland, Wales, Canada, Australia, New Zealand and the various other places England currently shares its monarchy with. And less subtly different with most other countries, where they've had revolutions and changes of constitution lots of times, and learned the largely happy lesson that they didn't lose their whole identities when they stopped having kings or gave their assemblies new names.

The English tradition of kings and queens has a lot riding on it and a lot to answer for. Its longevity, and the stability that that implies, has resulted in an England that doesn't have much else uniting it. Simply because the monarchy has never been removed, except for a brief experiment in the middle of the seventeenth century, we've never been forced to work out what else we might be other than a kingdom.

What do we stand for really? Freedom and democracy? Tradition and hierarchy? Bad food and sarcasm? Traffic and disappointment? Ships and factories? Rain and jokes? We've never agreed on anything and the royal family have long since stopped taking the lead. They just smile and keep it vague. This was the late queen's greatest talent: being the screen on to which everyone was invited to project their own views.

I don't really mean this as a criticism. I'm not sure it's healthy for a state to proclaim a unified sense of self. I used to enjoy feeling slightly contemptuous of the French and American habit of sticking their flags everywhere as if they can't get over themselves. We didn't do that in Britain. Then Boris Johnson announced, in his desperation to stoke nationalistic fervour to distract from his government's manifest failings, that the union jack must now be flown on the country's every available pole, and that small pleasure was denied me.

The fact is that, when millions of people are involved, any sense of a nation united in its values can only be portrayed by repressing the feelings and views of many. Humans don't often agree and it achieves nothing to pretend that they do. Genuine consensus is rare and open disagreement beats fake consensus. Whenever politicians mention 'British values', it's only ever to trick us. To flatter us with the thought that we're all paragons of liberty, fair play, common sense, justice, opportunity or some other concept that virtually no one outside Iran and North Korea would fail to pay lip service to.

Still, as we become less comfortable about our imperial past, and as Scotland and Wales seek solace in their own distinct cultural identities, the majority of Great Britain's citizens, the English, are left puzzling over what they're supposed to feel collectively. The ferocious interest that many of us are taking in the rift between Harry and Meghan on the one hand and Charles, Camilla, William and Kate on the other may be a side effect of this. Are we hoping that, in that row, we can find some answers? Is that why, even though it's just a family quarrel among strangers, we're drawn to it as if it's a soap opera made of crack?

We look to the royals because we look to the past and royalty emerged from the past. England's identity is England's history. More than with any other nation I can think of, the two concepts seem synonymous. Leaders talk of the future, about becoming a modern, thrusting, caring superpower of enterprise or greenness or science or education – and we nod along. But who really feels that's what England is?

As I confront my own puzzled sense of national identity, I have reached for the best way of explaining my own people, and people in general, and that's history. So this book may be about all the kings and queens who ruled England – and it's mainly kings, the olden days being, among many many many other flaws, extremely sexist – but it's not really about the past. It's about history. History the school subject, the hobby, the atmosphere, the wonky drawings of kings, the grist to heritage's mill-that's-been-converted-into-a-café, the sense of identity.

History is a very contemporary thing – it's ours to think about, manipulate, use to win arguments or to justify patriotism, nationalism or group self-loathing, according to taste. In contrast, the past is unknowable. It's as complicated as the present. It's an infinity of former nows all as unfathomable as this one. That's why historians end up specializing in tiny bits of it.

For England, in particular, history is about who we collectively are and how we feel about it. It's one of the attempted answers to the great human question: what the hell is going on? Most animals don't ask that question, which is why you can put a massive Ikea next to a field of sheep and they just keep on grazing. Not even twenty minutes of bleats and gestures and questioning looks, they're just not interested. But a vast amount of human endeavour is an attempt to answer it in different ways: all the sciences and all the humanities. Microscopes, philosophies, expeditions, religions and poems are all having a go.

Of all of those attempted answers, history is the one I reach for first. After all, if you walk into a room and someone's standing on a table waving a gun and someone else is having a wee in the fireplace and there's an enormous bowl of trifle in the middle of the floor in which a terrier has drowned and, on the TV, it's nine minutes into a DVD of *One of Our Dinosaurs is Missing*, and you ask that great human question, then the best answer is a history. What happened before is the best explanation of what happened next. It's more pertinent than getting into how dogs evolved or the functioning of the human kidney or the economics of 1970s cinema.

This book, then, is an anecdotal attempted explanation of England, focusing on what I find most interesting. More often than not, that has something to do with a person wearing a sparkly metal hat. If you think that sounds silly then remember: in Britain today, pictures of that hat are everywhere – on stonework, signs, documents and websites. The hat is still doing what the first bossy and brutal man who ever put it on meant it to do: conveying authority and asserting power.

PART ONE
Pre-Willy

1. King Arthur

He didn't exist. That's the headline. It's a disappointing start, I know, but it's an early sign of how tricky history can be. England's (though more usually Britain's, but often Wales's and Cornwall's, sometimes Brittany's) most famous king turns out to be fictional. That's putting it politely. Gandalf is fictional. King Arthur is a lie.

Some people will still say he might have existed, but the sort of person they say he might have been is so far removed from King Arthur in any of the forms we understand him that it feels like they're just saying he didn't exist in a different way. It's like they're saying, 'Oh yeah, there was a real Superman except he didn't have any actual superpowers and he dressed as a bat.'

For the avoidance of doubt, and of a catastrophic collapse in readers' confidence in the first chapter, let me make clear that I realize Batman also did not exist.

Who do people say 'the real' King Arthur might have been? Perhaps a Roman officer who served in Britain, or a Romano-British chieftain, or a Welsh king – some senior figure who lived at any point from the third to the sixth century (the 200s to the 500s). Someone like that, the idea goes, might have been the bit of real grit in the imagination oyster that turned into the Arthurian pearl.

Personally, I don't think imagination oysters need real grit any more than metaphorical bonnets need real bees. What caused the Arthur pearl was the persistent longing of humans, of almost all eras and cultures, to hark back to something better. It's a far more enduring psychological habit than a belief in progress. People found it much easier to believe in a rose-tinted view of the past than a utopian future. They still do: hence 'Take Back Control' and 'Make America Great Again'.

For most of the period covered by this book, any claims or attempts by leaders to change or improve things are most persuasively labelled, to the people of the time, as restorations of some kind. Saying that something was totally new often played badly. The ultimate, most glorious restoration would be to the golden age of King Arthur.

We get most of our sense of King Arthur from Geoffrey of Monmouth, who completed his *Historia Regum Britanniae* (*History of the Kings of Britain*) in 1138, and from Sir Thomas Malory, whose fifteenth-century *Le Morte d'Arthur* (*The Death of Arthur*) was, in 1485, one of the first books to be printed in England. That gave the Arthur myth wider circulation. There's now been so much talk about King Arthur over the centuries that many people feel, like they do with ghosts, that 'there must be something in it'. There is: it just happens to be deep-seated psychological need rather than historical reality.

The story of Arthur reflects our longing, as a species, for the ancient, concealed and magical. Towards the end of *Le Morte d'Arthur*, Malory suggests the title is not the spoiler it seems: 'Yet some men say in many parts of England that King Arthur is not dead, but had gone by the will of our Lord Jesu into another place; and . . . many men say that there is written upon his tomb this verse: *Hic jacet Arthurus, Rex quondam, Rexque futurus*' (Here lies Arthur, the once and future king).

This is great stuff and poses a haunting and exciting question: will King Arthur return? It's clever because, as well as being haunting and exciting, it's a leading question, of the 'When did you start taking cocaine?' kind. Whether you answer yes or no, you've accidentally accepted the premise that Arthur existed.

The dates of those two books explain why Arthur, supposedly a fifth- or sixth-century ruler, looks like a medieval king in most of the surviving imagery. To us, King Arthur is an olde-worlde figure – to the people of the middle ages he was in modern dress. They imagined him like a contemporary king but less shit – a paragon of justice, might and legitimacy.

He could be whomever and whatever they needed. What he was king of, in the most real sense, is Albion. And what is Albion? Its poetic and ancient connotations go beyond merely being the old name for Britain. It's pretty much whatever you want it to be: an English Britain, a Welsh Britain, a Scottish Britain, a Celtic Britain, an ancient British Britain – a nice version of here.

So, while King Arthur didn't exist, the idea of him is lurking, guiltily or inspiringly, in the minds of many of the rulers who did.

2. King King

Another thing that didn't exist in the sixth century was England. No one called it that for hundreds of years. It's impossible to know exactly how many years, though, as there was no official rebranding moment. It wasn't like when Royal Mail became Consignia, or Andersen Consulting became Accenture, or Consignia became Royal Mail. There wasn't a day when all the signs saying 'Britannia' got taken down. There was no signage. Hardly anyone could read. Those last two sentences can be applied to most of human history, so I hope you're not expecting this book to be about anything nice.

England was a word that gradually gained currency, like mansplain or staycation, and it was fully in use by the time William the Conqueror was king of it. I expect you've heard of him. Most people know that, in 1066, William the Conqueror (not at that point so named) won the Battle of Hastings and became king of England. When it comes to the likely readership of this book, that 'most' must rise to 'all'. If there is anyone reading this book who didn't already know that, I would love to hear from you because you are genuinely reading in a genre that was previously of no interest. You, if you exist, and I bet you don't, are an absolute confounder of the algorithms. It would be like someone reading a biography of Elvis Presley who did not already know that he was a singer. What you are doing is probably more statistically remarkable than what William the Conqueror did.

Perhaps that's where we should start: the Norman Conquest, the beginning of proper English history. You know, the normal sort, with the current monarch numbering. If Prince

William becomes king, and takes the name that people actually call him by as his regnal name (which they don't always, confusingly – cf. Edward 'David' VIII and George 'Albert' VI), he'll be William V and that's a fifth where the Conqueror is first. It's almost official that English history starts then.

A few months before that first William's arrival on these shores, King Edward the Confessor died. His posthumous career was more glittering than his living one because he became a saint. Trumps king, doesn't it? To be honest, I slightly disapprove of kings being made saints. It's like CEOs getting knighthoods, standing alongside all those dedicated charity volunteers who raised millions for incubators but only get MBEs. Still, there it is. Edward the Confessor makes saint, even though he was never burned to death or nailed to anything – and a saint in honour of whom a later King Edward was named. But that later one is still King Edward *the first*. Even the revered Confessor, as with all English kings before William of Normandy, literally doesn't count.

The only trouble with calling William the Conqueror the first king of England is that it's not what he called himself. It's not what he chose to identify as, you might say if you happen to be living in the early twenty-first century. William would have said he was the rightful successor to the Confessor, and not because he was the sort of idiot who assumed things were more true if they rhymed. I reckon that kind of thing makes an ass out of you and me.

Edward the Confessor would have said he was the rightful ruler from the royal House of Cerdic, which had consolidated its hold over what was beginning to be referred to as 'Engla londe' after expelling the Vikings a few times. Before that it had ruled the kingdom of Wessex since its establishment by Cerdic himself (he was supposedly a person) in 519, soon after the arrival in Britain of 'the Anglo-Saxons', an umbrella term for various tribes from what is now north Germany and

Denmark who started turning up once the Roman Empire withdrew its legions around 410, leaving lots of vulnerable Romano-British dignitaries wondering who was going to service the central heating in their villas – plus a few not particularly tough local warlords none of whom, as discussed, was in any meaningful way King Arthur, and all of whom had lived rather comfortably being looked after by the Roman Empire since it had taken the place over in the year 43.

Shit, this history's going backwards! Although, if you think about it, that's the logical direction to go in. It's how archaeology works. You can't start with stone age axes and work your way up through Roman pots to clay pipes and finally ration cards and an old Nokia. The starting point for our enquiries into the past is the present. Historical narratives proceeding chronologically are a bit like sets of directions that start with where you're going and then work their way back to where you are.

But I'm not the guy who's going to overturn the long-standing tradition of chronological historical narratives. I'm not that kind of iconoclast – you should see what I'm wearing. I still use a fabric handkerchief, for God's sake. I'll try and start with the first English king and go from there.

The mists of time

I'm going to throw a few names at you: Vortigern, Hengist and Horsa, Wehha, Aescwine, Aelle, Aella, Ida, Icel and finally Cerdic (whom I've already mentioned). You will be thrilled to hear that no one totally knows if any of these people existed. But it's more likely than King Arthur. If you like, you could say that King Arthur was based on one of them. Really, go ahead, there's no harm in it.

But who were *they* based on? Why do we have these names,

these noises? Have I made them up? No, I haven't. I like to think I'd have made them sound more plausible. They are the names that have emerged out of the mists of time as belonging to some early rulers in England.

Yes, the mists of time! Deal with it! It's not a cop-out, that's the situation. There was very little in the way of record-keeping. Why do you think archaeologists got so excited when, at Sutton Hoo, they discovered the body of a king and a few trinkets in a rotten old boat? All of it dating from hundreds of years later than the complete buried Roman leisure centre they found in Bath? It's because it was a rare sign of what might have been going on in the 300 years after the Romans left. Otherwise it's mainly rumour and guesswork.

This is how the (hi)story goes. Notwithstanding the Caraticus- and Boudica-led resistance to the early days of Roman control, by the time the empire left, the ancient Britons had gone completely Stockholm syndrome. They loved the Romans. In fact, they'd become the 'Romano-British' and, with the legions gone, their instinct was to try and keep things going in a nice comfy Roman way.

This strategy didn't work out. When the Western Roman Empire was collapsing, a lot of other things were going on. Huns, Goths and Vandals were moving around Europe in an upsetting way. In Britain, a king called Vortigern (but note that 'vortigern' means 'king' in Brittonic, the ancient Britons' language, so I worry someone might have got confused, but maybe there really was this King King) was beset by raids from the Picts, who came from what is now Scotland, and from the Scots from what is now Ireland. I know that sounds wilfully confusing but there's nothing I can do about it.

I imagine Vortigern looking anxiously out to sea over the North Kent marshes, trying to remember how to do up his toga. I also imagine a thick sea mist blowing in. I may be taking the mists of time thing a bit too literally. Baffled and terrified though he was, there's no reason to assume he didn't benefit from a normal amount of clear weather.

Vortigern seems to have been a bit of a Thatcherite. A believer in a small state. The British had successfully outsourced their defence requirements for hundreds of comfortable years and, in the absence of those wonderfully professional legions, he was looking for another continental corporate body that might bid for the contract.

Enter the brothers Hengist and Horsa. They were leading figures among the Anglo-Saxons over in Germania. Vortigern hired them plus three ships full of their followers, to come and sort out the security situation in Britannia. I don't know how and when the deal was done – mists of time, etc – but they duly turned up at some point in the second quarter of the fifth century, knocked a few Picts' heads together and then promptly turned on their employers.

Cue the arrival of many other Angles, Saxons and Jutes (the Jutes don't make it into the adjective, perhaps from a combination of mishearing and antisemitism). They gradually took over what is now (thanks to them) called England, setting up several kingdoms. Hengist became the first king of Kent (Horsa died in battle fighting the Britons) and now we can make sense of some of those other names: Wehha was the first king of the East Angles, Aescwine of the East Saxons, Aelle of the South Saxons, Aella of Deira and Ida of Bernicia (Deira and Bernicia later become the kingdom of Northumbria), Icel of Mercia and Cerdic of the West Saxons. There's no need to remember any of that – there's a high chance it's bullshit. And the rest, after a few more centuries of mists of time, is history at last.

That's a lot of potential first English kings. We're in an obscure region where truth and fiction, like the land and the marsh and the North Sea across which the Anglo-Saxons sailed, merge. Hengist and Horsa smack of fiction: the two brothers and the three ships, often referred to as the 'three keels', are very storyish. The brothers are reminiscent of Romulus and Remus, another foundation myth laced with notions of betrayal, and three keels are always turning up in Anglo-Saxon stories, much like men bursting through doors holding guns in film noir.

There will have been early Anglo-Saxon big shots. The kingdoms these 'kings' supposedly founded certainly came to exist. But the details of who those men really were have been forgotten.

Don't be afraid of the Dark

A remarkable amount of forgetting about stuff went on in the two or three hundred years following the collapse of the Western Roman Empire. People at the time forgot what had just happened and, because there are few reliable written sources, posterity did too. There is only a grim sense that everything went down the drain (or would have done if the drainage infrastructure hadn't fallen into disrepair) and, as a result, those centuries are commonly known as the Dark Ages.

Academic consensus has turned against that term in recent years because that's what academics are like. Their favourite thing is saying that previous academics have got it wrong, even if it's just about the naming of an era.

At one point 'Dark Ages' was used to refer to the whole medieval period up to when the Renaissance kicked off in the fifteenth century. That is simplistic, as well as being poor brand management of the late middle ages which, I don't know about you, but I think of as being absolutely slathered with heraldry. Perhaps I'm basing it too much on the eye-bruising Technicolor of Laurence Olivier's film of *Henry V*, but it feels like there's altogether too many shiny trumpety things and maidens with pointy hats and youths with pointy shoes to be dark. Daft maybe, but not dark. Plus there was a lot more going on that we know about by then, so using the term 'Dark Ages' about that era speaks more of some people having gone a bit nuts about how amazing the Renaissance was, as if we might as well not bother with any history until Leonardo started doodling helicopters.

The term has also been used to cover the centuries from the Romans leaving England right up to 1066, which again doesn't seem right. The ninth, tenth and eleventh centuries were not – by modern standards – at all pleasant, but they were different from the fifth and sixth centuries, for which 'Dark' feels eerily appropriate.

Also, there were parts of the world where things were going swimmingly in the fifth and sixth centuries, so it's silly to use it about those places. But England, or the bit of the world that's now called England but wasn't then, is not one of those places. With the withdrawal of Roman protection, society went to shit – quite literally, since it heralded a 1,400 year hiatus in the construction of sewers. There was vertiginous civic and economic decline. Manufacturing collapsed, coins were no longer minted, population numbers went into free-fall, and not because people were choosing to have fewer children in order to focus on their careers.

Villas were abandoned and, all over the country, hoards of coins and valuables were buried in the hope of being dug up by their owners when the situation improved. It was a vain hope. Instead they were dug up by metal detectorists over a thousand years after the owners had all rotted to dust. A civilian population which, under Roman rule, had been forbidden to bear arms, put up a feeble resistance in the face of the warrior peoples arriving from all directions.

This might have made less of a difference to subsistence peasants who'd always lived in (to us) unimaginable rural penury, but it screwed anyone even a tiny bit better off than that – anyone who wasn't screwed already. It was apocalyptic. If that's not reason enough to use the term 'Dark Ages', I dread to think what we're saving it for.

Particularly stupid is the implication that the expression is somehow rude to the age. As if an age can get offended. As if the people, whose standard of living plummeted with the retreat of the legions, would mind or object. I reckon they'd agree that the time they were living in was dire. I don't see that it's in any way more respectful to gloss over that.

What's the point of showing bland respect for all the ages? 'Oh, they're all lovely, all the ages – let's not be rude by labelling one of them "dark". The rubble and leaky roofs that no one could remember how to repair are, in their way, just as spiffing as building the Parthenon and inventing democracy. Let's say a big "well done" to all the people of history for being there at all. We won't get all analytical and judgy. It's patronizing to start telling people that, just because they all totally forgot how to do running water or dress stone and loads of people died, that's not a lovely positive choice they've made.'

This example of a civilization suddenly getting markedly worse, by any meaningful definition of the word, is extremely interesting and worthy of note. The fact that history took such a sudden and, yes, dark turn is important to emphasize. It's something every society might profit from remembering.

I don't mean to be a doom-monger but we could do with it now. A big threat to our current civilization is the persistent post-Victorian assumption of progress. This 'Whig Interpretation of History' has been regularly debunked ever since the term was coined by the historian Herbert Butterfield in 1931, a tough year for believers in things getting better. Still, most of us unreflectingly go along with it. You hear it in the way people rebuke each other for prejudiced remarks by saying 'Come on, it's the twenty-first century', as if the passage of time inevitably brings with it ethical improvements.

The pejorative word 'dated' shows how ingrained is our assumption that human civilization gets better over time. It probably has recently, technologically at least, but it's not a given. Is assuming that things improve the best way of ensuring they will? I doubt it. A healthy fear of societal cataclysm may be a good technique for avoiding it.

The going-to-shit qualities of the Dark Ages are important to emphasize – they're a handy warning. Plus it's a cool and attractive thing about studying that period. You don't specialize in it for the architecture or the plumbing.

3. King Ceolwulf of Northumbria

For me, the misty, dark, unknowable aura of fifth-, sixth- and seventh-century Britain is an enormous draw. Murkiness with a fleeting glimpse of gold. A crown, a sword, a hoard of Roman coins buried by a rich Romano-Briton fleeing his villa in panic . . .

What was that movement in the fog? A dragon, a dinosaur, a galley full of legionaries hurrying away? The sense of mystery and loss is overwhelming, long before anyone thought of inventing King Arthur.

Hwaer cwom mearg? Hwaer cwom mago?

That's the Anglo-Saxon language, also known as Old English. It contains hardly any words inherited from Brittonic, which suggests there was eerily little cordial interaction between the Anglo-Saxons and the people they displaced. It's a snippet from a poem called 'The Wanderer' that's preserved in a tenth-century manuscript but is believed to have been written much earlier. It's from a bit that translates as this:

> Where is that horse now? Where the rider?
> Where is the hoard-sharer?
> Where is the house of the feast?
> Where is the hall's uproar?

There's a powerful sense of missing something, which is a strangely sophisticated emotion to have been preserved for us from what, in our terms, seems like such a primitive and poorly documented culture. Longing and bereavement are surprisingly high in the mix, compared to, say, glory or sex or anger. From our perspective, this little medieval society is barely getting started and yet it's already steeped in as much moist-eyed nostalgia as last orders at a British Legion club on the anniversary of VE Day.

'The work of giants is decaying,' laments another poem, 'The Ruin'. It's reflecting on some crumbling Roman buildings, probably those in Bath. 'Bright were the castle buildings, many the bathing-halls, / high the abundance of gables, great the noise of the multitude, / many a meadhall full of festivity, / until Fate the mighty changed that.'

'A meadhall full of festivity' sounds a bit downmarket for a Roman night out, and the reference to 'castle buildings' is poignant. Magnificent though they are, the buildings aren't fortified. They didn't need to be for most of Roman rule. The Romans established reliable public order, a feat not achieved again in Britain for well over a thousand years. This was a luxury the Anglo-Saxons couldn't imagine.

Still, the point is well made. I suppose it's hard to live amid so much decaying infrastructure without feeling a bit glum.

The good news

Some people managed it, though. King Ceolwulf of Northumbria, for example, and his favourite historian, the Venerable Bede. They lived in the late seventh and early eighth centuries and they're quite upbeat about life. Plus they definitely existed. You can take that as read from now on. The mists of time have lifted considerably.

Bede is one of the main mist-lifters. He was a monk in the abbey of Jarrow in Northumbria and his *Ecclesiastical History of the English People* was the most famous thing to come out of Jarrow until a march protesting against unemployment in 1936. Bede's book predates the march by a cool 1,205 years and is one of the main reasons we know anything at all about

Dark Age England. He dedicated it to the King of Northumbria at the time, Ceolwulf.

Bede and Ceolwulf are also both saints. I don't disapprove of Ceolwulf's kingly sainthood as much as Edward the Confessor's, because he abdicated in 737 and lived as a monk for the rest of his life, so he put the hours in sanctity-wise. As did Bede, though the soubriquet Venerable seems to have stuck to him despite achieving higher-ranking saintly status. These things happen. People never really said 'Admiral Kirk'.

I have genuinely literally read Bede's *Ecclesiastical History of the English People*. So you don't have to. I'd take me up on that if I were you – it may be important but it's boring. It was written in Latin but an English translation was on the reading list I was given before going to university, so I gave it a go.

In my nineteen-year-old arrogance, what I felt was silly about Bede was that he characterized an age of comparative barbarism and misery as one in which humanity had advanced. He only did this, ridiculously it seemed to me then, because it was a good period for the church, an institution with which he was obsessed. In England, for the hundred years or so before he wrote his history, Christianity had been on the march. That's why Bede didn't see the situation in the same bleak terms as whoever wrote 'The Wanderer' and 'The Ruin'. I felt he was just plain wrong.

Looking back, I realize I was a bit hard on him. Religion both bored and unsettled me, and yet my history teachers were constantly exhorting me not to ignore it. In an A-Level history essay, I was taught, there should always be at least one paragraph on the church. I would dutifully stick one in but I didn't really get it. I was an agnostic who didn't like thinking about religion because I hoped there was a God but didn't have the confidence to commit. Plus the trappings of religion felt a bit embarrassing and weird, like properly putting on a French accent when saying things in French.

My religious views haven't significantly moved on, but what I am slightly more capable of understanding is that, the existence or non-existence of God notwithstanding, religion is real and powerful and not just something from the olden days. Moreover, in the olden days, it was, in pretty much every society, a bigger deal than we can possibly imagine.

Christianity, for Bede, wasn't merely something he was massively into, or he solemnly exhorted other people to adhere to, it was *everything*. It was the real underlying truth of existence, like science is today. It was very much not like religion is today, even for those who are very religious. If we don't accept that, we can't begin to understand the times he lived in and the attitude he took.

So, for him, a history of England that wasn't entirely focused on the spread of the Christian faith would be pointless, because nothing else mattered. This was a prevalent view at the time and one that gave a brutal existence meaning, purpose and hope. I'm thirty years nearer the grave than when I first read Bede and much less confident in rejecting this worldview.

The bad news

The Romans had been Christian by the end. Originally they'd been polytheistic and inclined to use Christians as lion food, but in 313 the Emperor Constantine put a stop to all that and declared he was a Christian himself. Soon Christianity was the empire's dominant religion, which meant that the Romano-British were Christian – hence King Arthur was Christian, even though he didn't exist. Over on the continent, Roman rule may not have survived but Roman religion did. Tribes like the Goths and the Franks were content to live in Roman cities and were soon worshipping the Romans' lovely big single

God. Despite repeatedly sacking Rome itself, these upwardly mobile barbarians were keen to live an increasingly Roman life. It was as if they were collectively willing into existence the expression 'When in Rome'.

It was different in Britain. The invading Anglo-Saxons weren't interested in Jesus or a free *limoncello*. The Britons were driven west, some remaining Christian and some reverting to a sort of iron age paganism, cities were abandoned and the newcomers settled down to a rural existence throughout the south-east of the island, hurling the occasional Roman brick at one another.

The Anglo-Saxons stuck with the form of paganism they'd brought over from the continent, which was a nice little bunch of gods who, as a helpful mnemonic, the days of the week are named after. There's Woden, king of the gods and god of wisdom – beardy guy with a cloak – after whom Wednesday is named. Then Thunor, their version of Thor, who you might know from the Marvel Universe. He's god of thunder, which feels like a comparatively small brief, and the etymological root of Thursday.

Then it's Frigg. I don't know if the 1970s expression for wanking derives from this goddess's name – though it seems unlikely as her portfolio includes marriage and childbirth – but the word Friday definitely does and I think we can all agree that the end of the working week is a lovely time for a jolly good frigg. The god of war, Tiw, accounts for Tuesday. Sunday and Monday are the sun and the moon and, weirdly, Saturday is named after the Roman god Saturn, which feels incongruous – a bit like having a parish church called St Mohammed's.

Back to the mortals: whatever the actual names of those early Anglo-Saxon big shots, it seems unlikely that any of them were kings in the sense we understand the word. What probably happened is that the new settlers appropriated areas of land and then, people being reliably unpleasant, some of those settlers would start pushing others around, demanding 'tribute' and offering 'protection'. Gradually, by the same method used by drug gangs to divide up LA, a system of government emerged.

The local hard guy had to stay in with the provincial hard guy who had to curry favour with the regional hard guy. It was out of this unjust and lawless maelstrom of violence that the Anglo-Saxon kingdoms coalesced. The kingly legitimacy affected by the relatively settled handful of rulers and regimes that were in existence by Bede's day is no more respectable than a mafia boss adopting the title 'Don'.

It's just dressing up a system based on violence in order to economize on violence. If you can get people to start calling you 'sire' and obeying you because they think that's the way of the world, or somehow right and proper and endorsed by God or the gods, then you don't have to raise so many bands of heavies or armies and incur all the risks and costs involved in asserting your supposed royalty at the point of a sword or knuckle.

In case this isn't sounding grim enough, in the 530s–550s there was a period of extreme cold weather, famine and plague. A series of volcanic eruptions in (what is now) Iceland threw up dust clouds that blocked the sun and made the crops fail all over Europe. Outbreaks of plague followed, probably because everyone who hadn't starved to death was hungry and cold and sad. All this suffering must have hastened the process by which power was consolidated into fewer and nastier hands. Many desperate people will have accepted the protection offered by anyone tough with a bit of spare food.

The true roots of English kingship are therefore so far away from the Arthurian ideal it's actually funny. The notion that pious legitimacy was the foundation of the institution is totally false. Everything those early kings possessed they, or their ancestors, had either stolen or demanded with menaces.

The veneer of legitimacy was retrospectively applied in order to keep hold of all the power and wealth.

By the late sixth century and early seventh, pretending to be a king was all the rage. The vague regions of strongman influence started to coalesce into kingdoms and the idea of a bretwalda emerged. The bretwalda, which literally means either 'wide-ruler' or 'Britain-ruler', was supposedly the dominant Anglo-Saxon king at any given time. We don't know if the term was used contemporaneously – it may be a ninth-century invention – but the notion of being a dominant ruler must have been understood. It would have been the gold medal in the Olympics of unpleasantness that these violent men were competing in.

Rulers' status was all about power deriving from violence, combined with a growing sense that a bit of regal showiness helped keep inferiors in their place and intimidate rival kings. So they energetically asserted their importance in other ways. That's what the elaborate burial at Sutton Hoo was all about. They also built huge wooden halls, full of booze and smoke and warriors. As you can imagine, they burned down, or were burned down, with tedious regularity, but they were major symbols of the new kings' power.

A king could put a roof over your head, at least for a few hours, and keep you warm and fill your stomach. In those bleak days, that was all it took. Rather poignantly, the modern English word 'lord' derives from the Old English *hlaford* meaning 'bread-giver'. In Roman times, there'd been circuses too.

For God's sake?

This was the environment into which Christianity was reintroduced by a monk called Augustine, now referred to as St Augustine of Canterbury, not because he got his head handed to him on a plate or was killed in a way that inspired a fire-work, but because it all went so well. He was one of the getting-things-done sort of saint rather than the getting-done-in kind. He'd been sent from Rome by Pope Gregory I to convert the Anglo-Saxons, landed in Kent in 597 and was given a cautious welcome by its king, Aethelberht, the domin-ant southern English ruler at the time. Aethelberht already had a Christian wife, Bertha, so he was less inclined than many of his contemporaries to murder Christians on sight.

Queen Bertha had been born a princess in the Christian Frankish kingdom across the Channel in what is now France (which may give you a clue to where the name came from) and she had married the barbarous pagan Aethelberht on condi-tion that she be allowed to practise her faith. Aethelberht ignored his wife's funny ways until they were explained to him by a man from Rome and suddenly he was into them.

Aethelberht's conversion gave Christianity its first foothold among the Anglo-Saxons, but the flame of Romano-British Christianity was being kept alight in western parts of Great Britain. In fact this Celtic church, as it tends to be referred to, had converted Ireland in the fifth century. It's odd that it's called Celtic because its root is as Roman as the pope's church. It had spread to Britain because of the Roman Empire, but had then become cut off because of the Anglo-Saxons. With-out the wifi of the empire, the app hadn't been getting the updates. Different practices had started to emerge.

Don't let the last sentence fool you into thinking it was any-thing interesting like human sacrifice or Jesus being a Martian. The main things were a different tonsure (monks' hairdo) and a different way of calculating the date of Easter. The argu-ment among prelates about this last tedious issue was so interminable it feels like they were just trying to prove they believed in eternal life.

It took the best part of a century for the Anglo-Saxon

kingdoms to convert, largely to the papal brand of Christianity. It was a century of relentless, brutal fighting. A succession
of kings, some Christian and some pagan, established themselves as bretwalda but they almost all died in battle, usually
fighting against the man destined to be the next dominant
Anglo-Saxon, though there was also fighting against British,
Irish and Pictish rulers.

I'm not sure the violence really had anything to do with
Christianity, even if it was often used as justification. There'd
been loads of fighting before Augustine turned up, and the
arrival of Christianity certainly didn't put a stop to it, or even
a dent in it. The whole vague Christian niceness agenda – love
thy neighbour as thyself, do as you would be done by, etc –
seemed to have absolutely zero impact, but neither was it the
real cause of all the unpleasantness.

If you're trying to decide whether religion is a good or a
bad thing (and people often claim they are, though they have
usually already decided), early Anglo-Saxon England is a
useful time and place to look at. These days atheists often cite
the murderous religious wars in history as proof that believing in supreme beings is a damaging and regrettable practice.
The fact that they're convinced none of those supreme beings
exist incentivizes them to make this argument. Personally, I'm
not convinced of the universe's godlessness; but, even if we
assume the atheists are right about that, I doubt religion is
responsible for as much death as is claimed.

Some people love to fight and steal and dominate – that's the
key. There are arseholes among us and, given half a chance,
they're going to start some sort of trouble out of ruthless self-
interest or bloodlust or both. The prevailing ethos of any
surrounding society is almost always that you're not supposed
to kill people without a good reason, or at least some sort of
reason. But the arseholes are clever, so they come up with reasons. To deeply religious societies, religious differences sound

like a very convincing reason for killing people. But that doesn't mean the killing wouldn't have been happening anyway.

If St Augustine hadn't provided the reason, Woden would, or family feuds, or just plain xenophobia. That said, a lot of the people fighting in seventh-century England sincerely believed they were doing it in Jesus's name (or alternatively to wipe out the heretical cult of Jesus that was pissing off Woden, Frigg, Thunor and the rest). But the fighting would have been happening regardless. Violence is a constant, the religious views are just the accompanying spin. The largest avowedly atheistic societies in all human history, the various communist states of the twentieth century, didn't stint on murder.

You could argue that, under Stalin or Mao or Ceauşescu, communism effectively was a religion, just without the promise of eternal life. That's a fair point, but it extends the anti-religious argument to cover pretty much any sort of big concept or philosophy. The logical conclusion is that people should in general refrain from getting any big ideas into their heads and restrict themselves to philosophies on the level of 'it takes all sorts' and 'funny old world' – though before you knew it there'd be a war over whether the world is deemed to be funny peculiar or funny ha-ha.

My point is that I don't think religions are themselves to blame for all the violence in the name of religion, though it has to be said that the religions also totally failed to stop it.

So, is religion a good or a bad thing? Perhaps the answer is no.

Christian? Well, you know, just Christmas and Easter and when I'm committing genocide

That wasn't Bede or King Ceolwulf's answer. For them, the advance of Christianity made sense of everything. The horridness and occasional goodness was all part of some plan. It was a nice plan even if it was counterintuitive and tricky to unpick.

A king who abdicates to become a monk is a very different sort of person from the warlords of a century or more earlier who came up with the notion of kingship to dignify their violent amassing of power and wealth. There's a sincerity to Ceolwulf's piety, an implication of duty that comes with his abdication, that would have seemed very strange to those self-proclaimed kings. He comes across as decent, is I suppose what I'm saying – though they seem more of a laugh.

In the seventh century there are several rulers who were splendidly cynical in their use of Christianity. For example, King Raedwald of East Anglia, who died in 624 and is probably the main Sutton Hoo corpse, hedged his bets by building a temple with two altars: one to the pagan gods and one to Christ. Bede is predictably contemptuous of this and, given a moment's thought, it's not as canny a strategy as it initially sounds. Whether it turned out to be God or the gods who really existed, you imagine He or They would be pissed off at this equivocation when Raedwald turned up in the afterlife. Perhaps that's why he thought it important to be buried with all that treasure – he reckoned he might have to tip heavily on arrival.

Similarly the Christian British King Cadwallon of Gwynedd, who reigned until 634 when he was killed in battle by the also Christian Anglo-Saxon King Oswald of Northumbria, had, a year earlier, been very happy to make an alliance with the very very pagan King Penda of Mercia in order to defeat Oswald's predecessor the Christian King Edwin of Northumbria. That's quite a sentence, I know. The point I'm trying to make is that, even by the time Christianity was very much around, it wasn't necessarily the dominant factor.

Another example: later in the century, the brutal King Caedwalla of Wessex was, with the enthusiastic support of

St Wilfrid, happy to use Christianity as an excuse for slaughtering everyone on the Isle of Wight (at that point the last pagan Anglo-Saxon kingdom) and taking the place over. But Caedwalla himself wasn't baptized Christian. He was hedging his bets as well. Though, to be fair on him, he then abdicated and went on a pilgrimage to Rome where he was baptized by Pope Sergius I in 689 before promptly dying.

Fifty to a hundred years later, leaders like Ceolwulf are a *lot* more serious about it, even when they didn't go on to become monks. A bit like smoking to look cool and then becoming addicted, medieval kings soon came to believe their own Christ-proclaiming hype. Most of the rulers after this time, brutal and self-interested though they may have been, were genuinely God-fearing. They turned that fear to their advantage by asserting that the very fact they were kings was a sign of celestial favour.

Ceremonial elements were gradually introduced, following trends already established on the continent where there hadn't been such a post-Roman pagan blip. The Old Testament mentions kings having crowns put on them and being anointed, and the word 'Christ' comes from the Greek meaning 'anointed one' – so the way of legitimizing, even sanctifying, secular power under the big new religion was obvious.

Hence, back in the fifth century, the emperors of the surviving Eastern half of the Roman Empire, which these days gets called the Byzantine Empire, had started getting themselves crowned by the Patriarch of Constantinople. This gave ecclesiastical endorsement to that ancient pagan office, and the trend had been spread westwards by the cool Byzantines' soft power. In the seventh century the Visigoth kings of Spain started being crowned and anointed in holy oil and, by the middle of the eighth, the practice had been adopted by the Frankish kings who held sway in most of what is now France, the Low Countries and western Germany.

This need outwardly to assert a massive holy link between God, Christ and some beardy guy with a sword and a colossal sense of entitlement was becoming entrenched on the mainland and followed Christianity into the lands of the Anglo-Saxons. Christianity and the right to rule were welded together. By the time of Bede, for a king to remain unbaptized, as Caedwalla had been, would be as unlikely and egregious a lapse in professional housekeeping as a presenter of *The One Show* forgetting to renew their television licence.

4. King Offa of Mercia

When my wife and I are visiting a nice town or village for the first time, the question we always ask is 'Where's the bit?' That's what we're looking for: the main bit. The nice bit. The bit you're supposed to go and walk round where the stuff is. The bit that, once seen, gives you the authority to say you've been to the place. Tourists judge a place by its bit, even if locals eschew the bit because they're inured to its beauties and obsessed with the difficulty of parking.

Anything from a substantial village to a small city will have one bit. Sorrento in Italy, where we have spent a few holidays, is blessed with two bits and we'd been going there for several years before we discovered the second one (it's the old port!). Metropolises like London and New York can have several bits, and LA has no real bit at all, but quite large places still have only one. Cambridge and Bath, for example, have relatively sizeable bits, but only one each.

The bit isn't really the place, though. It's only a small part of the place. It's just the bit you don't want to miss, because it's most characteristic of the place. Well, in the history of Anglo-Saxon England, we've finally found the bit. It's the mid- to late eighth century. That's the main bit, the normal bit, when the era of Anglo-Saxon England was properly up and running but hadn't started to run out.

During this bit, there were several stable kingdoms broadly covering the area soon to be known as England, one of which was, at any given time, in the ascendancy. The Britons had been pushed back into the west – parts of what is now Devon and Cornwall and pretty much all of what is now Wales.

In fact, the words Wales and Welsh are derived from the words the Germanic-speaking tribes all over Europe gave to the retreating and cowed citizens of the collapsing Roman Empire: *walas*, which meant foreigners or strangers, from which we get Walloon (the French-speaking Belgians) and Gaul, of Asterix the Gaul (somehow the 'w' turned into a 'g'), as well as the Old English *wealh* which became Wales and Welsh. (Hence the modern French for Wales is 'Pays de Galles', country of the Gauls, which is massively confusing. France, Gaul, is the actual country of the Gauls, you'd think. It's almost like the French are calling Wales France, as if, to the French, the Welsh seem more French than the French. And, having been to both France and Wales many times, that strikes me as an eccentric opinion.)

Meanwhile the Welsh word for Wales, Cymru, derives from a Brittonic word meaning 'fellow-countrymen'. Strangers or fellow-countrymen. The Welsh for Wales basically means 'us' and the English for it means 'them'.

Us and them. That sums up the relations between the Britons and the Anglo-Saxons at this point. Sharing a religion only seemed to divide them further and there were persistent differences over how to calculate the date of Easter despite the extreme disinclination of people on both sides to send one another festive eggs. (My strong advice is not to worry about the specifics of this difference because it is complicated and unimportant. Basically, the Celtic church calculated the date of Easter Sunday on an eighty-four-year cycle, while the Roman church that the Anglo-Saxons had largely adopted did it on a nineteen-year cycle. If that information is not enough to put you off further enquiry, then I think you should seriously consider putting this book down and developing a drug habit.)

Northern Europe enjoyed a significant economic recovery in the late seventh and eighth centuries that enriched the

Anglo-Saxon kingdoms but didn't much benefit the Britons, who had too many Anglo-Saxons between them and all that trade. This further boosted the Anglo-Saxons' increasing feelings of communality, of a racial and linguistic bond from which the Britons were explicitly excluded. The two sides defined themselves against one another and the Anglo-Saxon world was buoyed up by a consequent sense of unity.

This unifying enmity finds its physical embodiment in Offa's Dyke. You may have heard of it. People do walks along it these days. It's a very long earthwork – a ditch with an embankment – that runs roughly along the Welsh–English border or, at time of construction, the Mercia–Powys border. It's been called Offa's Dyke since time immemorial and, unusually for something like that, it's probably correctly named and was indeed constructed by order of King Offa of Mercia.

People don't exactly know why. The answer 'just for fun' can be ruled out because constructing a ditch that long would take a huge amount of effort and resources today – for a small eighth-century kingdom it would have felt as difficult as acquiring a nuclear deterrent. Was it supposed to be a deterrent, a defensive military line? Maybe, but it wouldn't be a very good one, unless it was manned and it doesn't seem likely that it was – it's too long. Assuming an invading army didn't require disabled access, it wouldn't stop them – they could scramble over it.

It would have made stealing livestock tricky, as herding lots of animals back over it would be difficult. Also, it will have been symbolically powerful. Perhaps it was just literally drawing a line, asserting power: the Anglo-Saxons hold sway up to here.

When Offa was king, from 757 to 796, Mercia was the dominant kingdom and had been for some time, certainly for most of the reign of his almost immediate predecessor, Aethelbald, who had been king since 716. (I say 'almost immediate' because another man, Beornred, ruled briefly and unsuccessfully between Aethelbald's assassination, possibly orchestrated by Beornred, and his own, definitely orchestrated by Offa.)

If you're looking for a way to remember the chronological order of dominance of the Anglo-Saxon kingdoms (and you might be – you could use it as the basis for a series of internet passwords), it's this: start at the bottom and then go round anti-clockwise. That's not how the Anglo-Saxons remembered it, though, as none of them had ever seen a clock.

It starts at Sussex, back in the mists of time when Aelle was king. He was supposedly the first bretwalda but may not have existed at all, so this Sussexian dominance could be fictional. Then, we move into fact and round to Kent, when Aethelberht was in charge, and then to East Anglia under Raedwald. After that, there were several dominant kings of Northumbria but this was fading in the time of Bede to be replaced by – we're moving down the left now – Mercia, which we've just got to, and finally (spoiler alert) Wessex.

Of the seven kingdoms that later historians, in an effort to tidy up this disordered era, referred to as the Anglo-Saxon 'Heptarchy' only Essex doesn't seem to have had its moment in the sun, even in myth. This slightly spoils the mnemonic but there it is. Perhaps we should just pretend that Essex briefly ruled the roost between Kent and East Anglia and I suspect there'll be insufficient evidence to comprehensively refute the claim.

An Offa you can't refuse

Boom! I've dropped the pun. I couldn't help it. It's been hanging over me all chapter. My justification for making it is – bear with me – that Offa asserted dominance over, or took over, all the Anglo-Saxon kingdoms except Northumbria. For those kingdoms King Offa's domination was what he *offered* and, if you refused Offa's offer, he would respond with lethal violence. So *you can't refuse* it. It's actually a completely apposite pun and, on reflection, I'm extremely proud of myself.

One of the main reasons Mercia was able to dominate was that it controlled London. That seems a bit strange. Mercia's heartland was the Midlands – the word is still used to refer to that part of England, as in the West Mercia Police that arrests people in Herefordshire, Shropshire and Worcestershire. London is in the south-east. To a modern perspective, it is the dominant core of the south-east. The south and east of Anglo-Saxon England were dense with other kingdoms. Kent, Sussex, Wessex, Essex and East Anglia all seem like much more natural kingdoms to centre around Britannia's old Roman capital.

Yet none of them cemented control over it while they had the chance. One of the reasons for this is that, throughout the early Anglo-Saxon period, London, or Londinium as the Romans called it (and they founded it, so it's actually quite offensive that we don't still call it that), was abandoned. I don't mean abandoned in the Sunday colour supplement sense of 'professional couples are abandoning the cities for a simpler life out of town'. It wasn't a drift, a trend, a thing about house prices. *Everybody* left. Or died, which is a form of leaving. London, a large walled conurbation, was simply empty for nearly 200 years. It was used as nothing but the inspiration for baffled and mournful poetry.

I know I've alluded to this abandonment before but it's worth pausing to contemplate it for a moment. It's really strange. It means there was a complete cessation of one form of human occupation of that part of southern Britain and the start of a new one. The original Londoners died, or fled, to go and gradually become Welsh, and the newcomers looked at what they'd left behind – a city way beyond their technical abilities to construct – and thought, 'We don't want anything to do with that.' They built hovels somewhere else instead and left London empty. I reckon that is weird. These are people who definitely wouldn't have taken the Covid vaccine. It's important to bear that in mind before we get too adulatory about the fact that a few of the knick-knacks found at Sutton Hoo came from Byzantium.

The beginning of the repopulation of London came in 604 when Augustine appointed a man called Mellitus as bishop of London and of the East Saxons – Essex the kingdom that controlled the area at the time. (Perhaps we could squeeze in its period of dominance soon after this? It only needs to be a few minutes.) Mellitus had been sent from Rome and wasn't afraid of buildings, so he set up his church inside the city walls. By that time, a trading settlement or *wic* as they were called in Old English, had already built up, not inside the city walls (too scary!), but just to the west, round about where the Strand and the Aldwych (or old *wic*) are now. This place was known as Lundenwic and, by the end of the seventh century, it was a major centre for the same reasons that Roman London had been and the city has prospered to this day: it's a very good place to put a port.

Once nominally under the aegis of the relatively feeble kingdom of Essex, then tussled over by Kent and Wessex, by the early eighth century it was being run by the Mercians whose king, Aethelbald, was making a fortune from the tolls he charged the traders.

This powerful and prosperous situation continued to improve later in the century under the reign of Offa. As with most kings at this time, we know pitifully little about him. We have lots of unrealistic images of him on the many coins that were minted in his reign (another sign that greater stability and prosperity were being enjoyed than at any time since the Romans left). We also know he kept most other Anglo-Saxon kingdoms in subjection to him and built a fuck-off great big dyke to say fuck off to the Welsh. Plus he corresponded with his illustrious contemporary Charlemagne, the dazzlingly successful European ruler who consolidated most of what is now France and a fair chunk of what is now Germany and Italy, into one empire. Offa borrowed from Charlemagne the idea of having his son consecrated as king while he was still alive.

This strategy was very fashion forward. It was another part of the transmogrification of the office of king from top thug into something supposedly sacred and noble. Offa wanted his son Ecgfrith to be anointed and proclaimed his successor because this would add a sense of grandeur to the whole family and might obviate the period of savagery and chaos which was the usual consequence of a reign ending. That's what had happened between Aethelbald and Offa.

The tricky aspect of Offa's plan was that such an anointing needed to be done by an archbishop and there were only two in Anglo-Saxon England: one in York, part of the entirely independent kingdom of Northumbria, and one in Canterbury in the kingdom of Kent, which Offa had treated with considerable savagery. Neither archbishop was willing to oblige. So Offa persuaded the pope to create a new archbishopric inside Mercia: the archbishop of Lichfield. It was not an archdiocese destined for a great future but it existed long enough to anoint Ecgfrith, which must have made Offa feel very secure about the future of his kingdom and his legacy.

That's the feeling his reign gives. The brutality of Anglo-Saxon kingship is still there, but it's less chaotic, more organized, with an increasingly stable and well-funded infrastructure and a strengthening religious and ceremonial underpinning to the notion of kingship. Offa doesn't seem too different from the monarchs of centuries later who were also corresponding with continental rulers, bargaining with the church and nervously securing their sons' succession. It's a much more relaxing picture. Perhaps history is going to be nice and normal from now on.

5. 'King Hell, it's the 'King 'Kings!

Sometimes things just happen. That's worth bearing in mind. It's a great get-out clause if you're writing a history book. 'Look it just happened, okay?' I can always say. 'Sometimes things do. Never mind why. Deal with it. It simply occurred, and that's that. Ask the scientists, they're up to their eyes in this stuff – butterflies' wings and so on. Everything's just a chaos of microparticles. Things just happen – don't get comfy.'

We're probably more than usually aware of this at time of writing because the coronavirus pandemic was like that, all the jokes about bat-eating notwithstanding. And, frankly, even if some bat-eating was contributory, I don't buy all that wise-after-the-event admonition. The whole 'Well, if you're going to eat bats, what do you expect?' attitude.

'Not this!' is the answer to that. 'I expected a delicious bat meal, not a global pandemic. I maybe had half an eye on food poisoning – perhaps that would have served me right. This is fucking insane.'

Now I'm talking as if I was the guy who ate the bat. Which I'm not. I am relatively confident I have never eaten bat, though I've had a fair few frozen lasagnes so it's hard to be totally sure.

From most of our points of view, the coronavirus pandemic was just a shit thing that suddenly happened, and not the inevitable consequence of the insufficient pandemic-preparedness of governmental structures that incentivize using public money for easing politicians' paths to re-election rather than for stockpiling PPE or maintaining a vast permanently mothballed emergency-vaccine-manufacture infrastructure. The pandemic might look inevitable in retrospect, but hardly anyone saw it coming.

The monks at Lindisfarne, as they were being chopped to bits by some Vikings, probably told themselves they should have prayed more. 'I could tell you weren't concentrating at Matins, Brother Edgar! Now look where we are!' The thought that disasters are your fault is comforting, on some level. It gives you the illusion of control when, in truth, something horrible came out of the blue and ruined your life.

The Vikings were a thing that just happened. From most people's point of view. There weren't Vikings, or not as far as any non-Vikings knew, and then there were Vikings. Ships with ferocious dragon heads carved on their prows, crammed full of savage warriors, turning up and being horrible. It started in 793 at the Holy Island of Lindisfarne, just off the Northumbrian coast. A nice quiet spot for a monastery, everyone had thought 150 years earlier. Good for a bit of prayer – you can look at the sea, think about stuff, get away from it all. Then 'it all' was abruptly redefined as gangs of scrappy pagans turning up in boats, hungry and broke. Lindisfarne became Ground Zero.

It was a massive shock. I expect people hoped it wouldn't happen again. But it did. It kept happening. Just think of the stress – the mental health cost. It must have done people's heads in. Then a lot of those heads were also smashed in, by Vikings.

He wasn't as horny as I'd hoped

What I'm attempting here is 'empathy', popularized as a historian's tool by the GCSE syllabuses of the late 1980s. It falls down because it's impossible for a child living in late twentieth-century Britain to get their head round how different the lives of the people they're trying to empathize with actually were. They haven't got much better at it by the time they've become, say, early twenty-first-century comedians, or . . . well, I can't really imagine what else they might have become. As I say, empathy's tricky. But we need to focus more on it and less on dates – that was the thinking among the GCSE boffins. I'm better with dates, to be honest.

So: 793 to 1066. That's the era of the Vikings. It's quite precisely defined for something so anarchic. Like a rugby match. 'Why are they so susceptible to the whistle?' I sometimes think. 'It's basically a fight.' Well, the final whistle in the match between the Vikings and the rest of the world (well, not the *whole* rest of the world – they didn't get to China, but they got to North America and Russia and Constantinople) was blown in 1066. Who won? It's not clear. It was sort of a draw. There were Vikings everywhere but most of them had become Christians – which, for a lot of the non-Vikings, was the point of everything. But everyone was very tired and cold and wet, and had long since given up on relaxing at the seaside.

I don't mean to imply, by the way, that the Vikings aren't fun. This is the problem with all the empathy. One can easily end up focusing exclusively on what it was like being a Viking (cold, scary, damp, desperate, navigational excellence worn lightly) or meeting one ('Jesus save me from the arsehole with the axe!') when, for the vast majority of humanity, and absolutely everyone reading this book, that's not the main thing at all. They were brilliant! Unless you met them personally, in which case they were awful. Bit like Peter Sellers.

From our point of view, the Vikings had great big boats and beards and gods and they smashed things up and travelled everywhere and had horns on their helmets.

They didn't have horns on their helmets. That might have been the first thing a teacher ever told me about the Vikings. As far as I recall, the order of events for me was: 1) Not having ever heard of any people called the Vikings; 2) a teacher said, 'Here is a picture of some Vikings' and showed me an illustration of some amazing warriors in a dragon boat with horns on their helmets; 3) the teacher said, 'They didn't really have horns on their helmets.'

The fact that history remained my favourite subject despite that moment is a real testament to how boring the other lessons were. I don't know where the idea of Vikings having horns on their helmets came from, but it's a brilliant one. In every possible way, other than the literal truth, they totally had horns on their helmets. Horned helmets was absolutely their vibe and I feel we all have a right to that deeper artistic truth. They had limited technology and manufacturing helmets was pretty tricky for them, I imagine, so putting horns on them wouldn't have been workable, and wouldn't have increased the functionality of the helmets, but I swear they'd have given it a go if they'd thought of it.

We can't know, though. Maybe they'd have given them peaks like baseball caps or warming earflaps or a single prong like the Prussians. We don't know that much about them, except how stressful it was to meet them, because they didn't write stuff down so we don't have much sense of their point of view. They came from Scandinavia, but nobody knows why they came and, conversely, before the late eighth century, nobody knows why they didn't. It's another mists-of-time thing, once again evocatively supplemented by imagining people literally emerging out of mists. Although the Vikings are likely to have preferred sunny weather for their inexplicable arrivals.

I mean, you can speculate about why they came if you want to – if you really hate yourself and can't stand a bit of mystery in your life. You can start thinking about their reasoning and ferreting around for the evidence. But I think it's a bit of a shame – rather George Lucas of you. You've got some horned warriors in dragon ships emerging enigmatically from the mist – why ruin it with the prequel? Why start asking, 'Ooh, what happened before this dramatic bit? What dry socio-economic causes can we root out?'

Need I say I am not a professional historian? I suspect that the view 'It's more fun to keep a bit of mystique about what's actually going on' is frowned upon in academic circles. In the case of the Vikings, the joyless search has gone largely unrewarded because nobody's sure. Their Scandinavian lands were getting crowded and fractious is one reason, as you'd probably have guessed. We don't totally know. Personally, I'm going to side with the atheists and blame Thor – he sounds like a very problematic role model.

All is lost but the irony

The Vikings made their presence felt all over Europe and gave the Franks, the Irish and the Picts just as much shit as they did the Anglo-Saxons. Still, for the Anglo-Saxons there was an irony about the Vikings' arrival that there wasn't for any of the other peoples being harassed. The Vikings were doing almost exactly what the Anglo-Saxons themselves had done three or four hundred years earlier: turning up in boats, all savage and pagan and fighty, and nicking stuff.

Newly Christianized as they were, the Anglo-Saxons had retrospectively justified their success over the Britons in terms of the latter's decadence or sin – it was the will of God that they should have conquered Britannia, even if it was a God they didn't believe in at the time they did the conquering. Now the tables were turned: the Anglo-Saxons were the Christian residents facing pagan invaders and, once again, God seemed to be favouring the infidel newcomers.

In the early ninth century, the giant geographical backwards-clock showing the dominant Anglo-Saxon kingdom had done its last mega-tick and moved on from Mercia to Wessex. This change was precipitated by the battle of Ellendun in 825 when Egbert, King of Wessex from 802 to 838, had defeated King Beornwulf of Mercia.

Despite Offa's careful succession planning, Beornwulf was not descended from him but had nicked the throne off another king who was also not descended from him. So the archdiocese of Lichfield was all a colossal waste of energy and, in fact, had already been abolished. Ellendun was the culmination of Beornwulf's invasion of Wessex and his defeat indicated a major shift of power to Egbert. By 830, Egbert was acknowledged as bretwalda, and was either directly in control of or had been acknowledged as a senior king by all the Anglo-Saxon kingdoms.

Sadly for Egbert, though, it wasn't possible to enjoy it. This early ninth-century squabbling between the Anglo-Saxon kingdoms is reminiscent of the way the BBC and ITV still tussle to win the Saturday-night TV ratings war. Like Wessex and Mercia in the 820s, they must find something comforting in that old, irrelevant conflict. It distracts them from the terrifying new threats they're facing. For King Egbert the equivalent of YouTube, Netflix, Amazon and the Conservative Party was the Vikings.

The raiding and killing and stealing from anywhere coastal went on throughout the early ninth century and, while there were periods of respite, usually when the focus of Scandinavian raids moved to Francia or Ireland, the trend was steadily worsening. More depressing still, the Vikings' range gradually extended inland. Many of the Roman walled towns were reoccupied by Anglo-Saxons who were now, like their Briton predecessors, more inclined to agoraphobia than claustrophobia.

The Anglo-Saxon response was a confused mixture of fighting back and trying to buy the Vikings off. Neither strategy worked. All military victories over the Vikings were temporary. More of them would pop up again, streaming from coasts and navigable rivers. And the Anglo-Saxons wouldn't have needed us to explain why bribing Vikings to go away was a counterproductive strategy over anything but the very very short term. Every time they did it, the cocktail of desperation and self-loathing must have been a bitter draught, particularly for a populace accustomed to mead, which is quite sugary.

It's easy to criticize the Anglo-Saxons for this response because it failed. But the tide was against them, literally and metaphorically. The Vikings were masters of the sea and ferocious fighters on land, and the Anglo-Saxons must have felt that they were being punished by God for something. Let's be honest, there were plenty of things to choose from – there's all the murder of course, but also they were *really* sexist. This formless guilt must have further sapped morale. What if they were as contemptible to the Almighty as those loser Britons about whom they were accustomed to feeling so contemptuous?

Fundamentally, though, the technology and martial practices of the time hugely favoured offensive action. It's not that the raiders were necessarily better at fighting, it's that raiding was easier than repelling raiders. Militarily speaking, the Anglo-Saxons were attempting the early medieval equivalent of reversing a blitzkrieg offensive without air cover. They were fucked.

6. King Alfred the Great

Then, in 865, they were saved. From the chapter heading, you might assume that the accession of King Alfred had something to do with it. Not really. That didn't happen until 871. What happened in 865 was that the Vikings decided to take over all of England permanently. They'd moved on from nicking move-ables; now they wanted real estate, somewhere to settle down.

Why did that help the Anglo-Saxons? In the short term it didn't. It was an absolute disaster, seemingly. First Northum-bria, then East Anglia, then most of Mercia were conquered, leaving a small puppet-ruled western rump. Edmund, the last independent King of East Anglia, was killed in battle by the Vikings in 869 and rumours of the brutality of his treatment were such that he was soon venerated as a Christian martyr.

The story goes that the Vikings tied Edmund to a tree and insulted him and beat him and fired arrows and spears at him while he refused to renounce his Christianity, so finally they chopped his head off and threw it deep into the forest where his followers went looking for it. The head called out to them, and they found it being guarded by a wolf, who out of respect was not eating it. They then popped it back on the body and it became miraculously reattached.

There are many issues with this account: why were these 'followers' allowed to stroll about in the wake of a Viking vic-tory? What the fuck had they been doing when King Edmund was trying to win a battle? Why did the victorious Vikings give a damn whether Edmund renounced his faith? How can we be sure that the wolf wasn't just pausing to work out how to eat a king's head without breaking a tooth? In fact, the disembodied talking head seems like the most plausible element. And as miracles go, reattaching a head to a dead body is pretty lame. What's the use of that? You wouldn't last long in the Marvel Universe with that superpower.

At some point in the next century or so, Edmund's remains were interred in a place that, but for the last 's', was named after precisely what people first went there to do: Bury St Edmunds. Another saint–king whose admirers focused on his celestial title. I suppose calling a town 'Bury King Edmund(s)' would have sounded like incitement to insurrection, which, if you've ever been there, you'll know is not the vibe of the place at all.

Catastrophic though this all sounds, in the long run it saved the Anglo-Saxons. Now both they and the Vikings wanted the same thing – to take large areas over and retain control of them. It was a fair fight. Trying to defend everything and everyone from tens of thousands of seaborne raiders who could strike anywhere and leave just as quickly was, a cool 1,070 years before the invention of radar, impossible. You can't defend everything at once from people who possess nothing that you can attack. As soon as the Vikings started trying to occupy areas of the country, however, the Anglo-Saxons had a chance. Still, when someone is repeatedly stamping on your face, it takes a while to realize that what you're being smashed with is their Achilles heel.

Everything seemed to be getting more ominous. Then, in 870, the great Viking army turned its attention to the last and most powerful Anglo-Saxon kingdom, Wessex.

That thing on your knob looks wrong

When I was ten the history teacher informed us that we were going on a school trip 'to see the Alfred Jewel'. This announcement, which would have confused me as an adult, was taken by the whole class in our world-weary strides. We were used to baffling stuff. Having to absorb weird thing after weird thing after weird thing is what being at school largely consists of. Whatever the empathy-drive in history teaching, no adult, however great a teacher – not even Robin-Williams-in-*Dead-Poets-Society* himself – can quite get their heads round the extent to which small children don't have the first idea what's going on.

Where do you start? With my own daughter, I quickly realized that my instinct to explain the United Nations, and then cover the structure of global human interaction downwards from there, had to be resisted. We may as well start with animal noises, even though, in adult life, they hardly ever come up.

It's the only trip to see a jewel I've ever been on, but at the time I didn't know that grown-up life wasn't full of jewel-seeing trips – or indeed that the world wasn't packed with jewels named after men. For all I knew, that's what tourism mainly was: 'Let's go down to Worthing at the weekend and have a good look at the Eric, Steve and Keith Jewels.'

I enjoyed the trip very much, partly because my expectations had been skilfully managed – I was only expecting to see one jewel but I also got to walk through a museum containing other artefacts on the way and through the far greater wonders of the gift shop on the way out – and partly because the Alfred Jewel is a very nice thing to look at. It's not really a jewel, it's a piece of jewellery: it's made of 'filigreed gold', which looks exactly as it sounds, all twiddly and intricate, is about 6 cm long and seems to have been made to put on the end of a stick, like a sort of knob. I don't know why they didn't call it the Alfred Knob.

It was discovered in Somerset in 1693 by people who didn't even realize they were living in the past themselves. It was assumed, probably correctly, that it was made for King Alfred the Great because it has the phrase 'Alfred ordered me made' written around it in Old English. It's from the late ninth century and is powerful anecdotal evidence that the Dark Ages were over – though nobody seemed to be able to draw a face that looked realistic at any point between the Romans leaving and the Tudors. Does thinking that make me a philistine?

There's a picture on the Alfred Jewel, in the middle of all the lovely gold work, that archaeologists think is supposed to be Jesus. Nobody knows what Jesus really looked like, but we can be pretty sure he didn't look like that. It's skilfully crafted in enamel under quartz, but the image itself is like something I might have done while drunkenly playing online Pictionary on my phone.

Maybe it's all equally valid, but I believe the thing with modern art is that it isn't supposed to look real but the artists could do it Michelangelo-standard if they wanted. Picasso puts the ears on the same side of the nose, but it's deliberate and he could totally have turned a profit doing funny caricatures for tourists in Montmartre if he'd needed the money. I don't reckon that holds with medieval art. I reckon they wanted it to look as good as a photo but they couldn't get it right. The craftmanship's there – the Anglo-Saxon jewellery and then all the cathedral building – but no one can draw.

The original owner of the jewel, King Alfred of Wessex, known as Alfred the Great, is a very famous king indeed – certainly the most famous to be covered in this book so far, apart from King Arthur. That's largely because, unlike any other Anglo-Saxon ruler, a biography was written about him during his lifetime and, with a little bit of chopping and changing and a few random additions, it has survived to this day.

It was written by a monk called Asser and it's very much an authorized biography – overwhelmingly positive. It says Alfred was . . . well, great. Capable and clever and wise and kind and nice and terrific at battles and admin, and that's basically the view of Alfred that's come down to us. Though latterly it has been questioned by the bloody 'let's try and work out what actually happened' killjoys, fresh from lopping Viking horns off.

While we're on that subject, I should mention that the Vikings weren't called Vikings at the time. It's not clear where the term Viking came from – there are a tedious number of competing theories – but it's very clear what it means now and, for that reason, I think it's a good word. Nevertheless, the terms in use at the time were, among others, Norse, Northmen, Norsemen or Danes, whether or not they originated from what we'd now call Denmark.

I'm going to start using those names too, mainly when I don't want you to think of them as having horns on their helmets. The trouble with the imagined picture of them with the horns is that it looks like a stag do, which is a bit negative and trivializing for something so geopolitical, particularly once, as is about to happen, they start converting to Christianity. That would be a weird vibe for a stag do. That's when the penny drops that the beatifically smiling best man, who seems like such a lovely guy, is a Mormon.

It made a great story

The fact that the Danes converted to Christianity was thanks, in part, to the efforts of Alfred. The youngest grandson of King Egbert, he became king in 871; his three elder brothers had all been kings before him and had brief, stressful reigns. At the point of his accession, the situation was terrible: a huge Danish army was roaming the south of England, winning more battles than it lost, and all the other Anglo-Saxon kingdoms had been overthrown.

By early 878, things had deteriorated further. Wessex was almost entirely taken over by the Danes, and Alfred was reduced to hiding in the Somerset Levels – a harder place to hide than somewhere more undulating. I mean, anyone can hide in the Alps. The Danes must have been surveying the horizon for suspicious Alfred the Great-sized pieces of cover, like in that Monty Python sketch 'How Not to Be Seen'.

Alfred came back from that low point of marshy guerrilla warfare, won the Battle of Edington in May 878, against the army of Guthrum the Dane, the new (Vi)King of East Anglia, made Guthrum convert to Christianity, reorganized the military, founded a navy, issued a law code and established himself as ruler of all of England south-west of a line drawn from where Essex meets the Thames up to the top right-hand corner of Wales. The other half was known as the 'Danelaw'. Alfred was established as the pre-eminent Anglo-Saxon. It was quite a dramatic turnaround. At some point, he also had a jewel made.

Is all that enough for him to be known as 'the Great'? Demonstrably it is. Still it's not quite Napoleonic. It's more the regal equivalent of rescuing the fortunes of a struggling regional chain of family-owned shoe shops. If 'Great' monarchs have parties in the afterlife, I reckon Catherine of Russia and Alexander of Macedon are going to be raising their eyebrows behind Alfred's back in the same way St Peter and St Mary Magdalene do when St Edward the Confessor walks into the reception for saints and starts troughing on the special canapés reserved for martyrs. These mediocre Brits get everywhere.

I remember being told at school that Alfred was the only British king who's called the Great. The ninth century seemed quite early for British history to have peaked. The best king over with before the proper numbering system even started. Let's not forget that if Prince William's grandson is named Alfred he'd become King Alfred I. There's no infiltrating Wantage's greatest son into the official post-Conquest numbering system, no matter how good he was at sneaking about in a bog.

It's impossible to know how great Alfred really was, but he got a lot of things right. His decision to call upon the defeated Danes to convert, and to make Guthrum his own godson, is clever. On the face of it, it looks like either an act of open-handed Christian clemency by a deeply religious man, or an aggressive and humiliating move to take away your foes' religion and culture. It's neither really: it's opening up diplomatic relations. It's establishing a situation of mutual acknowledgement, maybe even respect. 'Okay, we're both going to live on this island and we have to make that work somehow' is the key message.

Another message: forget about Mercia. Alfred styled himself King of the Anglo-Saxons; the ruler of the rump of Mercia not under the Danelaw, a nobleman called Aethelred, acknowledged Alfred's lordship and never styled himself king. Alfred frequently used the word *Angelcynn*, 'the English race'. He pushed the idea of Englishness and an Anglo-Saxon kingdom, in vague opposition not merely to the Britons, but also to the Danes. The remaining Anglo-Saxon bits of the island were coalescing into a coherent political entity led by the House of Wessex.

Alfred's greatest achievement, however, was his posthumous PR – maybe we should really be talking about Asser the Great. Like King Arthur, King Alfred later became a convenient repository for English patriotic feeling and, unlike King Arthur, he both definitely existed and isn't also a convenient repository for Welsh patriotic feeling. Some patriots can get really pissy about sharing the convenient repositories for their feelings – which is why it's a bad idea to tell a football hooligan that St George was from Turkey. An English football hooligan, that is. I don't suppose any other sort of football hooligan, even a Turkish one, gives a damn where St George was from.

Alfred's and Asser's efforts to lay down the basis for a nice positive Wikipedia page were useful to posterity. Alfred, said Asser, was English, pious, learned and militarily successful, so an obvious figure to want to associate yourself or your country with. This positivity developed a momentum that lifted Alfred above all the other Anglo-Saxon kings and meant random achievements were attributed to him like aphorisms to Winston Churchill. For example, in the fourteenth century the idea got round that he'd founded University College, Oxford, which is roughly as historically plausible as Mozart designing the iPhone. In the fifteenth century, Henry VI tried to have him made a saint. But he failed, which then counter-intuitively gave Alfred's reputation a massive boost after the English Reformation because, unlike other celebrated Anglo-Saxon monarchs – St Ceolwulf of Northumbria, St Edmund of East Anglia and St Edward the Confessor – he wasn't tarred with the papist sainting brush. Protestants were able to infer that Alfred's Christianity had been more English and less Roman and was therefore a precedent for Anglicanism. Needless to say, this was bullshit.

In the comforting story of English history that the Victorians liked to tell, a great king like Alfred, who they could assert was properly *English* (even though the term was only emerging in his day), defeating and converting the Danes and then sorting out his kingdom with some sensible laws and a nice fleet feels like a perfect starting point for a long and glorious narrative – with a few ups and downs to keep it interesting, but lots more ups than downs – leading with messianic inevitability to a lovely great big empire. There were huge celebrations around the thousandth anniversary of Alfred's death in 1899 with an enormous statue of him commissioned for the City of Winchester which was unveiled two years later at an event so massive and exciting that it was reported in the *New York Times* and Lord Rosebery came to speak. Yes! Lord Rosebery! (Lord Rosebery had briefly and unsuccessfully been prime minister – not as briefly or unsuccessfully as Liz Truss, more at the Theresa May level. Still, I think we have to accept that the prospect of a speech from him was more of a draw in 1901 than the prospect of one from May is today. Thank the Lord for TV.)

Alfred's reign rivals 1066 as a beginning, because there's no avoiding the fact that William the Conqueror seems a bit French. Alfred meanwhile, if he weren't entirely English, might have been, as an Anglo-Saxon, a tiny bit German – a very useful attribute during periods such as the eighteenth and nineteenth centuries, when the contemporary British royal family weren't quite as unGerman as could be wished.

History never stops

The trouble with the Alfred beginning is that, in terms of that Victorian narrative leading to a nice organized England, with the lions and the longbows, and then a nice organized Britain, with the empire and the gunboats, it's a bit of a false dawn. That gets in the way of the story the British in the late nineteenth century were trying to tell. From their point of view, it's obvious where the whole English and British thing is heading: it's towards everyone on the island of Great Britain being in the same country, very happy about that, ruling much of the world and, in general, being very rich and right about things.

That's how it must have felt to most British people who took an interest in the past around about 1900. There's an impatience, in telling the history, to get it all going. Never mind all the tribes and mini-kingdoms – the Picts and the Scots, the Danes and the Norse – we all know where this is heading. Get on with it!

Looking at things an eventful 1.2 centuries later, that

majestic narrative arc has got a bit chewed at the end. There's no longer any sense that British power was 'for the best' – plus most of it's gone. The sense of a Britain run from London, an effective enlargement of the former kingdom of England, as definitely the way events were always heading and would inevitably end up, has evaporated even while the UK remains nominally intact.

These days it's possible for us to contemplate the confusing events between the death of Alfred the Great and the arrival of William the Conqueror without getting distracted by the prospect of a nice British imperial happy ending, because we know about the Somme and the Blitz and Suez and Profumo and the miners' strike and Brexit and Covid. We can understand more clearly that history isn't actually a proper story. It's more like a soap opera. It never fucking ends. So it has to get cyclical. England comes together and then something has to happen next, and one of the options that the exhausted cosmic hack writers might go for is England falls apart again. The same goes for Britain. Together, apart, united, divided.

You wait till we get to all the attempts by kings of England to be in charge of France – it's *so* repetitive! Raising an army, getting it there, fighting – might go well, might not, again and again and again – cut a long history short, they *never really get to be in charge of France*. But they *keep trying*. Maybe it's not a soap, maybe it's a sitcom: 'This time next year, my son, we'll be kings of France.' They even *said* they were kings of France . . . for 460 years. In general, people who say they're kings of France, but clearly aren't, get sectioned – but, if you happen genuinely to be king of England, you seem to get away with it. Ironically it was George III, who *did* go mad, who finally dropped the delusional claim.

At the end of Alfred's reign then, the situation for the Anglo-Saxons was much better than it had been at the beginning, but that wasn't saying much. And when I say 'much better' I'm ignoring the main thing that hadn't changed at all: the fact that almost all of them were medieval peasants. Whoever happens to be king, that is a horrible thing to be. There was astronomical infant mortality, a 20 per cent death rate of mothers in childbirth and, if neither of those things got you, a grim life of toil and shortage.

Still, for the minority of Anglo-Saxons affluent enough to care, here was the state of play: half of them were still under Viking rule in the vast Danelaw and there still wasn't anything like a proper kingdom of England, whatever posterity reckoned. Alfred ruled most of the rest of the Anglo-Saxon area – an enlarged and stabilized Wessex, encompassing the south-western half of Mercia plus Kent, Sussex and London – though there was a small surviving fragment of non-Wessexian (non-Wessexy? non-Wessexual? awessexual?) Anglo-Saxon rule in the northern section of the old Kingdom of Northumbria, the bit we still call Northumbria today.

Don't feel bad that England still didn't exist – France didn't either. But, again, it's on the way. In 843, at the Treaty of Verdun, Charlemagne's grandsons agreed to split his vast empire into East Francia – which evolved into a state that, broadly speaking, was the precursor of Germany – and West Francia, which later started to be referred to as France. It's eerily appropriate that, 1,073 years later, Verdun was also the location chosen for Germany and France to fight a vast and fruitless nine-month battle of apocalyptic mechanized slaughter that still somehow failed to jolt them into a lasting peace. At the time of the treaty, Verdun itself went to neither of the Francias but to the third and thinnest slice of the imperial cake, called Lotharingia, which was squeezed between the other two and didn't last long for that reason.

In the late ninth-century, the kings of West Francia were having their own issues with Vikings, or Northmen. One of them, Rollo, had invaded and occupied the area around Rouen and, in 885, had nearly taken Paris. But, like Alfred, the West Francian ruler Charles III had accepted the new reality. In 911, in exchange for agreeing to be baptized, marrying Charles's daughter Gisela and leaving the rest of the kingdom alone, Rollo and his heirs were granted authority, under the West Francian crown, to all the land between the River Epte and the sea. Since it was now ruled by these Northmen, or Normans, the region became known as Normandy.

7. Kings Edward, Athelstan, Edmund, Eadred, Eadwig, Edgar and Another Edward, and Queen Aethelflaed

Two things are striking about the names of Alfred's successors and the notables of their courts: first the similarity – so many 'elfs', 'alfs', 'edgs', 'adgs' and 'ethels' that we're forced to conclude that the Anglo-Saxons found making those noises a lot easier than people do now. They're quite tricky syllables, if you ask me, but maybe in an age of, by our standards, catastrophically poor dental hygiene, ethels and adwigs tripped off the tongue comparatively easily. Perhaps it was a noise that came naturally and five or six would just slip out, accompanied by gloops of saliva, as a side effect of working a particularly fibrous chunk of turnip round to the last fully functioning molar.

And second, half of them survive as common modern names, while the other half look like a piece of software had those names typed into it and then generated the rest. On the one hand, there's the likes of Alfred, Edward, Edgar and Edmund – okay, fine – and on the other Alfweard, Athelstan, Aethelred, Eadred, Eadwig and Aethelflaed. Bless you.

There'll eventually be an England

This period, the early to mid-tenth century, is when the kingdom of England started. It feels like it deserved a bit more fanfare. The truth is it was something of a soft launch.

When Alfred died, in 899, the next king, his eldest son, was called Edward, known as 'Edward the Elder' by historians to distinguish him from another King Edward who briefly reigned later in the century, and another one in the century after that. (As discussed earlier, this is all long before 'King Edward the First' who didn't reign until the late thirteenth century, and was therefore, in reality, the fourth. This means Edward VIII was really Edward XI which, for reasons I can't quite put my finger on, seems more appropriate for a Nazi sympathizer.)

On accession, Edward was challenged for the throne by his cousin Aethelwold (a great name for an artisanal cheese), who was the son of Alfred's elder brother and predecessor as king. This kind of crisis happened more often than not between reigns. The tradition King Offa had tried to start, of getting the next king anointed during the reign of the current one, had failed to catch on amid all the Viking stress. When you're surrounded by death, the last thing you want to think about is death. That's why the troops at the Somme must have been reluctant to discuss estate planning.

They say history is written by the victors, and they're right whoever they are, which is probably why what little we know about Aethelwold makes him seem like a wanker. He rebelled against Edward, forcibly married a nun, holed up at the place where his father was buried (Wimborne, to be precise), swore he'd die rather than leave there (and this was long before they had a model village), then did in fact leave without dying (reason prevailed), but also without taking his poor wife, the nun, with him (what a wanker).

His next move was more impressive. He fled to the Danish kingdom of Northumbria, which was where Yorkshire is now (to the south of the surviving rump of the Anglo-Saxon king-dom of Northumbria which, as I've said, was where Northumbria is now), and persuaded its leaders to make him king. Nobody knows how. Maybe he wasn't such a wanker? Or maybe the Vikings *liked* wankers? Either way, he invaded

Mercia with a Danish army, did all the usual damage and then retreated into East Anglia. Edward followed him there with his own army to do some retaliatory smashing and grabbing but left without managing a proper battle. The proper battle happened soon afterwards, in 902, between Aethelwold's Danes and a force of Kentish men who refused Edward's repeated orders to stop pillaging and come home. It was called the Battle of the Holme and Aethelwold was killed at it. End of succession crisis.

Still, the Danish presence in what is now England was considerable – there was an East Anglian Danish kingdom, plus a large area in the east Midlands called the Five Boroughs (it centred on the towns of Leicester, Nottingham, Stamford, Derby and Lincoln) ruled by a coalition of Viking warlords, as well as the other Danish kingdom around York. Aethelwold's antics showed that these Vikings were very much still in the market for attacking, looting and otherwise destabilizing the kingdom of the Anglo-Saxons.

During Edward's reign, this situation shifted and the power of the House of Wessex was extended considerably. He was supported in this by his formidable elder sister Aethelflaed, known as the Lady of the Mercians. She was married to Aethelred, the non-king of the non-Danelaw bit of Mercia whom I mentioned earlier. He died in 911 but was in poor health for some years before that which meant that, for over a decade before her own death in 918, Aethelflaed was running the place and orchestrating military activity that relentlessly encroached upon the Danelaw.

In the chapter heading, I've referred to Aethelflaed as a queen, which isn't strictly true. But, as the daughter and sister of kings and the effective ruler of an Anglo-Saxon kingdom, she deserves the title, tonally speaking. Also I'm bitterly aware that this is the first mention of a woman in this narrative, apart from a brief one for Queen Bertha of Kent and an adjectival contribution from Queen Victoria. And actually I think my daughter got a nod, but that's really just nepotism as her impact on early medieval English history is tiny.

I'm sorry about that. It is one of the boring things about a lot of history. The towering sexism of many ages, and of many subsequent ages which have spearheaded the analysis of those earlier ages, has left the specifics of all the brilliant or shitty things women were doing largely unrecorded. You'd think that *all* they were doing was marrying kings, which the overwhelming majority were not.

I'm acknowledging this because I'm aware of the irony that, while I'm writing about an age in which almost all women (and men) were illiterate, in the current era of mass literacy, it is much more likely that any given book is being read by a woman than by a man. Men read less than women and instead commit more violent crime and listen to more audiobooks. These aren't necessarily the same men, I should add.

Back in the tenth century, after the death of Aethelflaed, the violence is once again almost exclusively being committed by men. By the end of Edward's reign, he had taken over East Anglia and four of the Five Boroughs. Only Lincoln and the kingdom centring around York were still in Viking hands.

The mite of Roam

This trend continued apace under the next king, Athelstan, who, after the traditional succession crisis culminating in the suspicious death of his half-brothers, mopped up the rest of the Danelaw. After 927, he styled himself in his various charters as *Rex Anglorum*, 'King of the English', rather than merely of the Anglo-Saxons.

Better still, his military dominance was such that he was able to assert a sort of pseudo-imperial superiority over the whole of Britain, with grudging endorsement from the various Scottish, Welsh or Danish rulers. He had sufficient clout to make them all assemble at councils to acknowledge his seniority, which caused a lot of bad feeling similar to that felt by the leader of the SNP whenever they're caught in traffic on the M25.

These resentments turned to rebellion, culminating in the brutal Battle of Brunanburh in which the Anglo-Saxons, led by Athelstan, defeated the combined forces of the kings of Scotland, Strathclyde and Dublin. The kings of Wales had wisely decided to suppress their disgruntlement and not take part. Athelstan carried all before him, declaring himself the *Rex totius Britanniae*, which you don't have to be much of a classical scholar to translate. It sounds like joke Latin made up by a child – something like *Imperius Completus Everywarium* or *Bossus Worldiae Massivum*.

There's something infantile about these post-Dark Age rulers' relationship with Rome. They seem to have only the sketchiest idea of what the Roman Empire actually was, but a strong sense that it was enormous and official and that the route to looking like you're allowed to be in charge of stuff was via affecting to be extremely Roman.

It's a bit like some nursery-school children trying to dress up as astronauts. There's lots of glue and glitter but it's all a bit crumpled. The whole business of having crowns was borrowed from the later Roman emperors' habit of wearing diadems. The objects were then infused with some handy religious significance when the Eastern Romans invented coronations based on some biblical references to crowns and anointing. What looks to us like an archetypically medieval ceremony caught on across Europe because of its associations with the mystique of classical antiquity – this ancient pagan superpower that was also somehow where Christianity came from.

Then Charlemagne decided he was going to have a bit of that. He had the brilliant idea of announcing he was the Roman emperor – or as the office was later referred to with garish hyperbole 'Holy Roman Emperor!' 'What is it, Boy Wonder?!' Since the original proper Roman Empire had split in half in the fourth century, the Eastern bit had been going pretty strong, but the Western half hadn't (see above) and the title of 'Western Emperor' had lapsed. So, having put together an extremely large early medieval kingdom (albeit still much smaller than the Western half of the Roman Empire had once been), Charlemagne twigged that a key part of becoming an emperor was saying you were one.

There's a pleasing irony to this. The first actual Roman emperors – you know, the proper ones like Augustus and Tiberius and Nero, when Rome was all-conquering and the whole notion of its decline was restricted to its own self-involved literature – always pretended *not* to be emperors. They still went along with the notion that Rome was a republic run by elected consuls, sometimes not troubling to become consuls themselves.

In fact, the term 'emperor' started as a euphemism. Rome, having become a republic, loathed the notion of kings. 'Emperor' derived from *imperator*, which means a 'military commander' – they weren't horrible kings, just trusty commanders, in the same way that Stalin was just a nice reliable general secretary rather than anything showy or threatening like a president or tsar.

A few baffled centuries later, the concept of a king had been detoxified, but the concept of an emperor, having been conceived to say 'Don't worry, I'm not a king or anything threatening like that,' had come to mean 'I'm a king among kings, full of the might and legitimacy of Rome, whatever that was!'

Alfred and his grandson Athelstan loved all this. Alfred had actually been to Rome as a boy on two occasions which, considering it was then a two- or three-month journey each way, will have taken up quite a lot of his childhood. While there, the pope had given him a *cingulum* (a sort of utility belt that officers in the Roman army wore) and the robes of a consul. Imagining this scene of a pope in ninth-century Rome, a feeble and impoverished city lurking on the outskirts of the ruins of its namesake empire's mega-capital, handing out shiny bits of old Roman clobber to random visiting children, is both poignant and hilarious. These items were then ceremonially handed on to Athelstan by Alfred, with how much understanding of the vast difference between the Anglo-Saxon system of government and that presided over for centuries by the polytheistic consuls of Rome we can't know.

Athelstan was the first English king who, at his consecration in Kingston in 925, had a crown placed on his head rather than the traditional helmet. This piece of Byzantine ceremonial had taken 500 years to reach England – almost as slow as the espresso machine – and was the first of many English coronations. It's a moment of childish blinging-up that we're still stuck with – a vulgarity as irreversible as when they started putting chocolates into advent calendars or TV presenters first wore sparkly poppies around Remembrance Day instead of normal ones.

Yet Athelstan's imperial pretensions, and claims in Latin to be *totius* in charge of everything, show confidence and success. England as a place and a kingdom – as a viable state – had finally started to exist. The England that Alfred was deemed by posterity to have 'reconquered' from the Danes didn't really exist before that – it was just a bunch of squabbling Germanic kingdoms – but the 'claiming of it back' had the effect of creating and defining it.

As so often in history, what is in fact a novelty is defined and justified in terms of precedent. The House of Wessex claimed to be restoring something, a pre-existing England, which didn't pre-exist, and a pre-existing Romanness, which their regime was absolutely nothing like and had no connection with at all.

Five more kings

The four decades after the death of Athelstan in 939 saw the accession of six kings. The next chapter is about the sixth of them and I'm going to rattle through the first five now. It may well be that, after this, no one ever mentions them to you again.

The first two, Edmund and Eadred, were Athelstan's half-brothers, sons of Edward the Elder by his third wife, Eadgifu. Then there were Edmund's two sons, Eadwig and Edgar – Edgar was known as the Peaceful, which makes him sound nicer than he was. Then, finally, Edward the (spoiler alert) Martyr. They all died young. None of them reached thirty-five and two of them died in their teens.

As I've said, the kingdom of England existed by this point, but they hadn't done the extension. There was still a viable Danish kingdom of York when Athelstan died, which had a revival under Edmund and Eadred and had to be repeatedly pushed back, but was finally knocked on the head in 954. During the troubled and fractious reign of the teenage Eadwig, there was such a split at court in favour of his younger brother Edgar that, in 957, the country was briefly partitioned between the two of them – along the line of the Thames, with Eadwig ruling Wessex and Edgar Mercia and Northumbria. This awkward state of affairs ended two years later with Eadwig's timely, and very possibly actively timed, death.

Edgar the Peaceful is the most significant of these kings. He was a great enthusiast for the monastic reform movement which was a big deal at the time, exceptionally dull though it sounds. Spearheaded by St Dunstan, Archbishop of Canterbury, and St Aethelwold, Bishop of Winchester, the idea was to sort out the rackety old Anglo-Saxon monasteries, also known as minsters, and make them conform to the Rule of St Benedict. This Rule was written by an Italian monk called Benedict in the early sixth century and is in fact *lots* of rules. The big ideas were obedience, humility, work and prayer.

In contrast, Anglo-Saxon monasteries were often more casual and public-facing than we imagine such institutions to be. Many of the people who lived in them, known as secular clerks, were free to marry and popped in and out, treating the place like a vaguely God-themed Club 18–30. The system of parish priests and churches hadn't yet developed, so it made sense to have a version of monasticism that wasn't entirely inward-looking. Still, there was an aura of flexibility and fun that's always vulnerable in a religious context.

Sure enough, Dunstan and Aethelwold, and many other worthies at the time, declared it vital to sort this out. In an era when most people sincerely believed that incurring divine displeasure could result in the ruination of the kingdom, by plague or famine or Viking, and the damnation of any specific displeasure-incurrers, this campaign was about more than virtue-signalling. People really thought it was important.

This seemed to suit Edgar's temperament. He founded, or refounded, loads of monasteries and was enthused by the new uniformity that was demanded of them. At the same time, under Aethelwold's influence, he was also introducing uniformity into his administration: he standardized the coinage, exported the West Saxon institution of the 'shire' to the rest of England where we can still find them – in fact they've since found their way into Scotland and Wales too – and established shire and local courts based on 'hundreds', areas of a hundred 'hides'. A hide was the amount of land deemed sufficient to support a family. Many of the familiar trappings of the English state were being put in place.

He does not seem to have been a peaceful man at all,

despite his moniker, but rather a self-important, ruthless and tyrannical one. His piety was extolled by contemporary churchmen almost to the point of worship: he was described in the charter of the New Minster in Winchester as 'the vicar of Christ', which is a bit crawly. Not to be left behind by continental royal fashion, he gave himself a second coronation, thirteen years into his reign. It was a special imperial one conducted in Bath with its Roman associations, in the hope of evoking Charlemagne's capital in Aachen and getting the whole *Rex totius Britanniae* vibe going again.

All in all, he doesn't seem very nice. Yet his reign was genuinely peaceful. The bitter truth is that it was peaceful because of his ruthlessness. He was rigorous and predictable. People knew where they stood. In the medieval era, when people's expectations of government were unbelievably low by modern standards, this was as good as it got. All kings did terrible things, but the ones who did so out of weakness, capriciousness, viciousness, favouritism or fear engendered uncertainty that led to violence and chaos. What helped daily life go smoothly was a straightforward, well-organized hard-arse. Edgar's ruthless and violent refusal to be questioned, his indomitable martial spirit and his readiness to deploy violence, engendered peace.

Then aged about thirty-two he suddenly died, there was a succession crisis and everything was immediately fucked again. Of Edgar's two sons, one was an illegitimate teenager called Edward and another a five- or six-year-old child called Aethelred. On balance, encouraged by St Dunstan, the leading nobles went with the teenager, but the situation was very unstable and culminated in Edward's murder by supporters of his infant half-brother. It was an inauspicious start to yet another new reign.

8. King Aethelred the Unready

There's no justice. Alfred's medium-sized achievements, thanks to his canny commissioning of a praise-packed biography, overshadow that of his more successful successors. Worse still, their fame is also dwarfed by that of the incompetent who came after them: King Aethelred, known as Aethelred the Unready. The nickname sums him up, though apparently 'unready' didn't mean what it sounds like it means, but derives from the Old English word meaning 'badly advised', while the name Aethelred means 'well advised'. It's a joke – Well-Advised the Badly Advised – and a message to posterity about the limited impact of nominative determinism.

He reigned, on and off, from 978 to 1016, and his hapless reputation as a man utterly unable to deal with the Vikings is projected down the centuries. Not delusional and hubristic, not aggressive and miscalculating, not idiotic, just a prat and a coward who couldn't cope.

This image isn't helped by the terrible drawing of him that always gets used. It's from a twelfth-century chronicle, so the monk who drew it had never laid eyes on the man himself. In fact, the monk who drew it shows few signs of having ever laid eyes on a human being of any sort – though the facial expression he gives Aethelred might have inspired cartoonists of later centuries who were trying to capture the essence of someone who's just been viciously bonked on the head. We find Aethelred sitting on his throne with this look of lopsided bafflement. His right hand is grasping what looks like an enormous inflatable green sword. His left scratches his crotch. One leg is slightly raised as if to facilitate a fart.

Unready and unwilling

Aethelred's problems were no more of his own making than he was subsequently able to make them of his own solving. What I'm saying is that, like Alfred, he found himself in a shit situation but, unlike Alfred, he couldn't find his way out. Soon after his reign started, and just when everyone thought it was safe to go back in the water, the Vikings started raiding again.

These weren't Danes from the northern or eastern parts of England. They were from Scandinavia, as they had been in the nightmarish ninth century. As the reign progressed, it became clear that they weren't random piratical raiders, but were organized by the King of Denmark and Norway, Sweyn Forkbeard (Forkbeard is Old Danish for Fuckface) (no it isn't). This time there was an unnerving undertone of invasion by a foreign power to the familiar high stress of everything getting smashed or stolen or occupied.

Aethelred was an unenthusiastic warrior. He was exceptionally unwilling to lead troops into battle and I feel a lot of GCSE empathy for that attitude. At the time, though, it wasn't on. It's the equivalent of a modern politician being afraid of public speaking. In refusing that element of the job, Aethelred was about 700 years ahead of his time.

In the alternative he found to fighting, he was a hundred years behind it. He reverted to the old and unsuccessful Anglo-Saxon Viking-repelling technique: paying them to go away. It's what I did when we had mice – well, I didn't pay the mice, but I wouldn't be amazed to discover that the mice and the mice-removers had struck some sort of deal. As with Aethelred and the Vikings, it was very expensive, but I needed the mice to go away and was willing to pay any sum they named that was less than or equal to all the money I had.

Aethelred showed a similar dearth of bargaining acumen

and exported a lot of silver as a result. That this was possible was a sign of the wealth and functionality of the kingdom he was ruining. England had an extremely sophisticated coin-minting infrastructure for the time which enabled huge numbers of tiny metal portraits of Aethelred, which were even less realistic than the twelfth-century monk's drawing of him but not quite as stupid-looking, to invade Scandinavia, which perhaps the king considered a sort of pictorial revenge.

To be fair, that wasn't Aethelred's only idea: he also ordered the killing of all the Danes in England. It's a very different approach, isn't it? This was the St Brice's Day massacre of 1002 and it gives a nasty spiteful tinge to Aethelred's harmless-idiot image. The whole notion of slaughtering people was a lot more acceptable in those days – nowadays we're really down on it, but they were really down with it (oh, the power of prepositions!). Still, Sweyn Forkbeard was disinclined to take the proposed genocide of his countrymen on the prongy chin and invaded.

Aethelred's third strategy was to try and build an alliance with Normandy and that indirectly led to the Norman Conquest and the final eclipse of the House of Wessex and Anglo-Saxon kingship itself. Goodness, he really is enjoyably unsuccessful. Not that he could have foreseen the consequences of his Norman overtures. He was just trying to find some support against the Danes, and stop the Danes unloading all their loot in convenient nearby Norman ports.

The Duke of Normandy, Richard II, half-heartedly agreed to discontinue this practice, a promise he intermittently kept, and Aethelred married Richard's sister, Emma of Normandy, to seal the deal. Aethelred's first wife, Aelfgifu, had recently died so, in her role as queen of England, Emma was also given the name Aelfgifu. This might have been less confusing for Aethelred but not for anyone else, then or since, enchantingly beautiful though the name Aelfgifu obviously is.

Emma of Normandy seems to have been an accomplished powerbroker, and much of what happened between her marriage to Aethelred and the conquest of England by her great-nephew revolved around her. In the intervening sixty-four years, it was ruled for thirty-three years by her two husbands and for twenty-five years by two of her sons. The husbands were called Aethelred (as discussed) and Cnut, and the sons were called Harthacnut and Edward. You might get an inkling of what was going on ethnically speaking.

A flurry of sad ends

Have you noticed how bankrupted former tycoons always end up somewhere opulent? Their troubles tend to play out in mansions, and somehow the electricity and gas have never been cut off. Someone's still servicing the pool, even as the desperate bankrupt paces round it, shouting, 'What about the *Swiss* accounts?!' into his mobile. They might get murdered, but the blood always trickles on to something expensive.

It's the same with deposed kings. They tend to keep their creature comforts which, for those of us who aren't kings, might seem like the main reason it's nice to be a king. Tsar Nicholas II and his family were shot in the basement of the nice country house with servants where they were imprisoned, and former King Constantine II of Greece lived peacefully for many years in Hampstead Garden Suburb. You might die, but the circumstances usually remain plush.

We know from the life of Alfred the Great that this wasn't always the case. He was literally hiding in a marsh. He would have been cold, wet, hungry *and* in fear for his life rather than just the last one. People with royal blood never undergo anything that uncomfortable any more, except at Gordonstoun.

When did this start to change? It's earlier than you'd think.

Aethelred, for all his incompetence and throne-losing, never ended up down and out in the Somerset Levels legendarily burning cakes. You may have heard that King Alfred was said to have allowed the cakes of a poor woman, whose hospitality he'd prevailed upon at his lowest ebb, to burn because he was distracted thinking about what to do about the fact that he was sitting in a hovel monitoring peasant bakery when he was supposed to be king of Wessex. I didn't mention it earlier because there is no contemporary corroboration of this story so it's probably not true plus, unlike the Vikings' horns, neither is it particularly fun. It's in a strange category of 'Boring Myth and Legend' that also includes the tale of Hannibal of Carthage's brief attack of conjunctivitis and the time Charlemagne was given advice about dealing with recurrent damp by an apparition of the Virgin Mary. Those last two myths get their first citation here.

Aethelred and co. didn't have to hide in a marsh. When, in 1013, they got chucked out of the kingdom by Sweyn Forkbeard, they hung out at the Norman court in Rouen, care of Emma, enjoying the hospitality. Under Emma's influence, Aethelred and the Normans got pretty close and their son, Edward (future king and saint), stayed there for twenty-five years. You are what you eat, they say, which must be why some suspected that he was never properly English after that.

Ex-kings, future kings and aristocrats who were out of favour in Britain would be sojourning on the continent forever after – the future Edward III, the ex- and future Edward IV, the future Henry VII, the future Charles II, the former James II and Bonny Prince Charlie, all the way down to ex-King Edward VIII who lived out his days in bitter elegance in Paris. They head off to (usually) France to lick their (seldom literal) wounds, enjoy the cuisine and dream out loud about coronation or restoration to anyone who'll listen. If the French, or in this case the Normans, reckon it might further their own interests, there's the possibility of serious military or financial support. If not, there's still croissants and sympathy. And, in Bonny Prince Charlie's case, booze.

Aethelred didn't have long to wait for his chance. Sweyn Forkbeard, who had swiftly conquered England in 1013 (greatly helped by how sick of Aethelred the English had become), suddenly died in early 1014. He'd been king for five weeks. Taking advantage of a sudden death was a viable career path for much of the olden days. If you're looking for promotion nowadays, hoping your immediate superior will snuff it just isn't enough. It's not very nice and it's likely to lead to disappointment. You have to get proactive and start sending out CVs. People don't die as much as they used to.

That's not quite true. People still die at exactly the same rate as they always have: once per person. It's not how it feels, though, because people used to die younger, on average, and more randomly. It jazzed things up, introduced an element of doubt, like the presence of all those hungry lower-league teams in the FA Cup.

There are all sorts of times in history when events seem to be going in a certain direction and you're wondering 'Will so-and-so manage to do this, or will they fail?' You're locked into the plotline. It could go either way and it's very exciting . . . Then they die at a really weird point in the story. And we're reminded it's not a story. It's soap opera. In soap operas people expire mid-storyline all the time, because of trouble with agents or scandal in the news. Well, whoever was playing Sweyn Forkbeard asked for his own Winnebago or got hooked on diet pills or accused of assault and was abruptly written out.

Back came Aethelred from Normandy. Sweyn's army wanted his son Cnut to be king but the leading English noblemen were up for giving Aethelred another go. This seems strange, but Sweyn's swift death made them suspect that God didn't dislike Aethelred as much as they did. Plus he'd hired a Danish army to come with him (fresh move – he usually paid them to go away). So he got to be king again, just about. He probably wouldn't have lasted long had it not been for the fact that he didn't last long. He died in 1016, by which point Cnut had returned and was already doing a solid job of conquering the place again.

Aethelred had a son – I don't mean Edward, who was still at this point a child in Normandy, or his little brother Alfred, ditto – but an adult, by his first wife Aelfgifu (not to be confused with Aelfgifu). He was called Edmund 'Ironside', the soubriquet in honour of the valour with which he unsuccessfully resisted Cnut. He became king but was then defeated in battle. Nevertheless they did a sort of rehash of the Alfred–Guthrum deal, but with no religious conversion needed because they were both already Christian. On this occasion, though, the Danes were calling the shots and Edmund only got Wessex and the title of 'King of England', while all of Mercia, East Anglia and Northumbria went to Cnut.

Very soon afterwards, still in 1016, Edmund also suddenly died (this is getting ridiculous – there must have been a new executive producer). Cnut took over the whole country and, to cement his leadership, married Queen Dowager Emma of Normandy aka Aelfgifu, despite the fact that he was already married to a woman called, yep, Aelfgifu.

9. See Next You Tuesday

Amid all this levity about the strange name Aelfgifu, which must have sounded perfectly normal to people in those days, don't think I'm unaware of the enormous vagina in the room. I am referring of course to Cnut's name, which is basically Cunt. It's very very nearly Cunt. In fact he's known – and my teacher at school didn't mention this when talking up Alfred – as Cnut the Great. I suppose the thinking was that he's deemed more Danish than English so Alfred was still the only properly English king called Great. Then again, Cnut was king of England, which Alfred never was, so I think he definitely counts and it's casual anti-Danish racism in the teaching establishment of the early 1980s that means his greatness gets ignored.

I digress. I'm getting distracted by analysis of history from the proximity of an exceptionally rude word. As a comedian, that's arguably a lapse of professional duty and would prove bitter and perverse reading to any of the learned academics who attempted to teach me history when I was at university, a time when I was focused pretty much exclusively on writing rude comic sketches and neglecting the historical analysis the local education authority was paying for me to go there and do. Those were the days.

Theses have been written, with no doubt more in the pipe-line (rude – pipeline could mean rectum), about why slang references to vaginas are deemed hugely offensive, while slang references to penises are considered less fulsomely impolite. But, for me, the presence of a king called Cnut in all the history books is the culmination of a long journey made by children which begins with the discovery of the word poo, continues through noticing the missing 'i' on every 'to let' sign (they've even left a gap for it) and reaches its greatest joy with the widespread usage of the word 'bosom' in hymn lyrics.

The bottom (fart) line is this: I don't want to become someone who will blithely carry on when a king's name is as close to the word cunt as Cnut's is. If I get to the point where that amusement is lost on me – the fact that a big important serious king is very very nearly called King Cunt, King Cunt the Great or the Great Big Cunt – then I think an important part of me will have died.

He's often known as Canute. Maybe that version of his name is a Hyacinth Bucket-style attempt in later centuries to distance him from genital connotations. You've probably heard the stories of King Canute failing to stop the tide. I've heard it told two ways: one in which the king is foolish for thinking he can stop the tide and the other in which he's brilliantly showing what vacuously craven yes-men his nobles are for falsely claiming that, as king, he can stop the tide. I don't know if either is true – but we do know that he couldn't stop the tide. Stupid cunt.

It seems Cnut was an effective king, despite his inability to influence lunar gravity. It's by accident not merit that William the Conqueror gets all the attention. Cnut conquered England and ruled it plus Denmark *and* Norway. William only had it and comparatively tiny Normandy. Also Cnut was genuinely king of the Anglo-Saxon kingdom of England. He didn't bring in a brand new Danish aristocracy and loads of Norwegian bishops – though under him the title of the most senior nobles charged with governing large areas of the country changed from 'ealdorman' to the ironically less-foreign-sounding 'earl'. Otherwise he largely worked with the people and institutions that were already in place. To my mind, this is both sensible and comparatively nice.

Taking all the weird soap-opera randomness of history out of the equation for a second, an Anglo-Danish kingdom made lots of sense. For the last five chapters, I've been banging on about the Vikings and the Anglo-Saxons (or the English as they came to be known). Surely, this regime is where all that has been heading?

Instead, the soap opera of England is going to take a sharp turn away from Scandinavia and towards what is starting to be known as France. At this point under the empire of Cnut the Great, that doesn't feel natural at all. It feels weird, random and like the producers didn't take the decision for creative reasons but because the advertisers of Cruises of the Fjords have been dramatically outbid by Bonne Maman. And that, I'd say, is a Lesson We Can Learn from History. Possibly the *only* one: You Never Completely Know What's About to Happen.

Damnation avoidance

I don't suppose Cnut *was* nice. It's hard to imagine any of these kings being pleasant people. They did so much killing. Some straightforward in-battle killing, which doesn't seem that sunny, but also quite a lot of having people executed, which is even less friendly, and, in many cases, a decent chunk of arranging for people to be murdered, which is downright spiteful.

For example, when Sweyn Forkbeard died in 1014 and the English opted to allow Aethelred back, Cnut was holding a lot of English noble hostages that his father had taken when invading the kingdom a few weeks earlier. Cnut returned the hostages, but only after he'd had their hands, ears and noses cut off. Can you imagine doing that? I really can't and I don't count myself a particularly nice person.

My faltering GCSE empathy lets me down again here.

Were these kings like driven CEOs in an age where murder and mutilation were deemed less serious? Or could be justified for religious reasons? Or could be atoned for by industrializing the process of getting monks to pray for your soul?

That's what 'chantries' were – big expensive religious buildings which rich people funded so that thousands of monk-hours would be put into praying for their souls, thus making sure they evaded hell and sped through purgatory, straight to lovely heaven where they'd presumably then bump into all the other rich nobles they were already accustomed to socializing with.

It seems like a weird notion – the religious equivalent of tax avoidance. Those rich guys must have thought that, like with the Inland Revenue, it was possible to game the system – that omniscient God wouldn't notice that the millions of prayers saying how lovely Duke Charles the Rapist was were all coming from monks living in buildings he paid for. They must have thought God was an idiot, a very powerful idiot. If your experience of government is exclusively medieval kingship, why would you expect the celestial realm to be a meritocracy?

Whatever his dearth of niceness, Cnut does seem to have been clever. By marrying Emma of Normandy, he neutralized the threat of her and Aethelred's two sons, Edward and Alfred, who were still sojourning in Normandy. By restoring and respecting Anglo-Saxon institutions, he was able to seem more legitimate and gloss over the fact that his only justification for being king of England was conquest. By being a Viking, he very effectively dealt with the Vikings. They were literally no trouble – because they'd won. Letting people win can be a great way of shutting them up. If only it had worked on Nigel Farage.

We still haven't got to William the Conqueror and yet there already seems to be an enormous amount of conquering going on: Sweyn Forkbeard and Cnut, and even poor old

Aethelred, who regained some sort of control in between the two. All of these men conquered England. And Vikings had been conquering bits of it, and Anglo-Saxons reconquering them again, for centuries. Conquering England doesn't look like that big a deal at this point – in fact, it seems like one of the main things that happened in England since everyone forgot how to build villas. 'Conqueror' is an unremarkable nickname for eleventh-century England – a bit like 'Setter-Up of a Website' would be in 2001.

All the conquering had not left England in tatters. On the contrary, it was a coherent and organized unit – hence Cnut's canny decision to govern it through its existing structure: shires, run by shire-reeves (sheriffs), divided into hundreds in most of the kingdom and wapentakes in the more Scandy bits, over which earldormen, later earls, exercised authority. Taxation was raised according to areas called hides (carrucates in Scandy), there was an advanced and regularly reissued coinage system, and written royal commands were routinely distributed to the whole kingdom. This is impressive stuff – it's not like they had email. Hardly anyone could read. In summary, it was a lot less shit than most places at the time. Not much in the way of stone buildings, but it was prosperous and administratively sophisticated. That's why lots of people were keen to nick it.

10. A Pair of Cnuts

There was a brief hiatus in the conquering between 1035 (when Cnut deid) and 1066. Cnut's son Harthacnut, a name which surprisingly means 'Tough Knot' not 'Hard Cunt', was all set to conquer England in 1040 but didn't have to in the end because the guy he was hoping to conquer it off suddenly dropped dead. This was another son of Cnut, not by Emma but by his first wife Aelfgifu, who was called Harold Harefoot (nickname not surname).

I wonder how Harthacnut felt. Relieved, I suppose. Still, it must have been an anticlimax. All that prep and then you don't have to do anything. Like when exams were cancelled during the pandemic (empathy attempt). Think of all the wasted adrenaline. The squandered food. Catering for an invasion is a much more important historical role than it gets credit for, as we know from the fact that the expression 'an army marches on its stomach' is attributed to generals not chefs (usually Napoleon, sometimes Frederick the Great – *never* Escoffier or Jamie Oliver).

What I'm failing to consider, of course, is that Harthacnut's main feeling might have been terrible grief that his half-brother had just died. I'm deliberately failing to consider it, because considering it would be a complete waste of time. This was not a loving family – or not in any sense that we'd understand. If it was love, it was tough love. Very tough. I'm thinking specifically of an occasion where someone was blinded. If that's being cruel to be kind, the resulting kindness is going to have to be *amazing*. 'In retrospect, I'm glad you blinded me because . . .' I'm struggling to think of anything that would follow that. 'Because it's given me the edge in my dream profession of being a piano tuner'?

The blinded person predeceased the invention of the piano by about 650 years, and in fact didn't last long after the blinding. I suspect it may not have been done that hygienically. We don't seem to deliberately blind people so much these days, which is good, except for the fact that we now have the know-how to do it much more safely. The royals of the eleventh century would look in awe at the efficiency and cleanliness with which leaders of the modern age would theoretically be able to blind their relatives, and find it hard to believe how seldom they take advantage of that facility.

The blinded man was a half-brother of Harthacnut, but just a stepbrother of Harold Harefoot who ordered the blinding. But I don't think we should infer that Harefoot would baulk at blinding a half-brother, or a full brother, or anyone at all except possibly himself. You're either up for things like blinding people or you're not, and an alarmingly large number of the political leaders of the middle ages fall into the former category, which puts the whole 'They all went to Eton!' issue we have with politicians these days into quite a relaxing perspective.

The blindee was in fact Alfred, son of Emma of Normandy and Aethelred the Unready, and younger brother of Edward the Confessor, future king and saint and all-round jammy sod, who came to England at the same time as Alfred but slipped back to Normandy and was happily munching camembert by the time Alfred was having his eyes put out. I don't like Edward the Confessor.

The agonies of choice

This all happened as a result of the confused situation after the death of Cnut. Another bloody succession crisis. At this point in English history, the rules about who should succeed when a king died were a fair bit vaguer than they subsequently became. If you were hoping to become king, being son of the previous king certainly boosted your cause, but it didn't clinch the deal. Neither did being the eldest son. Other things helped, like being accepted by the major nobles (when brought together to discuss such things, they were known as the 'witan' – just imagine the House of Lords, but not so modern), or claiming with some plausibility to have been nominated by the previous king, or having recently conquered the country by force of arms.

On the face of it, this seems like a better system than raw primogeniture because there's a small measure of merit in the mix. Alfred the Great became king after all his elder brothers but in preference to their sons and that seemed like a sensible decision: he was an adult, for a start, and quite clever and determined, while they were bereaved children.

The fun thing for us about primogeniture is that the person who ends up as king can be hilariously unsuitable. The way the poor Spanish Habsburgs meandered towards extinction, after centuries of dogged adherence to agnatic (male-only) primogeniture and intermarriage, led to some entertaining dribbling and crazily chinned figures, dutifully trying to find a way to impregnate various cousins and nieces (all of whom were equally riddled with underlying conditions) using what-ever enfeebled genitalia their lopsided genetic inheritance had bequeathed them. It's less fun for the people living at the time. And is fun the main thing you want from a governmental system? Storing up anecdotes for posterity makes sense for a character actor and raconteur, but it's not a sound basis for building a regime.

With that in mind, the eleventh-century English conven-tion of being able to choose a king, even from a small shortlist largely of members of the same family, seems helpful. It would have allowed the seventeenth-century Spanish to bene-fit from rulers who could feed themselves unaided. But there is a massive downside: uncertainty. When a king dies, you really want everyone immediately to know and accept who is going to be the new king. Civil war can do a lot more damage to the state and its inhabitants than the most befuddled inbred.

A fair bit of uncertainty is okay in states with a more stable governmental structure, where the various candidates for power don't have their own armies and there's an effective civil service and law enforcement system to keep things ticking over while the future leadership is decided. That's what happens in functional democracies. It's a prerequisite if you want to enjoy the luxury of choice without enduring the unluxury of constant violence. In comparatively unsophisticated medieval states, periods of murderous uncertainty, such as that after the death of Cnut and many many other occasions before, since and elsewhere, made people look increasingly favourably on primogeniture. At least then you *know*.

Not always – kings can die without sons, and daughters absolutely weren't seen as satisfactory alternatives. Then you're into a whole rival-claimants nightmare. But a lot of the time it meant that at least everyone knew which idiot was coming next. If your expectations of the state are low, that can be a comfort. There's not much to be said for a choice of idiots even when civil war isn't a realistic threat, as the recent politics of the UK has demonstrated.

A fiddly bit

The two candidates for king at Cnut's death were Harthacnut, his son by Emma of Normandy, and Harold Harefoot, one of his sons by Aelfgifu. Harold was right there on the scene, all ready to be king, with Aelfgifu on hand to promote his cause. In fact, some say he got his nickname, which means 'swift like a hare', from the speediness with which he put himself in front of the assembled witan to claim the throne. If so, it seems a snide compliment, a bit like calling him King First-to-the-Buffet.

Meanwhile Harthacnut was busy securing his father's other kingdom of Denmark, though his claim to the English throne was still being energetically advanced by Emma and the most powerful lord at the time, Earl Godwin. Godwin was an Anglo-Saxon but a massive Danophile. He'd hit the big time under Cnut, and thereafter worked tirelessly to end up on the right side of things in order to remain a major player. Was he a kingmaker or did he just back whoever looked like winning anyway? This question is often posed about Rupert Murdoch. Was it the *Sun* wot won it for Tony Blair in 1997, or did Murdoch and the *Sun* swap sides to back Blair when his victory started to seem inevitable? Same question for Fox News and Trump in 2016.

Godwin was very pro-Emma and Harthacnut in 1035, but that all went a bit phone-hacking for him because the witan gave the throne to Harold-with-the-Napkin-Round-his-Neck. Or they sort of did. It was a bit unclear, which must have been very annoying for the overwhelming majority of people who didn't give a shit who was king but wanted it decided. Harold was effectively king of most of England – though not crowned because the Archbishop of Canterbury was not a fan and point blank refused to – while Emma of Normandy and Earl Godwin were vaguely in charge of Wessex on behalf of Harthacnut.

This unstable situation put the willies up Godwin, who reckoned he'd backed the wrong horse. That's when Alfred turned up – remember him? The one who gets blinded – Harefoot's stepbrother and Emma's son by her first husband Aethelred the Unready. It's not clear why Alfred came to England then – Emma later claimed Harold forged a letter from her to lure him, but it's more likely she genuinely invited him hoping it would boost her position (but then regretted it because it didn't and he got blinded). What with Harthacnut stubbornly staying in Denmark, she may have fancied her chances of restoring the House of Wessex. She was an energetic woman.

Whatever the reason for Alfred's arrival, Godwin welcomed him as an honoured guest and then, in order to curry favour with the new regime, immediately turned him over to Harefoot, who had him blinded on the way to Ely, where he died without even having seen the magnificent cathedral for the combined reasons that he was now blind and it hadn't yet been built.

By 1037, Emma had fled to Bruges, Harold Harefoot's position was stable with the new-found support of Godwin, and Edward the Confessor, who had travelled to England at the same time as Alfred but separately and was able to leg it without being mutilated, was back in Normandy, probably praying or looking wise or going to calvados tastings, waiting for the kingdom of England to be served up to him on a fucking silver platter which, infuriatingly, was just about to happen.

Harthacnut hadn't given up on ruling a second kingdom and, once he'd sorted out Denmark, started planning the invasion I mentioned (the one that turned out not to be necessary thanks to Harefoot's narratively insensitive death). Harthacnut then arrived in England having collected his mother from Bruges, became king and had Harefoot dug up, beheaded and thrown into a fen, just to work off some of that unspent invasion energy. Plus, I suppose, to avenge the blinding and death of his half-brother, Alfred. So there *was* love in that family, but it tended to manifest itself in violent acts of vengeance rather than birthday cards.

Harthacnut swiftly made himself very unpopular, partly by raising taxes to cover the costs of all the ships he'd organized for the invasion. To shore up his position, he invited his other half-brother, Edward, over from Normandy, and, far from blinding him, proclaimed him his co-king and heir, before dying without issue after getting shit-faced at a wedding. It's possible he was poisoned. So Edward the Butter-Side-Up became king. I expect he thought he deserved it.

11. King Edward the Confessor

The Danish historical cul-de-sac in English history ends here. Or nearly. The days of Scandinavian kings and dragon ships thick with metaphorical helmet horns breasting the horizon are almost over. It's 1042 and the House of Wessex is back in charge as if it had never happened, as if it had all been a weird 250-year-long nightmare.

Not quite. Edward the Confessor, while on paper a straightforward Anglo-Saxon king and indeed a great-great-great-grandson of Alfred the Great if you can imagine anything so posh, was in reality a bit different. He'd gone slightly Norman. Because of the Danes, he'd been living in Normandy for most of his life – and his mother, his key advocate, was Norman, while his father, Aethelred, the previous proper Anglo-Saxon king of England, was long dead. The English regime was already turning continental under Edward, even before William turned up.

Despite this disconcerting whiff of garlic, Earl Godwin noticed which way the wind was blowing this time. Maybe the garlic made the wind more noticeable? Or caused the wind? Are you enjoying how I'm mixing tired meteorological metaphor with anachronistic xenophobic slur with fart joke? I have no idea whether any more or less garlic was used in the cookery of eleventh-century Normandy than that of eleventh-century England. I reckon I can get away with the mild xenophobia because of modern France's GDP. In my experience, people don't tend to object anywhere near as much if you're rude about affluent nationalities.

The problem I now face is thinking of the equivalent thing

that Danish people stereotypically smell of – which, come to think of it, might be a branding issue the Danish tourist board need to look at. Come on, guys! What's your 'when in Rome'? When in Copenhagen you eat . . . bacon? Lurpak? Rancid tinned fish? No, I think that's a Swedish thing. Perhaps you have a glass of . . . I'm desperately trying not to say Carlsberg.

Whatever it is, that's what Godwin would pong of, if Edward smelt of garlic. These two Anglo-Saxons would pick very different places for their holidays. Godwin was Cnut's man and looked to Scandinavia just as much as Edward favoured Normandy. Nevertheless, Godwin energetically supported Edward at the start of his reign and Edward pretended not to mind that Godwin had betrayed his brother to Harold Harefoot. But he did mind, deep down. Which, I suppose, given the brutality of the age, reflects well on him.

Edward vs Godwinsteam: pick a side!

While I'm grudgingly acknowledging positive aspects of Edward the Confessor, I should say that, in general, his reign seems to have been competent and peaceful. He doesn't appear to suffer from the standard monarchical vices. There's no sign that he was a boozer or overeater or womanizer (he didn't even have sex with his wife) or much of a murderer. He still liked hunting, of course.

It's remarkable how many kings over the centuries were obsessed with hunting. It's like American presidents with golf. It must have been weirdly addictive, like space invaders crossed with smoking. Loads of otherwise very different-seeming kings – Edward the Confessor and Henry VIII and Charles I and Louis XVI and Franz Joseph and George V – were chasing around after wild animals every moment they could spare.

Massive sections of the countryside were reserved for them to do it in, in a way that makes the madness of an emerald-green golf course in the Nevada desert seem restrained. Edward did even more hunting than he did praying, and he did an enormous amount of praying, and had Westminster Abbey built in the Romanesque style beloved of the Normans, for him to pray in. (That's not the Abbey that is there now, which was completed in the fourteenth century.)

Friend though Edward was to the Normans, they do him no favours with posterity; they reduce him to the indrawn breath before the inflation of their glorious balloon. Nothing he did seems to matter except insofar as it was a precursor to the Conquest.

What he mainly seemed to do was bicker with Earl Godwin and tip people the wink that they could be the next king. Those two activities are interconnected because the man who actually ended up being the next king was Earl Godwin's son Harold, often called Harold Godwinson for reasons you can probably grasp.

The Anglo-Saxons didn't have surnames in the sense we now understand them, but Harold being referred to by that patronymic suggests they're scratching around for some sort of system for distinguishing between the various Ethels, but haven't quite got there yet. 'Godwinson' feels like a short-term solution because it raises so many questions about what Harold's own son might then be called: Godwinsonson? And then his son Godwinsonsonson? That would make it easy to keep track of the generations but is going to be a drain on charter-writers' ink if the dynasty goes on too long. Haroldson? Makes sense but that's not really a family name because it's going to change as often as the first names. So stick with Godwinson? For ever? But hang on, why does Godwin get to stick his brand on all his descendants? His father was called Wolfnoth – why not Wolfnothson? We can only presume an

Anglo-Saxon would have absolutely no trouble enunciating that, and it might have the happy side effect of partially draining a dentigerous cyst.

The Godwinsons and the Godwinsonfather (aka the Harold-father or Wolfnothson) were in a very powerful position throughout Edward's reign and between them held more land than the king. This would have been *slightly* humiliating for a king under circumstances where this dominant family hadn't previously caused the mutilation and death of his brother. But they had, so it was *very* humiliating and it soon got even humiliatinger when Edward was forced to marry one of them.

In 1045 Edward married Godwin's daughter, and Harold's sister, Edith. It's unlikely to have been a love match – that was the reality of royal marriages for centuries. In this case, it's also unlikely to have been a no-hate match – and that was something that even medieval princes and princesses were permitted to shoot for. Okay, maybe you're only twelve and they're sixty-two, and you don't speak the same language, and you've never met, and yet somehow you're also cousins, but you can still be *civil*, right? You can be like cordial neighbours who say good morning and occasionally try to procreate heirs – it's weird but it doesn't have to be *horrible*: Margaret Theresa of Spain, a seventeenth-century princess whose strange fate it was to marry her own uncle, Holy Roman Emperor Leopold I, affectionately called him 'Uncle' throughout their marriage.

On top of all these stresses, Edward was very keen to bring some of his Norman chums over and put them into positions of power to try to counterbalance the power of the Godwins (that's what I'm calling them from now on) and to make things feel a bit more like Normandy – he must have missed it. The Godwins weren't at all keen on this.

This tetchy situation came to a head in 1051 when the monks of Canterbury put forward one of Earl Godwin's relatives to become archbishop. Edward wasn't having it and appointed one of his favourite Normans, Robert of Jumièges, instead. In the same year, Eustace II of Boulogne, a big shot from northern France who had married Edward's sister, and later fought with William at the Battle of Hastings – so very much on the Norman side of things – visited England and he and his men triggered some sort of (presumably horrendously violent) fracas in Dover, causing the locals to kill about twenty of Eustace's men. Dover was in one of Godwin's earldoms so Edward took the opportunity to make something of it.

He ordered Godwin to punish the townspeople for their treatment of Eustace and co. and, when Godwin refused, the king turned on him. Archbishop Robert accused Godwin of plotting to kill Edward just as he had his brother Alfred – I don't know if Robert's pitch was that Godwin was a sort of brother-killing completist, or just that he was generally murdery so why not the king too. But the reasoning didn't seem to get much immediate scrutiny and suddenly the Godwins were in very hot water. All the other major Anglo-Saxon earls sided with the king, Edward put Edith in a nunnery and the rest of the Godwins legged it.

Who are you rooting for at this point? I've made my feelings pretty clear, I know. Even though Earl Godwin seems a bit of a rotter, there's something about Edward that comes down the centuries as insufferable. He's *such* a virtue-signaller. I can totally imagine him on social media, taking pictures of himself praying or saying tasteful things about the architectural style of his new minster. This is projection on my part but I'm not a professional historian so I don't have to pretend I haven't picked a side.

In fact, I'd argue that historians telling themselves they haven't picked a side are more misleading in an insidious way, because they definitely will have done, even if they don't know it. People can't help it. We do it without thinking. I have a favourite eye – of my own eyes, that is. I prefer the left – I'm just fonder of it. I wear contact lenses and I put the right lens in first, with a sort of clinical coolness – and then I do the left, and it's more friendly. To me, my left eye feels like the underdog, but I'm on its side. Metaphorically. Literally, *it's* on *my* side. My right side, as you look at me.

The sides we're dealing with here are going to morph into the sides at the Battle of Hastings, when Edward's beloved Normans, led by his great-nephew William, take on Harold Godwinson. Perhaps that's the fundamental reason I don't like Edward – it's because I can't help cheering for Harold when I think about the Battle of Hastings.

Who wants to be king?

The Godwins were soon back and even more powerful than before. They'd scattered to Ireland and Flanders but, in 1052, they returned and raised an army of their supporters in the south-east. Strangely, there wasn't a fight. This time it was the king's support that melted away and the Godwins were restored to all of their roles, including queen of England. That must have been an awkward homecoming. Returning to a man who'd banished her to a nunnery six years into a marriage that he'd already refused to consummate. Hard to take that as a compliment. I like to think she coped by employing withering sarcasm.

Edward had to send his Normans home, including Robert of Jumièges, who was replaced as archbishop of Canterbury by an Anglo-Saxon prelate called Stigand. Genuinely. That's what everyone says he was called. To me, it sounds like a name someone has hastily invented while trying to conceal extreme drunkenness from a police officer. The last 'd' in particular reeks of falsehood and lager burp.

The king's attempt to assert control had failed. This is the point when the bickering-with-the-Godwins section of Edward's reign gave way to the suggesting-to-lots-of-people-that-they-can-be-king phase. Annoying though this must have been for many people at the time, it makes sense psychologically. There Edward was, totally under the Godwins' various thumbs, largely powerless. All he had left were the undisputed facts that he was king and that he didn't have any children. The throne was seemingly in his gift. Frankly, he might have started promising people they could be king just to get some attention, as an excuse for a chat. He wasn't going to be dealing with the fallout.

The precise details of whom Edward offered the throne to and when are lost. It's slightly a mists-of-time thing, but there are some extra mists that have been pumped in by the Norman dynasty who wanted to appear as legitimate as possible to posterity. Once again, history is written, and edited, by the victors (or, rather, by some nerds the victors have ordered to write it, the actual victors being far too macho and illiterate to be arsed to write it themselves). It seems likely Edward genuinely did offer the throne to Duke William of Normandy in 1051 during the Godwins' period of exile. In fact, one of the earl's sons and one of his grandsons appear to have been given to William as hostages. I suppose the idea was that Godwin would then support the duke's claim – but it didn't work and anyway Godwin died in 1053.

Next, in 1056, Edward tipped the wink to his half-nephew Edward the Exile, by inviting him back to England from Hungary whence he'd been spirited off as an infant to stop Cnut having him murdered. This Edward would have been the official heir by the rules of succession that developed later, the ones we're now familiar with. He was the son of Edmund Ironside and the grandson of Aethelred. But he died soon after getting home, leaving a five-year-old son, Edgar, always referred to as 'atheling'. That's the Anglo-Saxon word basically meaning 'royal prince who's certainly a candidate for next king but isn't anything as reassuring as a confirmed heir'. The fact that this status was sufficiently common to justify its own word is a key reason there was so much fighting.

The other major contender was Harold Godwinson, Earl of Wessex and the most powerful man in England since the death of his father. Edward allegedly left the throne to Harold on his deathbed in January 1066. The chief alleger of this development was Harold himself, but it seems likely that Edward did say he could take over, if only because the subsequent Norman chronicles, whose primary raison d'être was to make Harold look like a faithless dick, didn't directly dispute it. Their argument was that William had the prior claim and that Harold had visited Normandy in 1064 and sworn an oath to support that claim. It was the oath-breaking and the consequent displeasure of God that led to Harold's defeat and the general rightness of William's seizure of power – that was their point.

We can't know for sure what promises Harold made to William, if any. He probably did visit Normandy, possibly in an attempt to broker the release of the Godwin hostages the duke was still keeping, but we can't know the circumstances under which any oaths were sworn. There's likely to have been a bit of dodgy pressure involved, in which case a modern lawyer would call the contract illegal and thus non-binding. We can be more certain that, when Edward was dying, there were a fair few people hanging around the bedside to witness Harold's being named as successor and more of them would probably have asserted that it hadn't happened if it hadn't happened.

To be honest, Edward sort of *had* to offer the crown to Harold by that point. Harold was the most powerful nobleman, already running the kingdom. Edward was lying in bed, drifting in and out of consciousness. It would have been inconvenient of him not to suggest Harold take over on a more official basis, and might have interrupted the flow of sympathy and cooling head-flannels from the surrounding Godwinite magnates, and the warming foot massage he was getting from the Godwinite queen. With his bunions at the mercy of her thumbs, it was no time to mention the Duke of Normandy. Instead, on 5 January 1066, he died.

Harold knew there were other contenders who might cause him trouble. He got the witan to rubber-stamp Edward's bequest immediately and had himself crowned *the very next day*. The ceremony was a sort of extra session stuck on the end of Edward's funeral mass. The corpse wouldn't have been cold. It must have been tricky to strike the right tone at the drinks do afterwards.

12. King Harold of . . .

A friend once told me a true story about a swimming gala at her school. All the children who were watching the gala had agreed in advance among themselves that, at a certain moment – let's say when a whistle was blown to start the first race or something like that – *all* of the watching pupils, dressed in their uniforms though they were, would simultaneously go 'Aaaaaaaah!', run towards the pool and jump in.

Much anticipatory amusement was derived from this exciting and ambitious conspiracy. But when the moment came, and the whistle was blown, one solitary girl, all on her own, suddenly went 'Aaaaaaaah!', ran towards the pool and jumped in. She looked like a maniac. Few of the onlooking teachers will have had the perspicacity to think: 'There goes *that* child's faith in humanity.'

People don't always do what they say they're going to do. You've got to keep your eye on that and seriously consider not doing what you've said you're going to do yourself, in pre-emptive response. Don't be the first to jump in the pool. Or the last. These are important things to remember if you're a medieval baron. Particularly if the king's just died and you're not a huge fan of civil wars. Everyone's got to watch each other.

That's what must have happened at Westminster in January 1066 after Edward the Confessor died. A lot of the leading nobles were around at the time – for Christmas and the consecration of Edward's beloved new Westminster Abbey a week earlier, an event the old king was too ill for, which would make me feel sorry for him if I was of a more charitable disposition.

The nobles will have watched each other. Harold, the most powerful among them, will have watched too. Everyone will have been a bit worried, most just wanting a nice, stable government to come out of this. They certainly weren't all thinking, 'This is my chance to be king!' Perhaps only Harold was. And he was right.

Harold's other big worry

Harold's reign started smoothly. Nobody jumped in the pool. There was a nice consensus about the next king, which is remarkable considering that there were several claimants and the successful one wasn't at all royal. Yet he knew that there was trouble ahead, likely to come from one of two people. William, obviously – Harold knew the duke would respond in some way – and Tostig Godwinson, Harold's errant younger brother.

In general the Godwins stuck together – it was a key strength in that family. King Edward was the richest person in England throughout his reign – he held the most land. It was only collectively that the Godwins had more. Staying united was crucial to their rise.

England at this time was divided into earldoms – 'earl' wasn't just an aristocratic title, it meant you pretty much ruled a bit of the country. By the early 1060s, Harold and his three brothers held all the earldoms except Mercia. Harold himself was earl of Wessex, like his father before him, and Tostig was earl of Northumbria. Very nice.

Then Tostig screwed it up. Northumbria, which had been a major Anglo-Saxon kingdom and then a major Viking one, was different from the southern earldoms where Tostig had grown up. He was a bit heavy-handed and raised taxes too much and had a few of the wrong people killed and, in

October 1065, the Northumbrians rebelled. They chucked him out of York and killed all his officials and *then* – and this is the really embarrassing part – they called for the brother of the Earl of Mercia to be their new earl.

They asked to change service provider! Who ever does that? It's such a hassle. You start your life with Vodaphone and British Gas and HSBC and you're stuck with it unless you're a pervert who gets off on filling in forms. I can't imagine it was any easier to switch from a Godwin earl, not with their market penetration. They were the earls everywhere except Mercia, remember, and the rebellious Northumbrians asked for Morcar, the younger brother of Edwin, Earl of Mercia. That doesn't sound like a coincidence. It sounds like a snub.

The situation got more embarrassing for Tostig. Harold backed them up. He supported the rebels and persuaded the worn-out King Edward to sack Tostig and make Morcar earl. Around the same time, it should be noted, Harold married Edwin and Morcar's sister. Tostig, understandably, thought this all stank to high heaven. He refused to accept his deposition, went into exile and spent most of 1066 buzzing angrily around England's borders trying to screw things up for his newly royal sibling.

Harold, as he took the throne, seemed very secure within England – now absolutely *all* the earls were either his brothers or his brothers-in-law, and his treatment of Tostig the previous year probably looked even-handed and kingly to most nobles. But he had made a vicious new enemy in his brother.

Naughty Harold wanted to be king

Did Harold Godwinson deserve to lose? The Norman version of history, which William and his heirs energetically advanced after the Conquest, claimed he did. But not in the way we might imagine. They didn't say it was lack of hard work, or of martial and regal acumen, that meant he merited failure. That would have been hard to argue if they'd tried – he was a capable, canny and ruthless operator. For the Normans, what clinched their case against Harold was his lack of luck. That proved he didn't deserve to win, because it showed that God was against him.

The reason God was against him, they said, was that he'd broken his oath to support William – he'd committed the sin of perjury and there was no way lovely old God would allow such a rotter to continue in a position of power. This was drawing a veil over the large number of absolute scumbags who were merrily in charge of vast swathes of the world, then and before. In a time of deep and sincere religiosity, and terrifying, short and brutal human existences, the idea that the hand of God was moving in a mysterious way to ensure some sort of cosmic justice – so that when things seemed to go unexpectedly well or badly, that wasn't just the terrifying random nature of existence but a tiny, incomprehensible part of some vaguely beneficent plan – was key to keeping everyone's peckers up.

Despite all of the above, I'm definitely on Harold's side. I can't help it. He's the ultimate underdog so I always find myself rooting for him, as if next time I think through the events he might beat William and stay king. Futile, you might say, but millions of people support football clubs other than the four or five that ever win anything. They root week after week for unsuccessful teams with no more or less statistical hope of major silverware than Harold has of being the victor at the Battle of Hastings when you next check Wikipedia.

Plus, as a not very religious person from the twenty-first century, I won't buy into all the judgemental priggishness about oaths. Harold might have broken his word . . . So what? It was probably extorted under pain of death or mutilation, either for him or his brother or nephew whom William had been holding hostage for over a decade. The contenders for power in this era are depressingly willing to be vicious sadists to achieve their ends. In that context, the significance of Harold's alleged promise to support William is utterly lost on me.

Ambition aside, stasis wasn't really possible for Harold. He was an overmighty subject, the most powerful English earl by far. Kings don't like that. Even Edward the sanctimonious Confessor hadn't, and had attempted to destroy the Godwins fifteen years earlier. The failure of that plan created a brief period when it was relatively safe to be such a dominant earl because the king had lost heart. A new king, say William, wasn't going to have it.

In theory, Edgar Atheling, now in his early teens, might have done, for a bit. Harold could have popped him on the throne and said to everyone, 'Look, this little chap has clearly got the strongest dynastic claim. Any attempt by Duke William of Normandy to deny that is going to sound actively *funny*, whatever he says I swore. So little Eddie's the king. If you don't like it, you'll answer to me.' Harold might have been able to continue as the power behind the throne, now that the throne was an adolescent-size chair rather than a geriatric's deathbed.

But for how long? Edgar would grow up and want real power. William would probably have still invaded. The leading barons might not have thanked Harold – children on the throne are notorious catalysts for trouble. Hostile forces see it as a great opportunity to start chipping bits off the kingdom. It seems less likely to have worked out than Harold taking the throne himself.

For Harold, it's either promotion or demotion, and demotion might have been fatal for him even without a big battle. I'm sure Harold's primary reasons for seizing power were straightforward ambitious, brutal, egotistical ones, but it's worth bearing in mind that a life of pious and dutiful service to a new king wasn't necessarily an option.

It's odd, in light of the whole history-is-written-by-the-victors thing, that Harold should be such a sympathetic figure in the eyes of posterity. It's not just me. I think most British schoolchildren learning about the Norman Conquest root for Harold. When I was about seven, as part of the relentless cutting out and sticking with which primary-school teachers fill their charges' days, we all had to pick whether to make little versions of Harold's banner from the Battle of Hastings or William's. Almost everyone opted for Harold's valiant little dragon rather than William's pompous papal cross.

William's banner had been personally blessed by Pope Alexander II, who backed the duke's claim to the throne. More evidence of the Normans' assiduous self-justification campaign – as is, looked at in a certain way, my personal dislike of Edward the Confessor. Bear with me – this is a bit convoluted.

My starting point in this bit of history was as a Harold supporter. Before I'd heard of Edward the Confessor, I knew about the Battle of Hastings and who won and thought that was a pity. I only learned about Edward afterwards and didn't like him because he seemed pro-William. The fact that that's how he seemed is the victory of Norman propaganda. Central to William's claim was the assertion that Edward had bequeathed the throne to him. My dislike of Edward shows that I have bought that argument. Well done the Normans.

It doesn't make me think William should have been king, though. Since I'm a twenty-first-century comedian, the issue of royal legitimacy isn't that important to me (typical TV lefties . . .). I'm imposing anachronistic values. Some would say that's unfair of me. I reckon I've got the right to enjoy 1066 in whatever way I like.

More anachronistic values: I support Harold because he's

defending his homeland against an invader. What business has William got being king of England? He's practically French! If not French, he's a Viking! What I'm not also thinking is 'He was born out of wedlock so shouldn't have anything nice.' Mean though that sounds, it would be less anachronistic. Though still *slightly* anachronistic, as insistence on legitimacy of birth didn't fully kick in till the twelfth century. The events of 1066 happen on the tail of a slightly more relaxed attitude to it – possibly thanks to those Viking kings who had more than one 'wife' on the go (e.g. Cnut who was married to Emma of Normandy and also one of the many Aelfgifus) but all of whose king-sired issue might be in the running for next monarch.

Still, while the tenth-century rules of succession might have been vaguer than they subsequently became, that doesn't mean anyone could apply. You were supposed to have some sort of family claim. Otherwise there's no limit to who might have a pop, which, as discussed in the last chapter, has shitty consequences unless you've got a massive and stable infrastructure to stop the applicants turning the country into a battlefield. Such infrastructures were not available in western Europe at the time.

Some royal blood was expected. Harold had none. William, who was spitting tacks about Harold's swift coronation, had some. Little Edgar Atheling had loads, though the poor kid had little else.

Harold's seizure of the throne as nothing more than a very powerful aristocrat, while it might smack pleasingly of nascent meritocracy to us today, was, by the standards of the time, a far more egregious violation of how things were supposed to work than William's armed invasion. But it shows gumption, and he was defending the country of his birth, so he remains sympathetic despite all the subsequent Norman attempts to slag him off. They should have just said he was a paedo.

1066 – a good year for Harold

Things had been tough but satisfying for the new king – like an overdone steak when you really need the iron. The year had started well with his being crowned king, then he'd stabilized his position swiftly and relatively peacefully. He'd repelled Tostig's various raids, raised a large army in the early summer and divided it into sections stationed all along the south coast, while Harold himself set up his headquarters on the Isle of Wight. It was the height of the campaigning season and he was ready for William.

Annoyingly, William didn't turn up. By early September, Harold's troops had run out of food and he had to let them go home. Still, the year was getting on, the weather was likely to worsen, so there was a decent chance, the king must have thought, that William wasn't going to invade at all.

Harold then found out that someone else had: Vikings! That's a blast from the past, isn't it?! A bit retro, like that *Carry On* film that came out in 1992. Also like that *Carry On* film, this was the absolute last time, and it didn't work.

It might have done, though. Tostig had been making power-ful new friends. He'd persuaded the King of Norway, another Harold (though often called Harald to avoid confusion so I'm going with that), to attack England for old times' sake. That will have appealed to Harald, I suspect. He is known to pos-terity as 'Hardrada', meaning 'hard ruler', and he was an old-school Viking and renowned bruiser.

About fifty years old, which, given contemporary life-expectancy coupled with his lifestyle, makes him about 260 in our years, he was arguably the greatest warrior of the day. He'd spent much of his life fighting for the Byzantine emperors, exotically enough. These actual proper Roman emperors – none of your nouve Carolingian pretension – had an elite force known as the Varangian Guard, largely made up of battle-hardened Norsemen. After a successful career of banging Greeks' heads together, Harald returned to Scandinavia in 1045, made himself king of Norway and repeatedly attempted to make himself king of Denmark too.

He was running out of things to do. At the bottom of all our 'to do' lists is the last task: die. By implication, anyway. I suspect actually writing it on a list is a red flag mental health-wise. Perhaps Harald thought conquering England would be a good way of delaying the inevitable. He couldn't have been more wrong.

The news that the greatest Viking of the age, at the head of a fleet of dragon ships, had invaded the north, defeated Earls Edwin and Morcar in battle and taken York would have been enough to make King Harold doubt whether he'd ever get the chance to enjoy his long-awaited clash with the Duke of Normandy. Yet the new king's response was impressive. He reassembled his extremely recently disbanded army (which, apart from anything else, must have been very annoying to have to do) and marched north so quickly that he caught Harald and Tostig on the hop. At the Battle of Stamford Bridge, just east of York, the Norwegians didn't even have a chance to put on their chain mail. They were brutally and bloodily defeated. Both Tostig and the previously invincible Harald were killed.

That was on 25 September. On the 28th, William of Normandy landed with an army at Pevensey Bay in Sussex.

'That's not tremendously convenient,' Harold must have reflected as he wearily marched south. 'Though at least this time it's happened before I disbanded my army.' I like to think of him as a glass-half-full kind of guy.

13. ... Hastings

Battle is such a peaceful place. I've only been there once, about twenty years ago, but I thought it was delightful. A quiet and pretty Sussex town. I've just had a virtual wander round it on Google Street View and it still looks idyllic: it must have been a lovely sunny day when the dystopian droid car went through stealing everyone's data.

I was momentarily disconcerted to see that the tea room where I'd had lunch with my parents and brother around about the turn of the millennium seemed to have been turned into a Costa Coffee. I had another look and concluded that the tea room is actually still there but a nearby old pub – the 1066 – had been turned into the Costa, which still isn't great. They've put a swinging sign with the Costa Coffee logo into the fittings where there used to be a pub sign, which to me is worse than McDonald's taking over Notre Dame and having a big golden-arches 'M' done in the rose window. Pubs have been more significant in my life than cathedrals.

If that's a sad sign of the passing of time, how do you think William the Conqueror would feel? The abbey he founded in Battle to say sorry for all the killing necessitated by conquering England was closed down by Henry VIII in 1538. Or 'dissolved' as they say. Well, it didn't dissolve properly. Henry VIII should have stirred it more. Great lumps of it are still there. Standing jaggedly on Senlac Hill where Harold Godwinson died, possibly as a result of having taken an arrow to the eye – though possibly more boringly than that, some historians have felt constrained to point out. 'Dear oh dear, you appear to have accidentally captured someone's imagination! Put it down immediately and return to your research on crop yields.'

You've probably inferred, if you didn't know already, that a battle happened in Battle. Or near Battle. It was in fact, the Battle of Hastings, slightly untidily. It didn't happen in Hastings, it happened in Battle. Or near Battle. Quite near Hastings, but much nearer Battle than Hastings. 'Of' doesn't get a look-in.

Time is as crucial as place. You can stand in the same place and, depending on the time, you might find yourself on your own in the mud, run through by a Norman knight, praying for a king's soul, being made redundant by another king, having a nice pint or buying a nasty coffee. When the Battle of Hastings happened, Battle didn't yet exist, so they named the battle after Hastings, which did. Otherwise it would have been called the Battle of Battle. Except, it wouldn't because, if Battle had existed before the battle happened, it wouldn't have been called Battle. It was named Battle after the battle. Or rather after the penitentiary monastic foundation that was named after the battle (colloquially, anyway – officially William dedicated it to St Martin). Then William's (eleven greats)-grandson Henry VIII closed it down and now English Heritage runs it as '1066 Battle of Hastings, Abbey and Battlefield'.

I can neither confirm nor deny the existence of an afterlife – frankly, if I could, it would be on the cover of the book. But, if there is one, I wonder how kings William I and Henry VIII are getting on. That's assuming the afterlife isn't just airy-fairy spirits and feelings and nebulous niceness amid white light, but is something we can get our heads round: translucent figures chatting on clouds, or sweating in lava-dripping hell-caves. It's also assuming that both William and Henry would be in the same section of the afterlife, but that does seem reasonable. They were both ruthless and killed a lot of people – so if that matters, they're surely both in hell. On the other hand, they were both kings and incredibly well connected. If that helps at all, as it very much does in this vale of tears, they'll both be enjoying the ambrosia and harp medleys. An afterlife in which one of them is damned and the other saved would seem to be splitting hairs in terms of when it's okay to have people killed in order to get your own way. It also implies a God more engaged by the details of what the pope thinks than the most self-confident pontiff would dare to dream. William, even his worst enemy would admit, got on better with popes than Henry VIII did.

I rather like the image of William the Conqueror tearing a strip off Henry VIII for closing down Battle Abbey, and all the other abbeys for that matter. Or possibly roughing him up, like Michael Caine does to Bryan Mosley in *Get Carter*. Henry VIII seems all broad-beamed and martial, but in reality he was a pampered prince – born to a reigning king. Good at sport and jousting in his youth, but his later life was dominated by relationship troubles and a gammy leg. He wasn't a proper warrior like his Norman ancestor, who was born illegitimate, became duke of Normandy as a child, somehow managed to hold on to the duchy and then made himself a king. 'You're a big man,' the Conqueror would say, 'but you're out of shape. With me, it's a full-time job. So behave yourself.' Slap.

The massive year 1066 – the most famous in English history and the inspiration for a million guessable PINs – is dominated by – NOT MINE! – is dominated by the brilliance and luck of William of Normandy. He needed both to become king of England. That's a bit disconcerting. It's not how we like to view history or world events.

History is dominated by big themes and trends: capitalism, nationalism, colonialism, industrialization, communism, sexism, racism, Christianity, Islam. Enormous things that rise and fall like tides – that's what affects our lives. That's why the

USA has so many nuclear weapons and China manufactures so many objects. That's why we all have mobile phones and there's too much carbon dioxide in the atmosphere. This is all caused by the themes, not by a single human's personal drive and whether their toast falls butter side up.

What one clever bloke, William, did with his little life – and how the clash of metal between two groups of heavies in the Sussex countryside one October day panned out – isn't supposed to matter much. If William hadn't been ambitious in the first place or the fight had gone the other way, we like to think it wouldn't have mattered much, because the trends and themes were happening anyway.

Maybe that's true. Maybe England was always going to gravitate towards the French axis and out of the Scandinavian one. Maybe, with or without William, the England of, say, 1166 would have been more or less the same, and by the twenty-first century, the counterfactual history where William didn't exist, or died in infancy, is pretty much identical except maybe we have a different word for pork. We'd probably just call it pig.

Maybe the deeds of kings are just the details of how inevitable trends played out – the pattern of individual snowflakes, rather than the overall fact that there's snow. But it's not how it feels. It feels like important changes started partly because of what a small number of people decided to try to do and partly because of blind luck.

1066 – a shit year for William

The first three quarters of 1066 were an irritating and static time for the Duke of Normandy. With the news of Harold's coronation, the year did not begin happily. William immediately decided to pursue his claim to the English throne which,

4. A burial mound at Sutton Hoo, 'England's Valley of the Kings' according to the National Trust, which runs the site. If you go, do take advantage of the Trust's 17-metre-high viewing tower or 'England's Empire State Building'.

5. An Anglo-Saxon helmet from around 625, dug up at Sutton Hoo in 1939. I imagine there was a ladies' version without the moustache.

6. 'Going anywhere nice on your holidays?' 'No, I'm not allowed to go anywhere – I'm a monk.' This is a thirteenth-century depiction of one monk giving another monk a tonsure from behind.

7. A clipping from the *Anglo-Saxon Chronicle*. It's written in both insular script and Old English, two barriers to comprehensibility which, it seems, don't cancel each other out.

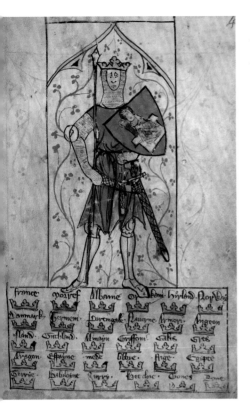

1. An absolute legend. A fourteenth-century illustration of King Arthur, looking worried because he doesn't exist. The picture of the Virgin Mary on his shield was meant as a compliment but seems uncomfortably like pinning her to a dartboard.

2. The arrival of the Anglo-Saxons: this drawing of Hengist and Horsa landing in Britannia with their 'three keels' is from 1605, over a thousand years after the events it depicts probably didn't occur.

3. The Venerable Bede from an illustration in a twelfth-century manuscript. He appears to be writing with both hands at once, a trick he passed on to the young Barbara Cartland.

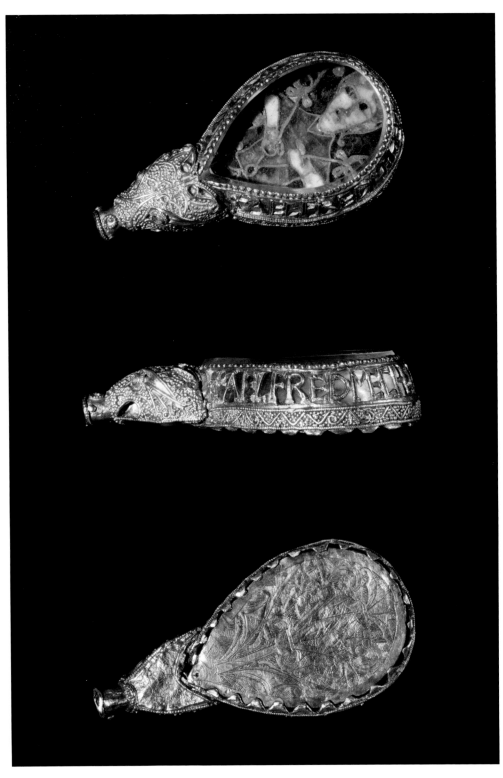

13. The Alfred Jewel, photographed against black to maximize its sparkly beauty. There's not much they can do about the little picture, though.

14. A chantry chapel built in 1056 by an earl called Odda for people to pray for his brother's soul. It fell out of use at some point in the thirteenth century, then someone converted it into a house, put up a TV aerial and let the garden get on top of them.

15. A thirteenth-century illustration of Emma of Normandy fleeing England, back to where she's of. She is being chased by her future father-in-law, Sweyn Forkbeard, whose famous facial feature is concealed by chain mail.

8. Offa's Dyke. This earthwork, which goes along the England–Wales border, was completed around 784 and then, in 1971, adopted for a popular rambling route. Nobody is quite sure what the point of it was for the intervening 1,187 years.

9. Manufactured at the same time as the dyke above, this was clearly mistaken for a chocolate coin by someone who then found out it wasn't the hard way.

10. You can tell this isn't a real Viking longship from the horns on the most prominent Viking's helmet and also from the fact that it's a photo. The most glaring historical inaccuracy, though, is that everyone pictured seems happy to be there.

11 and 12. These depictions of Alfred the Great and Aethelred the Unready were created hundreds of years apart and hundreds of years after the deaths of their subjects. They nevertheless provide an accurate guide to the two kings' relative levels of competence.

frankly, I wouldn't have done. Would you? He was nearly forty which, considering contemporary lifespans, must have felt like sixty. Plus he was already a very important duke. To my mind, that's a nice comfy laurel for a lovely rest.

History must be full of occasions where someone had a reasonable case for raising an army and invading somewhere and didn't, through either fear or laziness. Those people don't get the credit they deserve for the positive consequences of their indolence. By the same token, William's determination to go for it has to be factored in before dismissing the 'Great Men' interpretation of history. Actually, not 'Men' – it should be 'People'. I'm not happy with 'Great' either. Harold and the Anglo-Saxon aristocracy wouldn't have thought it was great. Is 'Annoying People' clearer? 'Ambitious People'? 'Pushy People'? 'Difficult People'?

Having decided to follow through on his claim to the English throne, William succeeded in rallying a lot of support. This is both impressive and understandable. William was good at waging war and had secured his duchy with constant and ruthless military action. The news that he was planning an enormous corporate takeover must have looked attractive to investors.

By early August, he had a large army and navy ready to go. Weather and wind were against him, so he had to wait. This was harder than it sounds. He had to keep supplying the army with food, drink and other incentives not to go home, as well as stop them all from dying of dysentery. This is at least as tough a challenge as marching lots of people to Yorkshire quickly and much less bracing. He kept his army in the field for longer than Harold could – the only trouble was that it was in the wrong field and there was a lot of water between it and the right one.

It was a change of wind, probably, rather than brilliant strategy that meant William turned up in late September. It seems likely that he would have crossed earlier if the weather had allowed. Autumn was a much less clement time for starting an important war. Still, it looked like *amazing* strategy. Not only had he waited for Harold's army to disband, he'd also waited for it, having been called back together, to be force-marched up and down the country and, in the middle of that, required to fight an exhausting battle in which quite a few of it were killed. It seems like inspired waiting around, but it was probably just luck. Bad luck with the weather turning out to be excellent luck for timing the attack.

This luck (which he will have thought meant God was on his side) and logistical excellence allowed William to plonk a large, well-supplied armed force on the south coast of England.

Annoyingly, it's not clear *how* large, or indeed how large Harold's army was. We can blame medieval chroniclers' rather rhetorical attitude to numbers. They're altogether too keen to say 'a squillion soldiers' to keep the reader's attention. Before you cut those poor olde-worlde idiots with their childish drawings too much slack, it's worth bearing in mind that they could count. It's not fucking calculus – someone just needed to tot up the numbers. It would have been nice if they'd bothered.

William's army may have numbered anywhere from a few thousand to a few tens of thousands. What seems clearer is that the army Harold scrambled back down the country at the head of, and lined up on Senlac Ridge, was roughly the same size. All the work they'd both put in and, when it came to it on 14 October 1066, they might as well have tossed a coin.

One in the eye for a defensive strategy

Harold didn't win the Battle of Hastings, but he didn't need to in order to stay king. He just had to force a draw. He was in control of England, England was literally and metaphorically behind him. The longer he wasn't comprehensively defeated, the greater the chance William would have to go home.

Therefore his battle tactic was simple: his army would stand at the top of a hill, barring the Normans' advance, and stay there until William gave up. It doesn't sound a very snazzy strategy but it's how Wellington defeated Napoleon at Waterloo and basically what happened in almost every single battle on the Western Front. In a sense, Harold was ahead of his time. Though he could have really done with a machine gun. As it was, he didn't even have many archers.

It's impossible to know how the battle played out because it happened a long time ago and nobody videoed it. Someone tapestried it, though. Most of our sense of how it went comes from that massive tapestry. The Bayeux tapestry: you may have heard of it. If you've only heard of one tapestry, it'll be that one. If you've heard of two, I don't know what the other one will be because personally I've only heard of one.

I haven't really even heard of one, because the Bayeux tapestry is, strictly speaking, an embroidery. I know. Why is it called a tapestry if it's not a tapestry? Why, for that matter, has the fact that it's the most famous object on earth to be referred to as a tapestry not resulted in the definition of the word 'tapestry' being widened to include it? I thought the English language was supposed to be governed by usage rather than arbitrary rules of the kind that have long hobbled French.

But then it is a French tapestry. Except it isn't, despite its location and the other part of its name. It's English. It's not a French tapestry, it's an English embroidery. It was commissioned by the victorious Normans, but they didn't have the skill base to commemorate their triumph in needlework, so it was made in England by English women. Another example of how disasters can boost GDP.

If you're planning a trip to see a tapestry or embroidery, or indeed any sort of cloth, I recommend the Bayeux tapestry. If you're passing *quite* near. It's worth going slightly out of your way for, but it's not Disneyland. Still, I reckon it craps on the Turin shroud. It really is a massive embroidery – the sense of a vast amount of embroidery done to a very high standard is undeniable. Though, as with most medieval art, it looks like it's based on pictures sent in by a nine-year-old *Blue Peter* competition winner. I can't help wondering whether the undoubtedly talented seamstresses who made it didn't look at each bit, as they finished it, and notice this.

'What do you think, Aelfgifu? I don't think we're getting the faces quite right? And the horses are too small.'

'Jesus Christ, Godgifu – get on with it! We've not got to the actual battle and I'm already bored shitless.'

Point taken. Initially, it seems the battle was going fine for the Anglo-Saxons – they had the advantage of higher ground and the cavalry charges of the Normans weren't having much of an impact. The Norman archers were being pretty useless for the amusing reason that there were so few Anglo-Saxon archers to fire arrows back at them that they quickly ran out of arrows. No use shyly walking up to the Anglo-Saxon line to ask if they could have their arrows back.

It's an insight into a more environmentally friendly form of warfare than we've had for centuries. Use a bullet once and it's ruined – whether or not it hit anyone. Whereas you can dig an arrow out of your own shoulder and twang it back at the enemy, assuming you're incredibly hard. Just like with single-use plastic, as a society we need to see single-use bullets as rather an irresponsible way of killing someone. There are lots of musket balls in museums that, in my view, we could seriously look at reusing.

Then a rumour went round the Norman army that William had been killed. This caused some of them to start fleeing. At this point, it was all looking pretty good for Harold and co.

A section of Harold's army then did the main thing they

had been instructed not to do. They charged down the hill after the fleeing Normans. I can almost taste Harold's frustration coming down the centuries about this. I mean, literally the *only* thing they had to remember was not to do that. William was gifted the perfect opportunity to show himself to his own side, who were buoyed up by the proof he was alive, and then able to kick the living shit out of the pursuing section of the Anglo-Saxon army. Many never got back to the depleted ranks on the ridge.

It was so successful that the Normans then used it as a tactic, pretending to flee several times throughout the day, punishing the Anglo-Saxons for their unshakeable credulity and grinding down Harold's numbers. The grinding went on for hours and hours until Harold was killed – probably by being shot in the eye with an arrow, though not definitely – at which point the English army collapsed and retreated, with a huge number of the major players in Anglo-Saxon politics left dead on the battlefield.

William was lucky to win but would have been unlucky to lose. That's the thing with coin-toss scenarios. However balanced Harold's and William's respective positions before the battle, it was decisive. Anglo-Saxon England was on its knees. At this point the ghastly nature of Normandy during William's formative years stood him in good stead. He was used to subduing truculent, powerful people. The remaining Anglo-Saxon nobility went down without much of a fight.

There was a desultory attempt by the surviving earls Edwin and Morcar, who hadn't been at Hastings, to rally round the teenage Edgar Atheling – 'Oh, *now* you want me to be king!' he must have thought – but William spent the rest of the year stalking round London with his army, defeating any forces put up against him and otherwise 'wasting' the area. This was a savage but effective military strategy, at which William excelled, where an army rendered the land unfit to support human life.

It didn't take much of this to secure the submission of all the remaining Anglo-Saxon big shots, at which point William entered London and had himself crowned king at Westminster Abbey on 25 December. Merry Christmas.

God and my right fist

We've finally got there: it's the setting up of the current English state, key component of the British state. The institution that is the UK today was 'established 1066'. On Christmas Day. It all began with people having to work on a bank holiday. How apt.

William the Conqueror wouldn't have expressed it as a beginning. He'd say it was a continuation, a restoration – much as Alfred and Athelstan had presented their own extensions of power a couple of centuries earlier. He would have stressed his legitimate claim as the rightful heir to Edward the Confessor, not a foreign invader at all. The Domesday Book, the survey of England that William commissioned towards the end of his reign, is full of references to 'the day on which King Edward was alive and dead'. It's a poetic if long-winded (and those are not mutually exclusive concepts) way of saying the day he died. That day, the Normans insisted, was when William's right to be king began. His regime was nothing more than a lawful continuation of rule from that day, after a regrettable blip caused by the perjuring usurper Harold.

But it *was* a beginning. Nothing illustrates it better than the fact, already noted, that the numbering of our monarchs starts then. Well, it didn't actually start then – English monarchs weren't issued with their numbers for several centuries. But when the numbering conventions were introduced, it didn't occur to anyone to include any pre-Conquest kings in the tally. That's how obvious it seemed to posterity that this was the start of something, not a continuation.

Early in William's reign, he made attempts to work with the remains of the pre-Norman aristocracy but, after the first few years had been beset by rebellions, he changed tack. The entire Anglo-Saxon ruling class was replaced by the Norman aristocrats William had brought with him. Ownership of England was passed to new people.

That's not something that the legitimacy claim justified. An entire ruling class being dispossessed didn't have anything to do with Edward the Confessor's supposed choosing of William, or Harold's alleged perjury, or the support of the pope. The premise was possession. We all risked everything to invade, and we might have got killed but we didn't. We won and now we're going to enjoy the country we've stolen.

They did. To this day, the highest born of the British aristocracy cite Norman ancestry. The Victorians, for all their fondness for Alfred the Great, were obsessed with 'Norman blood'. To have come over with William the Conqueror is as old-school as it gets.

Aristocratic one-upmanship is all about ancient lines and precedent – older equals first equals poshest. In theory, anyone who could trace their descent from the Anglo-Saxon nobility would be holding the ace of snobbery trumps (apart from anyone who could say they were descended from, say, Charlemagne or Julius Caesar or Jesus. Quite a few European nobles can claim descent from Charlemagne. The Habsburgs used to claim they were descended from Julius Caesar but, needless to say, it was horseshit. Whatever Dan Brown says, Jesus seems to have ascended to heaven without issue).

The Anglo-Saxon nobility were removed and driven into the sort of obscurity where no one's making a note of the genealogy any more, where the 'I'm posher than those brutish Normans' snobbery doesn't matter. England's most pukka lineage is a descent from thieving thugs. But it's okay because a) they were thieving thugs an exceptionally long time ago and

b) they were extraordinarily successful thieving thugs. (We should of course remember that the Anglo-Saxon kings and nobility were also, in all probability, though with a few more mists of time to spare their blushes, descended from thieving thugs.)

This fascinates me. It seems to be an admission that, fundamentally, everything's awful. There is no justice, just strength. The foundations of our state, the position of the family whose coat of arms hangs above every courtroom in the land, derives from conquest – militarized theft. The brutal reality of new people in charge, and owning everything, was quickly evident – and, after a few centuries, no longer really denied.

I don't say this against the royal family, or in a spirit of advocating republicanism. On the contrary, I think the deep-rooted and somehow openly acknowledged hypocrisy of our state's ostensible raison d'être is kind of great. 'Dieu et mon droit' – 'God and my right' – is the royal motto, but they got everything from a smash and grab. Not just the crown but pretty much all the land in the country.

The 'right' was a dubious claim to say the least and the God part, one papal banner notwithstanding, is inferred with hindsight from success. If you get away with it, God was on your side. When someone nicks your mobile phone, remember that: William the Conqueror would have argued that you deserved it because of something sinful you've done. God was with the thief and wanted him to have your property and the lovely heroin he's going to exchange it for.

I like all this. I reckon that, as soon as anyone starts seriously believing a system of government is at bottom rooted in justice and loveliness, they've let their sceptical guard down and are inviting the unavoidably imperfect to descend into the downright hellish. The world has never been fair, and cannot be made fair, and claims that it can are foolish or dishonest. It can be made fair*er* and attempts to make it less fair can be resisted. Optimistic realists seek improvement, not perfection.

England was invaded and conquered again later but, in all cases, the retrospective justifications said they weren't conquests. Restorations – of some sort – remain the official story. William tried making it the official story in 1066. That was his one failed endeavour.

Nope, it was a conquest, posterity has decided – a takeover by force of arms. There's a sense William was being too modest, saying he was the rightful king aided by God. He was more dynamic than that: invader, conqueror, successful sexy arsehole. The brilliant son-of-a-bitch nicked the whole place, something which, posterity also decided, is virtually impossible.

That's the presiding mythology, whatever actually happened subsequently. All the invading and toppling, the civil wars and regime changes, are blips. England was conquered in 1066 and that's it. That's the line: everything's been the same since. It was the beginning of English history and also, in a sense, the end.

PART TWO
The Dukes of Hazard

14. King William I

What happened to William the Conqueror in the end? Same as James Bond – he exploded.

It's a strange expression, 'What happened in the end?' Looked at from a historical point of view, it implies that the final thing to happen is what happened overall – it was the most important, the defining thing. But life doesn't have a tournament structure. For a mortal species, to focus on what happened last is a pretty downbeat way of looking at things. In the end, we die. But that's not necessarily the main thing about us.

Still, our ends often overshadow us. History bristles with examples of people who died in poverty despite being great artists or musicians or having invented vulcanized rubber. The penurious demise casts a pall over their achievements. It can make their efforts seem futile – those people get defined by the injustice of fate. Similarly when the people meeting grisly ends are nasty, we can feel that justice has been done – but that doesn't make sense either. What happened to Adolf Hitler in the end was no less than he deserved, but it didn't restore justice. It didn't make everything okay.

I wasn't expecting to find out what happened to James Bond in the end. He's not real. He doesn't have to end. Or begin. There's no need to make those things part of the story. So imagine my surprise, when tentatively venturing out to the cinema in post-lockdown London for the relaxing escapism of a Bond movie, at finding myself (spoiler alert) watching that character die.

I was fucking furious. I'd looked forward to that night out.

We'd been to Pizza Express first. We'd had popcorn and choc-olate buttons brought to our seats at a swanky cinema. And then, at the very end of *No Time to Die*, James Bond is killed in an explosion. Yes, he actually dies. In the middle of a pan-demic when death was feeling really unoriginal. I'm sorry if this is where you're finding that out but it's one of the most extraordinary creative missteps that Hollywood money has ever been lavished on.

James Bond not dying is the premise of a Bond film. It's the premise of the whole franchise. What you are supposed to watch and enjoy is the exciting manner in which he does not die. The fact that a movie that departs from this sound con-vention was deemed by many reviewers to be clever or interesting or dark or real – to be, in summary, good and indeed *better than the ones where he doesn't die* – is an index of how mediocre, joyless and self-importantly worthy our commen-tariat has become.

Honestly, the whole creative team right up to Barbara Broc-coli and Daniel Craig need to be lined up against a wall and criticized. Better still, they should have to answer to the ghost of Ian Fleming, who met his own death having left his famous creation alive and wise-cracking. He must have thought the lovable rogue was safe. But no, the daughter of one of the producers to whom he'd sold the film rights had another idea. She was going to leave him, depressed and alone, contemplat-ing the fact that he'd never see his own daughter again – oh yes, he's been turned into a family man by then! – while some Royal Navy cruise missiles bear inexorably down on him.

You may be thinking that there's more about James Bond in this chapter than you expected. Sorry. But my point is that giving Bond a sad and lonely end casts a shadow over every other moment in his life that we've seen portrayed. It's a proper canonical Bond film and so that simply *is* what hap-pened to him. That's the story and pretending it isn't would be like reading a Poirot novel but determining to believe a different solution to the mystery than the one provided by the detective. There's no getting away from the fact that everything Bond undergoes in every other film – every moment of suavity, action, humour or seduction – is happening to a man destined to die young, heartbroken and alone.

This lamentable situation is further complicated – and I promise I will get back to the kings of England in a minute – by the words put on screen at the end of the credits: 'James Bond will return'. This is a tradition of the franchise, like James Bond not dying, but what can it mean here? Clearly the producers are keen to keep the gravy train fully serviced for another journey, but will this be a prequel from earlier in Bond's life, so another film overshadowed by the knowledge of his bleak demise? Or will it turn out that he *didn't* die after all, in which case they have released a Bond film where, for the first time, they elected not to end with the exciting, heroic and miraculous nature of his triumph, but with a miserable and vacuous affectation of artistic significance which they will then reveal to have been a sort of leaden prank? Either way, the shit ending really spoils it.

It's the same with William the Conqueror. At least that was fate, not a creative choice. His bowels exploded while some monks in Caen were trying to cram his bloated corpse into a sarcophagus that was far too snug for him. The consequent stench rather ruined the solemnity of the remaining funeral rites.

So that was the very last anyone saw of him. The bit before that wasn't much more dignified. The bloating which necessitated the sarcophagus-cramming had partly happened pre- and partly post-mortem. William had put on a bit of weight in his declining years, which is not how one imagines the victor of the Battle of Hastings. There's a glum poignancy to it, a sign of mundane human frailty, which undermines the snapshot image of the victorious warrior. Suddenly you imagine a cross and red-faced old fat guy. From divinely inspired warrior to compulsively snacking gammon.

If he does have that altercation with Henry VIII in the afterlife, it might be a closer fight than I first imagined – like a couple of ageing regal sumo wrestlers. It all depends on what system the afterlife has for the corporeal manifestations of its inmates. Are they in their prime, or how they were when they expired, or how most people think of them? This would hugely influence how a King Bill vs King Harry punch-up might go, as well as raising other more philosophical questions about what the hell is going on generally.

These rulers' bodily frailty reminds me of Napoleon's piles. They stopped him being able to ride a horse at the Battle of Waterloo. He was a brilliant general, an administrator of unparalleled energy, a ruthless tyrant and a politician of dazzling opportunism. But he was also a portly chap who, on the day his fate was decided, was mainly thinking about his sore arse. If he's in the same afterlife as Kenneth Williams, maybe he can lend the emperor a tube of Anusol.

In 1087 William, by then nearly sixty, set off on a military expedition against King Philip I of the Franks (basically France, but it isn't called that yet). William, in defiance of his age and obesity, was attacking the town of Mantes and really got stuck in. And then, in turn, the pommel of his horse's saddle got stuck in him, right in his new enormous stomach. It caused a horrific injury and the best medical advice at the time was just to settle in for a long agonizing death. William had himself taken to a priory outside Rouen and proceeded to do so.

When he finally expired and all the important people had legged it to try and secure their futures under whatever the new regime turned out to be, his attendants stripped the room, and corpse, of anything of value, and then fled. There lay the Conqueror, naked and alone and beginning to decompose. Bleak.

A fairly lowly knight had to arrange for the body to be transported the 80 miles from Rouen to Caen, where William had said he wanted to be buried in one of the monasteries he founded. This was the only element of the funeral that went as he would have wanted. It was marred first by fire in the town, then by a weird heckling incident when a member of the congregation claimed the church had been illegally built on his family's land, and then finally by the aforementioned royal bowel-bursting. That's what happened to him in the end.

The language barrier and other barriers

There's a lot of discussion among historians about how radically the Norman Conquest changed England. The problem with it being historians having the discussion rather than, say, scientists is that historians aren't very good at measuring things. Scientists would say that, if you're working out the extent of anything, the first thing you need is an objective way of measuring it – in this case, of measuring the level of radicalness of a change. They would come up with an SI unit for that and then we could put a number on the effect of the Norman Conquest and compare it to, say, the level of radicalness of change wrought by the Russian Revolution or voyages of Christopher Columbus or the invention of the SodaStream.

All historians have is words – adjectives and the like. 'Small', 'huge', 'fundamental', 'superficial'. And phrases: 'not as huge as has been previously thought'; 'much more significant than was suggested by recent orthodoxy', etc. What historians say happened is often just stated in comparison to what other historians previously said happened rather than in comparison to not knowing what happened at all.

The reason there's controversy about something which, it seems to me, we could all agree caused 'reasonably major changes' is that historians' prejudices about each other start to play a part. This is because the section of society for whom the Norman Conquest was indisputably a massive deal was the ruling class. Historians who conclude that the Conquest caused an enormous change are suspected of only caring about the fate of posh people, out of either snobbery or laziness. Snobbery because they're only interested in the lives and fates of kings and earls and so on, and laziness because such people leave a lot more in the way of written records and statues and buildings, so it's much easier to keep track of what they were up to than it is with your average peasant or slave.

Yes, slave! It seems incongruous, doesn't it, in the middle ages? There were still quite a lot of slaves in England in the late eleventh century. Not serfs, not merely peasants whose freedoms were, by modern standards, massively curtailed, but proper full-on 'How much will you take for that big strong lad with the lazy eye?' slaves. Like the Romans had. It seems it was the one major aspect of Roman civilization that the Anglo-Saxons really took to. Funny people.

The Normans were comparatively anti-slavery. Not so much as to actively ban it – according to the Domesday Book over 10 per cent of the population in 1086 were slaves. But William did ban the sale of English slaves overseas, which stymied the export market and, under the influence of the Norman aristocracy, the practice went into decline. By around 1200, there weren't any.

'So it might not have been so bad for normal people,' say some historians to some other historians, 'as it was for the Anglo-Saxon aristocrats with whom you're obsessed even though they don't matter as much as millions of poor people and crop yields!' And it may well be that, for lots of the ordinary peasantry, the Norman Conquest didn't make all that much difference, and very little appreciable negative difference – particularly as William adopted the long-established Anglo-Saxon governmental and administrative system, the one Aethelred had managed not to destroy and the Cnuts hadn't tinkered with and which was still in pretty good nick. England was, by the standards of the time, a nice orderly kingdom to take over – like a house you move into where the fuses are clearly labelled. Frankly, that infrastructure was why a project like William's much vaunted Domesday Book was possible at all.

Still, it's hard to believe the peasantry didn't notice the new management. For one thing, it spoke a different language. Old English, the language of the Anglo-Saxons, ceased to be used by the nobility or in the administration of the kingdom. It was replaced by Latin and Norman French and all but disappeared as a written language.

This is a world away from leaders just having a posh accent. The subtly different way people such as David Cameron pronounce words like 'round' and 'pound' even from other people with RP makes us suspect that they're a slightly different sort of human from most of those they seek to govern. But imagine if, instead, Old Etonian cabinet ministers simply spoke French. Even that would make them seem too familiar – most of us learned some French at school or have visited France. It would be like all our political leaders were suddenly speaking Hungarian or Japanese.

This situation was not short-lived. Royalty and aristocracy in England continued to use a different language from the vast majority of the people for centuries. English (Middle English rather than Old English by that point) didn't become the official language of the English courts until 1362, or of government until the reign of Henry V in the early fifteenth century.

Its legacy is that, in modern English, we often have words for the meats we eat that are different from those for the animals they come from – beef for cow, pork for pig and mutton for sheep. This isn't out of delicacy – an attempt to conceal what docile creature's slaughter any given lunch has necessitated. It's because, in the middle ages, only rich people ate meat and, after the Norman Conquest, all the rich people spoke French. The French words for the animals – *boeuf, porc, mouton* – turned into the words for the foods, and the English words came to refer to the animals under the only circumstances where the peasantry encountered them: when looking after them until they were ready to be turned into posh people's dinner.

Another change that even the least posh must have noticed was the appearance of castles. I don't mean a change in what the castles looked like, I mean they appeared. There were no castles and then, pretty suddenly, there were castles.

The notion of castles being new is weird – perhaps young people today feel the same about CDs. Obviously fortification wasn't new. There'd been forts in the iron age, and the Romans built thousands of them, and the Anglo-Saxons developed fortified towns, known as burhs, as a way of defending against the Vikings. But castles as structures controlled by the local lord, or by the crown – as nodes for the imposition of power on the surrounding land and settlements – came with the Normans. Literally. They brought wooden ones as flat packs in their invasion fleet. Overconfident bastards.

Castles had existed on the continent for about 200 years and the Normans saw them as key to exerting control over the new country they'd stolen. They stuck up wooden ones everywhere, 500 of them in twenty years – usually overlooking towns and villages.

The standard design was a defensive central building, the keep, plonked on a little hill, which was often man-made, called a motte. This word is confusing because the castle would also have a moat, which went downwards, while a motte went up. I suppose you could make a motte by digging a moat. That's how sandcastles work. Next to the motte, and within the moat, was something called a bailey which was a walled courtyard with a palisade around it and other castle stuff – kitchen, chapel, chill-out room, etc – inside it. These are known by historians as motte-and-bailey castles in wilful disregard of the fact that the moat and keep are the more interesting features.

These wooden castles were gradually converted to stone, which is why we have so many lovely ruined ones to walk round today. And, in the case of the Tower of London and Windsor Castle, some lovely ones that the Victorians restored to how they reckoned history should have looked. You know, nice and tidy.

Unjust William

None of this gives an answer to the most pertinent question about the Norman Conquest from our point of view: how should we feel about it? The historians' answer is unhelpful. They say we should feel differently from previous historians. They *always* say that. It's relentless mild revisionism and is therefore endlessly comparative. The Conquest mattered more/less, was better/worse, than was previously thought. But what does that mean?

As you know, at Hastings, I'm on Harold's side like most British schoolboys. But after that the narrative of school history changes. Suddenly there's a lot of 'look at the lovely castles', Norman architecture in churches (curved non-pointed arches are the thing to look for – strangely the Norman stuff looks more modern than the Gothic architecture that came later) and the ruddy Domesday Book.

Let's be honest, the Domesday Book is not that impressive.

133

It's just a manky old book. Or rather two manky old books. An ancient pile of incomplete paperwork about what England was like. No one in the last 300 years is genuinely going to be wowed by that. Not instinctively or viscerally. I get more bumf from my financial adviser on an annual basis. Durham Cathedral is impressive, the Domesday Book is some rotting jottings.

The reason the Domesday Book is relentlessly cited as so bloody amazing is twofold: first it's very useful for researching what was going on in post-Conquest England. If your job is doing that, it's impossible not to feel grateful for this resource. You'd get fond of it. I feel the same about Google maps. And second because, in explaining why it is supposedly amazing, you end up illustrating the nature of the era quite effectively but without being overtly negative.

This was a time, everyone gets told and it's right, when producing this fairly modest bit of national analysis and research was a huge achievement. This did not happen by accident – the king must have really wanted this, because at this stage of history, being this organized, even briefly, was extremely unusual. It's an upbeat way of making clear what we're dealing with: quite a primitive society. England may have been more administratively sophisticated than most places in Europe but, by modern standards, that's not saying much. There's still a lot of fighting in the mud and no opera.

But was it worse than what went before? It was for northerners. The Domesday Book makes that clear with all its references to the areas of 'waste' in Yorkshire. This was a result of something called the Harrying of the North, which feels like it should be called the Williaming of the North, or possibly the Willying of the North, because it certainly left the north well and truly fucked.

It happened in the winter of 1069–70 and it was William's response to various uprisings in northern England in support of Edgar Atheling, who was on the comeback trail. The north was different and William knew it. The influence of the Danes was still strong there and the late Anglo-Saxon kings had never had as firm a grasp over it as they had over Wessex and Mercia. When putting together his rebellion, Edgar Atheling had appealed for support to King Sweyn II of Denmark, who was a nephew of Cnut, the man who had wrested England from Edgar's grandfather Edmund Ironside. It all feels like they were trying to get a pre-Norman gang together and, in 1069, Edgar and the Danes briefly occupied York.

You can understand why William completely lost his shit over this. He didn't know that, post-Norman Conquest, the whole Anglo-Danish thing was over. It was only three years since he'd seized the kingdom from a very tenacious Anglo-Danish usurper (from William's point of view). Like all English kings, he will have feared a Danish threat like the modern Germans fear hyperinflation. But, by the time William got to York with an army, Edgar had fled to the court of King Malcolm III of Scotland and the Danes were back in their ships.

William had been denied battle, so he paid off the Danes (it's confusing that, while this was often a disastrous strategy, successful kings like William and Alfred the Great seem to get away with it) and decided to 'waste' the north. His troops went around slaughtering people and burning villages, crops and crop stores. The hope was that the area would no longer be able to support the king's enemies. The side effect was that it was unable to support much human life at all.

Some historians say this was an act of genocide, others that it was merely the sort of brutal thing that went on back then. I don't reckon those conclusions are mutually exclusive. But it underlines William's ruthlessness. He'd had a tough upbringing, inheriting the dukedom as an illegitimate minor and being passed from magnate to magnate in an anarchic power struggle. Before he'd conquered England, he'd had to conquer what was nominally his own duchy – this took strength and the projection of strength. I'm not saying he'd become a psychopath numbed by trauma, but he wasn't the sort of person who, if they see a lamb gambolling across a field, turns veggie for six months. His mercilessness may have been the quality that was most vital to his success.

Doubt is a dangerous thing in medieval politics. We've seen how doubt over the line of succession bred violence and discord, and we're going to keep seeing that. That's going to get boring. A key skill in a medieval ruler is eliminating doubt, and ruthlessness is part of that. The knowledge that, if crossed, the king will respond with immediate reflex savagery, no matter who is doing it or why, is in a sense reassuring.

It reassures you that any rebels who might disturb the peace will be dealt with quickly, so you don't have to worry about lawlessness in the land. Plus, if you're a senior baron thinking of rebelling yourself, it reassures you that there's no point. You're not being a mug by not tilting at the throne, or supporting someone else who might and who would give you great honours if they succeeded with your help. You don't have to fret about whether or not to rebel because you know it's definitely not worth the risk. That's clear. Everyone knows who's in charge and can relax.

While, looked at one way, the Harrying of the North makes William a genocidal maniac, it also demonstrates his understanding of the contemporary rules of ruling. He knew that it was impossible to make it too clear that rebelling, and consorting with the Danes of all people, was not okay. This clarity banished doubt.

Still, if Harold had been king, things might well have been calmer. There's no reason to think he wouldn't have dealt with rebellion just as ruthlessly – he also seemed to have a strong grasp of what constituted professionalism in a ruler of the time. But he wouldn't have had so much dissent to deal with because he would broadly have been governing with the consent of England's Anglo-Saxon ruling class. There wouldn't have been as much harrying (more appropriately named in his case) needed, which would have made for a nicer time for most people. I think that's my conclusion about the Norman Conquest: it was a moderately major change and, in general for people at the time, it would have been nicer if it hadn't happened. I feel the same way when they make you upgrade your operating system.

I don't want to dwell on this because we're now stuck, for several centuries, with this French-speaking castle-dwelling ruling class who perpetually have half an eye on what's happening in France. Some would say we're *still* stuck with them. We might as well try and enjoy them.

Children of the New Forest

Do you have a favourite holiday destination? Perhaps somewhere you associate with sunshine and childhood? Cornwall or the Lake District or North Wales? Maybe sunshine is pushing it. Drizzle and ice cream. Personally I'm fond of the New Forest – I've had many happy times there with my family. Glamorously enough, it turns out this is something I have in common with the English royal family of the eleventh century. William the Conqueror's brood loved the New Forest – they really did. In fact it was William who, in around 1079, proclaimed it a royal forest, which is what it remained until it became a National Park in 2005. They spent a huge amount of time there. In fact they had a little place down there. It was called the New Forest.

Just when you're thinking that you might be able to get a handle on these strange people, because you've found something about them that you recognize other than the need to eat and oxygenate blood – in this case that they liked the New Forest – it only turns to greater weirdness. William had four sons and two of them were killed in the New Forest. In hunting accidents, of course. But not in the same hunting accident. William's second son, Richard, was killed there in 1070 and his third, William Rufus, in 1100.

This means, and this is what I reckon is weird even for someone who would give the north such a vigorous harrying, that *they kept going there*. It didn't spoil it for them, as a family, the fact that one of them had been killed there. It didn't then have negative, one might hazard traumatic, associations. There wasn't then something about that area that didn't feel quite so fun. These are people who had a wide range of other recreational options (by which I mean other places they could have gone hunting, because they certainly weren't going to do anything except hunting). But, oh no, they reckoned they'd stick with the New Forest. 'Ah well, we've all got to go some time, it's still a lovely forest' was the view.

Like learning to be impressed by the Domesday Book, these very different family attitudes are a good illustration of how alien this time was. Royal nuclear families back then were not close in the modern sense. They often treated each other with open contempt, if not open warfare.

William had seven children who outlived him – four daughters and three sons. The eldest son, Robert, had a troubled relationship with his father, which started with William giving him the nickname 'Curthose', meaning 'short stockings'. If this was ever meant affectionately, the name outlived the affection.

Robert first rebelled against his father at the age of about sixteen, as a result of an occasion when his two surviving younger brothers, William Rufus and Henry, emptied a full chamber pot on his head. Genuinely. I mean, they didn't know about germs, but still. One gets the sense that these people weren't just literally shitty. At the end of the ensuing unhygienic brawl, King William failed, in Robert's view, to sufficiently punish the two whippersnappers for befouling him, so he flounced off and tried to storm one of his father's castles. Unsuccessfully.

Despite this shaky start, rebelling became a bit of a hobby for Robert and he had a rackety time for the rest of his father's life. His mother, Queen Matilda, was keener on him than his dad was and, to William's fury, was discovered to be secretly sending her son money. She brokered a rapprochement between the two of them at Easter 1080, but they fell out again soon after her death in 1083.

By the time William was lying in a priory with a suppurating wound and nothing left on his to-do list except divide up his lands, die and explode, he was on the verge of disinheriting his eldest son. England, certainly, would go to William Rufus, his favourite child. However, the Norman lords pushed for Robert to inherit the duchy as planned. That's what William had declared more than once previously and Normandy, unlike England at this stage, had a firm tradition of primogeniture dating back to Rollo. In a spirit of banishing peace-corroding doubt, the dying duke relented and left his ancestral lands to Robert after all. His youngest surviving son, Henry, just got money.

This was a flawed outcome. Robert, while easy-going and affable (when not furious with his father), seems also to have been lazy, inconsistent, relentlessly impecunious and generally unlucky. William Rufus was made of sterner stuff. Meanwhile many major lords held lands in both Normandy and England and didn't want to have to choose between the two.

Robert, some nobles will have thought, was likely to be a soft touch. They were probably right – and he always needed money, which left him open to persuasion. But weak figures like that are enormous purveyors of doubt, the very thing William the Conqueror was trying to avoid by giving him the duchy, and, I'll say it again, doubt, particularly doubt about the future conduct of the ruler, is the greatest obstacle to the barons of a medieval kingdom having a nice quiet life. That is what I am resolutely insisting most people wanted.

Some say that all that is necessary for evil to triumph is for good men to do nothing. I find that an awkward principle because, in my view, allowing good men to do nothing is the purpose of civilization.

15. King William II

I don't mean to get into the habit of starting each chapter explaining how the ruler it's about died. Nevertheless, I've already mentioned this so there's no suspense to be ruined: William II died in 1100 as a result of a hunting accident in the New Forest. Some say it was no accident. But some say it was an accident. I reckon it's too late to dust for prints. So that's where this is all heading.

He was known as William Rufus. 'Rufus' means red-headed, so it was probably because he had red hair or was ruddy-cheeked. Either way, it feels fonder than 'Curthose'. He was unmarried and died without issue, and he has gone down in history as quite a bad king. Not the worst, but not one of the good guys. And the good guys, on closer examination, usually turn out to have killed more people than Fred West and blinded more than dog shit.

Why the dodgy reputation? I must say I don't entirely understand it. The chroniclers of the time say he did terrible things: embezzled from the church, allowed his entourage to steal from local villages when his court was progressing round the country, failed to appoint a new archbishop of Canterbury so he could keep the money, etc.

He eventually did appoint a new archbishop because he fell ill and assumed this was because God was cross with him. So, in 1093, he picked Archbishop Anselm to take the place of Archbishop Lanfranc who'd died in 1089 and was himself the replacement for the Anglo-Saxon Stigand whom I mentioned earlier. That's three archbishops in a row whose names ended in interesting juxtaposed consonants. Coincidence? Well, it means you have to pronounce them carefully, reverently even, to do justice to the last noise. It's a technique branding experts must be aware of -- I'm sure that's where Häagen-Dazs came from. I'm thinking of sticking an extra 'n' on the end of my own name in the hope of finally getting a bit of bloody respect.

Back to William's detractors: they also said, and obviously this was a scandalous accusation for the time, that he was gay. They didn't put it like that, of course. People at the time said William indulged in the sin of sodomy and encouraged 'effeminacy' in his followers. They said William did that sin lots, which was very bad of him and meant he was a terrible king who deserved to die young in a hunting accident.

We don't know if he was gay, or bisexual, or if the various forms of sexual abandon that he's accused of actually happened. Maybe it was just that he was mean to the church and so the chroniclers, all of whom lived in monasteries, accused him of sodomy to sully his reputation. But where would they have got the idea from, living in a monastery? At this time, almost all rulers found themselves at loggerheads with ecclesiastical authorities because of an ongoing international row about whether the pope or local kings got to appoint bishops. It was possible to represent *any* of them as enemies of the church, so it doesn't feel like it means much.

My scepticism about whether he deserves his bad reputation stems from two things: first the uncalamitous character of his reign. Most of the kings who we're encouraged to think of as bad demonstrably screwed things up: Aethelred the Unready, as we've already seen, and also Stephen, John, Edward II, Richard III, whom we have yet to enjoy. The shit hit the fan in all of those cases and there was no hiding it. But William II seems to have ruled with competence.

He inherited England under controversial circumstances. Many powerful noblemen wanted England and Normandy reunited and, at the beginning of the reign, they didn't see

William as the man to do it. In 1088 there was a major rebellion led by his uncle, Bishop Odo of Bayeux, in favour of Robert Curthose. Rufus dealt efficiently with this, and all future rebellions. He expanded England's borders, at the expense of Scotland, to include Cumberland and Westmorland, secured the border with Wales with a string of castles and, by the end of his reign, he had effectively become duke of Normandy too, thus reuniting his father's empire in the opposite way to that envisaged by Bishop Odo. This last was thanks to his brother's relentless incompetence and need for money: Robert leased the duchy to William for 10,000 marks, which paid for him to go on the First Crusade. You're going to be hearing a lot about these crusades over the next few hundred years (I hope I'm not over-estimating your pace of reading) and I'll get into them in more detail later. At this point, suffice it to say that it involved fighting in the middle east and Robert went on it and it was the best place for him.

So, unless you listen to all the anecdotal evidence about church funding and followers stealing things, all of which could have happened during most reigns, William's appears to be a functional regime. This leads me to the second reason for my scepticism, which is related to his possible sexuality: it's the fact that he died without issue. Nobody afterwards was motivated to look after his reputation. Many subsequent kings were careful to honour William the Conqueror's name and the righteousness of his rule, because they were his descendants and their rights rested on his.

But no subsequent regime derived its legitimacy from William Rufus, so his reputation remained an easy target for chroniclers with nits to pick. William seems, in general, to have had the strength, consistency, energy, ruthlessness and organizational competence required to keep fractious possessions together. He wasn't the best of medieval kings but neither was he one of the many who simply couldn't do the job.

On the other hand . . .

Sorry to be annoying and not come to a firm overall conclusion about William II – I'm really hoping it wasn't merely the prospect of a firm overall conclusion about William II that convinced you to read this book – but I'm afraid there is another way of looking at it. His reign was only thirteen years long and might even have ended in someone murdering him. Whether or not it did, there's a chance that the collapse of government that I just said was absent from Rufus's maligned regime was imminent.

The other, more disastrous kings I mentioned (Aethelred and co.) all, with the exception of Richard III, reigned longer than William II before everything fell to bits for them. So his reign could have been an unbearable tyranny. Or it could have been perfectly fine.

We can relax when making our judgement because, refreshingly, William himself didn't seem to care what anyone thought at all. He didn't care what posterity thought, what his subjects thought and, except when dangerously ill, what his boss thought. By his boss, I mean God. William certainly acknowledged no other, and he barely acknowledged Him. In this he was very different from his father.

William the Conqueror was very religious. As we've seen, by our standards everyone was back then and there's no suggestion that William Rufus was anything close to an atheist. But he wasn't pious. His father, on the other hand, really was. Tediously so. It was key to how he coped psychologically with an existence fraught with danger and risk. He'd had to fight all his life and, at the few points where he didn't have to fight, he'd chosen to fight. He will have been bitterly aware, from Harold's fate if nothing else, how a stray arrow could make everything suddenly go wrong. For him religion was the answer.

William Rufus wasn't like that. He wasn't naturally God-fearing and he wasn't a generous endower of the church. Very unusually for the time, the most enduring architectural legacy of his reign isn't religious but secular. It's not even a castle. It's Westminster Hall, still part of the Palace of Westminster today. It's an impressive building (though the best thing about it is the hammerbeam roof and that was put in three centuries later) and it was the largest hall in Europe at the time. In a sense that makes it a precursor of the Shard, though I earnestly hope that isn't still standing in 930 years' time. For William to dedicate that much stonemasonry to neither war nor God shows bravado.

He was a bluff military type – full of regal and martial self-confidence. There's a story about him needing to hurry to France in 1099 because the city of Le Mans in the county of Maine had fallen. When he heard the news, he was hunting in the New Forest (obviously) but headed directly for Le Mans – so directly in fact that he reportedly had a wall demolished that was in the way (to make some sort of point, one imagines, as I'm sure it would have been quicker to walk round it).

When he arrived at Southampton there was only an extremely rickety ship available and the weather didn't look too clever. The sailors counselled caution but William said: 'I have never heard of a king who was drowned at sea.' He commanded them to set sail, which they did and all was well – until the following year, when he was killed hunting in the New Forest.

This attitude is the opposite of pious or God-fearing. As William the Conqueror nervously waited on the French coast for a favourable wind to invade England, one suspects that he considered the drowning of a king, or a duke as he then was, to be eminently possible if you put God in a bad mood. His son, meanwhile, felt that there was something about him, something physiologically different, that made him undrownable. That's the difference a generation can make. What William

II had, and it can be both a strength and a weakness, was a sense of entitlement.

Was this entitlement the reason he never troubled to marry and beget an heir? It's a very unusual choice for a monarch at this time and the suspicion that he was gay isn't enough to explain it. Royal marriages weren't usually love matches. The business of impregnation could generally be managed within couples where there was no mutual attraction. Even the most undutiful of kings still tended to try to provide an heir, unless there was already an obvious successor.

Athelstan, the great Anglo-Saxon king, had no wife or children and some people think that may have been a deliberate, diplomatic omission because of all the younger half-brothers, all considered athelings, who were lining up behind him. The introduction of an infant heir into that dynastic context would've been destabilizing. But that concern isn't applicable to Rufus's situation. Robert Curthose was his nominal heir (as he was Curthose's), but William showed no desire for his elder brother and his progeny to inherit England – he probably expected to outlive him anyway. After that, what was the plan? Was William so entitled he thought he'd never die? Or did he just not care?

If the latter is true, he is an extremely unusual monarch. In general they *all* care about who will succeed them. They obsess over that, as if by getting it right they become immortal. You're probably aware of the lengths Henry VIII later went to in order to father a son. That need changed the whole country's religion and geopolitical orbit in a way that still partially defines Britain today. Henry also had a healthy sense of entitlement but, for him, the notion of leaving no ordered male succession was nightmarish. That's because he believed there was something bigger and more important than him: the crown, God, the dynasty, all that. William II doesn't seem to have given a shit about any of it. And who are we to say that was wrong?

16. King Henry I

If William II had a sense of entitlement, Henry I suffered from impostor syndrome. That was because he was an impostor. If Rufus was murdered, his younger brother Henry, or someone working on his behalf, is a major suspect. Even if his predecessor wasn't murdered, Henry still usurped the throne. William II had left it to Robert Curthose, albeit unenthusiastically. For the second time Robert would have expected to be king of England but he was still on crusade and Henry moved fast.

He rode from the New Forest – oh yes, he was right there when William was killed – to Winchester where he seized the royal treasury, and then to Westminster, where he had himself crowned king three days later. He had to make do with the Bishop of London officiating because Archbishop Anselm was in exile over a quarrel with William, but it still counted.

Only a few centuries after the Byzantines started making this shit up, coronations were now viewed as real and sacred and transformative. Once you were crowned and anointed, you simply *were* the king – that was the view. Maybe you shouldn't be the king, but you still were. That's why, in those days, no one hung about being uncrowned for months so the ceremony could be nicely organized with lots of pageantry. It wasn't worth the risk of a rival claimant steaming in with some biddable bishop and getting himself crowned while the rightful ruler was busy choosing bunting.

Even though Henry wasn't the rightful heir, by getting crowned he had sort of physically become a king and that was, to a certain extent, that. Robert Curthose could still fight to remove him, but he was fighting to remove an anointed king not a hopeful prince, and that felt very different.

It's still the situation with Roman Catholic priests. Once someone is ordained a priest, that's that – they can say the mass, they have the power of transubstantiation, whatever happens. If they're disgraced, imprisoned or lose their faith, there's nothing the church can do (it thinks) to reverse the transformation that occurred in them when they were ordained.

So stealing the crown isn't just like stealing an object – say a crown – something that can then be returned to its rightful owner. It's like stealing a sandwich and then eating it. The delicious sandwichy goodness of royalty was within Henry no matter what Robert did.

Still, you can understand the impostor syndrome. He knew he wasn't supposed to be king and this is only made clearer by the comical nature of his claim to the throne. Henry cited something called porphyrogeniture. Unlike primogeniture, which gives primacy to the first born, porphyrogeniture favours those born 'in the purple' (the word comes from the Greek *porphyrogennetos* meaning 'purple-born'). The purple in question is Tyrian purple, the expensive dyed cloth customarily worn by Roman emperors. This is another example of medieval kings borrowing some Roman notions they'd vaguely heard about to try and make themselves seem posh.

The idea behind porphyrogeniture was that, even better than being the first-born male of the previous king, was being born while your father was already king – 'in the purple'. It feels tied in with the notion of kingship causing a physical change in the human who becomes king. Henry was claiming that he was more royal than Robert Curthose because William the Conqueror was already king of England when Henry was born, whereas when Robert was born (and William Rufus for that matter) he was a mere duke of Normandy.

To me, this idea seems so mad and self-serving as to have barely been worth Henry expressing. It might as well have been people-whose-names-begin-with-H-ogeniture. He stuck with the theory though and, since he was unmarried at the time of his accession, both of his legitimate children were born 'in the purple' too.

The more societally useful consequence of Henry's impostor syndrome was his coronation charter. Fundamentally, this was a deal he was offering the leading nobility. It was mainly stuff about not charging exorbitant fees when a son inherited his father's lands, and not forcing rich widows to remarry. The sort of thing the barons got stressed about. But the key message was: I will be a reasonable king. Much more so than my brother, more like my father. I offer peace and justice, was the pitch. Like Magna Carta over a century later, this charter was an influential document and much cited in later decades when the barons were disappointed with the quality of kingship they were receiving.

The surprising thing was that, broadly speaking, Henry, the maybe-fratricidal definitely-usurper, was as good as his word. He kept that promise and his reign was stable and successful. Frankly, he was a born king. Except he wasn't, unless you're a believer in porphyrogeniture (and, if you are a believer in that, I bet I can guess what job your dad had when you were born). He was a natural. From a modern perspective, he was right to seize the throne, because he was very good at being king.

Being cruel to be king

Henry was good at being king but that's not to say he was good. By modern standards, he was horrible. Vicious and brutal and vengeful. But his reign in England, after a brief, inevitable and unsuccessful attempt by Robert Curthose to claim the throne in 1101, was peaceful. There was a flurry of punitive violence against the lords who had supported Robert and then calm.

If medieval England had been a democracy and all of its kings had been options on a ballot paper, all normal members of the public, and the overwhelming majority of aristocrats, would have been well advised to vote for Henry I. Under him, England was a placid and administratively efficient place to live where conditions, in general, were improving. Why?

He was predictable. That's the key. It's disappointing in a lover but, in a feudal overlord, it hits the spot. Henry made it clear what the deal was – what he wanted and what he expected – and then he was reasonable if he got it, and horrendous if he didn't. Like his father, he eliminated doubt. He did it even more effectively than his father, but then he didn't have to conquer a kingdom.

He did have to conquer a dukedom, though. Most influential Anglo-Norman lords at this point still held land in both England and Normandy and their wealth was always jeopardized by the possibility that the two regimes in which it was held might have a war with each other.

After Henry's coronation, Curthose, who was on his way back from the First Crusade, remained duke of Normandy. William II had only leased the dukedom and, by primogeniture and the bequests of both William I and William II (the wills of both Wills), Robert was the rightful duke. He was also the rightful king of England, until Henry persuaded him to give up his claim at the Treaty of Alton in 1101, in exchange for 3,000 marks of silver a year.

This was a lot of money, but it was still a good deal for Henry. And Robert frittered the cash away anyway. As I've already mentioned, he was one of those people who simply cannot hold on to money. He was constantly broke, despite his ability to get hold of vast sums. Some people can work their way through any amount. For all our sakes, may Jeff Bezos be blessed with such an heir.

Henry had Normandy off Curthose within a few years. Curthose wasn't a total idiot, and had fought well in the First Crusade, but his financial failings were part of a wider propensity to cock things up. Henry was pushing against an open door. He sowed a bit of discord in Normandy and, by 1106, many of the Norman barons were desperate for him to take over. Henry captured Robert at the Battle of Tinchebray in September and put him in prison for the rest of his exceptionally long life. He died in Cardiff Castle in 1134, well into his eighties.

William the Conqueror fathered his sons in reverse order of regal competence. If this isn't enough to make me endorse porphyrogeniture, it's still a massive rubdown for primogeniture. I wonder how it felt to witness it at the time. Our notions of meritocracy and equality of opportunity would have sounded incomprehensible to medieval ears and not just because there was nothing they could do about the build-up of wax. Kings were chosen by God and anointed by bishops. The way God chose them was to make them born to the previous king.

But did people not reflect on the obvious fact that Henry was really good at the job and Robert was terrible, and the other fact that the only way Henry got to be king ahead of Robert was via theft and violence? Did it not make them wonder about their system for running things?

I feel sorry for Curthose, though, living out long decades in prison, just a five-minute walk from Wales's only branch of the Ivy – though counterintuitively a 985-year walk would have been more convenient because that's how long he'd have to wait before it would open. I doubt there was even a chip shop back in his day, as it was centuries before the first potatoes arrived in Europe. Still, he wouldn't have been able to afford a meal anyway.

Poor guy, remembered to this day by the condescending nickname his father gave him. It sometimes feels like they're set up to fail, these eldest sons of powerful men. There's something in the arrogance, the need to feel indispensable and the fear of death of guys like William the Conqueror that makes it impossible for them not to be disappointed with their heirs.

Their own toxic mixture of self-loathing and narcissism stews inside them and comes out as contempt for their firstborn: 'This boy has my failings but will never learn to overcome them like I have' is often the sentiment. With younger sons, there seems to be more space for love. But the eldest is presumed to be trying to supplant the father and gets blamed for mortality itself. It feels like Curthose's failure to get his shit together was made inevitable by his father's low expectations. The younger sons were free to be themselves.

Robert Curthose's own son was also free to be himself. Known as William Clito – *clito* being a medieval Latin word meaning 'royal' or 'princely' – he was three years old when his father went to prison for being bad at his job. Henry uncharacteristically decided not to imprison his brother's heir.

That may sound like a fair way to treat a blameless infant. But Henry wasn't fair, any more than life is. He was just predictable. This was a lapse in his own policy: few would have predicted that he'd have left a male child with a better claim to be king of England and duke of Normandy than any man living toddling around the continent making friends. But he did. I wish I could say that Henry was rewarded for this unwonted kindness. But no. He bitterly regretted it.

Messing about in boats

Broadly speaking, you can divide Henry's reign into two halves: the first half in which most things went right for him, and the second half in which most things went right for him. But it is divided into these halves by an absolute catastrophe: in 1120 his only legitimate son and heir was killed in a shipwreck.

This was, above all, very very sad. The prince, whose name was William and was known as William Adelin (a corruption of 'atheling') was seventeen years old and had recently been endorsed as the next duke of Normandy by King Louis VI of France. Strictly speaking this was necessary, notwithstanding the hereditary nature of the duchy and Henry's complete military control over it, because the kings of France were the dukes' overlords. Still, it wasn't an act of generosity on Louis's part but the consequence of his having just lost a small war to Henry.

The whole English court was travelling triumphantly back from Barfleur, the preferred port on the Normandy coast for making swift crossings to England, but the cool kids, led by Adelin, decided to travel in a snazzy, new, fast vessel called the *White Ship*. The ghostly connotations of the name are entirely appropriate because they all died. An entire young generation of Anglo-Norman aristocracy was lost. The sole survivor, when the ship sank, was a butcher from Rouen. The shipwreck had a greater impact on the English ruling class than the Somme and achieved even less.

Instinctively one feels one should separate Henry's personal tragedy, and the hundreds of other personal tragedies for other leading families of the realm, and for the more ordinary families of the sailors and servants on board, from its colossal geopolitical impact. Then again, I'm not sure. For

Henry, such a capable and successful king, so conscious of his dynasty and legacy – all the more because the justification for his own kingship was so dodgy – the personal loss and the dynastic disaster were inextricable.

His grief at the loss of a child will have been supercharged by his feeling that his legacy was in ruins, and the succession crisis made more nightmarish by the enormous personal pain that had caused it. The death of children, or teenagers, was so much more common back then that, on some level, it's impossible to believe that the pain felt as unbearable as it does in societies where such tragedies are much rarer. Everyone lost children, so everyone had lots of children. And they coped. Henry, while he had only two legitimate children, had over twenty illegitimate ones whom he freely acknowledged and lavished with favour.

William Adelin was obviously Henry's favourite son, but he also personified his father's strategy for the future: a prince, named after the Conqueror, but given the old Anglo-Saxon heirs' soubriquet to signify his descent, through his mother Queen Matilda of Scotland, from the House of Wessex. He was to unite Normandy and England, in one royal house under one rightful king, by both primogeniture and porphyrogeniture.

He gave all of Henry's prudent brutality, his administrative reforms, his building of an aristocracy he could trust and who trusted him – in a word his struggle – a reason and point. The prince's death was more than the tragic death of a son, it was also Henry's death. It represented the whole horror and inevitability of death as a concept, its inescapability for kings as well as for peasants, and the lurking futility of all human endeavours.

And it was such a stupid cock-up. Everyone on the *White Ship* was pissed. Adelin, young, hot-headed and the star of the court, had inaugurated a party boat – bringing on board large quantities of wine and encouraging passengers and crew alike to indulge. They spent the whole evening drinking in the harbour, while the other ships, including the king's, set sail. Then they decided it would be a laugh to beat them all home. They raced out of the harbour straight into a rock and slipped screaming into the freezing sea. Dead from youthful foolishness. It's the pointless, heartbreaking fate of millions of beloved teenagers throughout the ages and, though Henry would never know it, it doomed his peaceful, ordered kingdom, his life's work, to chaos.

Smile though your heart is aching

Henry reputedly didn't. They said that he never smiled again after he heard the news of the *White Ship*. I don't know how they kept such a close eye on him – they must have worked in shifts. Another thing they said was that he died of a surfeit of lampreys – a lamprey is a weird jawless eel-like fish which was considered a delicacy. You never see it on a menu any more, even at those places that make it their mission to concoct dishes out of nostril and ball and bladder, so perhaps, in any society that has access to chips, asserting the lamprey to be delicious is no longer credible. Whatever its objective tastiness, it was a dish quite susceptible to accidental food poisoning, so it may have been the quality rather than the quantity of the lampreys that did for Henry.

That was fifteen unsmiling years later. In the meantime, he worked hard to deal with the catastrophe. He must have been kicking himself at his failure to father more than one legitimate son, and his wife had died in 1118, two years before the shipwreck. He got married again, in 1121, to a very attractive young woman called Adeliza of Louvain whom he spent the rest of his life failing to impregnate. She subsequently had children with a second husband, and Henry had had kids with loads of different women, so it's odd they remained childless. Somehow the urgent necessity of an heir militated against the likelihood of begetting one. The whole 'Okay, quick, let's get a son fathered ASAP and then I can buckle down to the arduous task of living until he's old enough to be king' vibe didn't maximize fertility. Plus a smile might've helped.

Henry also had to deal with William Clito, who had grown up into an impressive and capable young man and increasingly looked like the undeniable heir to all of Henry's dominions (if you don't count Robert Curthose, who was still kicking his heels in Cardiff, dreaming of Deliveroo). The Norman barons, more truculent than the English ones, were keen to make Clito the official heir. This struck Henry's enemy the King of France as a delightful idea now that Adelin was dead and, in 1127, he made Clito count of Flanders.

Henry seemed to feel nothing but enmity for his nephew and was determined that his direct descendants would inherit the kingdom and, in the end, he got his way: King Charles III is his (twenty-seven greats) grandson and not a direct descendant of Clito. To screw things up for Clito, Henry supported a rival claimant to the county of Flanders, called Thierry. Clito defeated Thierry in battle in June 1028 but then, out of the blue, died as a result of wounds incurred in a different battle the following month. The premature-death luck had started to go Henry's way again.

The question of what was going to happen when Henry himself died remained. Unlike his elder brother William, Henry was obsessed by this question. He had one legitimate heir remaining, his daughter Matilda. I should warn you that, as a name, Matilda was very much the Aelfgifu of the twelfth century. Henry's mother, first wife and daughter were all called Matilda. Henry's daughter Matilda is going to spend much of her life fighting to be queen of England but I'm not risking any spoilers when I say that one person or another called Matilda was queen of England most of the time from 1066 until the middle of the following century.

So the best way of distinguishing Henry's daughter Matilda from the others is to call her the Empress Matilda, and that's what she liked to be called. It wasn't just a mad whim – she was married to the Holy Roman Emperor Henry V until he died in 1125. The couple were childless and Matilda then headed back to her father, whom she hadn't seen since she was packed off to Germany at the age of eight as the emperor's intended bride. (Obviously she didn't marry him when she was eight. That would have been barbaric. They waited until she was twelve.)

Not long after Matilda's return, Henry took, for the time, a rather eccentric decision. He decided to make her heir to England and Normandy. For a woman to take on this role was unprecedented for the House of Normandy. The examples of women ruling anywhere at all were few and far between, and usually it had occurred when they were acting on behalf of a husband. There was a widespread feeling among all the powerful men of the time not necessarily that women *couldn't* rule but that they wouldn't be accepted as rulers.

But Henry, more out of an obsession with his own bloodline than any glimmer of proto-feminism, decided to name his daughter as his successor. This was in preference to several illegitimate sons, notably Robert Earl of Gloucester. Henry may have seen qualities in Matilda that made him think she'd be a more capable ruler. Despite only being twenty-three when she was widowed, she was politically experienced and had acted as her husband's regent in northern Italy.

So Henry had a plan. His daughter, the dowager empress, would rule after him. She would secure his legacy and the immortality of his bloodline. At the Christmas court in

Westminster in 1026, Henry made all of his leading barons swear an oath to support Matilda as his heir in England and Normandy. They obediently queued up and did so. In 1131 he made them do it again just to confirm that they meant it. After his fishy-breathed death in 1135, it turned out that they didn't.

17. King Stephen

The next reign began exactly like the previous one: an opportunistic usurper raced to get himself crowned and became king as a fait accompli. The opportunist in question was called Stephen of Blois. He was the fourth son of one of William the Conqueror's daughters, so wasn't a legitimate king by primogeniture, porphyrogeniture or people-whose-names-begin-with-H-ogeniture.

Stephen had been knocking around Henry's court all his life and was a charming and popular figure. He was lucky as well: he had been on board the *White Ship* in Barfleur before it set sail but a violent case of the shits forced him to disembark. Whatever fetid privy he settled on to once he'd hurried ashore turned out to be a far more auspicious enthronement than his subsequent one in Westminster, and made much less of a mess.

The old king liked Stephen and five years after the *White Ship* disaster, by which point he was pooing normally, Henry had arranged for him to marry the rich heiress to the county of Boulogne, who, like Henry's first queen, was a descendant of the kings of Wessex. Her name was Matilda too, I'm afraid.

Matilda may be a common name for a queen at this time, but Stephen is an unusual one for a king and, to a great extent, that's thanks to this Stephen. He's so badly thought of that no one would touch that regnal name with a sterilized sceptre thereafter. For a king's name to catch on, you need one or two successful ones to get it going. There are quite a few Williams and Henries, but only one Stephen and one John.

The main reason people don't like Stephen is his rivalry with the Empress Matilda. She was clearly the person her father had wanted to succeed him. *Very* clearly. However, Stephen and a few others wouldn't have admitted as much, and would have cited the schism that existed between Henry I and his daughter at the time of his death.

It was a row about some castles in Normandy that Henry was refusing to hand over to Matilda and her second husband Geoffrey, Count of Anjou – they'd been part of her dowry. Henry was probably concerned that Geoffrey would use them to try and take over Normandy. It was a classic case of an old man refusing to loosen his grip on power as much in defiance of approaching death as anything else. It seems vanishingly unlikely that this spat, coming as it did in the wake of Matilda giving birth to his first two legitimate male grandchildren, an event which delighted Henry (not that he can have smiled – maybe he gave a sombre-faced thumbs up), would have led the old king to rethink his succession plans.

There's little doubt that Stephen was defying his uncle and mentor's wishes when he took the throne. And *no* doubt that Stephen had sworn an oath, twice, to support Matilda as the next sovereign. This behaviour has gone down badly with posterity because Empress Matilda is a sympathetic figure.

A woman in a man's world – robbed of her rights, accused by contemporaries both of lacking the traditionally male strengths to rule and of being unnatural and unfeminine whenever she displayed those strengths – but refusing to give in and let Stephen be king. All in all she's a Crufts-winning underdog. While Stephen, a man who stole the throne and then held on to it ineffectually, is hard to like.

Except, I suspect, if you met him. He's talked of as a very nice guy in person. Having myself once met and warmed to Boris Johnson, I'm aware of the limitations and fickleness of this attribute – but it's interesting. Stephen's life was defined by one opportunistic moment of colossal self-interest. But it seems likely that, had he not stolen the title of king, Stephen might have qualified for that of 'nice man'.

Meanwhile Matilda gets called haughty. Contemporary descriptions of her personality are less reliable than those of Stephen, though. Her alleged haughtiness was probably more about the attitudes of the age: the very thing she was trying to do — be the ruler of a kingdom — was deemed by most to be unbearably haughty behaviour before she'd even opened her mouth, and the fact that she called herself empress is unlikely to have defused that impression.

The most frustrating thing about Stephen was that, despite following Henry I's example closely in the manner of his seizing power and the promises he issued to powerful people in the realm, he then completely departed from his predecessor's strategy of kingship. He couldn't stick to being firm but predictable. He lacked ruthlessness and he displayed favouritism. He needed to be clear and unwavering in his conduct, vicious to those who opposed him and even-handedly generous to supporters. But he wasn't and this created bad feeling, uncertainty, rebellion — it stoked the fires of guilt for those who'd sworn to support Matilda and sparked opportunism in those who reckoned they'd do better if the regime changed. All of this was succour to Matilda's cause.

The conflict that this led to, when Matilda finally came over to England to pursue her claim in 1139, has been referred to by historians, since Victorian times, as the Anarchy. It won't surprise you to hear that this term has since fallen out of favour. Apparently it's a simplistic label. I'm sure it is, but that's pretty much the deal with names. I'd say 'Brian' is a simplistic label for the guy who came to fix our washing machine, but it's still his name. I don't reckon we'd get to the root of the man any better by calling him Adrian.

It wasn't nice, the Anarchy. It was a big and brutal civil war and my main feeling about it, throughout — and this must have been the sentiment of the overwhelming majority of people in England at the time – is a desperation for one side or the other to win. It really didn't matter which, except to two people.

If Stephen had a quarter of the usurper-competence of his predecessor, Matilda wouldn't have had a look-in and millions of people, men and women alike, would have had a much nicer time in the 1140s. It would have been so much better all round if he'd managed to secure the throne properly and there hadn't been a civil war. It wouldn't have been fair on Matilda, but nothing had *ever* been fair on Robert Curthose and, if he'd been king of England, he'd have ended up mortgaging the rivers. Justice for people who are already beneficiaries of a massively unjust system becomes difficult to give much of a damn about.

The snow empress

Oxford Castle, I felt when visiting it in the late 1980s, gives a powerful sense of incarceration. I grew up in Oxford and, as a fan of castles, it had always seemed weird to me that this otherwise extremely historical city didn't seem to have a proper one. It had tea rooms and museums and the country's first ever branch of Past Times. But, instead of a castle, there was just a small artificial green hill with nothing on it, that you could glimpse over the top of a tall stone wall, just down the road from Marks & Spencer's. 'That's Oxford Castle,' my parents would say. No one was allowed to go there.

The reason for this inaccessibility was, ironically, continuity of use. At that point, Oxford Castle, unlike almost every other Norman fortress, had not yet been abandoned to the elements and then tourism. When it fell out of military use in the late middle ages and its fortifications started to fall into disrepair, it nevertheless continued as an administrative centre for what became Oxfordshire county council, and as a courthouse and jail. The site had been redeveloped piecemeal over the centuries to accommodate these continuing functions.

This is what it was like by the 1980s: next to the hill, which was a Norman motte from which the stone keep had been removed in the early eighteenth century, was a building that looked very castly indeed – it was covered in arrow slits and crenellations and mini-turrets. It was protesting far too much and clearly wasn't actually a castle. The stonework was too even and there was parking in front. It was merely castle-themed, like a Vegas casino. It was in fact the County Hall, built in 1841 in the Gothic Revival style.

Next to this, constructed in 1973, was New County Hall. This was built not in the Gothic Revival style but in a style that I pray will never be revived. I no longer have the energy to think that buildings like this are anything but ugly. Wilfully ugly: 50 per cent concrete and 50 per cent tinted glass. The sort of thing that features in the title sequence of *The Office* or would be the headquarters for the secret police in a cash-poor totalitarian state. It feels like the architect either wanted it to look horrible or was worse at his job than King Stephen. It's almost penitential, the architecture of that era – a deliberate rejection of aesthetic convention which I'm now resigned to being too bourgeois to enjoy.

Speaking of the penitential, behind them all, incorporating the only bits of medieval stonework that remained above ground into a part-eighteenth-century and part-Victorian structure, was HM Prison Oxford. Brimming, I imagined at the time, with the nemeses of Inspector Morse. This was why the castle mound wasn't open to the public – it directly overlooked the prison. Allowing people on to that hillock was deemed a security risk. My visit in the 1980s was a one-off, part of a scheme, I seem to remember, to open just for one day of the year places that were usually closed. I took the opportunity to help a couple of fraudsters to freedom.

I remember two things about the castle: first, the amazing vaulted well chamber that was concealed inside the motte – a genuinely haunting space that is presumably genuinely haunted. And second, the view of the wing of the old prison. It looked grimmer even than the New County Hall and whoever was giving us the tour explained disapprovingly that it was massively overcrowded and was supposed to have been closed years ago. It was like an illustration by Phiz, a rebuke of the Victorian era. Except, to be fair on that era, the 1980s prison contained many more prisoners than its nineteenth-century designers ever intended. That's Thatcher for you.

As I remember it, I could see glimpses of inmates through the windows – tattooed forearms thrust through the bars. It feels unlikely but that's what my brain tells me I remember. So, as I say, incarceration was very much the ambience. It felt like a troubled place.

In general, it's a troubled part of Oxford, the south-west of the centre, between the castle and the river. Wracked by relentless redevelopment. In his enormous book *London: The Biography*, Peter Ackroyd writes evocatively about the rookeries, London's early nineteenth-century slums, located around the church of St Giles in the Fields. This church was on the route from Newgate Prison to the gallows at Tyburn and, from the fifteenth century onwards, the churchwardens developed the rather fun tradition of standing the condemned prisoners a drink, known as St Giles's Bowl, at the Angel pub next door on their way to being executed.

These themes of crime, alcohol and death continued to dominate the area as it descended towards its Dickensian nadir. Then in the 1840s an attempt was made to sort this out by constructing New Oxford Street, an extension of Oxford Street eastwards through the rookeries. Ackroyd's point is that this redevelopment never quite took – the area was too broken, its unhappiness too ingrained, to let it shake off its past and become a merry extension to the capitalistic confidence of Oxford Street or the twinkling bustle of Covent Garden. He's right about the neighbourhood – New Oxford Street, dominated by the enormous Centre Point building, is windswept and bleak – yet the idea that its history, almost its aura, is what prevents it from shaking off a grim ambience is fanciful but also attractive.

The Oxpens area of Oxford, as the section between the castle and the Thames is known, reminds me of Ackroyd's idea. It feels like scar tissue. This was the monastic area of Oxford, home to Osney Abbey, Rewley Abbey and St Frideswide's Priory, rich and prestigious institutions that were destroyed in the sixteenth-century dissolution of the monasteries. They had been founded at the time when the first students were beginning to form a university. The university had grown up alongside them and their sudden eclipse changed the centre of gravity of the city.

Oxpens, which was outside the city walls, became the city's seamier quarter. This was where there were slums, pubs, brothels and, in the nineteenth century, industry: a brewery, a factory and a gasworks, all on the same side of town as the council offices and prison. None of it very 'Oxford'. This was the part of town chosen for the railway station.

In the mid- to late twentieth century, when industry was declining but expectations of housing standards were on the rise, the planners razed much of the area and moved the residents out to new housing estates on the edge of town. And the area was redeveloped again: a shopping centre, multi-storey car park, further education college and ice rink all appeared, with a new road, the Oxpens Road, bleaker even than New Oxford Street, built through the wasteland. That's how it was throughout my childhood.

They've redeveloped it again since, when the prison finally closed in 1996 and became a Malmaison hotel. That castle precinct, given up to tourism with no intervening centuries of picturesque decay, teems with chain restaurants. The shopping centre and car park have been demolished and replaced with a different shopping centre and car park. Plus there's still a large area of waste ground. Maybe someone will start a Benedictine monastery there now that's allowed again.

This feels like the least historical part of Oxford. Apart from a hill, a tower and a few foundations, there's nothing old here. The rest of the city centre is crammed with ancient buildings that seem untouched – the colleges of the university, the stone quadrangles of which have been cleaned and repointed, had Virginia creeper and wisteria grown up them and latterly electricity and wifi installed, but otherwise have been left in peace. The Oxpens area hasn't seen much peace; history keeps happening to it. It's not picturesque but to stand in it and see what it is now, while knowing all the things it has been, brings you closer to understanding history than the quiet of an untouched cloister.

I'm talking about this area because, from my schooldays onwards, I was taught that here, before the traffic and the sculpted verges and the FE college and the ice rink, before the pubs and slums and factories and brothels, back when the monasteries were new, an empress escaped from the castle through the snow and fled across the frozen river wrapped in a white cloak. The castle had become a prison for her, just as it would be for thousands after her, but her jailers were outside the walls. King Stephen and his army had placed it under siege.

I'm an empress, get me out of here

With Oxford in Stephen's hands and his army settling down for a long siege, Matilda had realized her best bet was to run for it. In the middle of December 1142, she used the cover of night and snow, and the fact that the river was frozen, to slip out of one of the castle gates (or, according to some of the more helmet-horn-inclined chroniclers, be lowered down the castle walls) accompanied by a handful of white-clad knights, and steal through Stephen's unsuspecting army, across the ice of the river to the friendly fortress of Wallingford. It was daring, dramatic and slightly magical.

But the fact that Matilda's choice was between staying in a castle and escaping from a castle is illustrative of a big problem England faced during the Anarchy: castles. They'd only been around for seventy-five years but they were making the country ungovernable. What had been devised as an instrument for asserting Norman control over a foreign land was – under new circumstances where the Normans weren't all on the same side any more – becoming a catalyst of chaos.

The trouble was it was very difficult to get people out of them. Not impossible, but an enormous hassle. Assaulting or laying siege to a castle took a large amount of time and resources and you could only do that so many times before you lost the will to live or, it being the middle ages, stopped living. If you had errant barons holed up in dozens of castles all over the countryside, you were screwed.

Castles are like the twelfth century's asbestos. Seemed like such a great idea, got put in everywhere and then the lethal and resource-hungry consequences dragged on for decades. Because of the complete collapse of central governmental control, this asbestos kept being installed even as its damaging effects became clear. In fact it was introduced at an accelerating pace, because the advantages of it were enjoyed by the castle-builders, while the metaphorical toxicity – the thing that poisoned England's governability – affected only the already enfeebled state. (Like an impregnable castle wall, my asbestos simile survived the paragraph . . .)

More castles kept being built. Henry, Bishop of Winchester,

a major powerbroker at the time and King Stephen's younger brother, built six himself. With help, obviously – he got guys in. And some castles never fell. Wallingford, for example, where Matilda fled to, was a thorn in King Stephen's side throughout the war. It was far to the east of Matilda's area of influence, which centred around Bristol and Gloucester, and uncomfortably close to Stephen's heartland, in London and the east, and Stephen could not get into it. He built two castles of his own nearby in an attempt to neutralize the impact of its presence. You can see that things have gone a bit crazy when it's easier to build two new castles than gain access to one.

When Matilda reached the haven of Wallingford in December 1142, she'd been in England for three and a half years. At one point, she'd nearly become queen. She had arrived in 1139, accompanied by her half-brother Robert Earl of Gloucester. He had been a trusted adviser to his father Henry I and was a capable general who had never been keen on the Stephen regime and couldn't quite put the oath he'd sworn to support Matilda from his mind, so had rebelled against the king the year before.

On arrival, Robert headed straight to his power base of Bristol while Matilda stayed at Arundel Castle as a guest of the dowager Queen Adeliza, who was now married to the Earl of Arundel. Stephen swiftly arrived with an army but, on the advice of his younger brother, Henry, that castle-building Bishop of Winchester, he decided to let Matilda go. This seems bonkers. But there are other ways of looking at it. It wouldn't have looked great – laying siege to the castle and, if successful, which was by no means guaranteed, imprisoning his cousin. It wouldn't have seemed very chivalrous. Plus, by escorting her to Bristol, Stephen had his two main enemies, Matilda and Robert, in the same place, so he wasn't fighting on two fronts.

I still think it was bonkers, though. In a game, when you

don't know what to do, a good rule of thumb is to do whatever your opponent wants least. In this case, I'm pretty sure Matilda didn't want to be under siege, and did want to be escorted safely to Bristol. I reckon this is a case of Stephen suffering an ill-timed and self-defeating bout of decency. If he wanted to be chivalrous to Matilda, he shouldn't have stolen the throne from her. It was an eccentric moment to suddenly give a shit about her feelings. Matilda may have been pleased but she was well short of grateful. Stephen must have subsequently concluded it was a mistake because, a few years down the line when he had her trapped in Oxford Castle, no offer of safe escort was forthcoming.

Fighting the bad fight

Once Matilda and Robert were settled in the West Country, Stephen's problems started mounting. Lords were defecting to her cause in dribs and drabs, encouraged by both her presence in England and the progress her husband Geoffrey of Anjou was making conquering Normandy.

The situation in Normandy had a constant and unpredictable impact on the one in England because the nobility was still motivated by that desire for the same person to be in charge in both places. That was much more important to them than who that person happened to be. This had been demonstrated every time Robert Curthose was in the frame for either job. Ultimately it was the clear fact that Curthose would never oust either William II or Henry I from the English throne that made the barons happy to get rid of him as duke of Normandy.

Another clear illustration of the Norman barons' priorities came soon after Henry I's death when Stephen's elder brother Theobald, Count of Blois, was briefly acclaimed as duke. He was a viable candidate and the powerful men of the duchy settled on him (just as in England the oaths to support Matilda were put from their minds). Then the news of Stephen's coronation arrived and Theobald was hastily unacclaimed and Stephen acclaimed instead of him. Unlike Matilda, Theobald went along with this. But it's a reminder: most of the barons don't support Stephen or Matilda, they just want one of them to win big in both places because that's what will bring them peace and prosperity.

This means that, as well as attending to their own personal interests and supporting whichever faction is most likely to reward them, or least likely to punish them, they're constantly on the look-out for momentum, for the right bandwagon to jump on. But, as we've seen, the momentum in this civil war came crashing against the near-immovable objects of a dozen castle walls.

An important and illustrative figure in all this was Ranulf de Gernon, Earl of Chester. He, and his father before him, had enjoyed an almost semi-regal status and controlled a large area of the north. Unfortunately it became a much smaller area of the north when King David I of Scotland invaded in support of Matilda at the start of Stephen's reign. Stephen decided to appease David by granting him much of northern England. While the Scottish king, a protégé of Henry I, was pro-Matilda, the huge enlargement of his kingdom was a higher priority, so this saw off the Scottish threat for the time being. Ranulf, on the other hand, was pissed off and looking for an opportunity to regain his former position. He defected to Matilda.

This was what led to the Battle of Lincoln on 2 February 1141, the closest the war came to a decisive clash. An army led by Robert of Gloucester and Ranulf of Chester faced King Stephen's army outside the City of Lincoln, defeated it and captured the king. At this point, Matilda nearly achieved the seemingly impossible and got crowned queen – queen regnant, not just queen consort, so the actual boss. She was declared, by an assembly of clergy and nobles in Winchester in April, to be 'Lady of England and Normandy', as a precursor to a coronation.

This declaration was organized by the city's bishop, Henry of Blois, the king's younger brother who had given him that dodgy advice at Arundel. He's a slippery figure who evokes Michael Gove in my mind. He was quite sanguine about his elder brother's imprisonment and content to work with the new regime. He even handed the royal treasury, still kept at Winchester, to Matilda. Sadly, there was hardly anything in it.

The situation looked good for Matilda, but things didn't work out. Stephen may have been imprisoned in Bristol Castle but his queen, the other main Matilda on the scene, was working hard on his behalf. She, together with Stephen's most prominent military commander William of Ypres, raised an army in the south-east. Meanwhile Empress Matilda, who went to Westminster to prepare to be crowned, was rejected by the citizenry of London, who were pro-Stephen. They rose up and she was forced to flee to Oxford in the middle of dinner. Henry of Blois pointedly fled somewhere different, Winchester, and changed sides again. There would be no coronation.

A disastrous attempt by Matilda to take Henry's castle in Winchester followed and ended in defeat and the capture of Robert of Gloucester. So vital was he to Matilda's cause that she released King Stephen to get him back. Stephen and Queen (as opposed to Empress) Matilda were back in business and the pre-Battle of Lincoln stalemate restored. The two of them had themselves recrowned at Christmas 1141 and, the following year, Stephen marched north and persuaded Ranulf de Gernon to change sides again.

This was the situation when Matilda found herself

surrounded at Oxford Castle and her daring escape, and re-establishment of her rival court at Devizes Castle, just reaffirmed the stalemate. Stephen was very much still king, even if he didn't control the whole country, and the only good news for Matilda was her husband's gradual conquest of Normandy, which Stephen had no time or money to prevent. This culminated in Geoffrey being proclaimed duke in 1144. In 1147 Robert of Gloucester died and the following year Matilda went back to Normandy, never to return.

It was a grim and futile period. It's tempting to pick a side, and then it's tricky not to pick Matilda who was wronged by Stephen and overall a more effective political operator coping manfully with the disadvantages of being a woman in the twelfth century. But my feeling is that we shouldn't be distracted from the bigger truth that they were both twats. They may not have been able to help being twats – the mores and values of the time and of their class may have made them twats. But they were twats and terrible things happened as a result.

Having kings is an awful system. Henry I, for all his brutality, draws the eye away from this truth because he was capable and professional. In modern parlance, he gave a good service to the community. When Stephen seized the throne in exactly the same way as Henry did, one is tempted to see a basic intra-dynastic meritocracy developing. Then it turns out that the opportunistic cheek/gumption/amorality needed to steal a crown doesn't correlate with the skills required to use its powers wisely. Stephen was a twat.

And Matilda was a twat. She was more competent than Stephen as a ruler, but she knew, once he'd taken the throne, how slender her chances of ruling instead of him were. She still went for it and, if it didn't always cause anarchy, it definitely caused the Anarchy. I can't see her decision to fight him as striking a blow for women's rights. The notion is much more of an anachronism than being a twat, which is an eternal problem. Stephen and Matilda were just colossally entitled posh people whose incompatible ambitions caused enormous suffering.

The poor barons often get a bad press for changing sides in the conflict as they desperately tried to protect their own interests. Failing to find a sincere preference and then stick to it through thick and thin, apparently makes them morally suspect. Protecting their own position isn't deemed a sufficiently ethical justification for action. Except it is for the twats. Oh yes, they're important throne claimants. Their interests and desires and rights are elevated to a point of principle. Everyone else has a duty to pick one side or another like in a debate on Twitter.

Resist it! They were both as bad as each other! The fact that they didn't know it should only be added to their failings. I can't forgive either of them for thinking that the question of which one of them ruled England was so colossally important that it was okay for everyone else in the country to have such a horrible time.

18. King Henry II

In 1149 Geoffrey, Count of Anjou and Duke of Normandy, did an unusual thing. He gave up his dukedom in favour of his son. The son was called Henry and he was also Empress Matilda's son, and Henry I's grandson. Henry was sixteen years old and Geoffrey in his late thirties. This was selfless, self-controlled and very rare. Normandy was Geoffrey's greatest possession and putting it in the hands of his son was taking a risk with his own future.

The levels of trust within royal families at this time were not high. Stephen and Matilda were first cousins. Fathers were often betrayed by ambitious sons. In time, Geoffrey's own son would be betrayed by his ambitious grandsons. Geoffrey's father-in-law, Henry I, for all his exhaustive succession planning, remained, even when he started to feel the end of his life approaching, bitterly opposed to ceding any power at all pre-mortem. Geoffrey's decision is unusual. In dynastic terms, it was an excellent piece of estate planning.

Geoffrey was nicknamed 'Plantagenet' because he had the habit of wearing a yellow sprig of broom blossom, or *planta genista*, in his hat, and that name has been given by historians to the English royal house that descended from him. The Plantagenets officially reigned from the accession of Geoffrey's son to the death of Richard III. They are England's longest-reigning dynasty, it is proclaimed, lasting far longer than the Normans, Tudors or Stuarts. In the English royal houses championship, they are way ahead on points.

This seems a bit of an arbitrary accolade, as the name wasn't used by anyone between Geoffrey himself and Richard 3rd

Duke of York, who lived in the fifteenth century. By that ducal Richard's time, the royal family had acrimoniously split into Yorkist and Lancastrian branches, and Richard resurrected the name to emphasize that he was directly descended from a line of kings. So I don't see that it really means anything to say that the kings after Stephen and before Henry VII are all Plantagenets and the ones on either side aren't, when they're all related to each other. Most Plantagenet rulers didn't identify as Plantagenets at the time, only as legitimate kings.

This is not to say that the accession of Henry Plantagenet, as he wasn't then known, or Henry FitzEmpress, as he was, didn't feel new. It did. It had a tremendous aura of novelty. There was an enormous sense of optimism, strength and unity about the accession of the young king.

But how did he get to that point? He wasn't King Stephen's son and, when Henry became duke of Normandy, Stephen had two legitimate sons still alive. It was Geoffrey and Matilda's decision to make their son duke of Normandy that put him in the position to win the crown.

The nobility in England and Normandy continued to want what they'd wanted since the Conquest: one strong king of both places. Stephen was not a strong king, had patchy control of England and patchier control of Normandy. Matilda was a woman, had less control of England than Stephen, and Geoffrey, the man who came to control Normandy on her behalf, wasn't trusted. He was from the ruling house of Anjou, the Angevins, and the Normans considered them dodgy: it was said they were descended from a demon countess – a literal fiend of hell who was frightened of going into churches, though was presumably dead sexy. It was also said, more plausibly, that they were powerful and ambitious neighbours and competitors. The situation was finely balanced: hence civil war.

Once he was made duke, young Henry's prospects started

to tip the balance in favour of Matilda's party. His reputedly demonic Angevin blood notwithstanding, he was a young and plausible-seeming fellow, in complete control of Normandy, with a major power base in England thanks to his mother, and indisputably Henry I's male heir. He looked like a better bet than the ageing and ineffectual Stephen or his eldest son Eustace, Count of Boulogne.

The position only strengthened in the early 1150s. First Geoffrey suddenly died in 1151, so that Henry became count of Anjou, Touraine and Maine as well. Then, in 1152, he made a stellar marriage to a rich heiress who had just split up with King Louis VII of France. To complete her exotic allure, she wasn't even called Matilda. Eleanor of Aquitaine had her marriage to the King of France annulled in March and, narrowly evading those who sought to kidnap and marry her, she sent a message to Henry Duke of Normandy to come and marry her himself – which, on 18 May, he did.

Dynastic marriages are, in general, a boring subject. The endless betrothing of eight-year-olds to twelve-year-olds, of English princesses to German princes, Spanish princes to Burgundian countesses, etc etc, all in a bid to create or cement alliances. Half the marriages never seem to happen and less than half of the alliances ever stick. In an environment where brothers fight wars against each other, where sons try and overthrow fathers, I've never quite understood why there was any expectation that you could rely on your in-laws.

But this one's different. This was very cool. Eleanor was the most eligible woman in Europe, had just sloughed off the King of France and now Henry was her chosen consort. No one's fathers were organizing this – this was the conscious decision of two intelligent and powerful adults. It was an act of confidence and irreverence on both their parts. It showed contempt for Louis VII, so recently Eleanor's lord and master and nominally Henry's feudal overlord. Only nominally, though: through Eleanor, Henry now ruled the vast duchy of Aquitaine on top of his other possessions. He controlled a larger area of France than its king, and a larger area in general than the King of England.

In the face of this power couple, the ageing Stephen cut a feeble figure. When Henry arrived in England with a small army in 1153, all the momentum was with him. In July, Henry and Stephen's armies met outside Wallingford Castle, rather appropriately. But the nobles on both sides refused the fight. They'd had enough; the enraged king and duke were forced to talk. They did a deal: Stephen would stay king but Henry would be adopted as his heir. There you go, guys! Was that really so hard?

The main obstacle to this working was Eustace, Stephen's son, but he was so furious that the deal was even being considered that in August he conveniently died, apparently 'in a fit of madness'. Stephen's formidable wife Matilda had died a couple of weeks before Henry married Eleanor, so the king was now comprehensively out-wifed and an increasingly lonely figure. He spent what remained of his reign a bit like a constitutional monarch, parading around in royal regalia. He died in October 1154 and Henry's succession was so assured he didn't even bother to come to England to get crowned until late December.

It's all a bit stressful

As a child, I had a poor sense of drama. It didn't feel to me that stories particularly required events. I was comforted, not by fictional narratives, but by fictional contexts. Narnia, the Tardis, the cave where the children make a base and eat tinned fruit in *The Valley of Adventure*.

I would have happily watched an episode of *Star Trek* that

depicted the USS *Enterprise* on an unremarkable day. I just wanted to see the ship driving from planet to planet, the crew going about their business, a bit of beaming up and down. Perhaps something getting phasered at some point, but it could just be target practice on an uninhabited moon. The space ship was amazing enough, why the need for all that jeopardy and things getting damaged?

So when I was first taught about Henry II and the Angevin Empire, as his vast dominions of England, most of France and, nominally, Ireland are sometimes called, I was most comforted by the thought of this huge realm just *being*. And that's how it was taught to me: Henry ruled all those realms with energy and intelligence. He was constantly on the move with his court, hurrying from one area to the next. He made important and intelligent judicial reforms and he didn't suffer fools gladly. That's what I wanted to hear. That sounded cool and mighty, but also calm and organized, like the USS *Enterprise*.

Unfortunately, as the 'constantly on the move' bit implies, it may have been organized but it wasn't calm. Henry's empire was like lots of plates spinning on poles all over western Europe – he had to keep going round them to keep them going round. This was a preferable situation to Stephen's reign – which in the same analogy was the constant sound of breaking china, then the groan of Stephen bending down, then the smell of inexpertly applied glue – but it was dependent on energy and motion, on ambition and war. One of the ways Henry kept his huge realm together was by trying to extend it.

There was none of the stasis of him just being in charge like Captain Kirk or Aslan – there was a literal and metaphorical direction of travel. Something was always fucking happening. But what really spoils the ordered vision of successful kingship that I crave is that his reign was dominated by his falling out with people. His falling out with his wife and children and his falling out with his best friend. And the church – like most medieval kings, he fell out with the church, but Henry's way of doing it was really awkward and unfortunate.

I'm talking about Thomas Becket, Henry's hotshot administrator. (You may well have heard him called Thomas à Becket, but the 'à' is a random sixteenth-century addition, possibly motivated by a Protestant desire to make a major Catholic sound daft. It stuck, probably because it doesn't sound daft but actually works very well rhythmically.) The king had plucked him from obscurity and made him chancellor. When I say obscurity, I don't mean to suggest Becket was a peasant. He was, in the overall scheme of things, quite high up the social ladder, as is made obvious by two facts about him: first, he was literate. His ability to read and write was crucial to his being in a sufficiently unobscure bit of obscurity for Henry to be able to see clearly enough to pluck him. When he was plucked, he was already archdeacon of Canterbury having been previously plucked from a more obscure obscurity by Theobald of Bec, the Archbishop of Canterbury.

The second sign that he'd have looked pretty posh to a slave, serf, peasant or general tradesman was that he was from a Norman family. The things he could read and write were French and Latin, not Old English, which, as we know, people had basically stopped reading and writing a hundred years earlier after all the Anglo-Saxon posh people were killed or dispossessed. His family had come over with the Normans and settled in London, where Becket was born in around 1120 on Cheapside. He was middle-class at a time when there hardly was a middle class – and, if there was one, it would only have existed in London. So he was the metropolitan elite.

Still, Becket may well have been the least posh person a king at this time would ever actually speak to, so he'd done well for himself. And he behaved like he had, decking himself in the finery of his office. In 1157, he went to Paris to negotiate the betrothal of Henry's two-year-old son Henry to King Louis VII of France's one-year-old daughter Margaret. This diplomatic marriage led to a lasting peace between the governments in London and Paris which began only 747 years later.

The futility of the tedious dynastic marriage aside, Becket travelled in what sounds like ridiculous splendour. He took twenty-four outfits, had twelve packhorses to carry his silver dinner service, eight wagons of baggage and horses with monkeys riding them. That last is particularly flamboyant and was surely Becket's idea: 'If I don't have horses with monkeys riding them, the King of France won't take me seriously!' He sounds like the twelfth-century equivalent of a rap star.

King Henry, in contrast, liked to keep things simple and rarely displayed his riches. That's social confidence for you. He was as posh as they come, son of an empress and a count, and grandson of a king. Meanwhile Becket had the classic nouve's instinct to show off, to demonstrate to the world how far he'd come. He would definitely have got a personalized numberplate.

It seems Henry used to take the piss. There's a story about the two of them riding through London when they saw an old man in a ragged coat. I don't know what everyone else in London was doing, but that's the scene: the king and his chancellor, on horses, and an old man in a shit coat who gets talked about.

'It would be an act of charity to give that man a cloak,' said Henry in naturalistic Norman French.

'Yes,' replied Thomas. 'As king, you should do something about that.'

Henry then tried to take Thomas's very expensive and fine cloak off him and give it to the man. There was a bit of a tussle but Henry won (surprise surprise) and the old man got a weird blingy garment that was totally inappropriate for his lifestyle.

It's a grim anecdote. The tussle is the mortifying bit – I

can't help imagining a red-faced Thomas, with his hair all ruffled, trying to laugh it off as he shivered on his horse afterwards. Kings can be tricky. But it seems the two men were sincere friends, or Henry thought they were.

For all Henry's military skill, administrative energy and overall intelligence, he showed poor judgement of character when it came to Becket. He thought their friendship and Becket's personal loyalty to him were so solid that it would be a good idea to make Becket archbishop of Canterbury.

Render unto Caesar

I'm afraid it's time for a few paragraphs on the church. Right. Medieval kings really like being in charge of things. Not just lots of things, but everything. All the things in their kingdom. The poor kings of France were miserable for hundreds of years because there were times, like the one we're talking about now, when there were hardly any bits of their kingdom that they *were* in charge of. England is different and English kings really do aspire to run the place in quite a control-freaky way.

It sounds obvious, but I actually find it strange. Personally, I don't want to be in charge of much. It's an admin hassle and it makes things your fault. I'd much rather carp from the sidelines. Political leaders today, in Britain at least, are increasingly of my way of thinking. Many politicians seem to want to hold high office but for most of the things that actually happen, which inevitably go a bit wrong and piss people off, to be someone else's responsibility.

David Cameron was great at this. His government did lots of things that people didn't like – austerity, NHS reform, hiked tuition fees, a new national curriculum, police cuts – but they were all portrayed by the prime minister as someone else's policy: George Osborne, Andrew Lansley, the Lib Dems,

Michael Gove and Theresa May were the people actually doing this regrettable stuff. Cameron just stood outside Downing Street looking plausible.

At one point, when he was still prime minister, he even wrote to Tory-controlled Oxfordshire County Council complaining about cuts – as if they had nothing to do with him. Over the really big issues where it might otherwise have been tricky for the prime minister to show zero political leadership, he got around it by holding referendums. Say what you like about the man, but he wasn't power-crazed. He took a very different attitude to your standard medieval king. He would have been happy for many policy areas to have been in the remit of, and therefore the fault of, the church and the pope.

This was not Henry II's view, or the view of any rulers at this time. In the late eleventh and early twelfth centuries there'd been a huge row, and by row I mean war, between the Holy Roman Emperor and the pope over which one of them got to appoint bishops and abbots, and indeed future popes. Over the preceding centuries this had tended to be done by local powers, despite the fact that the church nominally had jurisdiction. The authorities in Rome had decided this wasn't on. Broadly, and perhaps surprisingly, the church succeeded in shifting the position in its favour and the centuries of bishops and abbots being picked by local rulers, and the pope by the Holy Roman Emperor, came to an end.

For the kings, this situation rankled. They felt a keen sense of ownership of their kingdoms, and for the pope to be deciding things within them was deeply intrusive. It was an awkward state of affairs because they were very religious people. They acknowledged that the pope mattered, and his power to excommunicate them, to cut them off from the church's route to salvation, was formidable to them. But they felt that, as anointed kings, they possessed their own measure of ineffable ecclesiastical power: they were holy too.

Under these circumstances, there are obvious advantages to a king of having the senior prelate in the land, the Archbishop of Canterbury, in his pocket – or, you know, pouch. Tied up in a bit of cloth. Stuffed in a scabbard. Theobald of Bec, the archbishop who crowned Henry and had been in office for much of the Stephen and Matilda shitstorm, was a fairly pro-Angevin primate. He had done Henry a favour by refusing to crown Stephen's son Eustace while Stephen was still alive.

This habit of getting the next king anointed ready for the current one to die was a continental technique for avoiding succession crises but it hadn't caught on in England (though, as you may remember, King Offa of Mercia had done it centuries earlier). Stephen's motivation for wanting to give it a go was obvious. The main thing that had scuppered Matilda's chances was the fact that Stephen had got himself crowned so quickly. The presence of a pre-crowned heir from the House of Blois could have scotched her son's chances in the same way. But Theobald wasn't having it, so that was fine.

In 1161 Theobald died and Henry was worried that a less amenable cleric would be appointed in his place. Then he thought: wouldn't it be great if my best mate Becket who does absolutely everything I tell him to, really efficiently as well, and I actually like spending time with, which I couldn't say about Theobald if I'm honest, nice old duffer though he was, became archbishop of Canterbury? Wouldn't that be *amazing*?! He could be archbishop and chancellor at the same time and then I'll be in charge of everything, which is as it should be.

So Henry threw everything at Becket getting the job, apparently failing to notice that Thomas himself didn't seem that enthusiastic. And, as he did in most of his aims in his career, he succeeded. In May 1162 the appointment was confirmed, even though Becket wasn't even an ordained priest. So, on 2 June he was ordained a priest and on the 3rd he was consecrated as archbishop of Canterbury. A meteoric ecclesiastical rise that continued apace because (spoiler alert) ten years later he was canonized a saint. By now, he must be an archangel at least – that's if he isn't the current God.

Henry was pleased. Then he was disappointed when Becket immediately resigned as chancellor. He was going to be a very different archbishop to how the king had imagined.

This was a monumental cock-up for Henry. As soon as Becket was installed at the head of the church hierarchy he went native and became an intransigent defender and maximizer of the church's rights in the face of the crown. To Henry, it seemed like he'd completely changed personality. Maybe he had, or maybe he was revealing his true self.

Workplace bullying

Henry and Becket, as king and archbishop, had an abysmal working relationship and it made the king very angry. The thing that made the Becket situation particularly infuriating was that it was Henry's own fault. Becket hadn't promised to be an easy-going, biddable archbishop, Henry had just assumed he would be. Every disobliging action of Becket's was something that, on some level, Henry had done to himself through his own colossal misjudgement.

He had a bad temper to begin with. There's one story of Henry getting so angry about someone saying something nice about the King of Scotland, with whom he was at that point displeased, that he tore his own clothes off and ended up sitting on the floor chewing straw. Historians sometimes refer to this as 'the Plantagenet temper' – apparently Geoffrey had a temper too – and later kings are also said to have 'inherited the Plantagenet temper'.

My feeling is that there's a slight nature–nurture confusion going on here. Henry I had a temper and he wasn't a Plantagenet and Eustace of Blois reputedly got so cross he died. My feeling is that all these kings and princes who fly off the handle when they don't get exactly what they want are the product more of circumstances than of genetics. They've been spoiled by lives in which no one ever shows disapproval of their behaviour. So I don't buy the Plantagenet-temper-as-hereditary-affliction argument, as if it's a bit like an allergy. What was hereditary was the state of affairs in which they had all spent insufficient time mastering the art of getting over themselves.

The key issue of difference between Henry and Becket was over whether royal courts had jurisdiction over clergy who were accused of secular crimes, the so-called criminous clerks. The archbishop was adamant that secular courts had no business trying priests. Henry felt the opposite. For him, the judicial system, his attempt to impose law and order on his realm, was a major part of what kingship entailed. He recoiled at the thought of the clergy letting each other off the hook for all the shitty criminous things they were getting up to. You know what I'm talking about.

Henry's view was encapsulated in a set of legislation called the Constitutions of Clarendon, which curbed church power, and in 1164 he persuaded all the bishops, including finally Becket, to agree to them. Then Becket changed his mind and fled to France, where King Louis VII was delighted to help him continue to foment trouble.

But it was when Becket returned from exile, in early December 1170, that things really got nasty. In Becket's absence, Henry had prevailed upon the Archbishop of York to crown his eldest son, Henry, just as Stephen had wanted for Eustace. The pope had okayed this, but Becket was furious and, on his return, excommunicated the Archbishop of York, together with the bishops of London and Salisbury who were also at the ceremony, for infringing his right to do all of England's crowning. Coming hard on the heels of a long and tortuous period of negotiation and grudging rapprochement between Becket and Henry, this was a kick in the teeth. The excommunications called the coronation's legitimacy into doubt and jeopardized the king's succession planning.

So, in a furious meeting at court, Henry said something angry. The wording is unclear, and it would have been in Norman French, so it certainly wasn't the famous phrase 'Who will rid me of this turbulent priest?' It was something more along the lines of 'What sort of a bunch of saps have I surrounded myself with that they let me get treated like shit by this fucking oik?' Four enterprising knights took it as their cue to go to England (Henry had been at Argentan in Normandy on the occasion of this particular flying off the handle – it was the site of a huge tank battle in 1944 and then, in 1988, I went there on a French exchange, so now you're up to speed). On 29 December 1170, they savagely murdered Becket in front of the altar of Canterbury Cathedral.

They weren't snowflakes, people in twelfth-century Europe. It was a brutal and messy time, but this action was as abominable to them as it would be to us. More so, possibly. They minded murder less back then, but thought being a priest was a bigger deal. So maybe it balanced out. I'd say, as a rule of thumb, if you imagine how we'd feel if four men murdered the current Archbishop of Canterbury in front of the altar apparently by order of the prime minister, that's basically how people felt back then. I reckon even Boris Johnson might have resigned.

Henry II didn't resign, of course. But he was under no illusions about how terrible the act that had been done in his name was. It seems very unlikely that it was something he sincerely wanted to happen, and his repentance of the words that had caused it seems genuine. He was also, as an astute politician, aware of how dreadful it looked and how much it weakened his rule.

It's goodnight from him

The coronation of Henry's son, known thereafter as Henry the young king, turned out to be a mistake. Not only did it indirectly lead to Becket's murder, and the grief and humbling of Henry that came from that, it also precipitated a nasty family row.

The two Henries, it transpired, had quite different views of what the younger one's coronation meant. For the father, it was just succession planning: everyone knows who'll be king after I die, so there won't be any nastiness. But Henry the young king reckoned it meant he was a king *already*.

He had a point – he'd been crowned. That was the deal back then. That's all Harold had over Edgar Atheling, or Henry I over Robert Curthose, or Stephen over Matilda. Coronation and anointing were a bit magic – it meant you were a king by divine right.

In a telling incident after the ceremony (which happened in June 1170 in case you're keeping track of time) Henry II had served his son food at the celebratory feast in order to mark the young lad's elevation. This was obviously a bit of symbolic ceremonial that someone thought would be nice. The Archbishop of York, wanting to be a good guest, and feeling lucky to have got what was usually Canterbury's gig, piped up politely saying what a distinguished servant young Henry had. I imagine there were chuckles. Then the young king replied that it was entirely proper that his father should serve him as he, the son, was of higher rank being the child of royalty on both sides, rather than the son of a queen and a duke. Silence. A cough.

This was quite a cunty remark for a fifteen-year-old to make. It sounds to me like an appeal to porphyrogeniture, but it's tactless to say the least – he was lucky his dad wasn't in a clothes-tearing mood. It was a sign both of the boy's unhelpfully high self-esteem and of his low astuteness. And another example of his father's poor judgement of character.

Gradually it became clear that the young king wasn't going to be allowed any real power. Then, in 1173, the old king gave three castles to his youngest son (and the young king's younger brother) John as part of some marriage negotiations he was engaged in on the boy's behalf, and for some reason this was the last straw. Henry Junior ran off to the court of his father-in-law, and his mother's ex-husband, Louis VII. There he started a rebellion with which the King of France was delighted to help out.

Also joining the rebellion were two more of Henry II's sons, Richard Duke of Aquitaine and Geoffrey Duke of Brittany. These teenagers were incensed that their father hadn't yet given them any real power either, and they were egged on, if not put up to it in the first place, by their mother Eleanor of Aquitaine.

All in all, they're a right bunch of inheritors of the Plantagenet temper. The only son who didn't rebel was John, who was six. He rebelled later though, despite being his father's favourite – another example of terrible judgement of character by the king, as we'll see.

But if his judgement of character was poor, the course of the rebellion was a resounding endorsement of Henry II's other kingly skills. He looked like he was screwed but he totally vanquished them. A masterstroke within this conflict came in the summer of 1174 when he declared the rebellion a punishment from God for what had happened to Becket and went to Canterbury to perform elaborate penance. He walked barefoot through the city, was thrashed by the monks of the cathedral and spent the night fasting and praying. As efforts to avoid cancellation go, it was extremely dramatic.

Regardless of the sincerity or otherwise with which Henry entered into it, this was a powerful piece of political theatre. He established a narrative turning point, a reason for people to believe the momentum was going his way, and the belief that this was true made it true. He understood that people wanted his stable kingship, and they wanted to be given a reason to think it was going to be restored. It was vital to tipping the balance in his favour.

Soon all his sons were humbly seeking forgiveness, which the king had the good sense to grant. His marriage never recovered though, as he found Eleanor's role harder to forgive, and so he imprisoned her for the rest of his reign, only occasionally letting her out for ceremonial purposes.

A fictionalized version of one of these away-weekends is dramatized in the film *The Lion in Winter*, in which Eleanor is played by Katharine Hepburn and her husband by Peter O'Toole. It's an interesting film. It's set at Christmas and they have a Christmas tree in the castle but with no fairy lights. I can't understand this as it wouldn't have significantly worsened the anachronism but it would have looked nice and twinkly.

The main problem with the film, for me, is that it inextricably links my imagining of Henry II to O'Toole and of Eleanor of Aquitaine to Katharine Hepburn. Hepburn seems so wise and warm and noble, and O'Toole so headstrong and chaotic, that you end up thinking Henry was a lucky but barbaric idiot and Eleanor a wronged goddess, which I don't think is fair. Henry had many mistresses, which must have upset Eleanor, but her relentless egging of her sons on to rebellion is quite annoying.

Henry may have triumphed in 1174, but he was fighting his sons, in various groupings, on and off for the rest of his life. It exhausted him in the end. His energy, his ability to appear at opposite ends of his realm only a few days apart, had always been his trump card. In 1189 illness and his current conflict against Richard and a new improved King of France were not going his way. He died, alone and betrayed, in Chinon Castle in Touraine. Then again, if he'd wanted his wife to be with him, he shouldn't have put her in prison.

The obvious question about all this is 'Why couldn't they just wait?' These sons were going to be fine, weren't they? It's your dad's kingdom, but you'll get it when he dies. Isn't that reasonable? The answer, I suppose, is that they were cash rich but time poor. It was the middle ages and they could die at any moment. Eleanor, her marriage over in all but name, wanted to see her sons fulfil their potential. As it turned out, she outlived her husband by fifteen years, but she probably didn't expect to because she was eleven years older than him.

Henry II's grip wasn't just on the kingdom of England and vast territories in France, it was on time itself. His sons must have thought him a glutton for life, living theirs as well as his own. It turns out their feelings were justified: both Geoffrey Duke of Brittany and Henry the young king predeceased their father. The young king's irksome instinct to rule from the moment he was crowned is recontextualized by the fact that he didn't have long.

19. King Richard I

Nowadays we seem to have a strange and spiky relationship with King Richard I, and I reckon it's all about lions. Richard was the first king to bear a shield with three lions on it – the three lions we now associate with England. And 'associate' is an understatement. They're like a hieroglyph meaning England. I'm talking about those golden ones that are still on the royal coat of arms as well as the England football shirt (though those ones aren't gold) and are sort of lying down while mugging to camera – or 'passant guardant' to put that unnatural pose in the jargon of heraldry.

Heraldry, all the shields and badges and coats of arms, was just getting going in the late twelfth century, so it's understandable that that's the time from which the basic badge of our monarchy dates. The problem for Richard's legacy is that the badge is deeply, inextricably linked to the notion of England. Those lions are English lions, we think – without pausing to ask why we should associate our country with a non-native animal. If we do, we just assume that England adopted lions in the same way that Wales did dragons. From an English perspective, lions might as well be fictional. You don't need to have seen a real one to appreciate the power of the symbol. And it's a thoroughly English symbol, it seems to us.

That, in turn, made it a thoroughly British symbol, and then a British imperial symbol. (It was convenient, in this regard, that the Scottish crown had independently adopted a lion 'rampant' – standing on its hind legs – as its main badge.) There are enormous lions in Trafalgar Square and a lion as one of the 'supporters' of the royal coat of arms, as well as those original lounging lions on the shield.

The lion symbol went everywhere the British Empire conquered, an emblem of European control of many areas where, ironically, real lions actually live. Also you have the lion as a symbol of England, or Britain, in political cartoons, scaring Napoleon or having its tail glued on by Gladstone. And there's British Lion films, and British Lion eggs and the British Lions rugby team, and the lions that were led by donkeys in the First World War . . . and it's got to the point where the lion and the union jack have somehow merged in our heads, and have been physically merged in things like Olympic team logos – they've become pictorial synonyms.

So that's the hinterland when we come to contemplate King Richard the Lionheart of England whose symbol was those three lions. It sounds like he's putting himself across as pretty fucking English – he's basically calling himself England McEnglishface. Then, when we find out that (along with England's entire ruling class at the time) he didn't even speak English and he spent only six months of his reign in England, almost all of it feverishly extorting as much cash as he could to spend on foreign military exploits, we feel a bit let down. We feel like he's been passing himself off as something he's not. 'So much for being English, he doesn't give a shit about the place!'

This is quite unfair on Richard the Lionheart. He never claimed to give a shit about England. On the contrary, he apparently said, on the subject of his ruthless fundraising drive, 'I would have sold London if I could find a buyer.' If only he'd known some Russians.

Some say that the three lions on Richard's shield represent not merely England, but Normandy, Aquitaine *and* England, Richard's main three dominions. This makes sense. Why have three of them otherwise? It's a bit random. A lion is a cool badge, but three lions isn't any cooler. It may be that two-thirds of the symbol of the England football team actually represent regions of France.

We need to get away from the notion that Richard was, in any way, trying or claiming to be English. He was the scion of a major French noble house who were such big shots they had their own rainy north European kingdom as a sort of country retreat. They went there for a break from continental politics and as a convenient place to have hunting accidents. For Richard, it was a splendid source of funds to pay for his main priority: raising a big army to take part in the Third Crusade.

This was the fashionable and righteous thing to be doing at the time – like going vegan is now, but with the opposite impact on the amount of blood that gets shed. Richard was determined to travel to the Holy Land (as the middle east was enticingly known before everyone gave up any attempt to make it sound nice) with enough of a force to maintain and extend the Christian kingdom there and reconquer Jerusalem.

To my mind 'Lionheart' is an entirely appropriate nickname for him, once we dissociate the lion from its fictional and heraldic manifestation. Lions are not really noble beasts. They are not proud. They do not have principles and they don't stand up for weaker people and defend island races. They don't like England – they find it too cold and rainy. The lion is a ruthless predator who deploys awesome violence in its own interests. As with the finger that shares its colour, its heart is cold.

Some sort of personal crusade

Richard's key attribute was being extraordinarily good at fighting. And, by fighting, I mean large-scale fighting. Making war. He was physically brave, a resourceful general, a cunning tactician, and he was conscientious about logistics. This was why he bled England dry of money and resources. He realized that, if he was to go on crusade, he would need a hell of a lot of stuff. Courage and praying weren't going to cut it on their own.

The crusades were a series of chaotic and vicious attempts by western European Christians to wrest the control of what is now Israel, Palestine and bits of Lebanon and Syria from Muslims – 'the infidel' as Christians called them and as they called Christians. Crusades were all the rage between the late eleventh and late thirteenth centuries, and rage is the operative word. Various popes initiated them, incensed as they then were (in both senses of the word) by the existence and geographical spread of Islam. It developed into a great scheme for posh murderous people, who were struggling to find meaning in their lives, to secure their places in heaven. Robert Curthose went on one, you may recall.

They're grim – a manifestation of what today we'd call religious extremism that resulted in thousands of horrific deaths in battle and from disease. Personally, I can't imagine any of the Christians who went on crusade not perpetually having the shits, while wearing full armour, in the baking sun. It's a bit gross. The combination of western Europe's ignorance of the principles of food hygiene with maintaining an army in an alien climate must have made it an absolute field day for dysentery bacteria, though I suppose the crusaders had stronger stomachs than we do, having reached adulthood in a culture with no reliable system for separating sewage from drinking water.

It sounds disgusting and lethal even if you don't factor in all the battles you might get killed in if you were lucky enough to win your game of food-poisoning roulette. Every single thing they did, it seems to me, must have attracted an enormous number of flies. If there's anything picturesque about the middle ages – and there is: stone crenellations silhouetted against winter skies, galloping horsemen with steaming breath, vast cathedrals echoing to muttered devotions – it vanishes at the contemplation of excrement and extreme heat.

Conquering and then permanently occupying a large area of the middle east, which may have been sacred to Christianity but was also sacred to the religion of all the people who lived round there, is a famously difficult and uncomfortable thing to do. It's even uncomfortable writing a paragraph about it, here and now in London, because some eagle-eyed readers will be analysing it for inappropriate views on the Israel–Palestine situation. If this were a website instead of a book, I'd have installed cookies so that this section could manifest exactly the same views on that situation as the reader has previously betrayed with their browsing history. But I can't, so let me just say that I am passionately committed to whatever it is you think.

If it's all a bit tricky now, it was worse then. The crusaders were travelling vast distances without any maps worth the name and trying to keep armies fed and watered as they went. Plus the people whom the survivors of the journey had come to fight not only had colossal home advantage, they also hadn't endured the economic and technological knock-back of the Dark Ages in the way western Europe had. The Franks, as western Europeans were often collectively known, were a backward civilization compared to the Islamic states from which they tried to conquer the Holy Land.

The fact that the crusaders kind of managed, off and on, to maintain a collection of Christian states near, and occasionally including, Jerusalem is a real testament to how nuts they all were. It's a major example from history of the energizing power of insanity – like when a tiny, maddened terrier nearly succeeds in killing a postman. Thousands and thousands of Christians became convinced that waging this distant, impossible and savage war was the right thing to do – that it was vital, that it would bring them salvation. Suddenly all the shitting and killing were worth it.

Richard may not have cared about England, but he cared passionately about his crusader vow. He was sincerely devout, but then why wouldn't he be? The church authorities had announced that there was a way he could do his favourite thing – attacking lots of people with an army – in a really holy way. It was as if the pope had told George Best that what Jesus really wanted him to do, what would make him an absolute saint and hero, was to get pissed.

Richard's crusade, known as the Third Crusade, failed in its aim of reconquering Jerusalem but otherwise went pretty well, and reconquered the cities of Acre and Jaffa on behalf of 'Outremer', which is the weird name given to the collection of tottering Frankish states in the middle east.

Richard, who arrived in June 1191 having suavely conquered Cyprus and used it as a wedding venue on his way, was the star of the whole enterprise. The other major participating monarchs were the Holy Roman Emperor, Frederick Barbarossa, most famous for having Hitler's cataclysmic attempt to destroy the Soviet Union named after him, and Philip II of France, subsequently known as Philip Augustus, but he would never have got that cool nickname on the strength of his crusading form. Richard totally overshadowed him, so he left early in a fit of pique. Emperor Frederick, meanwhile, drowned before he got there. Richard enjoyed all the military success, developing a mutual grudging respect for the Muslim sultan, Saladin, with whom he corresponded. He headed home in 1192 only because he got wind that Philip II and his brother John were conspiring to steal England.

The crusades were pointless in the end, of course. Outremer was finally snuffed out in 1291, and Constantinople itself – the new Rome and centre of the Byzantine Empire – fell to the Turks in 1453. The attempt to reverse the tide of the world's newest global religion by the world's second newest global religion was a colossal waste of energy. That tide kept rising for nearly 500 years, and lapped against the gates of Vienna before it turned.

Kidnapped, betrayed, shot, cuddled

Speaking of Vienna, it was near there, in the run-up to Christmas 1192, that Richard was captured. He was then held to ransom. He was vulnerable to this because he'd had a terrible journey. Bad weather had forced his ship to put into Corfu, which was part of the Byzantine Empire where he was *persona non grata* for the understandable reason that he'd recently nicked Cyprus off it. He left swiftly and in disguise, with only four attendants, which would be lots for you and me but is a pitiful number for kings and rap stars. He then got properly shipwrecked right at the north end of the Adriatic Sea and was forced to continue his journey overland, much of which was run by other people he'd managed to piss off by being so haughty and successful.

Leopold V, Duke of Austria, was one such person. He'd been on the Third Crusade too, but the two of them were unlikely to be seated together at any reunion dinners. Richard had infuriated him, on the occasion of Acre falling to the crusaders, by removing Leopold's banners from the city walls on the basis that Leopold wasn't important enough. This was petty of Richard but no pettier than Leopold, who stormed off back to Austria to concentrate on bearing a grudge. The following Christmas, Richard turned up like a lovely present, unguarded and wearing an unconvincing disguise instead of wrapping paper. Leopold captured him and, in March 1193, handed him over to the Holy Roman Emperor, Henry VI.

This period of incarceration doesn't fit with the rest of

Richard's career because he didn't do anything cool or valiant to get out of it. He was passive and trapped, reduced to working on his music like a teenager in his bedroom. The emperor charged an enormous ransom of 100,000 pounds of silver and Richard's mum, Eleanor of Aquitaine, had to go about organizing for it to be paid. The phrase '100,000 pounds of silver', or '150,000 marks', which is apparently the same thing, doesn't really convey any meaning to me other than 'big'. It was a lot of money, and not just for a king or nobleman, but for a large European state.

I'm afraid I glaze over at historians' attempts to explain money in the distant past, and say what pounds, shillings and pence were worth in modern terms, or explain the difference between a pound and a mark, and an English pound and an Angevin pound, and an Imperial mark and an English mark. So let me summarize: it's extremely confusing.

Money is so different now that it's frankly unhelpful that the same word applies both to what Eleanor of Aquitaine sent to the Holy Roman Emperor and to what I would use to buy a Twix. It's not just the quantity that's different. The use of and access to currency has totally changed. Plus a Twix, unremarkable chocolate bar though it seems to us, would be more magical and delicious than anything anyone in the twelfth century, even the Byzantine or Chinese emperors, had ever laid eyes or decayed teeth on.

So we might as well dispense with the numbers and express sums of money in terms of the pain that extracting it caused. And this would have been an 'aargh' of the size that Thor would emit if he stood on a plug – and he wouldn't know what a plug was, so you can mix some bewilderment in with the pain. It was another huge drain on the reserves of Richard's dominions but without the supposed celestial upside of bankrolling Islamophobic mass murder.

Richard didn't get back to his realm until February 1194.

When he was released, Philip not-yet-called-Augustus of France reportedly said to his co-conspirator, Richard's brother John, 'Look to yourself – the devil is loose.' They both hated Richard, and Philip must have been bitterly aware that, with Richard around, the whole 'Augustus' thing just wasn't going to happen. I mean, not that specific soubriquet, but the success from which it might spring. On crusade or off, Richard always bested Philip II of France.

As well as introducing the lions of England, Richard was the first monarch to adopt the royal motto 'Dieu et mon droit', 'God and my right', which I mentioned earlier and which is used to this day, written proudly in thousands of public places and on the front of everyone's passport. His reign is structured like the motto. The first half he spent fighting for God, and the second for his right – i.e. all the dominions he'd inherited from his father, many of which Philip was attempting to purloin. It took Richard most of the rest of his reign to secure his 'right' back from Philip, but he never looked like he wouldn't manage it.

He forgave his brother John, whose meanness, greed, cowardice and treachery are the only part of the Robin Hood story that's factually accurate. Richard couldn't really take him seriously and John tended to behave while Richard was around. Richard eventually named John as his heir, which wasn't entirely uncontroversial because, by primogeniture, the throne would have gone to Arthur, the son of John's elder, and Richard's younger, brother Geoffrey, the late Duke of Brittany. But Arthur was a child and John was a fully matured horrible adult, so it was obvious to Richard who ought to be king.

By the spring of 1199, Richard's position was secure and he was relaxing by laying siege to a small castle, Châlus-Chabrol, in the Limousin region of Aquitaine where there was a small rebellion going on. The castle had a tiny garrison and Richard was inspecting the castle walls, not wearing his chainmail because he was super-cool, when he noticed a valiant sentry high on the battlements, defending himself from the besiegers' arrows with a frying pan.

Richard paused to applaud this bravery in a foe for just long enough for the pan-wielder to pick up a crossbow and shoot him in the shoulder. Undaunted by this flesh wound, Richard calmly rode off to get some terrible medical attention before dying of the consequent raging infection in less than a fortnight. He'd always been Eleanor of Aquitaine's favourite son and she made it to his deathbed in time for him to die in her arms, which was nice.

20. King John

> King John was not a good man –
> He had his little ways.
> And sometimes no one spoke to him
> For days and days and days.
> And men who came across him,
> When walking in the town,
> Gave him a supercilious stare,
> Or passed with noses in the air –
> And bad King John stood dumbly there,
> Blushing beneath his crown.

I couldn't resist starting the chapter with that. It's from 'King John's Christmas', a poem by A. A. Milne. It uses the key thing we all know about King John – that he was bad – and reimagines him amid the values and references of early twentieth-century children's literature. It continues:

> King John was not a good man,
> And no good friends had he.
> He stayed in every afternoon . . .
> But no one came to tea.

It's a world where there is nothing to fear from bad people. They get their comeuppance when no one wants to go to tea with them and Father Christmas won't give them any presents. Though that reminds me of the occasion in 1937, only a few years after the poem was published, when a couple of the Mitford sisters went for tea with Hitler. It seems that Milne's system of social sanctions, the withholding of company over scones as a means of ameliorating the conduct of international leaders, wasn't always observed, even by the most pukka members of society.

Still, it's a comforting thought and you can imagine King John walking carefully along the pavement, avoiding the cracks, while passing schoolchildren regard him sternly, and then Mr Toad zooms past in his new car and soaks King John with puddle water and Peter Pan pokes him in the bottom with a sword. It taps into the haplessness that King John projects down the centuries, as if his badness was an affliction from which the poor fellow couldn't escape.

Well, he *was* bad and he *was* hapless. Delightfully, his reputation is deserved and the debunkers of all the fun and clear notions about the past, the revisionists, the revisers of the revisionists, have failed to put even a scratch on the gleaming paintwork of King John's famous shittiness. Efforts have been made, but the best the narrative-clarity police have managed is to point out that John was unlucky in some respects and, at times, displayed various forms of competence. What no one has sought to deny, though, is that he was a horrible person and his reign was spectacularly unsuccessful.

So poor was the management he provided that it famously spurred the English aristocracy into unionizing. That's what led to Magna Carta. Magna Carta just meant 'Great Charter', though now it means so much more: some would call it the foundation stone of English liberty. If that's true the architect of English liberty should be struck off by whatever organization regulates the metaphorical professions because it's a bloody wobbly foundation. But English liberty has no architect – it just got thrown together by various accidents, one of which was John's personality.

Temporarily agreed to by John in 1215, Magna Carta was a relatively ambitious attempt to rein in the monarch's power and tentatively introduced the idea that kings don't just make the rules, they should also abide by them. Or make some effort to abide by them. Or at least acknowledge that that would be nice. There should be some sort of thing – the law, the constitution, the customs of the realm – that existed separately from the person of the king and the surprisingly malleable tenets of Christianity. This was quite a big and tiring idea, but the barons were forced to come up with it by John's relentless deceitful cruelty and incompetence.

John agreed to Magna Carta only because he was in such deep trouble that he'd lose his crown if he didn't. He repudiated it a few weeks later. In his view, the kingdom was his personal property so the idea that it could generate rules that he would then have to obey was as absurd to him as if a billionaire found a 'No diving, no bombing' sign by the side of his private swimming pool. 'I'll do what I fucking like,' he thought. In fact 'I'll do what I fucking like' was, broadly speaking, John's policy. If translated into Latin or Norman French it would have made an arresting and appropriate motto for the royal family.

That said, some of John's more competent predecessors, his own father among them, would have explained to him that, whatever the legal situation pre-Magna Carta, there were enormous practical limits on kingship. Behind all the 'I'm the Lord's anointed' projection of entitlement and ownership, the clever and successful monarchs knew the score. The nature of their power fluctuated hugely and depended on other people going along with their rule.

John, on the other hand, seems to have been an instinctive believer in the hype of early medieval kingship. That misplaced confidence is what nearly brought the whole unjust edifice crashing down. His failure to question it in his own mind led to the barons starting to question it in theirs. They were reluctant to do so, because kingship was a reassuring idea and felt natural. But John forced them to think.

King John was not a successful man

Magna Carta happened near the end of John's reign and life, and he'd got a huge amount of failure under his belt first. John was Henry II's youngest son and was the old king's favourite. This has the same quality of embarrassing comic weirdness as when, in *A Midsummer Night's Dream*, Titania falls in love with Bottom when he's got a donkey's head. No one else seemed to like John and the fact that he was Henry's son doesn't really explain his father's enthusiasm because Henry wasn't particularly keen on any of his other sons. And they were all nicer than John. That sentence may win the world record for the smallest compliment ever paid.

Despite his father's favouritism, an aura of misfortune surrounded John. Having made his son Henry a nominal co-sovereign, and earmarked Aquitaine for Richard and Brittany for Geoffrey, Henry II had nothing much left for the apple of his eye and, consequently, John was given the nickname 'Lackland'. This was as humiliating as calling him 'loser'. And, in retrospect, 'loser' would have been more apt. Specifically 'landloser'.

At the age of ten, he was made lord of Ireland. If you think that sounds more problematic and less fun than being made duke of a nice sunny part of France, then you're right. Angevin control of Ireland was shaky and Ireland was a long cold sea voyage in the opposite direction from the centres of power. Even when you got there, it was very rebellious and rainy rather than relaxing and calm. I expect there were nice walks and a strong local artistic tradition, but the Angevins were more into clubbing – in every sense.

English control of Ireland has never really worked out, as you'll know if you've watched the news at any point since the invention of television, and, with John's lordship, it got off to a bad start. In 1185 he went over there as a teenager to try and extend his power but succeeded only in offending the local rulers by taking the piss out of their unfashionably long beards.

While Richard had been away on crusade or in captivity, John relentlessly and unsuccessfully attempted to nick all his brother's lands, by colluding with the King of France and claiming that Richard was dead. He was warming to his theme of being neither nice nor successful. As soon as Richard actually *was* dead, King Philip seized the opportunity to earn that 'Augustus' soubriquet fate had earmarked for him. Now that John was his useless competitor rather than his useless ally, he turned on him. He started by recognizing John's rival claimant to the throne, Arthur, the son of Geoffrey, as Richard's heir.

As previously noted, by strict primogeniture Arthur would have been the next king, but the fact that John was accepted as the rightful successor in most of Richard's domains, including England and Normandy, is a sign that the rules of succession were still fluid. The previous king's wishes are a real clincher. This is interesting because it shows that the notion that these kingdoms and dukedoms were merely a powerful man's personal property was very strong. This is the very interpretation of kingship that the barons who drafted Magna Carta were trying to get away from.

John's accession is also a sign that, as an adult man, he was deemed a safer pair of hands than Arthur, who was still a child. The potential hazardousness of Arthur's pair of hands was, conversely, his claim's key selling point for Philip. He wanted Angevin power to founder – that's why he'd backed John during Richard's reign. As it turned out, backing John would have remained a sound policy for screwing the Angevin Empire because John's pair of hands, despite their comparative maturity, turned out to be deeply unsafe – as Arthur found out when John used them to murder him.

Possibly. We can't know. Arthur died in 1203 while being

held captive by John. Capturing Arthur was one of John's few successes. Arthur probably died by John's order and there's a real chance it was an order he gave to his own hands. Even measured against the low level of niceness expected of rulers at this time, murdering your own teenage nephew was still dastardly. Keeping him imprisoned for the rest of his life was regarded as the done thing.

By the end of 1204, after a couple of years fighting against Philip, John had lost all Angevin possessions in France apart from the southern section of Aquitaine, and had retreated to England, where he focused on alienating the ruling class.

We don't want the same thing any more

John was understandably obsessed with finding a way to reconquer Normandy. Duke of Normandy was, in a sense, what he primarily was – he was William the Conqueror's great-great-grandson. He must have felt that getting Normandy back was his destiny, and relatively achievable. The English throne had been separated from Normandy several times since the Conquest – during the reigns of William II, Henry I and Stephen – and the Norman realm had always been subsequently reunited.

But this was different. During the previous separation periods, the dukedom had been ruled by another member of the family, albeit a rival: Robert Curthose, Geoffrey of Anjou or the future Henry II. This time it was held by the actual King of France and, to cut a long story short, that situation didn't change, except for a brief period in the early fifteenth century, until 1792 when the King of France was put in prison during the revolution as a precursor to being decapitated.

This is an important moment. It put the Anglo-Norman aristocracy in an awkward position. Over the many decades since 1066, some families had split their lands so that the English ones were held by one branch and the Norman ones by another. The sense of a joint aristocracy was less strong. Still, lots of powerful people hadn't been so prudent. They had estates in both places and didn't know what to do.

There was one obvious idea circulating. In May 1204, before John's position in France had quite collapsed, William Marshal (a top Plantagenet retainer, of whom we'll hear more later) and the Earl of Leicester (one of history's many earls of Leicester, of whom we won't) were sent to Philip to negotiate a truce. While doing so, they took the opportunity to enquire of the French king about what the deal might be, going forward, with their Norman lands. Philip said they could keep them if they paid a fine of 500 marks each (which, in modern money, is lots) and swore homage to him for those lands by Easter 1205.

This Easter deadline offer was open to all Anglo-Norman barons with Norman lands and was tempting. From Philip's point of view, it was a good idea because those who swore homage to him couldn't really then join a military campaign by John to reconquer Normandy. The opportunity played on the barons' minds and, just before Easter 1205, a group of them tentatively asked John if it would be okay with him if they did this.

I can barely imagine a more awkward scene. The barons sidling up to this bad-tempered king, who'd just fucked up his ancestral inheritance, and asking if, in the light of His Majesty's Monumental Recent Cock-Up, they might swear allegiance to his nemesis so that they could keep all *their* stuff even though he had lost so much of *his* stuff. They said they would swear allegiance with their bodies but their hearts would still be with John. Nice try.

John obviously was not okay with this for the very reasons that Philip was in favour of it – it would hugely weaken his chances of reconquering Normandy. The truth is, though, that they were weakened anyway. Some barons stayed in Normandy, swore allegiance to Philip and forfeited their English lands. More common among John's barons was to stay in England and forfeit their Norman lands. The most loyal of these were compensated with lands forfeited by the lords who'd stayed in Normandy and sided with Philip.

This had the effect of reducing the number of barons with cross-Channel possessions. So, even though they weren't prevented from fighting against Philip in Normandy by having given homage, they didn't have much to gain from it any more. They'd cut their losses. Now their possessions, and therefore their priorities, were Anglocentric. This was an increasing obstacle to the ambitions of John and his successors to reconquer the Angevin Empire. They had become solely royal ambitions, no longer shared by the aristocracy. In time, they seemed less and less realistic and, to the English ruling class, more and more enervating.

This shift in the status quo manifested itself early. In the summer of 1205, less than a year after fleeing Normandy, John energetically set about assembling an invasion force to win everything back. He requisitioned an enormous fleet, raised men, minted coins and got all the invasion stuff together – food, arrows, etc. It was to be an ambitious pincer movement. John would lead an invasion of Normandy from Portsmouth while his illegitimate half-brother William Long-espée, Earl of Salisbury, would simultaneously take a force from Dartmouth down the west coast to La Rochelle and invade Poitou from there.

John got everything ready in Portsmouth and the barons arrived and John said, 'Okay, let's go,' and they wouldn't. They didn't fancy it. William Marshal and Hubert Walter, the Archbishop of Canterbury, did the talking for the barons, citing various reasons why the invasion was unwise: Philip's wealth

16. The Bayeux Tapestry. When these images were embroidered, the events depicted were within living memory so they must have known it didn't really look like this. Here (*left*), King Edward the Virtue-Signaller tells Harold to offer William the throne.

17. (*Above*) Naughty Harold gets himself crowned despite this. See how he's got a similar stick and ball set to Charles III?

18. (*Right*) King Harold is slain. He might be the one taking an arrow to the eye, or the one falling over in front of a knight. Some say both pictures are him but, if so, he had time to change his socks between injuries.

19. This is what someone whose identity is lost but who lived in the late sixteenth and early seventeenth centuries guessed William the Conqueror looked like. Who are we to say they were wrong?

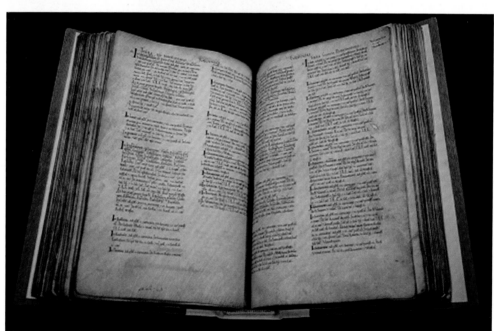

20. The Domesday Book, which looks and sounds like what it is: a magical book of ancient spells. Correction: it's a tedious and incomplete inventory.

21. Henry I thinking sadly about the *White Ship* disaster. The expression on his face is the one tabloid photographers tell OAPs to adopt to accompany articles about how they were tricked out of their life savings.

22. Henry's daughter, Empress Matilda, holding a charter. 'Put that charter down!' the patriarchy was screaming.

23. (*Left*) Matilda's husband, Geoffrey Plantagenet, looking a right dork. Surprisingly, this picture is on his tomb and not in an episode of *Family Guy*.

24. (*Below*) Matilda again, fleeing Oxford Castle, as imagined by illustrator Charles Ricketts in 1903. He's gone for moonlight and snow falling but no consequent lunar snowbow.

25. Was the idea that you could make these kings seem like upholders of the church by having them literally hold up churches? Here are Henry II, Richard I, John and Henry III in an illustration from the last's reign. The little chap in the middle is Henry the Young King, who is accurately represented as not really counting.

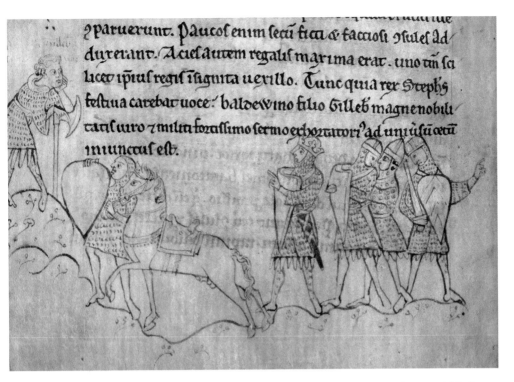

2ꝑaruerunt. paucoſ enim ſecũ fiꝛꝛ ā faccioſi ꝛſuleſ ad
duꝛeꝛant. Acieſ ꝛautem regaliſ maxima erat. uno tñ ſa
liceꝛ ipſiuſ regiſ iſignita uexillo. Tunc quia rex Stephſ
feſtina carebat uoce: baldeꝛwino filio Gilleꝛ magne nobili
tatiſ uiro ꝛmilitr foꝛtiſſimo ſermo exhoꝛtatoriꝰ ad univſũ cetũ
iniuncttuſ eſt.

26. King Stephen and the guys have a team talk just before the Battle of Lincoln of 1141, which they
are about to lose.

27. The murder of Thomas Becket, from
a fifteenth-century chronicle. Note the monk
on the right doing fuck all about it.

28. The fall of Acre in 1191. Richard the
Lionheart and his pals spread the good news by
dressing up as robots and attacking two unarmed
Muslims.

29. A parliament of Edward I. A lot of astronomically posh men with the recent addition of some very posh men.

30. That's what I call a proper castle. Conwy Castle, one of Edward I's state-of-the-art mega-fortresses, was completed in 1287. It appears to be flying a Welsh flag, precisely the opposite of what it was put there to do.

31. A contemporary portrait of Edward I. It really brings out his sensitive side, something for which there is otherwise no evidence at all.

32. History is doodled by the victors. A marginal drawing of Llywelyn ap Gruffudd, the last independent Prince of Wales, being slain.

33. A sculpture of Edward II from his tomb, which heavily implies he used to put curlers in his beard. Yet another homophobic slur.

34. (*Below*) Isabella, Queen of England, meeting her brother Charles IV, the King of France. A right pair of nepo babies.

and military strength, the notoriously treacherous nature of the Poitevins, the fact that Philip might invade England if it was left undefended.

What it amounted to was: look, your majesty, we don't have enough to gain from this plan considering the likelihood that you will fuck it up. John was furious and humiliated. He even put to sea and sailed up and down the coast for a few days in the hope that they'd follow him – it was a sort of maritime version of storming out. Everyone must have found this pretty embarrassing. No one got in a boat to go and check that he was okay.

Apart from his obsession with continental reconquest, the other source of tension between John and the English barons after 1204 is that he was *always* there. Have you heard of the phenomenon of long and apparently happy marriages foundering after the couple retires because, for the first time, both husband and wife are spending all day together? The English aristocracy were like an old-school housewife, accustomed to packing off their old man to work/France and not expecting him back for ages. Every king since William the Conqueror had been more often out than in. Suddenly John was there the whole time, getting under their feet.

Plus he hadn't retired, he'd been made redundant. And he was determined to get his job back. Now the simile collapses because the way he needed to get his job back was by lots of expensive fighting for which the wife/aristocracy would have to pay in blood and treasure. It was a fun few sentences while it lasted.

John's best friend, the pope

John did manage a couple of decent goes at reconquering his old bits of France, but they didn't work. He had a relatively successful campaign in 1206 and stabilized his position in the last bit of France he still possessed, inconveniently placed in the bottom left-hand corner down by the Pyrenees. But he never got close to restoring his enormous losses of 1204 and his final campaign to do so was decisively ended by the Battle of Bouvines in Flanders in 1214 at which John's allies, led by Otto the Holy Roman Emperor, were defeated by Philip Fair-enough-he-does-now-seem-quite-Augustus. John wasn't even there. He was hanging around La Rochelle with another pincer movement in mind. But Philip had snapped off the top pincer, so John was reduced to being a lone bottom pincer. Just a prick, basically.

All this fruitless campaigning had necessitated a great deal of brutal and unscrupulous money-raising in England, so when John got back there in October he wasn't met by a lovely supportive aristocracy telling him he mustn't feel bad about himself. They were livid and broke. So was he. The barons demanded that King John be less of a dick and abide by Henry I's coronation charter and his own coronation oath. There were unsuccessful talks, and both sides wrote to Pope Innocent III.

Relations between John and the papacy had been volatile, as you might expect. But volatile beats consistently shit, so in the end John's dealings with the pope amounted to one of his most successful professional relationships. There were problems of course. The king's whole 'I'll do what I fucking like' vibe was fundamentally antithetical to papal thinking, or to any religion really. In 1209 he'd been excommunicated for relentlessly encroaching on the church's prerogatives and taking its money and, by 1213, the pope had declared him deposed, which meant that any other ruler, say Philip Augustus, had a perfect right to come and nab his kingdom. In light of this, John changed tack and swore feudal vassalage to the pope.

This dramatic U-turn shows even greater cynicism about religion than invoking and then ignoring excommunication. To my mind, John seems unusually irreligious for his time, something I find no easier to warm to than his other traits. It genuinely seems possible that he was an atheist. In our current age, atheism is a coherent and reasonable response to the human condition. To be an atheist in thirteenth-century Europe was very different. At this time, Christianity was the self-evident truth. It wasn't a conclusion many people came to, it was the starting point of everything. It was also the rationale and justification of kingship. To be anointed a king at this time while secretly thinking it's all horseshit is sociopathic.

Still, Pope Innocent was thrilled with John's change of policy and insufficiently self-doubting to question its sincerity. The pontiff remained staunchly in John's camp until his death, only three months before John's, and repeatedly told the barons to stop rebelling and pay whatever taxes John fancied levying. In March 1215 John put a delicious hypocritical cherry on the top of his big cake of pope-courting bullshit by 'taking the cross'. This was supposedly a commitment to go on crusade at some point, but what it effectively meant was that, now he was a crusader, it was even more sinful for the barons to behave disobligingly towards him.

Nevertheless the situation descended into civil war. On 5 May a group of barons renounced their allegiance to John and on the 17th they took London. It was an awkward civil war because the barons didn't really know what they wanted. During the Anarchy, the options had been clear: Stephen or Matilda. But what was the alternative to John? A republic?

Maybe it goes without saying, but I'm going to say it just in case: nobody was thinking of a republic. Really nobody. They probably hadn't even heard of the notion and, if they had, it would have been as a sinful ancient Roman concept like lions eating Christians and anal sex. Countries had kings and that was that. They were anointed and crowned and, as such, endorsed by God. And John was the king – there was no doubt about that. *We* know it was an idea cooked up by some thugs in the Dark Ages, but they didn't.

So the rebel barons' awkward demand was simply for John to be better. It was a civil war dedicated to getting one man to try harder and to be more reasonable. But John was forty-eight. Forty-eight-year-old men seldom change. It was all a bit hopeless.

A bloody liberty

Magna Carta was the barons' attempt to address this problem – to come up with a framework to constrain this furious and infuriating idiot they were stuck with. It's got some big ideas in it, most notably clauses 39 and 40, which are still part of British law today: 'No free man shall be seized, imprisoned, dispossessed, outlawed, exiled or ruined in any way, nor in any way proceeded against, except by the lawful judgement of his peers and the law of the land' and 'To no one will we sell, to no one will we deny or delay right or justice.'

To us, these are resonant and inspiring principles. 'Now they're getting the idea!' we think. 'Democracy and freedom, here we come!' That's true, in a way. At the time, though, it must have been very worrying. These self-evident truths, that the authors of the American Declaration of Independence had in mind five and a half centuries later, were flying in the face of a bigger, more mystical and more reassuring principle – the one that was supposedly the basis for all medieval government and indeed the ordering of the entire universe: divine providence.

The barons must have found it unsettling to have to write a document to rein in a king who was endorsed by God. They must have worried that they were doing something terrible. And they must have worried even more that the whole basis for existence they'd been brought up with was somehow failing. Libertarians must feel the same whenever they notice some arm of the state or set of regulatory laws help avert catastrophe. It reveals flaws in the big comforting idea that's supposed to make everything okay.

Clause 61 of Magna Carta provided for a council of twenty-five barons to ensure the king's adherence to the charter. It was empowered to confiscate his castles and lands if he strayed. This was a massive affront to the concept of kingship – the regal equivalent of what happened to Britney Spears – and John had no intention of abiding by it, whatever he said. This clause was omitted from the many reissuings of the charter after John's death, the versions that eventually found their way on to the statute book, and played little subsequent part in history. Until recently, that is.

In 2020, during the Covid pandemic, as part of the general internet-fuelled stupidity of our time, some lockdown refuseniks took to citing clause 61 of Magna Carta as a justification for ignoring lockdown rules. Their reasoning was that the clause made it legal to rebel against government that the people considered unjust. I'm quite fond of this sort of bullshit – a little learning can be a hilarious thing, and the same goes for a little googling.

Clause 61 of Magna Carta only gave twenty-five thirteenth-century barons the right to rebel against unjust laws, not anyone at all, and it was only in the 1215 version of Magna Carta, which was repudiated by all signatories and the pope within three months and never became law. So they were wrong twice: they were wrong about what the clause said and they were wrong in thinking that it was ever a law. Of course if two wrongs genuinely make a right, they have a point.

The barons and King John met to sign Magna Carta on

10 June 1215 at a place between Staines and Windsor called Runnymede. It's named after how nervous King John was about the occasion. No, it was already called Runnymede, from the Anglo-Saxon *runieg* meaning 'regular meeting' and *mede* meaning meadow. So the 'runny' bit has nothing to do with either diarrhoea or the proximity of a river, which is a pity. It was a place where important outdoor meetings had happened before and was one of the venues where King Alfred's witan used to meet. What a felicitous precedent for a coming together of ruler and aristocracy!

John must have been apprehensive though, so he turned up wearing his grandmother Empress Matilda's imperial regalia to emphasize what a big shot he was. Whether wearing some ninety-year-old clothes that were designed for a woman had that effect we can't know. He signed the charter, but within weeks the pope had condemned it as illegal and ordered John not to abide by it. In the short term then, it was a failed peace treaty. But, like Henry I's coronation charter, it was influential and was reissued (without the anti-lockdown clause) several times in the following century, in 1297 ending up on the statute book where shards of it still remain.

Nevertheless the barons' attempt to find a middle way between John and not-John had failed and they had to resort to the more old-fashioned civil war strategy of supporting a rival claimant to the throne. They plumped for Philip Augustus's son, Prince Louis. He was married to one of Henry II's granddaughters so he did have a sketchy claim to the throne, plus he was a capable young man and he wasn't John. The rebel barons invited Louis over, and he landed in England in May 1216 and started conquering it. Pope Innocent III excommunicated him.

By the end of the summer, Louis controlled the south-east of England, but John went on the counterattack and frenetically marched around the country relieving sieges. But his situation was still terrible. To add to his woes, the King of Scotland had also invaded, taken Carlisle and then paid homage to Louis, thereby suggesting he was the rightful king of England, not John.

It was around this time that John both contracted dysentery and supposedly lost the crown jewels in the Wash. This was the Wash, as in the weird square tidal estuary at the top of East Anglia, not a laundering process necessitated by the sovereign's raging diarrhoea. We don't know exactly what was lost, but certainly a section of the king's baggage train misjudged the tides or the quicksand and was swallowed. This all adds to John's aura of haplessness as he raced around the place, his illness getting worse. He died at Newark Castle on the night of 18 October 1216. He didn't make it to Christmas.

PART THREE

Here Comes the Reign Again

21. King Henry III

Dying was by far the most astute and successful thing King John did in his entire reign. In general, when kings died that was bad news for the royal dynasty and the security of the regime. But John had contrived to inoculate the realm against that affliction, so his sudden absence had no negative impact whatsoever. In fact, it was an unqualified boon.

Had he been an iota less unpleasant or more competent, the barons might have been concerned by the replacement of an experienced forty-nine-year-old man, who'd been on the throne for seventeen years and fought many campaigns in the British Isles and France, with a nine-year-old boy. As it was, a crowned turd would have been preferable, so a biddable child under the guardianship of William Marshal, the elder states-man of the Plantagenet court, looked like a comparatively safe bet.

Nevertheless, at the point when Henry III acceded to the throne, the Plantagenet situation was bleak. London and the south-east were under the control of Prince Louis, so Henry couldn't be crowned at Westminster and there weren't any archbishops nor even a crown available. The bishops of Exeter, Worcester and Winchester, plus the papal legate, did the honours at Gloucester Abbey using a coronet belonging to his mother, Queen Isabella. It was one of her few gestures of maternal support for young Henry: the following summer she went back to Angoulême in France, where she had come from and where she remained for the rest of her life, having children with her second husband Hugh X of Lusignan.

Henry is a pitiable figure, and the aged William Marshal an

inspiring, likeable, avuncular champion. 'If all the world deserted the young boy, except me,' he apparently said, 'do you know what I would do? I would carry him on my shoulders and walk with him thus . . . and never let him down from island to island, from land to land.' The image of an old man carrying a child to safety on his shoulders cuts through all the dynastic and regal bullshit. It's simple and human – it bespeaks love.

We can't know what their feelings really were. There are so many centuries between us and them and their world was, by our standards, weird. But they still ate and drank and lived and died and hoped and lusted and feared and felt lonely. William Marshal was a warrior and a politician, hugely rich and hugely successful. He'd been a Plantagenet loyalist his whole life, had been in and out of favour with John – who hadn't? – but had shown consistent support of the principle of Angevin kingship.

Earlier in his life, he'd been on crusade and served both Henry II and 'Henry the young king', so it was apt that he ended his career serving Henry the even younger king. He was about seventy by the time Henry III became king, which was pretty old even to be alive in those days, so it seems likely that he was fond of the kid. As a supporter of John, he knew what a disaster his son had been born into and must have looked on this child, wearing a woman's fascinator and carrying a man's sword amid medieval military turmoil, with a grandfather's fondness. Similarly, the fatherless child, suddenly told that God had appointed him in charge of everything, must have loved the indomitable old man who turned up and cared.

Their love conquered all. Or England, anyway. As I've said, the momentum was going Henry III's way, however helpless he seemed, because the prospect of Prince Louis, son of an ambitious and aggressive king of France, becoming king of England only looked attractive as an alternative to John. With

John's replacement by an innocent child, all reasons for supporting the Frenchman evaporated.

At the Battle of Lincoln in 1217, seventy-six years after another Battle of Lincoln which had nearly handed the throne to Henry III's great-grandmother Matilda, William Marshal's army decisively defeated the rebel barons and supporters of Prince Louis. For Louis the jig was up and he headed home. By the Treaty of Lambeth later that year, he renounced his claim to the English throne and received 10,000 marks. The rebel barons were given an amnesty. Marshal, as regent of England, and protector of the king, had done his young sovereign proud.

Throne alone

William Marshal died in 1219, but Henry III's minority was far from over. In some ways, it continued for his whole reign. He never quite stopped being a child. But then why should he? He hadn't asked to be king.

This is something many of us feel about the current royal family: they're trapped. They didn't ask for this. Theirs is a thankless role, and if they do get thanks they're stressed and obsequious ones from anxious people holding flowers and reeking of shower gel. Few of us would swap places with them, for all their wealth and fame. Many people don't want fame at all, but even those who do want it wouldn't want the shit sort the royals have got – a fame you're landed with and can't take any credit for. They've earned it even less than reality TV stars – or, rather, even less than *other* reality TV stars.

We feel this absence of monarch-envy all the more keenly because we're lucky enough to live in a time and place where the basics of a pleasant life – food, shelter, entertainment, freedom – are available to millions. The royals' riches and luxury count for much less than in more squalid eras. For most of history the king, however overworked and unhappy, whatever the agonizing RSI from endless crown-wearing he endured, at least knew where the next meal was coming from, which put him in the most fortunate section of society.

The potential undesirability of being king hasn't been an issue in this book so far. Almost all the kings seemed to want to be king. Possible exceptions: Aethelred the Unready came to the throne as a child and had a very unenjoyable reign, and Edward the Confessor was far too holy to enjoy anything. But, in general, the preceding kings wanted to be king. They were into it and ambitious for it, however good or bad they were at it.

Since the Conquest, they also all got a decent amount of training for the job. William the Conqueror schooled his sons in the martial and political arts of the eleventh century and even the worst of them, Robert Curthose, was relatively pro-fessional. William II, Henry I, Stephen, Matilda, Henry II, Richard I and John were all keen on the job and grew up with major regal role models: close relatives who were actually rulers. The only ruler little Henry III knew was himself.

His minority was a success – the kingdom was stabilized in his name, the rebellion ended, the French expelled. And that was his training in kingship: a period where everyone scraped and bowed to him but grown-ups, adult men, replacement fathers, made all the real decisions. It reminds me of the skewed life experiences of those child actors who make it big, like poor old Macaulay Culkin – not that he's likely to be poor and, ridiculously, he's *still* not old. Weird childhoods, even if they're ostensibly successful, can screw you for life.

So when Henry III tentatively embarked on his personal rule, it soon panned out as a dispiriting mixture of the weak and the delusional. He was often dominated by a chief adviser whom he would follow to the point of alienating other major barons, and he showed divisive favouritism, in terms of

money, lands and offices, to various groups of his relatives –
initially the Savoyard relations of his wife Queen Eleanor of
Provence, and then his Lusignan half-brothers, sons of his
mother the dowager Queen Isabella of Angoulême. These are
classic ways not to be a successful king, later honed by Edward
II with disastrous consequences. Henry III hadn't quite perfected this brand of shitness, which is why, unlike Edward II,
he didn't die in prison.

On top of these failings, Henry had big dreams and
schemes, but lacked the focus, resources or talent to carry
them through – except when it came to expensive architectural plans. He spent a lot of money on Westminster Abbey,
the Tower of London and Windsor Castle, striking a grand,
regal yet pious style.

Beneath that style, there was no substance. He was very
keen to reconquer the Angevin Empire, but the baronage was
even less receptive to this agenda than during his father's
reign. His three feeble, underfunded expeditions, in 1230,
1242 and 1253, all failed and weakened him at home. More
than ever, the English aristocracy viewed the monarch's
attempts to defend or extend his French possessions as a private matter. It was not something they wanted to get involved
with or help pay for.

In 1254 he tried to make one of his sons, Edmund, king of
Sicily. If you're struggling to get a sense of how realistic an aim
this was, just work out how realistic it would be to make yourself
king of Sicily and multiply that by 1.6. Not very realistic then.
This was an attempt by Henry to support the pope on whom, as
one of those extremely pious kings, he was dead keen.

For all sorts of no doubt holy reasons, the papacy wanted
to stop the Sicilian throne remaining in the hands of the
Hohenstaufen family – this was the dynasty that dominated
the Holy Roman Empire before the Habsburgs got going.
King Henry III of England gleefully got involved, offering

troops and 135,000 marks he didn't have to help the papal cause in exchange for Edmund being declared the next king of that very distant island. Henry had no way of delivering on this promise and yet, if he didn't, the pope was threatening to excommunicate him, something which, as one of those extremely pious kings, he would find unbelievably upsetting. It was a terrible deal.

SDMV

If you were wondering when parliament was going to get invented, it's now. Thanks to the Magna Carta crisis, the concept of reining the king in, of expecting a certain amount of consultation on issues of major national fundraising and expenditure, had already been explored. The next king's long minority only intensified the magnates' expectation of being kept in the loop.

Back in 1225, during that minority, a relatively successful campaign to shore up Gascony – the English king's remaining section of Aquitaine – had been financed off the back of the reissuing of Magna Carta. The deal that was being done between the crown and the powerful people of the realm was clear: it was money in exchange for consultation, rights and limitations on royal prerogatives.

About five and a half centuries later George III, the then King of England (and Ireland, and by that time Scotland too), lost most of his North American possessions to a rebellion based on the idea of 'No taxation without representation'. That whole principle originated in the era we're talking about now, when cash-strapped medieval kings, with territorial ambitions beyond their means, realized that they'd have to consult their prominent subjects, and give guarantees of reasonable government, if they wanted those lords to contribute to royal schemes. In 1236, the word 'parliament' was first used to refer to one such consultation session.

By the time of the king's Sicilian fantasy, these parliaments are the established form of interaction between impecunious monarch and angsty aristos. At this point, the king would only summon his ministers and council, plus the leading magnates and churchmen – the archbishops, bishops and heads of major monastic houses. It only amounted to a few dozen men. In 1258, as the ruinous nature of Henry's delusional geopolitical scheming became apparent, and as the barons despaired at the favouritism Henry continued to show to the unruly and contemptuous Lusignans, parliament resolved to take on the king.

The key mover and shaker in all this was a man called Simon de Montfort, who was Earl of Leicester and after whom De Montfort University in Leicester is named. He himself was named after his father, Simon de Montfort, who was named after his father, Simon de Montfort, who was named after his father, Simon de Montfort, who was named . . . you get the idea. The main one is the fifth Simon de Montfort of six: he named his son Simon de Montfort but that one then died without issue, which I can't help thinking was for the best. Otherwise there'd still be one now.

The reason SDM the fifth has a university named after him is that he founded parliament, which is a jolly good thing to have done, leading as it did to democracy, freedom and the British Empire. That's what the Victorians reckoned, anyway.

Obviously, it's not entirely true, which, in retrospect, the Victorians might be relieved to hear because one thing that is undeniable about SDM is that he was French. He'd only arrived in England in 1230. I don't think they would have been too keen on that: the whole British parliamentary tradition being kicked off by a Frenchman might have made their recent gargantuan struggle against Napoleon feel like a lot of wasted effort. Another undeniable thing about SDM is that he was a colossal antisemite. The Victorians would probably have minded that less.

You may suspect that his antisemitism was standard for the middle ages, but it wasn't. It was standard for the thirteenth century, but it wouldn't have been for the twelfth. Let's not get overexcited: the twelfth century wasn't exactly woke, but the various Jewish minorities around western Europe were generally left alone. Then, in the following century, the mood changed. It's one of the many historical examples of the weird way antisemitism waxes and wanes for no clear reason, with little warning and with cataclysmic consequences for Jewish people. It's why those who nowadays accuse Jews of hysterical sensitivity to the slightest undercurrent of antisemitism need a fucking history lesson.

Rising Christian piety and consequent extremism made the thirteenth century a time when persecuting Jews was suddenly on the rise. Powerful people started doing it as a way of proclaiming their Christian virtue, so when SDM expelled all the Jewish people from Leicester in 1231, he said he was doing it 'for the good of my soul, and for the souls of my ancestors and successors'. That's a pretty twisted view of the Almighty: if you don't persecute the Jews, you'll go to hell. It's essentially a form of Christianity that imagines God to be like Hitler.

The good news, though, is that SDM's action earned a stinging rebuke from Leicester City Council. I'm sure it would have made him think again if it weren't for the unfortunate fact that it came 770 years later.

It's a tricky business appointing heroes from the past. You can see why SDM was latched on to when they were looking to name a new university. He orchestrated the Provisions of Oxford in 1258, which hugely limited the king's power, providing for a Privy Council to oversee the government of England in light of Henry's burgeoning incompetence. The king accepted the Provisions at a parliament in Oxford.

(Parliaments in the middle ages were held all over the country, wherever the king summoned them, rather than exclusively in the Palace of Westminster as they are today.) Judging by this, SDM seems to be a successful pioneer of both parliament and an early form of pseudo-cabinet government. How brilliantly anachronistic! It's like he's a time-traveller signalling to us across the centuries. Very exciting for Victorian historians and people looking to name institutions in the Leicester area.

Then it transpires he's been murdering Jews. That's torn it – turns out he's a monster. Maybe parliamentary democracy isn't such a great idea after all.

This is obviously unfair. Nobody completely escapes their own era, except Shakespeare. It would be a tall order to expect SDM both to invent parliament and to buck the antisemitic trend of the century he lived in. But when you're looking for a hero, the latter does cast a pall over the former.

I reckon the debunking of SDM is quite helpful. The development of a parliamentary system isn't like a battle – it's not the sort of thing that heroes do. It's not even like the invention of a new spinning machine or hoe. It comes out of circumstances, not the head of one person. But people are interested in people, in stories about the doings of people, so it was an attractive idea to say parliament was the product of one great man's great life. But it wasn't really and the man they chose was just a major magnate of his time: capable, intelligent, ambitious, militarily skilful, antisemitic, like dozens of others who lived around the same time.

Let's keep talking

In a way, parliament was just a new name for a process that had been developing since before the Conquest. The Anglo-Saxon witan had been crucial to endorsing royal power. That all changed when William arrived with a new aristocracy to whom he gave most of England. There was an implied deal: you helped me win so you get a piece of this. That deal changed over time – Henry I and Henry II had a working arrangement, again not overtly stated other than in Henry I's coronation charter, with the powerful people of England that both sides were usually content with. Stephen obviously didn't, Richard pushed his luck but was very good at fighting and John pushed his luck but wasn't.

However, with the loss of Normandy, the priorities of the king and his barons diverged. There was stuff to discuss, primarily about money and resources. Magna Carta was an attempt to kick that process off – parliaments were the continuation of it. The old deal was dead and new deals needed to be made.

This was embarrassing for Kings John and Henry III but it was inevitable. The financial balance of power was transformed because the English monarchs had lost control of huge amounts of territory and all the potential money that came with it, and the French kings had gained it.

Back during the reign of Louis VII, Philip Augustus's father, the King of France only directly controlled an area around Paris about the size of East Anglia, while Henry II ruled an area nearly half the size of modern France (albeit nominally as the French king's vassal) and this was on top of England and Ireland. By Henry III's reign, the Plantagenets still aspired to cut a Henry II-style continental dash, but only had Louis VII-scale royal resources. So they needed money and support from their magnates. Henry I's approach wouldn't work any more, even if John or Henry III had been able to rival Henry I's competence.

This new status quo wasn't SDM's doing, but he had the nous to exploit it. He wasn't a great legislative innovator, just an opportunistic overmighty subject, like many before and since. His insight was to use parliament as a tool in his power grab. He pointed out the flaws, corruption and unaccountability of royal government, but only in order to wrest control of the country from Henry and set up his own flawed, corrupt and unaccountable regime.

. Still, he did invite shire knights and town burgesses to the parliament of 1264 as well as the barons. These influential commoners had also been invited to a parliament in 1254, and SDM was only repeating the experiment in an attempt to shore up his support base rather than out of a commitment to representative government. But it powerfully reinforced a precedent which has led inexorably to Grant Shapps having a full-time job.

This nascent House of Commons didn't come close to including anyone common. Even the burgesses, the lowest down the new parliamentary pecking order, were big players back where they came from – merchants or senior craftsmen, the beginnings of an urban middle class. But the word 'middle' can be confusing. They were in the middle in the sense that they were between the aristocracy on one side and the peasantry on the other, but the two slices of bread in this sandwich were of wildly contrasting size. The melba toast of a few dozen toffs on top and, underneath, a 6-foot-thick doorstep representing 3 million peasants.

Most of the English were growing their own food. That's what really happened in the middle ages: subsistence farming. The new commoners admitted to parliament were well above that vast-majority experience, though they were more involved in trade than their baronial superiors – above all in wool, England's most lucrative export commodity. Yet it's the House of Lords, not Commons, whose chairperson (for centuries the lord chancellor, though today the lord speaker) sits, not on a chair, but on a woolsack in acknowledgement of wool's economic importance to the realm in which parliaments first assembled.

Witnessing these developments was Henry's eldest son,

Edward. You may think Edward sounds like a standard name for a Plantagenet prince but, at the time, it provoked considerably more comment than Princess Beatrice calling her daughter Sienna in 2021. Edward was not an Anglo-Norman name – it was an Anglo-Saxon name and Henry had chosen it because of his obsession with former king and by then saint Edward the Confessor. The confessor's relentless virtue-signalling had echoed down the centuries and, like a cheap jingle, become lodged in the head of poor, humourless, unimaginative, unsuccessful and bewildered Henry. So he gave his heir this strange, and to the Anglo-Norman aristocracy, alien-sounding, ethnic name.

Edward was nineteen years old at the time of the Provisions of Oxford and aware of the flaws in his father's government. At one point, he became a supporter of SDM's faction. He realized that many of the reforms proposed by rebellious barons needed to be made. Unsurprisingly though, he ended up on the royalist side – and then pretty much ran it. The last regent and replacement father of Henry's long and hapless reign turned out to be his own son.

In the early 1260s, everything descended into civil war – the Second Barons' War is what it's sometimes called, the first one being around Magna Carta. Edward was then involved in two major battles against SDM: Lewes in 1264 and Evesham in 1265.

They won one each, but the result was not, in any meaningful sense, a draw. SDM was killed at the Battle of Evesham by a royalist lord called Roger Mortimer. As a reward, Mortimer was permitted to cut SDM's head and testicles off and arrange his balls so that they were hanging either side of his nose. He then sent this cold collation to Wigmore Castle as a gift for his wife, Lady Mortimer. I wonder what her reaction was. 'You shouldn't have!'? I can only hope that she found it all very sexy.

22. King Edward I

King Edward I loved parliaments. That's surprising because they were quite new and in general are seen as a constraint on royal power. I'd say it was the most remarkable thing about him, which makes it strange that his two main nicknames are 'Longshanks' and 'Hammer of the Scots'. Being tall and trying to take over Scotland seem to me less unusual attributes for an English king than a fondness for parliaments.

It wasn't because he was a fan of free and frank debate that Edward liked parliaments, but because he wanted things to be properly organized and he needed money to go and conquer places. He realized that a strong king with a reforming parliamentary agenda of attractive organizational stuff he wanted to get done, which would be of benefit to the major players in the realm, could reap rewards in terms of taxation. This was vital to his reign's main aims of sticking it to Wales and Scotland, and to his hopes of going on crusade again.

He was on his way back from the Ninth Crusade when his father died, and for the rest of his life he was desperate to go back. He never did, which was definitely for the best. I mean, *Ninth* – for fuck's sake! It had overtaken the number of French Louis. The continuing issue of the crusades is tedious and futile. So many people seemed desperate to pitch in barbarously to the general ongoing murderous mess.

It's like when actors put 'actor and activist' in their biogs in an attempt to detrivialize their existences. In the same way, Edward remained 'king and crusader' until he died, as part of the muscular and murderous piety that was fashionable at the time and was used to legitimize a lot of horrible behaviour, all in the name of someone whose big pitch was kindness and eternal life.

For example, in 1290 Edward expelled all the Jews from England, an edict that remained in force until 1657. This is grim, but was par for the course – all the European kingdoms were expelling Jews around then as a result of a heady mixture of nasty piety and a desire to renege on debts. Jewish people, who unlike Christians were not prohibited by their religion from charging interest on loans, provided a useful financial service. But many who had availed themselves of this facility, as the enjoying of the lovely loan money morphed into the making of the horrible repayments, saw the light in terms of how terrible it was that not everyone in England was Christian.

This expulsion doesn't come close to being the main thing about Edward, which is a savage indictment of the times he lived in. It was just a shitty thing that was happening every-where that he joined in with, probably certain in his mind that it was morally the right thing to do. That's what's so chilling.

There was financial interest involved, but a lot of Chris-tians will have thought that excising all Jewish people from Christian society was what *ought* to be done. They won't have felt guilty, they'll have felt virtuous. People on their deathbeds, when contemplating their interview at the pearly gates, will have been thinking, 'I'm a bit worried all the wanking will get mentioned, but at least I was consistently horrible to Jews so that should count in my favour.'

Their certainty that they were right is worth remembering because it means there's probably stuff *we're* certain is right that future ages will correctly judge to be monstrous. The fact that everybody is convinced of something is no guaran-tee that it isn't evil horseshit.

Zero shades of grey

Edward was tall, strong, energetic, capable and intelligent, but his drawback was that he was unsophisticated. I don't mean he only liked plain foods and struggled for conversation at refined soirées. Having been brought up posh, he was probably okay at the medieval versions of that sort of stuff. But he wasn't great at detecting, or perhaps bloody-mindedly refused to acknowledge, nuance.

If he'd been a batsman in cricket, he would have played spin badly. I remember this about Robin Smith, an England batsman who hit fast bowling all over the place, driving and cutting all around the field, but was troubled by the emergence, in the early 1990s, of the brilliant Australian leg spinner Shane Warne.

All batsmen were troubled by Warne, but Smith seemed utterly bamboozled, while some lesser players came closer to coping. It was the bewildering nuance of top-class spin that troubled Smith – the absence of certainty. He was used to seeing the ball, albeit moving extremely quickly, and whacking it – or missing it because it was going too fast. But when it came out of Warne's hands, it slipped and slithered like a snake. It couldn't be played in a definite way. Batsmen had to soften their wrists, play it flexibly, accept that they could never be entirely on top of everything that's going on.

Edward was a renowned sportsman, a champion of the medieval tournament, who would have been a powerful cricketer if he'd lived five or six centuries later. But he would have been a smasher of the ball, not one for glancing or nurdling, or using his pad. Any edge he got on a delivery would have flown straight to the slips. So it was with his kingship: things that went right went very right, but, when he was making a mistake, he made it big.

It's even stranger, in light of this, that he was such a fan of parliaments, supposedly forums of discussion and compromise. But, for him, they weren't about compromise, they were about enforcing ordered government, about making things official. He set up a national survey of Domesday Book-rivalling scale to establish what privileges landholders enjoyed and why. He legislated energetically to stamp out corruption, reform the currency and stabilize royal revenue. He was using parliament to wage war on nuance.

As a result, hugely greater financial resources became available to him. He was extending governmental scope, and it's almost a law of physics that that provides the leverage to get tax money and banking credit. People will go along with giving much more to the state if they feel they have a proper say over how it's run. They will contribute to a process they're involved in. It's 'No taxation without representation' again and it was a sufficiently two-dimensional concept for Edward to master.

These are significant advances in the nature of government. It brings to mind Richard the Lionheart's quip about wanting to sell London if he could find a buyer. In that Angevin era, the rulers' domains were like estates, theirs to buy and sell. Richard didn't think there was any better way of making money out of them – the notion of taxing them in exchange for various governmental services and guarantees would have seemed too fiddly and time-consuming when he was itching to travel east to murder some Muslims. A century later, the now parliamentary England has shaken off that notion of royal ownership. Things have become more complicated – there's a dialogue between king and subjects, albeit with a strict hierarchy within it. That system is accepted, indeed embraced, by Richard's great-nephew who was a no less enthusiastic Islamophobe.

The French crown never sorted this stuff out and, come the eighteenth century, was still desperately trying to balance the books through established royal revenues, selling offices and daft local taxes. At that point it was trying to run a huge and populous country while regularly fighting international wars. Throughout the Seven Years' War (1756–63 – I assume they waited until it ended before coming up with the name) Britain, a much smaller and less populous state, was able to outspend France almost effortlessly. That was because of Britain's long parliamentary tradition whereby more of the fundamental strength of the country could be brought to bear financially.

The French kings never resigned themselves to doing that, and consequently held greater direct power within their country than the British kings. But money-wise, they were screwed. All they could do was borrow and borrow and borrow until the credit even of such a major state began to falter. Still, they did everything to avoid calling the French equivalent of parliament, the estates-general. By 1789, when Louis XVI finally had no option but to do so, it was too late. There was such rage at royal incompetence that the meeting of that assembly led to violent revolution.

Who's in charge here?!

Edward's rejection of nuance cost him most dearly over the issue of homage. I've alluded to this concept earlier in a way I hope wasn't baffling. It's part of the system of sovereignty and ownership that prevailed in western Europe at this time and is referred to by historians as feudalism.

Basically it's a hierarchy. At the top there's the king, whose major subjects hold lands 'from' him as his tenants-in-chief, who in turn have major tenants, knights and the like, who in turn have their own tenants among the wealthier peasantry, and then there are those tied to the land by serfdom. It's a system supposedly held together by bonds of mutual obligation: the tier above protects the tier below which, in recompense, provides labour, military service and/or money in lieu.

In practice it must have been horrible, though I suspect Julian Fellowes might have a go at a picturesque drama in which all the peasants are much happier being protected by a kindly lord (possibly played by me – just a thought, if you're reading, Julian) than being troubled with nasty state benefits that they just fritter away on alcopops and the lottery while losing their ancestral skills of planting crops and grooming horses.

Unless you're a king, you don't really own anything at all – everything is held 'from' the king to whom the major nobles have got to swear homage and keep on good terms with. That's why it was tricky for those who held lands in both Normandy and England when Philip II took over Normandy – it was impossible to be both Philip's and John's devoted vassal.

The issue of homage also affects the rulers themselves. The King of France was understood to be the feudal overlord of most of the area that's now modern France even though he often hardly controlled any of it. The rulers of Normandy, Brittany, Anjou, Flanders, Aquitaine, etc all have to do homage to the French king. This is bonkers because often these rulers are also fighting wars against him, but they still fight those wars with an understanding of the French king's nominal seniority.

A similar system had developed in Britain whereby the King of England was deemed to have feudal seniority over the various princes of Wales, and indeed over the King of Scotland. This sense of seniority dates back to some of the powerful late Anglo-Saxon kings such as Athelstan and Edgar the Peaceful. The King of England's writ did not run in north Wales or Scotland, but still there was an acknowledgement that he was the island's most important monarch.

As you can appreciate, these are waters made opaque by the pollution of nuance, and yet Edward was determined to snorkel through them looking for treasure. Initially, it went well: he conquered Wales.

To be fair on Edward, this wasn't an act of unprovoked aggression. Llywelyn ap Gruffudd, the ruler of Gwynedd, also known as Llywelyn the Last (spoilers!), had done well out of the confusion of Henry III's reign. As well as directly ruling the north-west quarter of Wales, under the Treaty of Montgomery of 1267 he was the feudal overlord of most of the rest of it, and official holder of the title of prince of Wales. He felt that the tide of history was flowing in his direction and he started to push his advantage/luck. He invaded lands held by English lords, drove his brother Dafydd to find refuge at the English court, refused to do homage to Edward, also refused to pay him 15,000 marks that he owed him and, just to put the tin lid on it, got himself engaged to SDM's daughter.

In 1277 Edward launched a massive invasion, which was entirely successful. By the Treaty of Aberconwy in November of that year, Llywelyn lost half of Gwynedd, much of it to Dafydd, and all of his feudal overlordship rights in mid-Wales. Then in 1282 Dafydd started a rebellion against Edward, because he felt hard done by in the 1277 deal, and this led to a much more widespread Welsh rebellion against English incursions. This was a trickier military challenge for Edward but his organization and credit were good and the war was wrapped up in his favour by July 1283.

At this point, Edward had had enough of his feudal relationship with Celtic Wales. He took the country over, building massive new castles, as well as new towns for English settlers and introducing English laws and a county structure. No independent Celtic prince of Wales ever ruled again. To make all this official, in 1301 Edward made his son, Edward of Caernarfon (named after where he was born, not where his heart was) prince of Wales. Ever since, the title has been held only by the heir to the English throne.

Edward's other key bit of PR where Wales was concerned was to appropriate the legend of Arthur. This was a bit rich coming from a French-descended royal with an Anglo-Saxon name. The Welsh, as descendants of the Britons, considered King Arthur a part of their history – they hoped he might return one day and lead them to glory. Edward countered this with two arguments: i) Arthur is dead and ii) I am Arthur.

In 1278 he attended a ceremony at Glastonbury Abbey at which the supposed tomb of Arthur and Guinevere was opened. The bones inside, which must have been put there by some monks at some point in the preceding centuries (they can't really have been Arthur's and Guinevere's because no such people ever existed), gave him the opportunity to show his reverence for Arthur while making it clear that the guy was deceased. He also took 'Arthur's crown' from Llywelyn and, in 1284 and 1302, held 'Round Table' tournaments at which everyone was encouraged to think of Edward as a new Arthur.

So the Wales project worked out. It was very expensive but Edward had a large amount of new territory to show for it, so parliament and his bankers were unconcerned. He had blasted away the old feudal relationship between English kings and Welsh princes. Plantagenet rule looked menacingly out over the Welsh from hundreds of state-of-the-art arrow slits in the walls of Edward's gleaming new castles. The trouble came when he tried to apply the same principles to Scotland.

Incidentally, arrow slits were genuinely, at this point, the latest thing. Edward had brought them home from crusade – God knows how he transported so many of them. It's a reminder of how different this age was, in terms not just of technology but of technological change. People had been firing arrows from castles for over 300 years and they've only just thought about making a nice thin defensible window to do it from.

That's a pretty relaxing pace of change. It's one of the

reasons that, in our own terrifying era, caught as we are in a world-wide-web awaiting the arrival of the AI arachnid, we find history so comforting. This struck me after my own visit to Caernarfon Castle, perhaps Edward I's mightiest state-of-the-art fortress bristling with the new advance in narrower wall-gaps, when I checked into a boutique guest house; there I had a very nice room, with atmospheric lighting and comfortable furnishings and, on the bedside table, a brand-new radio alarm clock with the obsolete sort of iPhone charging port.

Everything goes horrible with Scotland for ever

Strange to report but, up to this point, relations between the English and Scottish monarchies had generally been friendly. There'd been the odd spat, as when King William the Lion joined in with Henry II's sons' rebellion in 1173, or when Alexander II invaded the north during the First Barons' War in support of Prince Louis, the rebels' candidate to replace John on the throne. But, on both of these occasions, the Scottish king was merely taking part in the overall Anglo-Norman political situation, just as when King David I had supported Empress Matilda to replace Stephen.

Scottish monarchs were part of the general post-Conquest English political community. They often held English earldoms, usually Huntingdon, and spent time at the English court. There was an understanding that the kings of England were slightly higher up the feudal pecking order, but it didn't cause much controversy. For the Scottish regime the real struggle for influence was in the north, where they contested dominance of what are now the Scottish islands with the kings of Norway.

Alexander III, who was king of Scots for the last third of Henry III's reign and the first half of Edward I's, had been married to Edward's sister until her premature death, and relations remained cordial through the premature deaths of all his children and right up to his own premature death when in 1286 he fell off a horse.

Thanks to all the previous premature deaths, he didn't have a viable heir. In fact the fatal horse fall had happened when he was riding through the dark to visit his new queen on the eve of her birthday – a gesture as romantic as it was urgently procreational.

All that remained of the Scottish royal line was Alexander's three-year-old granddaughter, Margaret. She was known as the Maid of Norway for the sensible reasons that she lived in Norway and her father was the King of Norway. All the major Scottish aristocrats deliberated over what to do, in consultation with Edward, who was putting on all the feudal overlord airs and graces, and they decided on a plan. Tiny Margaret could be queen but she would marry Edward's even tinier son Edward of Caernarfon and then there would be a lovely joint monarchy. Sorted. No need for the next 400 years of dynastic history. They called for the Maid of Norway to be sent back from Norway. She stopped off in Orkney on the way and died of food poisoning.

Sorry to end that paragraph with the sudden death of a child but, grim though it is to relate, nearly half the children in the middle ages died before the age of ten. Wealthy children didn't have a much better survival rate than average – of Edward I's eighteen children, ten died during childhood – because, while having enough food and some decent shelter helped your chances a bit, medicine certainly didn't. Conventional western medicine was probably doing more harm than good until the nineteenth century, so people were better off not being able to afford it.

The Scottish royal family had lost the knack of keeping anyone alive at all and Edward scented opportunity – as it turned out, it was the opportunity to fuck up Anglo-Scottish relations for the rest of time. A new king of Scots had to be decided on and Edward was invited by the Scottish barons to organize that process, which is known as the Great Cause. That strikes me as a fun but slightly inappropriate name as there's no cause involved – no ideology, just wealth and power.

As with most party leadership elections, there were loads of candidates but only two of them had a chance: they were called John Balliol and Robert de Brus. Edward was determined to use the selection process to make the nebulous nature of the relative feudal standing between the kings of England and Scotland explicit in the English king's favour. That was his agenda throughout and that was why he made sure John Balliol got picked. He would be a king who fully acknowledged English suzerainty. He probably also had the best dynastic claim but that absolutely wasn't why he got the job.

At this point, Edward had done well: the new Scottish king, who was crowned in November 1292, was a viable appointment and was happy to tip his cap to the King of England. Then Edward's failure to grasp nuance screwed things up. He kept pushing his luck. He heard appeals to cases that had been ruled on by Scottish courts and he summoned Balliol to appear before the English parliament. This was extremely tactless.

As Edward should have known from his own position as duke of Aquitaine, the homage thing was embarrassing for rulers. It always worked better when the nominally senior royal was weaker – as when Henry I and Henry II did homage to Louis VI and Louis VII. That's more like the relationship between monarch and prime minister in modern Britain: it's good for the soul of the more powerful figure that there's someone they have to pretend to look up to. It helps keep them honest, like the slave who, it's said, in Roman triumphs would stand behind the victorious general whispering, 'Remember you are just a man.'

When the weaker ruler is doing homage, it's a bit humiliating. Balliol was trying to establish himself as a king, which was tricky enough anyway because he'd been appointed rather than born to it and he had a surname which is infra dig for a king – like a pop megastar having to keep hold of their own front-door keys. In order for him to remain a nice Scottish king, amenable to Edward's sense of superiority, he also had to disabuse the Scottish aristocracy of their understandable suspicion that he was just some bloke. It was not in Edward's interests to make Balliol seem pathetic.

Yet he did. The final straw was when he tried to make Scottish barons serve under him in a war against France. They weren't having it, but concluded that Balliol couldn't protect them from it. A twelve-man council took over the government and, far from supporting Edward against King Philip IV of France, in 1295 they signed a treaty of friendship with Philip.

This new alliance, subsequently known as the Auld Alliance, would last for over 300 years. Edward had made a new enemy to the north and driven it into the arms of his old enemy to the south. The Franco-Scottish pact was a problem for him and a problem for every single one of his successors. It was a monumental cock-up.

Hammer of the Scots

What will sort this out, Edward decided, is to give those Scots a damn good hammering. Both literal and metaphorical. And, to supplement the literal hammering, some literal swording and arrowing and militarized arson. An enormous English army invaded Scotland in 1296 and did an impressive job of conquering it. John Balliol was deposed and sent to the Tower of London, and the Stone of Destiny at Scone, on which

Scottish kings had been crowned for centuries, was taken to Westminster Abbey where it remained, but for fifteen months in the 1950s when it was stolen by some Scottish students, until 1996. As far as Edward was concerned, Scotland was now part of England and he was king of all of it.

He was wrong about that. Scotland wasn't having it. The problem never went away – not just for the rest of Edward's reign, but ever. What Edward wanted to do was to go and have a war against the King of France. That's what kings of England did. But the constant Scottish problem and consequent financial pressures meant he managed only one unsuccessful continental campaign in 1297 and many of his most powerful magnates refused to go with him.

When he returned to England, he had to mount a huge charm offensive to get the barons back onside. Only with another confirmation of Magna Carta, and the defeat at the Battle of Stirling Bridge of an English army led by the Earl of Surrey, who was supposed to be running Scotland on Edward's behalf, by a Scottish one led by a knight called William Wallace, did the English aristocracy unite again behind the king.

Edward went back to Scotland to do more hammering several times in his reign, but Scottish rebellion could not be snuffed out. Wallace led it for a few years, before Edward managed to capture him in 1305 and have him publicly torn to bits. Those bits were then displayed all over Britain – I suppose it got people out of the house.

It didn't do any good. Robert de Brus had a grandson, Robert the Bruce – the surname had evolved, but certainly not been anglicized. Bruce had been on the English side off and on over the previous decade but, in February 1306, he finally showed his hand. In it there was a dagger that he used to kill a rival claimant to the throne called John Comyn. This moment of brutality signalled Bruce's intention to seize the throne and he got himself crowned, the absence of the Stone of Destiny notwithstanding, the following month. Edward responded with vicious brutality against Bruce's family and allies – he had his brother hanged, drawn and quartered and kept his sister in a cage for four years – but this further galvanized Scottish resistance to his rule.

These are deep waters. Nationhood, nationalism and patriotism are complex issues, weaving together positive and negative elements: broadly speaking, on the one hand there's cultural identity and 'Freedom!', as William Wallace put it, and on the other there's xenophobia. They're also complex in terms of how they emerge and evolve. Not all groups of people who see themselves as different from their neighbours, culturally, socially, religiously or racially, come to define that as a sense of nationhood or an aspiration for political self-determination.

I was brought up to think of myself as British. I was born in England but my mother is Welsh and my father, though born in England too, comes from a Scottish family. I was aware that Scotland and Wales were parts of my country that were a bit different from the bit I lived in, which was Oxford. I was also aware that the way they were different from Oxford was different from the way, say, Cumbria, London or Devon were different from Oxford. Not necessarily *more* different, but *differently* different. But I assumed that a large majority of the people in England, Scotland and Wales were happy to be part of the same country. (I think I knew, even then, that that was not true of Northern Ireland.)

Clearly I was wrong. Many Scots do not share my sense of a Britain and I no longer seek to argue with that. It doesn't feel like it's my business any more. People say – and there's obviously truth in it – that recent events such as how the Thatcher government imposed the poll tax on Scotland before the rest of the UK, and even more recently Brexit, which was deeply unpopular in Scotland, have increased Scottish nationalistic feeling. But there was something deep and ancient for those events to work on: an old feeling, an old wound.

Yorkshire and Kent are examples of places with strong senses of identity and an inclination to define themselves in terms of their differences. But few people in either county resent being part of England or Britain. There's something about the Scottish sense of identity, which is not significantly older than Yorkshire's or Kent's, that's different. Is it because the Anglo-Saxons came to Kent and Yorkshire but not Scotland? But then, the Danes dominated Yorkshire and not Kent, which explains a lot of the ancient differences between northeast England and the south. And yet an overall English identity still covers both – differences are asserted but within a shared sense of nationhood.

I think what I'm stumbling towards is that modern Scottish nationalism, the rise of the SNP, are phenomena for which Edward I may be responsible. His hammering, and his inclination to see relations between England and Scotland in unnuanced hammerish terms, made him an unwitting blacksmith of the sword of Scottish independence. His brutal intransigence caused a deep cultural pain, and evoked a shared, defensive national emotion, a self-definition of Scotland as a place defending against, and in opposition to, England. This feeling will outlast his Welsh castles. But it didn't have to be that way. Aquitaine is a settled and contented part of France.

Edward died in July 1307, once more heading north in the hope that one last frenzy of hammering might do the trick.

23. King Edward II

You may have heard that King Edward II died when someone pushed a red-hot poker up his bottom. It's one of those famous kings' deaths like 'of a surfeit of lampreys' (see above) and 'immediately after saying "Bugger Bognor"', reputedly George V's last words. The lampreys one is partly true and the other two aren't – though George V's end is interesting because it was hurried along by his doctor, Lord Dawson, who wanted it reported in *The Times* rather than the evening papers which were deemed less prestigious and therefore beneath the dignity of an expired king-emperor. So he was euthanized to meet a press deadline – very regal.

Unlike the Vikings' helmet horns, the red-hot poker demise is a colourful historical myth that I'm content to debunk, partly because it's homophobic. It doesn't add to the gaiety of nations. Still, the story emerged in the decade after Edward's death and everyone was homophobic back then, so my tutting at it doesn't get me anywhere. There's no point wishing people in fourteenth-century England had thought homosexuality was okay – that kind of toleration of differences is such an alien concept for the era that I might as well wish them better wifi.

Another reason I don't like the poker myth is that, in its implied rebuke of Edward II, it misses what was wrong with him. The problem wasn't that he was gay. (He wasn't necessarily gay anyway. He fathered children, both in and out of wedlock, and the notion of a person's 'sexuality' is an anachronism.) The problem was his propensity to have 'favourites'. Not favourite foods, pastimes or colours, but people.

Kings shouldn't have favourites. That's one of the principles of stable kingship. Edward II's reign provides a ton of anecdotal evidence to show why. Edward had favourites and couldn't hide it – or didn't hide it, anyway. He became infatuated with men in a way that made him think they were brilliant and then give them lots of wealth and power. This was a catastrophe for the political dynamic between the king and all the leading aristocrats he hadn't taken a shine to.

So whatever fucking he did, didn't do or wanted to do isn't the issue. If he'd just rewarded his crushes with booze and a few jewels all would have been well. He could have had as much sex with men as he liked – the problems came when he started handing out earldoms.

Piers Gaviscon

People don't change. That's a decent rule of thumb, but it's depressing if the king is a twat. Edward II was twenty-three when he became king and there was no reason to hope he'd die any time soon – except that it was the middle ages and anyone might drop dead at any moment, but we can't really expect the barons of the time to take much comfort from that. 'Don't worry about the king – he'll die in a minute, everyone does. Just look at the place' would have been altogether too fatalistic an attitude.

Worse still, Edward's accession had been unquestioned so there was no hope on that front. You may have noticed that the principle of primogeniture has bedded in a fair bit more since the reign of John. His eldest son, Henry III, was hastily crowned in a country almost overrun with allies of a French prince but, once Louis had headed home, there were no rival claimants from within the Plantagenet family. Similarly Edward I was the unquestioned heir to Henry III and felt so confident of his inheritance that he delayed his coronation for more than eighteen months.

The days of the likes of Harold Godwinson, Henry I or Stephen, men with a dodgy claim scrabbling around to get in the same room as an archbishop and a cracker hat, so that their crowned kingliness became a fait accompli, are over. That chaotic element of gumption, nerve and, to a certain extent, merit has been excised from the process. Birthright has started to trump coronation. This is hugely stabilizing when a king dies, but it really does seem to mean: you get who you get. And people don't change.

Edward II wasn't crowned until seven and a half months after his father's death. He'd spent the intervening time going to France to sort out the details of his marriage to Philip IV's daughter Isabella (the dowry, the accompanying treaty, is it okay that the bride's twelve and the groom seems gay, that sort of thing), and demonstrating what a terrible king he was going to be.

The latter demonstration was all to do with Edward's favourite, Piers Gaveston. Have you heard of Piers Gaveston? It's quite a famous name, though it's become confused for me by the even more famous, but much more recent, brand of antacid, Gaviscon. I was aware of Gaveston first but then Gaviscon did a big TV advertising campaign at some point in the 1990s that really fronted up with the name.

'Gaviscon!', a big authoritative voice would say stomach-calmingly, and it sounded so close to the surname of Edward II's favourite that it felt like it can't have been an accident. Was sounding a bit like a familiar historical figure a deliberate branding choice, like using subliminal imagery? By softly ringing a bell in the brains of those with a passing interest in medieval history, did Gaviscon's owners hope more quickly to spread awareness of Rennie's new rival? Wouldn't Simon de Comfort have sounded more settling, or were they worried about the associations with antisemitism? Thomas à Better?

It turns out the name is a conflation of Gastric Viscosity Control, a reflux suppressant technique developed by Swedish radiologist Dr Stig Sandmark in 1964, so has no connection with Piers at all. No one would describe Piers Gaveston as a reflex suppressant technique. In fact, many of his contemporaries found him positively emetic.

Gaveston was a knight from a perfectly posh family from Gascony, an area not named after its impeccable gastric control, who would have been a totally reasonable member of Edward's circle if it wasn't for his and Edward's personalities. Edward I had banished him from his son's company, thinking he was a bad influence, but then Edward I died and the new King Edward immediately recalled Gaveston and made him earl of Cornwall.

In a way, this is all you need to know about Edward II. He made his recently banished favourite earl of Cornwall the moment he became king. Edward was then, and remained for the rest of his life, someone who was capable of doing something that stupid. Earl of Cornwall was a major title – its equivalent today, duke of Cornwall, is, like prince of Wales, held only by the heir to the throne. Making Gaveston earl of Cornwall was a staggeringly tactless, undiplomatic, unnerving and annoying act.

He got away with it at that point because he'd only just become king, but why do it? The downside was evident: all the magnates' fears about the king's judgement and his threateningly close, possibly homosexual, relationship with Gaveston were instantly realized. What was the upside? What did Edward gain from this? Would Gaveston have dumped him and flounced off to France if he *hadn't* been made earl of Cornwall? It doesn't seem likely – the King of France didn't fancy him. Did raising Gaveston to that earldom shore up Edward's power in some way? Absolutely not – quite the reverse.

The only conclusion is that Edward made Gaveston earl of Cornwall just because he wanted to. It was a lavish sign of honour and approval that he wished to publicly make and he figured that, now he was king, no one could stop him. This is exceptionally thick, vain and self-absorbed. He was using a huge piece of royal patronage not to increase his own power but to diminish it. It's like an act of political arson: it would have been no more daft to set fire to a royal palace merely to enjoy the pleasing effect of the flames.

His next move was to give Gaveston an absurdly prominent role in the coronation. At the coronation feast, specially commissioned tapestries displayed the coat of arms of the king and that of Gaveston but not, as far as we know, the new queen's. It looked like the whole event was about the bringing together of Edward's and Gaveston's families, rather than England and France, which was supposedly the point of marrying the King of France's child and getting crowned alongside her.

The effect of all this was to make the magnates just as obsessed with Gaveston as Edward was. They mirrored his infatuation with hatred; Gaveston's name was rarely off their lips and they demanded he be exiled. Edward agreed to this grudgingly but then allowed him back again.

The situation was not improved by Piers Gaveston's own twattishness. He delighted in the king's favour and called the major barons by offensive names. Edward seemingly did not instruct him not to do this. In 1311, parliament, despairing of Edward's regime, imposed some 'Ordinances' on the king, new rules that curtailed his power, and appointed twenty-one 'Lords Ordainers' to oversee the government. This was another Magna Cartaesque attempt to cope with the failings of an unarguably legitimate sovereign. Gaveston was exiled again.

Then Gaveston came back again and Edward renounced the Ordinances. By this point, in early 1312, a group of major barons led by Edward's cousin Thomas Earl of Lancaster, who was the richest and most powerful aristocrat in England, were fizzing mad. Thomas hated Gaveston so viciously that it's impossible not to suspect it was slightly sexual. That's another problem with the poker-violation myth – it makes you think too much about who fancies whom, which in general is a more useful thought process for analysing reality TV than for understanding medieval baronial politics.

Civil war was about to break out – again. There've been at least a couple in the thirteenth century and another couple in the twelfth, one of them lasting twenty years. This all makes the famous seventeenth-century event, which is simply called the English Civil War, seem rather presumptuously named. How come that historical titular web address hadn't already been taken? English civil wars, it seems to me, are what mainly happened in English history.

But not on this occasion. Gaveston, who was under siege at Scarborough, consented to surrender to the earls of Pembroke and Surrey on the condition that he wasn't harmed. Pembroke was given the job of escorting him south, and didn't harm him, but then popped off to visit his wife, leaving his prisoner poorly guarded. This, in turn, gave the more rabidly anti-Gaveston Earl of Warwick the opportunity to kidnap him and take him to Warwick Castle, where he and Lancaster did a shitty sort of mock trial, had fun getting really angry, declared Gaveston a traitor and had his head chopped off at the top of a hill by a couple of Welshmen. I expect they told themselves they weren't turned on by any of it.

More inevitable disaster

This chaotic and murderous sequence of events left Edward devastated. Even in a medieval context, the pseudo-judicial beheading of an earl was savage and taboo. It all feels messy and lamentable and unnecessary, and recasts both the king's and Gaveston's previous idiotic behaviour in an almost poignant light. In general, the evidence we have of what was going on in this era tends to be about conflict and charters and wars and homage. We hear a lot about what powerful people wouldn't stand for, and very little about what they liked. It's all very grand and cold.

Weird and destabilizing though it was, there is something warm about Edward's feelings for Piers Gaveston. Through the huge and distorting filter of time, one person's liking for another comes through. We get a glimpse of frivolity, humour – the half-witted antics of two overentitled young men. We don't really know what the relationship was like – whether and to what extent it was sexual, how sincerely Edward's feelings were reciprocated, where admiration, friendship and the baffled insecurity of being an heir to the throne played a part. But we know there was love. It's not particularly admirable, but it's human and it's powerfully recognizable and it doesn't feel like it meant anyone's head needed to get chopped off.

Did it change Edward? Well, as I keep saying, people don't change, so no. But obviously a bit yes. I hope you're pleased with the level of historical nuance you're getting: no, but a bit yes. That'll see anyone through A-Level.

When the Bourbon monarchy was restored after the French Revolution, Talleyrand, the extraordinarily clever, successful and untrustworthy French statesman, said of that regime, which was in power from the final defeat of Napoleon in 1815 till 1830, that it had 'learned nothing and forgotten nothing'. It's a great phrase, which Talleyrand probably ripped off someone else. It encapsulates how that royal house was so conscious of the myriad wrongs that had been done to it (most notably the chopping off of a king's head) that it missed the bigger picture: the fact that the revolution had revealed France's true character as a society, and a state, to itself. No restored monarchy could survive without respecting that.

Like the returning Bourbons, Edward never forgot the beheading of someone close to him. He never forgave the earls of Warwick and Lancaster. The former died in 1315 but Edward managed to capture the latter in 1322 and had him tried and executed for treason. That's understandable, but he failed to draw any broader conclusions from what had happened other than that he and Gaveston had been horrendously wronged.

I'm getting ahead of myself: lots more stuff had gone wrong by then. Most dramatically, the Battle of Bannockburn in 1314 when a large English army led by Edward was thrashed by a smaller Scottish one led by Robert the Bruce. The regime change between Edward I and Edward II hadn't helped the Anglo-Scottish situation. All the resentment and nationalistic feeling invoked by Edward I's intransigent viciousness was given the space to grow and develop by his son's ineffectual regime.

Bruce was able to consolidate his position as Scottish king, picking off Edward's castles one by one, and relentlessly raid and plunder the north of England while still representing himself and Scotland as the wronged party. It was seven years into his reign before Edward got round to doing anything about this. But then he seemed to get his shit together: he assembled an enormous army of between 15,000 and 20,000 men to head north and relieve the siege of Stirling Castle, one of the English king's few remaining fortresses north of the border.

Bruce's army was less than half the size of Edward's and so, on paper, his victory is surprising. But Edward had very little military experience, was leading a divided aristocracy and Bruce was, effectively, a self-made king. Bruce wouldn't have given battle if he didn't think he had a good chance of causing an upset. Bannockburn was a disaster and a humiliation for Edward II but, seen in context, it was just a dramatic event in an irreversible process.

Scottish national identity, under an ambitious and capable monarch, was not something English kings were capable of suppressing. Edward I, who caused the whole problem, was more effective at dealing with it than his son, but neither of them could really manage. In many ways, Bannockburn just clarified the way things were inevitably heading.

Six years later, King Robert's regime issued a document called the Declaration of Arbroath. It was addressed to the pope and was partly an attempt to get Bruce's long-standing sentence of excommunication lifted, but it also stridently asserted Scottish sovereignty and nationhood. It's expressed in terms of the Scots' ancient rights and independence – as ever, novelty is spun as restoration – but it really *is* a novelty. In general, the previous custom was for Scottish kings to accept that English kings were slightly higher up the pecking order. Then Edward I pushed his luck and that was the end of that.

In 1324 the pope recognized Bruce as king of an independent Scotland. Then, in the Treaty of Edinburgh–Northampton of 1328, England renounced all claims to superiority over Scotland. After Bruce's death in 1329, the next Scottish king, David II, was, by permission of the pope and for the first time, anointed with oil at his coronation. Previous Scots kings had merely been enthroned. The last vestiges of English or Plantagenet feudal superiority were wiped away.

The other novelty in the Declaration of Arbroath is the sense of a nation as distinct from a ruler or royal family. The Scotland that the Bruces now ruled was not merely their possession, but a community with an identity independent from its ruler or crown. This is the way things had been going in England too – Edward I's commitment to parliament is a world away from Henry II's or Richard I's attitude to their possessions. These are the first steps towards the concept of a country or nation that's familiar to us today. It's very different from the feudal hierarchy and system of ownership, and brings with it a huge range of problems, challenges and opportunities which I will summarize thus: liberty, equality, fraternity, Nazism.

They made themselves indespenserble

In the meantime, Edward had found himself a new favourite, someone called Hugh Despenser, and a second one, who was also called Hugh Despenser. There was a bit of an age gap between them because they were father and son.

The Despensers are hard to like – maybe harder to like than Gaveston. Gaveston was an idiot, contemptuous and arrogant, but he wasn't cynical. The Despensers were: they were on the make and had decided that total loyalty to the king would be their route to advancement, immense riches and power.

In more effective reigns 'total loyalty to the king' wouldn't have made you stand out from the general mass of noblemen. Under Edward II, the nobility's loyalty was all over the place, thrown off by the king's unreliability. Hugh Despenser the Elder's policy of just backing Edward, no matter how stupid his actions, was quite unusual and, to the king, extremely welcome.

After the death of Gaveston, Despenser the Elder spotted an opening for his son (I am *so* sorry). Hugh Despenser the Younger was not only younger, he was attractiver. With the elder Despenser as an unquestioningly supportive father figure, and the younger one fulfilling the Gaveston role, all of Edward's requirements from a favourite were met.

In the end, they were victims of their own success. They grew in influence so infuriatingly that the country actually *did* descend into civil war when, in the time of Gaveston, it had only threatened to. Somehow the king won that war, which is how he managed to have the Earl of Lancaster executed. In 1322, for the first time in his reign since his disastrously undiplomatic coronation, Edward was properly in charge. Lancaster, the greatest magnate in the land, had been defeated.

Finally given the chance to rule, Edward turned out to be a horrible, miserly tyrant, stockpiling cash which was of no real use to him without the confidence of the powerful people in the realm, and heaping ever more honours on the Despensers.

This annoyed everyone, but the most important person it annoyed was the queen. Up to now, Queen Isabella had been amazingly tolerant of Edward's dickish behaviour. But she hated Hugh Despenser the Younger and felt humiliated within her own marriage. Quite how badly he must have behaved, considering what she had previously gone along with in the days of Gaveston, we can only guess.

Edward, being an idiot, didn't realize the extent of her anger and unhappiness so, when a war with France was going badly, he thought Isabella would be the perfect person to go and negotiate on his behalf. Just to give a further insight into the kind of slapdash fool Edward was, he asked this of her even though a year earlier, at the outbreak of the war, he had confiscated her lands on the basis that she was French. But the new King of France, Charles IV, like the two previous kings of France, was Isabella's brother – so he'd be nice to her, Edward presumably reasoned.

He *was* nice to her. She successfully negotiated a truce, but Edward was still supposed to go and pay homage for his French possessions. Edward wasn't keen to do this, partly because he considered it beneath his dignity, and partly because he didn't want to leave England where most of the barons were screaming for the Despensers' blood and, in the king's absence, might obtain it. So it was suggested that his eldest son, also called Edward, might pay homage on his behalf. The king thought this was a very good idea which, as a general rule, suggests it was a terrible plan. It was: ultimately, it destroyed him.

In 1325 twelve-year-old Prince Edward went to France to join his mum and pay homage to his uncle Charles. And there he and Isabella stayed. She wrote to her husband saying she had no intention of coming back to England while Hugh Despenser the Younger was around and that she considered herself a widow. She took to wearing black clothes and a veil to signify how badly she felt her husband had let her down. She had with her the heir to the throne, and newly confirmed Duke of Aquitaine, her son Edward who, if and when she really became a widow, would be king of England.

In England, Edward senior raged, while in France, Isabella attracted around her many English nobles who had been living in exile from Edward's tyranny. Soon she had a favourite of her own: Roger Mortimer, grandson of the Roger Mortimer who had draped Simon de Montfort's balls over his severed head. This Mortimer had been condemned to death for treachery at the end of the recent civil war but managed to escape from the Tower of London to France.

Unlike Edward and Piers or Hugh, we absolutely *know* that Isabella and Roger 'became lovers', as historians put it when they want screwing to sound tasteful. The couple were quite open about it. I mean, I think they actually had the sex behind closed doors – or drawn tapestries – but they were fine with everyone knowing. Isabella probably hoped it would wind her husband up even more, which it did.

In the autumn of 1326 Roger, Isabella and Prince Edward landed in Suffolk with a small army. This freaked the king out. He was convinced that the tininess of the force meant the invaders were convinced they'd get a lot of support after they landed. He was right and they were right. His reign was finished. By the end of the year, the Despensers had been hung, drawn and quartered – or eighthed, I suppose – and the king was in prison.

In January 1327, a parliament convened, despite no king having summoned it. Edward refused to take part, hoping his absence would undermine its legitimacy. On paper, it did, but everyone was in a practical, non-theoretical mood. Hastily, and without pausing to contemplate the troubling ramifications for the whole system of government the country had been relying on for the best part of a millennium, the parliament decided that the indisputably legitimate, crowned and anointed king was incompetent and had to go. Instead of taking this to its logical conclusion and instituting a republic, it resolved that the terrible king's teenage kid would do the job splendidly. Oddly, he did.

24. King Edward III

If you're looking for a glorious medieval English king – a proper one with swords and flags and horses and everything's going terribly well – then Edward III is your man. Or rather, he's your best bet. It was problematic being a medieval English king, as we've seen, and medieval England was pretty awful by our standards, and disappointingly unlike a nice medieval-themed festival such as they might hold on the grass next to Warwick Castle, with lots of brightly coloured pavilions and stalls and refreshments and flags and a bouncy dinosaur and proper loos.

I remember going to an event like that at Warwick Castle, just as puberty was beginning to rob me of my unreflecting joy in such things but before I quite knew why. 'The Age of Not Believing' is what the Sherman Brothers called it in their Oscar-nominated song from *Bedknobs and Broomsticks*. Sadly for them the Academy Award that year went to Isaac Hayes for 'The Theme from *Shaft*', a fact which shines a penetrating light on the futility of awards for creative endeavours.

Some important, serious people, who had forged successful careers in Hollywood, sat in a room and tried to work out which was *better* out of the song 'The Age of Not Believing' and the theme from *Shaft*. They were willing to give that a go. They didn't insist that neither is better and that the notion that such works of art can be reduced to the quantifiable level of the 100-metre sprint is so contemptuous of the noble endeavours of composing music and writing scripts and directing and acting that it's completely

counterproductive to the whole aim of the Oscars ceremony. You might as well ask which is better out of a fish
finger and a ladder. It's an absurd way for busy people to
spend time – they'd have been better off playing 'I spy' and
then tossing a coin. I hope that's what they did.

Speaking of absurd ways to spend time, I went to this festival at Warwick Castle and stood there awkwardly while a
man dressed as a knight spent ages explaining the proper
way to use a broadsword. It's not what they do in the films at
all, he said. The man was of the view that the people in films
make themselves look quite foolish with all that dramatic
clashing. The real thing was much less picturesque and more
brutal.

The same is true of Edward III. There was a lot of glory.
Not just glory that's been subsequently projected on to
the reign, like Richard I's lionhearted Englishness or Alfred's
enormous greatness, but real glory, plus the notion of glory
that Edward himself deliberately broadcast to his subjects
and posterity. He was a successful warrior but also a powerful image-maker. Success, victory, martial valour, chivalry,
Englishness – these were the ideas that Edward promoted.
He'd set out his stall, so you might as well queue up and buy a
venison burger with special Plantagenet sauce and an iced
mead. There's a joust at 2, but don't worry – the lances are
made of sponge.

What's so great about glory? It's often gory. Edward III's
almost always was. Glory is overrated. People get hurt in the
quest for glory and not just the glory-seekers. Then the glory
itself is fleeting. There's a moment and then it passes. It's not
a film: the broadswordsmanship is too realistic and the climax
isn't the end. The credits haven't rolled, so life goes on and all
that glory is gradually whittled down to something only old
people remember.

Fraying at both ends

Let's start at the two ends of Edward III's reign and work inwards. The two ends weren't great.

The first end was, as with a piece of string, also the beginning and it was a strange one. Edward's father was still alive which, under more normal circumstances, would have been a nice thing. As it was, it complicated matters. In late January 1327, after parliament had decided the country desperately needed to move on to the next king even though he was a pubescent boy, a delegation of noblemen went to Kenilworth Castle, where Edward II was being held, in order to talk him into abdicating.

He made a bit of a fuss about it, as you might expect – he became tearful and had to be held upright because the shock had made him weak at the knees – but he was persuaded when the noblemen started saying that, if he resigned the throne, his son would succeed him and the Plantagenet dynasty would continue but, if he didn't, both he and his son might be sidelined and a new candidate found.

So he agreed to abdicate and his steward of the household, Sir Thomas Blount, ceremonially broke his staff of office in front of everyone. Dramatic. Good work, Sir Thomas – that's a nifty bit of protocol to come up with on the spur of the moment. And it's risky. You've got to be sure people will get what you're doing rather than think it's an accident or a weird moment of temper. It could easily have resulted in a terse 'Tom, can you *please* keep still – this is actually quite a stressful moment for everyone.'

Not only did they all realize what was going on but now there was a thing that must be done when kings stop being kings – staffs of office get broken. How reassuring that must have been for the anxious magnates. Suddenly there's a system and a ceremony, almost like a coronation, so what they were doing can't be an offence against God and nature after all.

Also, it answered the question that must have occurred to Sir Thomas and many of his predecessors: what is a staff of office actually for? How much of the day-to-day stewarding work involves the use of a stick? Very little, I'd have thought. The stick must, more often than not, have been an impediment – just something you have to put down somewhere in order to do anything that involves two hands. Now everyone knew what it was for: it's there to be broken when the reign ends. It could act as a warning to future kings – you're just one snap across the knee away from being busted back to civilian, your majesty! I wonder if, six Edwards later, Wallis Simpson's fiancé had a stick broken in front of him. Yet another thing for him to whinge to Hitler about.

On 1 February 1327 Edward III, just fourteen years old at that point, was crowned king. Meanwhile his dad was in prison, thinking *he* should still be king, and his mum, Queen Isabella, was both running the country and very publicly shacked up with her new boyfriend, Roger Mortimer. The teenage king must have been *so embarrassed.*

If they'd been competent regents, Edward might have been able to cope with it all until he reached the age of majority. But they weren't. They made a humiliating peace with France and another with Scotland, having fought a terrible military campaign that nearly got Edward himself captured. Plantagenet territory and rights were being frittered away to north and south.

Former King Edward II was also nearly captured, but in his case the attempts were made by well-wishers hoping to restore him to power. He was moved from Kenilworth to Berkeley Castle, which Mortimer hoped would be more secure. But the hoping didn't quite hit the spot so, in September 1327, Mortimer had him murdered just to be on the safe side. Almost certainly, that is. It's almost certain that it was murder by order of Mortimer and/or Isabella, just as it's almost certain that the method employed was not red-hot poker up the bottom.

The most disappointing failing in Mortimer and Isabella was that they were obsessed with increasing their own personal wealth, awarding themselves vast new estates and, in the case of Mortimer, inventing the new earldom of March (as in the Welsh 'Marches', or the border areas) to give to himself.

I don't understand their reasoning. What were they feathering their nests for? Weren't they comfortably off already? Didn't Mortimer realize his only future lay in retaining power and he could do this only by appeasing and ideally impressing the rest of the aristocracy and the adolescent king? Was he hoping to retire on these riches? He was a usurper of royal power – people like that don't retire. They're either still running the show or they're dead.

As Edward got older and more frustrated by the position he found himself in, Mortimer became more presumptuous and tyrannical and deferred to the young king less and less, even in public. When, in March 1330, Mortimer had the Earl of Kent, a son of Edward I, executed, the king realized he had to do something. In October that year, he launched a coup to gain control of his own kingdom. This involved creeping into Nottingham Castle with a bunch of mates, bursting into his mother's bedroom and arresting Roger.

'Fair son, have pity on the gentle Mortimer,' said Isabella, but Edward didn't. Mortimer was hanged as a traitor at Tyburn, the famous London gallows, roughly where Marble Arch is now, on 29 November 1330. Edward III's proper rule had begun. It lasted for nearly half a century.

At the other end

Edward III lived too long. His eldest son didn't live long enough. Those were the big problems at the other end of the reign.

There'd been a hell of a lot of glory, and I'll get to that, but it had petered out. Then, in 1369, Edward's wife, Queen Philippa of Hainault, on whom he was exceptionally keen and who had been a very effective partner in his rule, died. The following year, his eldest son's eldest son Edward who, all being well, would have been Edward V one day, also died. By then his father, Edward Prince of Wales, who, all being well, would have been Edward IV one day, was already ailing from a mysterious chronic illness. In 1376 he died.

Meanwhile Edward III who, all being well, would have stopped being Edward III by now was still just about going. But he was a shadow of his former self, possibly suffering from dementia, or perhaps he'd had a stroke – either way he was relying heavily for the location of his marbles on his mistress, Alice Perrers, and she didn't always act in the national interest.

The government had been spending vast sums on military campaigns which were no longer proving successful and there was widespread suspicion of corruption in the doddering king's council. In 1376 a parliament, subsequently known as the Good Parliament, during which the Prince of Wales died (those two facts are not connected, though the name implies the parliamentarians managed to keep their grief under control), made a decent stab at sorting all this out. For the first time, senior royal officials were impeached for corruption and new ministers imposed on the king and an attempt made to separate him from Alice Perrers.

Towards the end of the session, soon after the prince's

death, the commons, an increasingly powerful and confident force within the Good Parliament, made a demand. They wanted his surviving son, Richard of Bordeaux, who was then a nine-year-old boy, to be brought before them and confirmed as the heir apparent. They were worried that Edward III's eldest surviving son, John of Gaunt, Duke of Lancaster, who had been heading up the regime's responses to the parliament's complaints, might otherwise attempt to usurp the throne.

This is interesting. As it happens, John of Gaunt didn't try to usurp the throne, though he probably considered it. He swore an oath on the Prince of Wales's deathbed, along with his father, to honour and protect young Richard's accession. What's weird is how convinced everyone seems to have been that Gaunt becoming king would be such a terrible idea.

He wasn't a brilliant man, but he was okay. He was a competent and experienced military leader and politician. In his dealings with the Good Parliament he was a bit unreconstructedly pro-crown, but members of the royal family tend to be like that. The next parliament, Edward III's last, which is known to posterity as the Bad Parliament, was dominated by Gaunt and reversed many of the Good Parliament's reforming steps.

So he wasn't very parliamentarian in his outlook, but still there's no reason to think he wouldn't have made a decent king and was surely a better bet than a child? But by now the principle of primogeniture was carrying all before it. The realm had got so used to that certainty, that complete knowledge of who the next king is going to be, that it won't entertain the notion of any other ruler.

John of Gaunt was a senior international figure, a loyal son of Edward III and a major part of the very successful regime Edward had run for the last several decades. Yet the idea of Gaunt becoming king had become heresy because the child

Richard, helpless though he was, had the magical primogeniture fairy dust that now trumps the anointing-oil coronation magic. Clearly there was a feeling that, if you go against the righteousness of primogeniture, things might go badly wrong. Needless to say, they did anyway.

Perhaps parliament was now sufficiently self-confident that the magnates and knights actively wanted a child on the throne because they reckoned that would give them the chance to run the country for a bit – keep a control on spending and prevent dynastic ambition on the continent from making everyone go broke. A key figure here was a knight of the shire called Sir Peter de la Mare, the first elected speaker of the House of Commons.

More than anyone else, Peter de la Mare set the Good Parliament's agenda and he was, by the standards of the day, a very ordinary bloke. He wasn't an aristocrat or a magnate or anything close to it. He'd been a toll collector and the Earl of March's steward, and now he had been elected to a position of considerable importance. Doesn't that have a pleasing, tingly, anachronistic ring to it?

Obviously he was very very high up the social order compared to most people, but it shows that the influence of the commons was giving a much wider cross-section of society access to power, even if it was still a very narrow cross-section by modern standards (the number of Etonians in most contemporary cabinets notwithstanding).

The idea that someone as unposh as de la Mare might be able to instigate rules that directly affected the behaviour of big players like Gaunt and even the king would have been unthinkable a century earlier. The commons were comfortable wielding this power – no sense of deferring to their 'betters' seems to hamper them. Primogeniture and coronation carry weight – the king is treated with enormous reverence, but it's not unthinking reverence. Meanwhile notions of royalty and aristocracy seem to be carrying less weight. As the vertiginous hierarchy of feudalism became simplified – rulers were increasingly holding their lands in full sovereignty, directly below God rather than by paying homage to more senior rulers – there was less respect for aristocrats and relatives of the king. They, the commons seem to think, are not to be trusted.

I'm talking about the confused and discontented end to Edward's reign before I get to the good bit, because the end makes much of what went before seem futile. It felt splendid at the time but it led nowhere and, for me, it helps to keep that in mind. Edward inherited and bequeathed a bankrupt kingdom, failing to live up to its own unrealistic expectations on the international scene. What happened in between is a detail.

The glorious middle

In between these two periods of disappointment and corruption, there were some stellar triumphs. Edward III and his son Prince Edward were great strategists, warriors and propagandists. They furthered Plantagenet claims in France more forcefully than anyone since Henry II.

The aspect of their success that is most treasured by posterity, in Britain at least, was their knack for winning battles when outnumbered. At Crécy in 1346 and Poitiers in 1356 smaller English armies thrashed larger French ones due to the senior English royals' strategic excellence and the brilliance of the English and Welsh longbowmen. The French only had crossbowmen who were comparatively shit, plus men in armour on horses who you'd imagine, from their habit of repeatedly riding into blizzards of arrows, actively wanted to get shot to bits.

As a result of these battles a huge proportion of the senior

French aristocracy ended up lying around the French country-side, dead in their armour. And there were other English triumphs: Calais was conquered in 1347, after a long siege, and remained in English hands for over 200 years. At the Battle of Poitiers, King John II of France was captured and taken back to England. In 1360, as part of the Treaty of Brétigny, his ransom was set at 3 million crowns (which roughly equates to 'Oh mother of God, you are fucking kidding me!' in today's money) and he was allowed to go home to try and raise it, on the condition that he left his son, Louis of Anjou, as a hostage.

This was all quite humiliating for the French monarchy, but it got worse. In 1363, Louis managed to escape before the ransom had been paid. Well done him, you might think. That's not what John II thought. He considered the escape to be dishonourable – it was reneging on an agreement – so the king voluntarily returned to English captivity himself. We can only imagine how annoying the people of France, and his son Louis, found this extravagant act of virtue-signalling. This is finding 10p on the pavement and insisting on handing it in at a local police station raised to the geopolitical level. Then, in 1364, John died in English captivity.

For the French royal family, this was a time of deep crisis. It was compounded by the fact that not everyone accepted that that family, the House of Valois, really *was* the French royal family. Edward III didn't. In his view, *he* was the rightful king of France.

This was a strange state of affairs. On the face of it, Edward III was about as unlike the king of France as it was possible for a king to be. He styled himself, very definitely, as the king of England. He was the first ruler since the Conquest who stressed this Englishness. He was still a French-speaking inter-national blue blood by background, but he spoke and promoted the English language. In the Statute of Pleading of

1362, he changed the language which was to be spoken in England's law courts and in parliament from the Norman French of the royal court to English.

As with the Declaration of Arbroath, this is a sign of a nascent pre-nationalism developing in Europe. The king was citing and valuing – declaring ownership of – the concept of Englishness. It had taken three centuries for the descendants of William the Conqueror to start doing this. Previously, they emphasized their royalty, their kingliness, their righteous possession of their lands, but didn't trouble to lay claim to having anything in common with the millions of people whose fate they controlled. God and their right was the order of the day, not issues of nationality, which were deemed beneath the contempt of Plantagenet internationalists. That was changing and Edward was using that change and driving it.

It seems perverse, perhaps hypocritical, that at the same time he was making a dynastic claim to be king of France. Let me try and briefly explain this dynastic claim while we're here because, as I mentioned before, it resulted in the ludicrous situation that every ruler of England from the mid-fourteenth century until the start of the nineteenth claimed also to be the rightful ruler of France. Half a millennium of delusional bullshit rested on this, which makes the couple of decades for which the United Nations pretended Taiwan was China pale into insignificance.

For all this time, from Edward III onwards, the lions of England on the royal coat of arms were quartered with the fleur-de-lis of the French royal family. And if, as some think, those three lions aren't all English, but one is for Normandy and one for Aquitaine, lands which the English crown controlled only for fleeting periods during the subsequent centuries, that would make the symbolism of the royal coat of arms over 80 per cent delusional. Well, why not? The first kings, as we've seen, were just successful bullies – all the talk of religion and legitimacy is a distraction from that fundamental truth. I find the absurd claim to France of the English monarchs an amusing reminder that all these people with crowns are just chancers.

Now then, the dynastic claim. In itself, it was reasonable: when Charles IV died in 1328, there was no direct male heir. It was the end of the line for the House of Capet, which had been the French royal house for nearly 350 years. Edward III's mother, Isabella, was Charles's sister, and the daughter of Philip IV. By Edward's reckoning, that made him the next eligible male in line. Women were officially not allowed to be the sovereign in France (rather than merely *effectively* not allowed, which, as we know from Matilda's experience, was the situation in England), so Isabella was out of the running, but Edward argued that she could still transmit eligibility across the generations from Philip IV to him.

The counterargument, put forward by the French, who reckoned the King of England also being their king would be less than ideal, was that a right can't be transferred by someone who can't hold it. If you can't carry it, you can't pass it on – it makes sense in physics. So in 1328, after a brief pause to see whether Charles's pregnant widow would give birth to a boy – it was a girl – Philip VI of Valois was crowned king. He was Charles IV's cousin, and Philip IV's nephew, so he was a more distant relative than Edward III, but was related entirely through men.

That was why, in 1340, a few years into his reign, and after he'd paid homage to Philip VI for Aquitaine, Edward suddenly turned round and said he was king of France. It's opportunism, albeit based on an arguable dynastic claim. (By the way, in case you're trying to keep track of this blizzard of French kings, the John II I mentioned as having been captured by Edward was Philip VI's son.)

Edward didn't behave at all like a Frenchman trying to

reclaim his birthright. It would have been tricky to do that, I suppose. He was pushing his Englishness hard at home. He couldn't claim to also possess an innate Frenchness to go with his innate Englishness. So he didn't bother to try. He put the fleur-de-lis on all his stuff and went to war – a war in which, whatever the dynastic argument, what was really happening was that the King of England was trying to conquer France.

That's what spoils Edward and his son's valiant-underdog image. Yes, they were often outnumbered, and yes they were very brave and militarily astute, but they were also invaders and aggressors. If burglars find themselves outnumbered by the residents of a house they're attempting to clear out, that doesn't necessarily make them particularly sympathetic.

Being away from home put the invaders at a disadvantage some of the time, but it also gave them carte blanche to trash the place without destroying their own homes. They perfected a tactic known as the *chevauchée*, which was basically wasting, that beloved technique of William the Conqueror, but done at speed: an army on horseback cutting a swathe of destruction through the countryside, killing, burning and ruining the lives of hundreds of thousands of French peasants. Edward Prince of Wales used the *chevauchée* particularly effectively and mercilessly, and there is speculation that this is why he came to be known as the Black Prince.

Heart of darkness

In 1348, right in the middle of Edward III's reign, after Crécy but before Poitiers, two things happened. The king founded England's highest order of chivalry, the Most Noble Order of the Garter, and the Black Death reached England.

The Knights of the Garter, whose founder members were the king, the Black Prince and twenty-four other spunky worthies, are still a big part of British establishmentarian imagery. The monarch and the heir to the throne are always members, as well as other ageing big shots: retired generals, admirals, governors of the Bank of England, heads of MI5 and former prime ministers. There was a bit of a stink recently about Tony Blair being made one on the basis that he was a warmonger. The idea that that might disqualify him couldn't be more out of keeping with the spirit of the order that Edward III founded.

The dashing yet august aura of this institution, with just a touch of sexiness coming from its association with a saucy item of clothing, is a testament to Edward's skill as an image-maker. The order was dedicated to St George, who was then elevated to co-patron saint of England, alongside St Edward the Confessor. It's delightful to see the tedious old Confessor shunted aside, and great fun to have a patron saint whose most famous act, killing a dragon, is literally impossible. But, for Edward III, George's USP was his martial valour.

The Order of the Garter was key to the king's branding of his regime as English and also, as epitomized by St George, warlike. And the place the English were supposed to be war-like, according to Edward, was France. Ever since King John lost Normandy, Plantagenet kings had struggled to get their English magnates to become involved in, and agree to bank-roll, wars of (re)conquest in France. Once the major aristocrats ceased to hold lands on both sides of the Channel, fighting on the continent stopped being in their own interests.

Somehow Edward got over this problem. His stunning successes, his inspiring leadership and his conscious evocation of chivalry and nationalism, turned the English magnates into hawks. They wanted to fight in France – it had become something they were *supposed* to do. Indeed, Edward's successor, Richard II, found himself in the opposite position to most of his predecessors: he didn't want to fight in France but his barons pressurized him to do so. That's how influential Edward III's regal marketing strategy was. The Garter was all about warlike Englishness, but it also had a French motto just to underline Edward's claim to the French throne.

That motto, 'Honi soit qui mal y pense', usually translated as 'Shame on him who thinks evil of it', doesn't really mean much but, insofar as it means anything, is completely self-serving. It's basically 'We're great and, if you don't agree, you can fuck off' or possibly 'I'm King of France and, if you don't agree, you can fuck off and I may try to kill you.' It's wrapped round the royal coat of arms to this day, long outlasting the nonsensical fleurs-de-lis, so it's on all British passports, birth certificates, the adverts of any company with a royal warrant, the front pages of every edition of *The Times* and the *Daily Mail* and the walls of all courtrooms. As a piece of branding and image-making, it shits on any hashtag.

Even as this order was being founded, in the midst of English triumphs in France, something far more significant was happening that doesn't seem to find a place in Edward's narrative. Bubonic plague was sweeping the world. Emerging in Eurasia in about 1346 and spreading westwards with trade and rats, the Black Death, as it was known, condemned just under half the population to an excruciating death. And that was just the first wave.

It's worth taking a moment to contemplate what that means. Nearly half of everyone suddenly died. Or pretty suddenly. Over a few months to a year. And it wasn't just poor people, or just rich people, or just soldiers, or just children, or just men, or just women. It was every other person going all hot and screaming and covered in agonizing swellings, and then totally still and stinking.

They'd already had rough lives, these people, by our standards. Most of their kids died, just as standard, and people who made it to adulthood didn't live long. Random death was always a possibility. They were tough back then – life was viewed differently, valued differently. But even taking all that into account, the impact of the Black Death must still have been so terrible as to be almost surreal. It's probably the worst thing that has ever happened to humanity.

It must have driven everyone who was left alive absolutely mental with grief and post-traumatic stress. They seem weird, the people of the past, but for a few decades after the Black Death they've got a bloody good excuse because everyone, the whole of society, had just undergone a horrific experience on the level of being stuck in a particularly bad bit of the Battle of the Somme. Not as noisy, but even more deadly. It's impossible to understand how or why they coped.

Being human, a key coping mechanism was guilt – but a sort of arrogant self-aggrandizing guilt. 'This must be our fault,' everyone thought, in a maelstrom of self-loathing and self-involvement. God is angry with us and that's why this is happening. Aren't we careless, powerful fools?! Curse us for we have become too mighty!

I am thoroughly convinced by the overwhelming scientific evidence of humanity's role in climate change and the consequent need to inhabit the planet less impactfully. That fact is beyond doubt and those who do doubt it imperil our survival. Let me get that on record first. However, the only meaningful counterargument that could be made is that humanity *always* thinks it's responsible for everything. We always reckon it's about us. We love taking credit for things but, where no credit is available, we'll settle for blame rather than entertaining the horrendously humbling notion that something, anything at all, might have nothing to do with us.

The reason the climate-change deniers seldom make that potentially persuasive argument is that they're even more weak-mindedly obsessed with human significance than average, so their arguments are all based on conspiracies and secrets and other malevolent aspects of human agency. They're not up for the 'We had nothing to do with this' narrative at all — they just opt for a different pattern of blaming humans because they're delusional fuckwits who don't understand science.

The Black Death had nothing meaningful to do with humans. Human trade drove its spread, the close cohabitation of humans incentivized its emergence, but no person or people had done a stupid or sinful thing to cause it. It existed because we existed. I don't think you can blame humans any more than you can blame chickens for foxes. Still, I hope the solemn self-important guilt that people resorted to in their bewilderment and grief gave them some sort of comfort, some feeling of significance in the face of a bacterial tsunami for which they were no more than a fertile shore.

This happened at the core of Edward III's reign. In the middle of the first phase of what's going to be known as (spoiler alert) the Hundred Years' War. Under such circumstances, some people might forget about trying to be king of France. It might feel like it didn't really matter, like all those battles and slaughter were a bit hollow now half of everyone, both in England and France, had dropped down dead like it was the Rapture but smellier.

It spoils the glory, which isn't Edward III's fault. He didn't cause the Black Death and his government responded to it about as well as any. The Statute of Labourers of 1351 sought to control wages which, by the law of supply and demand, were sky-rocketing now so many people were dead. It feels a bit spiteful to deny poor survivors the pay rise that was the silver lining of the nation's infinite cloud of grief, but it stabilized the situation for the ruling class. Stability, peace and competence were hallmarks of Edward's domestic regime. He probably deserves more credit for that than for his showier but more ephemeral military successes.

Edward III had a bloody good go, an extremely bloody good go, at taking control of France. At his height, he was in charge of a similar area to Henry II but, unlike Henry II, he had taken the step of claiming that he ought to be in charge of all of it as the rightful king of France. In the Treaty of Brétigny of 1360, however, he temporarily dropped that claim, in exchange for holding all of his vast lands in full sovereignty, rather than having to pay homage, and for the vast amount of cash that was John II's ransom. By the end of his reign, Edward had reverted to saying he was king of France while controlling hardly any of it.

But the Black Death is such a reminder of mortality, of the futility of human endeavour, that it makes the grandiose enterprise of conquest, successful though it usually was during Edward's reign, seem dafter than ever – dafter than during Henry III's failed expeditions, dafter than when John or Edward I couldn't persuade any barons to come to France with him. All that dying makes you fall back on vacuous truisms: nothing matters more than health and family. Edward III had both, then he had neither.

Did he understand that? Possibly. He was no fool. Unlike his grandfather, he understood nuance. Chivalry, the notion of such honour in a murderous martial context, is a nuanced idea.

The Black Prince may have understood it too. This renowned warrior's tomb is in Canterbury Cathedral, where there is a bronze effigy of him in full armour, looking almost exactly like a Cyberman. In his will he asked for the following poem to be inscribed around it:

> Such as thou art, sometime was I.
> Such as I am, such shalt thou be.
> I thought little on th'our of Death
> So long as I enjoyed breath.

On earth I had great riches
Land, houses, great treasure, horses, money and gold.
But now a wretched captive am I,
Deep in the ground, lo here I lie.
My beauty great, is all quite gone,
My flesh is wasted to the bone.

In his slow decline from renown into sickness he must have realized that, when it comes to the human condition, glory only treats the symptoms.

25. King Richard II

It is a lamentable fact that the care system fails many of the children entrusted to it. A family environment needs to be exceptionally terrible – murderously, malevolently endangering – before a child isn't better off there than in care. It's a sad failure of the state and calls into question the extreme fastidiousness of the adoption process. Good luck adopting if you smoke, but the outcomes for children brought up in the households of smokers are far better than for those whose childhoods are spent in care. But the adoption system is not held accountable for the failings of the care system, only for the shortcomings of any parents they allow to adopt. It's the same principle as not allowing someone to get into your lifeboat because it has insufficient fire extinguishers.

Richard II was brought up in care and it fucked him up. I don't think John of Gaunt smoked – he'd have been ahead of his time – but the 'system' considered him an inappropriate influence on the young king. Parliament and the magnates jealously protected Richard from Gaunt and his other uncles, afraid of the power they might concentrate in their own hands if given control of the young king. As a result, the child was denied the consolations of family.

The previous king, his grandfather, also acceded to the throne as a minor and his home life was far from ideal – his mother was shagging an ex-con with whom she conspired to imprison and murder his father. This should have been a red flag for social services. But Edward, despite having his mother's lover executed, had a better upbringing than Richard and this may have been one of the reasons he was a far superior king.

One of the many strengths of Edward III's regime was that his own family, his wife and children, were close and loyal, so we must suspect loving. Unlike Henry II's sons, none of Edward III's ever rebelled even though he was greatly enfeebled for his last few years – Henry, conversely, had remained a competent and energetic king until his final weeks, but was run ragged by his own children's determination to supplant him. The sons of Edward who survived him, Gaunt plus Edmund of Langley and Thomas of Woodstock, weren't like that.

Nevertheless, when Richard became king at the age of ten, parliament and the magnates swerved any sort of official regency run by his uncles and pretended that Richard could exercise power for himself. He couldn't, but that was the pretence. He was nominally conducting affairs with the help of a series of 'continual councils' from which Gaunt was excluded.

From the start then, Richard was denied a replacement father figure but was surrounded by groups of older men who were eager to please him, and to exploit any influence they gained over him. The plan to stop Gaunt having too much influence may have succeeded, but it resulted in too much influence going to other men, most notably Michael de la Pole and Robert de Vere, whose power the magnates then feared and resented much more than that of Gaunt, who was at least a prince.

As well as this absence of a focal figure of guidance and love, the other destabilizing oddity of Richard's childhood was the crazy level of reverence with which he was treated. His coronation in 1377 was an eye- and ear-bruisingly splendid occasion – a vast and glittering ceremony emphasizing Plantagenet power and legitimacy and the new monarch's claim to divine favour. The underlying nuances and political expediency of the event will surely have been lost on the lonely boy at the centre of it. It must have felt, quite simply, like he was being worshipped. He knew he wasn't a god, by which I mean he knew that the word could not properly be applied to him, but he must have *felt* like a god. The way he was treated can't have been far off the experience enjoyed in ancient Rome by Caligula, who officially declared himself a god.

This isolated sense of divinity did not turn Richard into a team player. It was the very opposite of teaching him about the reality of kingship. None of the principles by which successful kings governed – even-handedness, predictability, immediate ruthlessness when required – were being conveyed to Richard. He was hearing only about his divine right. The absence of close family will have confirmed his feelings of singularity. No political common sense, no humility and no empathy were being instilled.

These people are revolting

Richard's greatest triumph happened early in his reign. It probably didn't do his damaged personality any good. I'm referring to his role in the Peasants' Revolt of 1381.

Everyone's pretty used to the idea that there was an event called the Peasants' Revolt in the middle ages. Even if you haven't heard of it, it sounds plausible. 'I'd revolt if I were a medieval peasant,' we say to ourselves with the self-confidence of people unafraid to complain about slow service in a Pizza Express. An uprising by the relentlessly shat-on rural poor sounds like the sort of thing that happens.

But it's not. It hasn't been happening so far. This isn't the nineteenth century. For 1381, this is remarkable and very different from the other disasters befalling medieval English governments. This violence and threat to the regime have nothing to do with either the magnates or the commons in parliament. It's much closer to an attempted popular revolution and, in history's eerie way of echoing and foreshadowing itself, it has striking similarities with events that feel pretty modern, like the French and Russian revolutions.

'When Adam delved and Eve span, who was then the gentleman?' That little rhyme is from a sermon given by one of the revolt's leaders, John Ball, a priest who had been disgraced and imprisoned for his egalitarian views. It's a haunting couplet, its ghostliness coming not from Ball's past, but from his future – an ethereal notion moving back through time and settling in the clergyman's mind. I like the way the rhyme makes you stress the last syllable of 'gentle*man*' in a subtly contemptuous way.

'From the beginning all men by nature were created alike, and our bondage or servitude came in by the unjust oppression of naughty men,' the sermon continued. The idea that no person is fundamentally better than anyone else, plus the implication that the Bible and Christianity are rooted in that principle, feels anachronistic. Most of the kings we've looked at in this book wouldn't even understand the concept. It was absolutely not the way Richard II had been brought up to think. People were not considered to be, in any sense, all the same.

The revolt was sparked off by the enormously unpopular poll tax. You may be familiar with this phrase from Margaret Thatcher's late 1980s/early 1990s version, which I mentioned earlier and was officially called the community charge. By the end, though, not even government ministers were calling it that. The poll tax label stuck and it wasn't meant as a compliment.

It was an insult in Thatcher's time, partly because of the precedent of the disastrous fourteenth-century version and partly because of what the nickname implied. 'Poll' is an old word for head and a modern word for vote. Either way, that makes it a tax on people's existence and rights as a citizen. In both twentieth- and fourteenth-century incarnations, it was a tax that everyone had to pay, and everyone had to pay the same amount. This wasn't the type of egalitarianism John Ball had in mind. These days, those who believe in that sort of equality tend to favour the free availability of guns over the free availability of health care.

In the 1380s, no one believed in either. This poll tax was first raised by parliament just before Edward III's death in an attempt to pay for the war in France. It was payable by everyone over the age of fourteen, no matter how impoverished, at the rate of 4 pence per person. This trivial payment for the rich was an intolerable burden on the poor. When a third poll tax started to be collected in 1381, it caused a huge uprising in Kent and Essex led by, among others, Ball and a man called Wat Tyler.

While the poll tax was the immediate cause of the insurrection, there was something else going on. The Black Death had changed the economic structure of rural England. Despite the government's attempt, in the Statute of Labourers, to control wages, the deeper law of supply and demand meant that the financial prospects of rural workers were much better than they had been before half of the population carked it. Yet the ruling class was determined to restrict wages, keep serfs tied to the land and even, through the 'sumptuary laws', to prevent affluent peasants from buying clothing too lavish for their social station. It was this more well-to-do and ambitious peasantry who led the revolt, frustrated by the attempts of the government, through local justices of the peace, to keep them in their place.

It's telling that among the rebels' first targets were places where government and tax records were kept. They sensed instinctively that, in trying to collect and hold information about ordinary people – what nowadays we'd call their data – someone powerful was depriving them of something. It's an instinct we do well to listen to when going online. The whole 'if you've got nothing to hide, you've got nothing to fear' approach to private information is predicated on state power being held in honest and ethical hands. That's not always the case – it certainly wasn't in 1381 – and, as a general rule, trusting the state doesn't make it more trustworthy.

After assembling in the home counties, huge numbers of the rebels marched on London where they nearly overthrew the Plantagenet regime. The Tower of London was stormed, John of Gaunt's Savoy Palace on the Strand was burned down and many important people were lynched, most notably Simon Sudbury, who was both archbishop of Canterbury and chancellor of England, and Robert Hales, the Lord High Treasurer. John of Gaunt himself was out of town, in the north of England, but his teenage son Henry Bolingbroke, of whom we'll hear much more later, escaped the rebels only by hiding in a cupboard.

It was clear to the boy king that all the grown-ups were losing their heads, either metaphorically or literally. The power and rage of the revolt was something the magnates around him didn't know what to do about. There weren't anywhere near enough royal troops in London to deal with the rebels, so the king had to go and meet them and listen to their demands. It was at this point that his weird upbringing and personality came to the fore. Most children would have been frightened under such circumstances, but Richard had been brought up to believe that there was something special about him that no one else in the country possessed.

This belief is probably why, when Richard met the rebels at Smithfield on 15 June, he saved the day. When the royal party arrived, Wat Tyler came over and addressed Richard with scandalous familiarity, calling him 'brother'. By this point in the crisis, some groups of rebels had dispersed in response to the government's agreeing to all of their demands, so Richard asked Tyler why he and his followers had not done the same. Tyler replied angrily to this and demanded refreshment, which was duly provided.

Next, an argument broke out between him and some of the royal entourage – the details are lost in the mists of time, obviously – but it culminated in Tyler being stabbed by the Mayor of London. He was mortally wounded, but not actually dead, and seemed very likely to cry treachery and call on his followers to attack the Plantagenet party. This was Richard's moment: he spurred his horse and rode towards the crowd declaring, 'I am your captain, follow me!' They did. And that sorted out the Peasants' Revolt, basically. He was fourteen years old.

It was extremely brave and well timed and was the most successful moment of Richard's entire life. Part of the reason it worked was that the rebels were opposed not to kingship but to the class system. They didn't like the notion of gentlemen, they were suspicious of royal advisers and taxation, but they believed in monarchy. They considered themselves 'the true commons' who had been kept away from their noble and rightful king by his dishonest advisers. They bought into the notion of Richard's righteous leadership as much as the poor addle-headed young king did himself. That was the one aspect of the regime that the peasants didn't question.

His majesty?

In the end, the magnates did question it, though. Over the next few years, they questioned it like they'd never questioned it before. And, having questioned it, it couldn't be unquestioned again. The process that England underwent in the last decade and a half of Richard's reign fundamentally weakened the institution of monarchy.

That sounds like good news, doesn't it? It's a bit shit, the institution of monarchy. It's not fair. Some guy gets to be in charge of everything just because of who his dad was. It's not a good system. But it is a system of some sort. It's not anarchy. Richard is in charge and that's that. One day he'll die but until then he's king – we know where we are and we can work on a coping strategy.

Up to this point, it's all been about the coping strategies. Those august foundation stones of the great British tradition of liberty, Magna Carta and parliament, are methods for dealing with kings who turn out to be arseholes or idiots. And while nobody designed this system, it does make a certain amount of sense: accept who the king is but rein him in so he can't screw things up too badly.

The long-lasting and widespread literary genre of 'Mirrors for Princes' was another approach to this problem. Its most famous example is *The Prince* by Niccolò Machiavelli, written in the early sixteenth century, but it had been going for over a millennium by then and there are dozens of these self-help guides for rulers, obsequious and patronizing in equal measure. The flaw in this approach, obviously, is that the monarchs most in need of instruction are often those least aware of the fact and so least likely to read an instructional manual.

Nevertheless, accepting who the king is and, crucially, who the king is going to be – gripping the notion of primogeniture ever more tightly – is a good way of maximizing stability. It means you don't really need to have a civil war *every* time a king dies, on top of all the civil wars you're having anyway. The idea is: you stop things like the Stephen and Matilda situation with a totally inflexible and preordained line of succession, and you stop things like the King John situation with Magna Carta and parliament. Both kinds of mega-crisis are precluded.

But if you *don't* unquestioningly accept who the king is, everything gets a bit wobbly. There's a frightening new potential coping strategy: change kings. That's sort of been tried once before when Edward II was made to abdicate, but the next king was his eldest son, so it wasn't fully stress-tested. The new king's accession was hastened, no more. The certainty of succession was maintained.

When the magnates got rid of Richard – and, as you are probably inferring, they are going to get rid of him – and he didn't have a son, and someone else became king . . . well, suddenly the position of that king, and every other king for ever, is weaker. Kings can be got rid of. But there's no system in place for how that's done, or who gets to be the new king. As a result, English history in the fifteenth century is an absolute shitstorm. There's no way that it wouldn't have been better all round if they'd stuck with crappy Richard until he died.

They could always have just murdered him. That would probably have gone better, for everyone except Richard – and not significantly worse for him. He ended up getting murdered anyway, just not until after he had been deposed. Yes, he was deposed. The magnates tried to do it by the book. But the book didn't exist. They were writing the book as they went along. All the previous books said: he's the king, deal with it.

Unfortunately Richard made it very difficult for the magnates to deal with it. He was awful. Feeble, petulant and narcissistic. Then, in the last few years of his reign, lethally vengeful.

He was intensely status-conscious – he was the first English king to insist on being addressed as 'your majesty', in emulation of the more twatty French court. And he was quick to fall into contemptuous rages – another bloody 'inheritor of the Plantagenet temper' – once declaring to a parliament that wanted to change his circle of ministers and advisers that he wouldn't dismiss one scullion from his kitchen at their request ('scullion' is an archaic term for a 'McJob'). Obviously, the commons didn't give a shit who his scullions were. At that point (1386) they wanted him to sack his chancellor, Michael de la Pole, and dismiss his favourite, Robert de Vere, whom Richard, in an act of magnate-baiting largesse, had just made duke of Ireland.

Duke of Ireland? Seriously?! That's like earl of Greece or marquess of America. It sounds made up. And of course it is, as are all aristocratic titles. The trouble with this one is that it had only *just* been made up and it's pretty clear what the agenda was. Duke was the highest noble title – it had only started being used in England by Edward III, also in emulation of the French, and ranked higher than earl and baron. And Ireland is bigger than the other places people tended to be dukes or earls or somethings of. They're usually locations on the scale of Warwick or York, maybe Sussex or Cornwall at most. Ireland is an altogether bigger entity. The lack of proportionality in the title inflamed the magnates' fear that Richard had lost his sense of proportion about the merits of Robert de Vere.

It had unfortunate echoes of when Edward II, just under a century of aristocratic titular inflation earlier, made Piers Gaveston the earl of Cornwall. Richard was fond of the memory of Edward II and tried to get him canonized. The notion that that idiot was in any way saintly is so absurd as to make Edward the Confessor seem momentarily worthy of the status. This enthusiasm of Richard's was another worrying sign that he didn't get what it took to be an effective king.

His court was magnificent. He and his queen, Anne of Bohemia, to whom he was devoted, wanted everything to be opulent and intellectual and what today we'd probably call bohemian in a way that has no connection with Anne, who just happened to have been born in what is now the Czech Republic. They invested lavishly in jewellery, fine textiles, metalwork, art and crazy clothes. Westminster Hall was redeveloped with fifteen life-size statues of kings and a hammerbeam roof which remains amazing to behold, and the royal palaces were made sumptuous.

Plus there were emerging writers in the English language at this time – Geoffrey Chaucer, John Gower and William Langland are the most prominent. They're often referred to as the Ricardian poets, in a rare positive note from posterity about this king. It's ironic because Richard doesn't seem to have been that into poetry, though Gower's 33,000-line *Confessio Amantis* says in its prologue that Richard commissioned it. Doesn't say he read it, mind you. But I can't talk. I haven't read a single syllable of any of those writers' work and certainly won't until I've watched the box set of *The Sopranos* that has been gathering dust in my possession for a decade and a half. Still, it's good to have writers and the fact that their works aren't exactly easy-reading to the modern eye doesn't mean they weren't great, nor that the advance in English vernacular culture wasn't significant.

So the lovely court, in itself, wasn't a problem (except that it was expensive and Richard utterly lost his shit when asked to account for his expenditure). A magnificent court can be a good way for a monarch to demonstrate and increase their power. Louis XIV of France created a dazzling court in Versailles which meant that all his major noblemen were right there, under his thumb, not interfering with the actual government of the country. Louis used display and fashion cannily as a way of uniting people behind his rule, and of making foreign regimes fear and respect him as a figure of intimidating grandeur.

Richard had no such political strategy in mind, however, and his expensive court was just prissy and alienating to the powerful men of the realm. A good example of this is the Wilton Diptych, a work of art Richard commissioned towards the end of his reign. It shows how he wanted to project himself to other people and posterity. It's a picture of three saints – the patron saints of England, St Edward the Confessor (grrr) and St Edmund (as in Bury St Edmunds – the martyred king), plus St John the Baptist – presenting a piously kneeling Richard to Mary and Baby Jesus, who are surrounded by angels all wearing Richard's badge, which was a white hart with a golden crown round its neck and a golden chain.

It's very pretty, but it's not how Edward III or Henry II put themselves across. It fails in two ways: in one sense, it makes Richard look a bit pathetic. For a king with no martial inclination, it serves only to reinforce his critics' view that he was a soft-skinned weakling. He looks small and slight and childlike – very odd self-presentation for a time when going to war was seen as the monarch's primary duty.

But, in another sense, he looks like a megalomaniac, with three saints hanging out with him, Jesus and Mary apparently thrilled to meet him and, astonishingly, an angelic host already wearing his branding. If you went into the office of the CEO of, say, Adidas and there was a big picture of him (or her – but it'll be him) accompanied by some saints, meeting some angels, and they're *all wearing Adidas-branded gear*, then you'd make a mental note that the guy was tyrannical and tasteless in equal measure, and expect a scandal about the dysfunctional working environment in the upper echelons of the Adidas corporation to break any day.

Total eclipse of the hart

In Richard's reign, a scandal like that broke twice – in 1386 and 1399 – and both times it resulted in a small civil war. In between those little wars, there was a period of competent government, which is boring so I won't dwell on it.

By the end of 1386, Richard's ineffectual and militarily unaggressive regime was causing consternation. The teenage king hadn't done anything brave since the Peasants' Revolt. As noted, Edward III's dashing reign had put an end to the magnates' disinclination to fight expensive wars in France. On the contrary, it was now something they felt English kings absolutely ought to do. King Richard disagreed.

In his early reign there'd been an unsuccessful attack on Flanders led, bizarrely, by the Bishop of Norwich, and then a fruitless expedition to Scotland, led by Richard himself, which had resulted in the king falling out with John of Gaunt. Gaunt had then left the country in high dudgeon to go and try to become king of Castile. Meanwhile, the French were threatening to invade. This crisis, coupled with the general dissatisfaction with Richard's circle of favourites and advisers, led to the emergence of a group known as the Lords Appellant.

There were five of these lords, namely Thomas of Woodstock, who was Duke of Gloucester, a brother of Gaunt, uncle of Richard and son of Edward III, plus the earls of Arundel, Warwick, Nottingham and Derby. This last earl was Henry Bolingbroke, son of John of Gaunt and hide-and-seek champion of the Peasants' Revolt. The word 'Appellant' is Norman French and meant 'one who is appealing'. Richard, however, found them unappealing because what they were appealing for was the prosecution of his ministers for treason.

The Appellants took control, imposing a commission on the king at the so-called Wonderful Parliament of 1386. Richard found this humiliating and initially refused to attend parliament at all, railing against his disobedient subjects and, according to some reports, threatening to seek help from his cousin the King of France. This was an incredibly dickish thing to say. England had been at war with France for decades and the French seemed about to invade. The King of England turning round and saying that he'd be in favour of that because his French counterpart was a relative, and he'd rather submit to a posh cousin than a bunch of uppity oiks, is a level of faux pas even Donald Trump couldn't get away with.

In the end Richard came to parliament and submitted to the commission with very bad grace. But he was soon fighting back, touring the country to drum up support, establishing a personal power base in Cheshire and getting some lawyers to say that the Appellants were treasonous. This led to a very short civil war, in December 1387, in which Robert de Vere raised a pro-Richard army in Cheshire and marched it south to be defeated at the Battle of Radcot Bridge by the earls of Nottingham and Derby.

The Appellants were more in charge than ever and, at the Merciless Parliament of 1388, purged the king's administration, condemning Richard's most senior ministers to death – this included de Vere and de la Pole, but they had fled to France so escaped execution. This might have been exciting if they hadn't both died quite soon thanks to medieval Europe's narratively insensitive mortality rate.

The king was now a puppet of the Appellants. This, he must have thought, is the lowest ebb of my entire reign. It turned out to be the second lowest. The lowest came in the summer of 1399 when Henry Bolingbroke (who by this time was duke of Lancaster as well as earl of Derby because John of Gaunt had just died), landed with a small army on the Humber estuary and took over England pretty much unopposed. This was a sign of how unpopular Richard had made himself.

For much of the previous decade, Richard had seemed like a reformed king. He still wanted peace not war, and fancied himself High Majestic Ruler of the Universe as well as the most holy little slip of a boy in Christendom, but he ran a competent government from when John of Gaunt returned in 1389 until the late 1390s.

However, his confidence was growing, which did him no

good. Then, in 1394, his beloved wife died, which also did him no good. He became increasingly obsessed with his power base in Cheshire, which he ran like a private sub-kingdom, and by vengeance against the Appellants.

In September 1397 Richard orchestrated a very dodgy parliament. It was held under the armed guard of Richard's Cheshire archers, had a cravenly pro-Ricardian speaker, Sir John Bussy, and was seemingly packed with loyalists – or at least those who were put in quite a loyal mood by having a bow and arrow pointed at them. It swiftly accused three of the Appellants of treason: Arundel was executed, Warwick begged not to be executed and was dispossessed of his estates and imprisoned, and Gloucester, the king's uncle who had been imprisoned in Calais, was murdered before he could even get to parliament. This was by order of the fourth Appellant, Thomas de Mowbray Earl of Nottingham, who had defected to Richard's side. He was made duke of Norfolk a few days later.

It's all gone a bit Stalin. There are two of the Appellants left standing – Mowbray, who had murdered Gloucester to show his loyalty, and Bolingbroke, who was John of Gaunt's son. They didn't feel safe and, in 1398, this very fact apparently became the subject of a quarrel between them, though we only have Bolingbroke's subsequent account of what was said.

According to Bolingbroke, Mowbray warned that the king's pardons for their role as Appellants were worthless and that he was going to turn on them, while Bolingbroke declared that Richard would not break his word like that. This strikes me as an implausible conversation, particularly Bolingbroke's part in it. Mowbray's fears are pretty obviously justified and Bolingbroke's response either naive or insincere.

Nevertheless the quarrel was genuine and could not be resolved by parliament. Richard, thrilling to the tyrannical power of it, declared that the two of them must settle their differences in a trial by combat. Then, just as the joust was beginning, he halted the proceedings and exiled them both, Mowbray for life and Bolingbroke for ten years. As it turns out, Mowbray's was the shorter sentence; he died of plague in September 1399. Although, as it also turns out, Mowbray was still in exile for longer because, by the time he died, Bolingbroke had returned to England and taken over the country.

Richard was in Ireland when this happened, which was stupid of him. By the time he got back to England in July, he had no choice but to submit to his cousin. Bolingbroke had nominally come to England purely to claim his Lancastrian inheritance, which Richard had unwisely confiscated, but his ambitions were growing fast.

Nobody liked Richard and everyone liked Bolingbroke. He was the son of John of Gaunt, a great figure of stability for many years. He was pious and brave, he had fought a crusade in Lithuania and been on a pilgrimage to the Holy Land. He was of royal stock and martial inclination. Also, he had the support of the magnates, particularly the powerful Percy family, the earls of Northumberland. Despite having sworn that he had no intention of taking the throne, Henry Bolingbroke had every intention of taking the throne.

A parliament of September 1399 made it so. Richard was taken to Pontefract Castle and, on 13 October, the feast day of St Edward the Confessor (in your face, Richard!), Henry, Duke of Lancaster, was crowned King Henry IV. What could possibly go wrong?

PART FOUR
Everything's Coming Up Roses

26. King Henry IV

Everyone would have been delighted by Henry if only he'd been the rightful king. He had all the qualities the magnates and commons were looking for in a ruler, except the one that would have qualified him for the job: being next in the order of succession when the previous king died. The previous king hadn't died and, even if he had, Henry wasn't next in the order of succession. Or probably not, anyway.

I mean, he might have been. It depends how you look at it. 'Strange women lying in ponds distributing swords is no basis for a system of government,' it says in *Monty Python and the Holy Grail*. Well, neither is 'it depends how you look at it'. Once a line of succession becomes open to different interpretations, it has ceased to function. That's what Edward III did to the French line of succession in the first half of the fourteenth century and, as a result, France spent most of the next hundred years hosting a war – an even more costly and dispiriting event to host than Eurovision.

Henry's claim to be next in line after Richard II was based on his being the eldest son of Edward III's fourth son. Richard was the only surviving son of Edward's eldest son, but he had no children. Then there was Edward's second son, who died in infancy. So far so good. Henry's problem was that Edward's third son, Lionel, Duke of Clarence, who was long dead himself, had a surviving male descendant, Edmund Mortimer, 5th Earl of March.

Edmund was only seven years old, and was Lionel's daughter's grandson, so descended partly via the female line. But, since he was male, and Lionel was born before John of Gaunt, this little boy had a strong claim to the throne. In summary, Edmund would have inherited under common law, but Henry was the rightful heir under what's known as Salic law, the even more sexist regal inheritance system favoured on the continent. (This was the law that undermined Edward III's claim to the French throne, on the principle that if, being female, you don't have the right to inherit, you can't pass on that right, even to your male heir. While observing this rule in asserting his rights in England, Henry, like his predecessors and successors, conveniently forgot it when saying he was the rightful king of France.)

The small earl posed no immediate threat – though Henry put him and his brother into a sort of genteel imprisonment, just to be on the safe side. Neither did the man he grew into, who became a loyal retainer of the next king, Henry's son Henry. But Edmund's sister, Anne, later married a descendant of Edward III's fifth son, the Duke of York, strengthening the monarchical hopes of that line, if not its genes. The foundations of several dynastic claims were being spread like fragments of asbestos in the lungs of the body politic.

What Henry really needed, as his reign started, were some strong signs of divine favour. Everyone was worrying about what God thought about the whole deposition thing. Kings ruled by divine right – they were crowned and anointed but also, via the line of succession, God was deemed to have selected them. God had very clearly selected Richard II – his claim to the throne was unquestionable. Was God going to be cross that He'd been overruled? Or was God cross with Richard for being so shit? The nation anxiously awaited the answer. A few signs that God was okay with Henry being king would be very welcome.

I knew I shouldn't have believed him

Such signs were not forthcoming. Just a few weeks after the coronation, in January 1400, a group of senior supporters of Richard tried to seize the king and his son in order to murder them and restore Richard to the throne. Known as the Epiphany Rising, because it coincided with the Feast of the Epiphany at the end of Christmas, the attempt failed, but it cast into doubt Henry's policy of comparative leniency to the Ricardian camp. Henry did a swift U-turn on this and had Richard starved to death by Valentine's Day. This rather undermined any goodwill that his former approach may have garnered.

It clearly wasn't safe for Henry to tolerate a more rightful king remaining alive in the kingdom and, to make the point that this state of affairs had changed irreversibly, Henry had Richard's body displayed in St Paul's Cathedral on 17 February. Despite this, rumours that Richard wasn't dead persisted throughout Henry's reign.

In 1400 there was a harvest failure, and in fact there were four others in the thirteen and a half years of his reign. In these pious times, this was seen as a sign of divine displeasure and it caused widespread discontent and unrest. Henry exacerbated this situation with taxation, despite having promised to run the country using his royal revenues only.

This was a silly promise to make which, if he'd had more political experience, he would have known he'd be unable to keep. It wouldn't have helped matters for him to explain that the reason for his inexperience of the heart of government, compared to many of his royal predecessors, was that he was a usurper rather than the previous king's son.

There were lots of rebellions, most notably led by the

Percy family, whose influence had been instrumental in getting Henry the throne. As a result, they expected to be the power behind it and reacted violently to Henry's unwillingness to give them everything they wanted. There was also a long-running rebellion in Wales, led by Owen Glendower, who had himself crowned prince of Wales, the first non-Plantagenet to do so for over a century.

The reign was going terribly. Henry was perhaps the first victim in English history of the now familiar phenomenon of public opinion being disappointed by a newly elected government. When a new party is swept to power on a huge wave of fragile optimism and then faces the predictable setbacks of actually having to govern rather than just talk about it, there's a peculiar bitterness to the nation's disappointment. It's peculiar because it's tied in with self-loathing. We blame ourselves for our naivety. 'We might have known.' 'We should have known.' 'We fell for it.'

The political nation of England – from the major magnates down to those with a small measure of local influence – had consented to Henry's usurpation. They'd been in favour. He was such a golden boy of the 1390s and Richard was awful. Their anger and disappointment seem to follow the inevitable sine wave of the mood swing. When things didn't pan out perfectly, when the new king made mistakes, and perhaps even more when he was unlucky, they shook their heads and muttered 'Of course'. They felt stupid and guilty for dispensing with the long-held principle of sticking with the anointed king.

It's a bit bleak. Henry had long acrimonious parliaments in which he appealed for money and got slagged off. His court was dull and pious. He said he was going to go and fight in France, like everyone now thought English kings were supposed to, and had made Edward III seem cool even in the face of millions dropping dead covered in buboes. But he never did it. He fought only at home, against other Englishmen and the Welsh.

One of the few positive, non-reactive moves of his reign was an act of parliament that ordered all heretics to be burned. It hardly elevates the mood. This was a response to the rise of the Lollard movement, which was like an early form of Protestantism: they wanted a vernacular bible, they didn't believe in transubstantiation and, in 1395, they even nailed their beliefs to a church door, though this was in Westminster not Wittenberg. They were often followers of John Wycliffe, an English priest and academic who had translated the Bible into English and of whom Henry's father John of Gaunt had been an admirer. But Gaunt was dead and now Henry wanted all Wycliffe's other admirers to die too.

Henry was sincerely pious, but drawing attention to that quality by ordering some burnings was a canny move. It kept the church onside, which was particularly important when people suspected that God might not be. Henry and Thomas Arundel, the Archbishop of Canterbury, were very close and Arundel had supported the usurpation. In contrast, Henry's relationship with the Archbishop of York, Richard le Scrope, culminated in the latter's execution. Scrope had taken part in the second Percy rising against Henry.

Despite all this grimness and crisis, Henry's regime was not overthrown. It continued. He weathered every storm, suppressed every rebellion, got through every parliament. It's tempting to call him a survivor, except he didn't survive. He suffered serious and deteriorating health problems from 1405 onwards and died in 1413 at the age of forty-five. But he died as king of England and was more secure on his throne at his death than at any other time in his reign.

His poor health was also taken as a sign of divine displeasure. In particular a skin disease, which may have been leprosy, was linked to his having killed an archbishop. Skin problems aside, he had several acute attacks of illness, which may have been cardiovascular or even epileptic – it isn't really known. But it was clear that he wasn't going to make old bones and, paradoxically, this had a stabilizing effect. There was no need to get rid of him – God was doing that anyway – and his son, Henry the Prince of Wales, Prince Hal of Shakespearean fame, was accepted as the heir and relatively untarnished by involvement in the usurpation.

Things got more stable, but no less bleak: a glum court surrounding a king beset by horrible skin problems and persistent life-threatening fits or attacks, figuring they might as well let him die with his crown on. Henry's opening speech in Shakespeare's first play set during the reign encapsulates the man's tiredness and fading hope.

> So shaken as we are, so wan with care,
> Find we a time for frighted peace to pant,
> And breathe short-winded accents of new broils
> To be commenced in strands afar remote.

He had promised to fight in France. He had dreamed of going back on crusade, back to Jerusalem. It never happened. In a final weak joke from God, Henry died in the Jerusalem Chamber of the abbot's house at Westminster. The new broils in strands afar remote were left to his son.

27. King Henry V

Henry V is pretty similar to Edward III. They were both sensationally militarily successful, mainly in France. They were both outwardly chivalrous but with a thick streak of military brutality when required. They both promoted English national feeling through success in war abroad. They both encouraged use of the English language and hastened its journey to become the language of all classes. They both used their military success to dazzle the magnates and commons back home so that they caused very little trouble and provided lots of money for more fighting. And they both insisted that they were the rightful king of France. This was even cheekier of Henry than it had been of Edward because, looked at a certain way, he wasn't even the rightful king of England.

The key difference between them is that Henry achieved a fair bit more in the French war than Edward did, and he achieved it in under ten years while Edward took over fifty.

Henry probably needed it more. He has presented himself to posterity as a glorious leader, brave, pious, honest and successful, a uniter of the nation and a provoker of intense loyalty in his followers – and these things are pretty much true about him. But his energetic projection of those qualities was also a diversionary tactic. He was distracting everyone from the weakness of his dynastic claim.

His father had usurped the throne – the Plantagenet line, stretching back to Henry II, had been broken. Henry IV and Henry V are considered to be from the House of Lancaster, which is merely a 'cadet branch' of the House of Plantagenet.

This was a much weaker dynastic position than that of any English king since Stephen, and a very similar one to the kings of France who, since Charles IV died in 1328, had all been from the House of Valois, a cadet branch of the ancient House of Capet. The weakness of that Valois claim was the basis of Edward III's assertion that he was the rightful king of France, rather than any of the various men who were actually king of France.

Henry had been heavily involved in government in the second half of his father's reign because of Henry IV's recurrent bouts of illness. He remembered the rebellions well and, as a teenager, had been wounded at the Battle of Shrewsbury when an arrow hit him in the face. This is said to be why the famous portrait of him is in profile, though it offers no explanation of his horrible choice of hairdo. All in all, he was well aware of how fragile his family's grip on the throne had been. Turning the regime outwards, taking the fight to France, was his technique for making everyone forget about all that grubbiness with Richard II starving to death and the recurrent rows in parliament and fights with the Percies.

First he sought to defuse as many festering resentments about the Lancastrian usurpation as possible. He started the reign pardoning a load of enemies of his father, returning titles that had been stripped from families in the wake of various rebellions and having Richard II's remains taken from King's Langley where Henry IV had stuck them, ignominiously near those of the reviled Piers Gaveston, and reinterring them in the tomb Richard had designed for himself at Westminster, where his beloved first wife was already buried. This last move provided another opportunity to proclaim, 'Look, Richard really is dead!' to the hard core of conspiracy theorists still eager to follow any old tramp in a gold hat willing to proclaim himself to be the former king.

35. (*Left*) A nice one of Hugh Despenser the Younger being executed. We've missed his genitals being cut off but join the action just in time to catch his heart being plucked out and thrown in the fire.

36 and 37. Battle of Bannockburn: This nineteenth-century engraving (*below*) shows Robert the Bruce addressing his troops while some of them don't listen. He still wins, though, so in 1877 this monument (*right*) is erected.

38. An unrealistic depiction of the Battle of Crécy, which makes it look like the Mexican stand-off in *Reservoir Dogs*.

39. Edward III looking old and worried, possibly because this illustration is from the 1440s, by which time his great-great-grandson Henry VI was making a monumental hash of everything.

40. The Bubonic Plague from a fifteenth-century illustration. Apologies for being a plague nerd but, if this is meant to be the Black Death, they've put the buboes in the wrong places.

41. The Peasants' Revolt. The man on the horse is John Ball, the preacher who was executed because of his egalitarian views. This was terribly unjust. They should have killed him for wearing that hat.

42. (*Left*) This is the earliest-known contemporary portrait of an English monarch. What a shame that it's of the dreadful Richard II.

43. (*Below*) This is supposedly a picture of parliament replacing Richard II with Henry IV. To be fair, I wouldn't be able to draw that either.

44. *The Wilton Diptych.* Bearing in mind what happened to Richard II, this makes Jesus look like a bit of a fair-weather friend.

46. Joan of Arc. She's a saint now, which I hope in some way makes up for having been burned to death.

45. Henry V looking incredibly creepy. I once stayed in a Malmaison hotel with that wallpaper.

47. The Battle of Agincourt inexplicably depicted with roughly equal numbers of archers on each side, which is like depicting Goliath wielding a sling.

48. Henry VI, a kindly prat who caused chaos.

49. Edward IV, a capable leader when he wasn't being led around by his penis or stomach.

50. The court of King Henry VI and Queen Margaret on a day when Henry wasn't in inert-blob mode.

51. Richard III. The Tudors said he was awful. Coincidentally he was probably awful.

52. The Princes in the Tower, worrying about getting murdered for their amazing hair.

53. Henry 'the VII' Tudor. Basically a normal member of the public who somehow managed to make himself king.

55. Mary I. She was the first proper female sovereign of England and yet, for various reasons, most of them incinerated Protestants, she has not been adopted as a feminist icon.

54. Henry VIII. Not a normal member of the public, by any means. What a difference a generation makes.

56. Elizabeth I. That's more like it! They should get a stand for that globe and then she wouldn't have to keep her hand on it to stop it rolling off the table.

Agincourporate manslaughter

Henry V's most famous triumph was his victory at the Battle of Agincourt on 25 October 1415. This is the last of the big three battles of the Hundred Years' War – Crécy and Poitiers are the other two – in which vastly outnumbered English armies thrash the French, and the most famous thanks to Shakespeare's play *Henry V*, of which it forms the climax.

I used to find these victories very enjoyable and now I don't so much. Does that make me a better person or just a curmudgeon? I'm not sure the fact that I can no longer summon any jingoistic glee from a medieval battle is much help to the thousands of Frenchmen who were once slaughtered as a result of their leaders' colossal strategic miscalculations. My sincere hope is that you can still get some fun out of it and it hasn't all been spoiled by empathy and Brexit.

Henry had landed in Normandy the previous August and spent weeks laying siege to the fortress of Harfleur (not to be confused with Barfleur, from which the *White Ship* set sail 205 years earlier – that's at the other end of Normandy. There's also an Honfleur near Harfleur, but no Bonfleur near Barfleur, so it's no use thinking there's a system). The siege involved the earliest use of cannon by an English army, which damaged the town's walls, but the weapon that clinched the encounter was surrounding the place and waiting. It surrendered on 22 September, Henry garrisoned the town, noted that quite a bit of his army had died of dysentery and wondered what to do next. It must have seemed that he'd gone to an enormous effort to little effect.

He resolved to march to Calais, already an English possession, in the hope of negatively impacting the lives of a lot of ordinary French people on the way, but also of not being engaged by a much larger French army. This latter hope turned out to be futile, hence the Battle of Agincourt.

The French army numbered between 15,000 and 25,000 men, mostly heavily armoured cavalry, and the English was between 6,000 and 8,000, mostly longbowmen. It had rained the night before; the ploughed land was wet and boggy and provided the perfect conditions for the French to move slowly so the English could shoot at them. It would also have been ideal for long-exposure photography of the French advance if only the technology had existed but, as discussed, we're still in an era when waiting was more deadly than guns.

So the French advanced more slowly than they would have liked and were relentlessly shot at. Lots of horses were hit and started rearing and panicking and trampling. Meanwhile other knights were trying to advance from the rear, pushing the broiling death-melee towards the English archers, who were protected by stakes that had been driven into the ground and were free to keep shooting. The whole thing turned into an abattoir, albeit quite a labour-intensive and unhygienic one.

Thousands of Frenchmen were killed, as against a few hundred Englishmen, and thousands more were taken prisoner. Many of these were slaughtered after the battle when Henry got nervous that the French reserves might renew the fight against his still-outnumbered force. This is an excellent example of Henry's selectivity when it came to being chivalrous.

Perhaps the most important consequence was this: among the dead were a lot of very important Frenchmen – and many of the bigwigs who survived were taken away and usually ransomed. Not always, though; Charles Duke of Orleans remained a prisoner in England for twenty-five years. The battle weakened France much more deeply than one lost battle would suggest. After Agincourt, Henry was in a hugely stronger geopolitical position than when his exhausted, diseased and outnumbered force had been hammering stakes into the ground in the rain on the night of 24 October.

Burgundy and Armagnac don't mix

Even before Agincourt, France was in a terrible state. King Charles VI, who had been reigning since 1380, was severely mentally ill. He'd acceded to the throne as a child but started to have acute episodes of mental incompetence a few years after beginning his personal rule. This prompted a struggle for power among the major players at court, which resulted in a civil war at the end of which Charles was left a pitiful and befuddled figure, cared for only by his wife, and whose son had been disinherited. His grandson was Henry VI, the next king of England, and the reason I've written this potted biography of Charles is that Henry VI's life story turned out to be almost identical.

That's England in the middle of the century – back to France at the start. Charles's issues were the kind that put the stigma into mental illness that nowadays everyone's trying to remove. 'People who are suffering with their mental health aren't running around screaming with their clothes off, shitting themselves, refusing to wash, not knowing who they are or who other people are, or thinking they're someone they're not!' Well, Charles VI was. The only stereotypical symptom of insanity Charles didn't suffer from was thinking he was the king of France. On the few occasions he thought that, it meant he was having a good day. Instead, he spent long periods thinking he was made of glass and behaving with neurotic caution in case he shattered.

These delusional problems for the king caused severe real ones for the large country of which he was the absolute ruler. For long periods government had to be handled by a regency council, presided over by his wife Queen Isabeau but fought over by two groups of princes and aristocrats: the Burgundians, led by the Duke of Burgundy, and the Armagnacs, led initially by Louis, Duke of Orleans until he was murdered in 1307 (he was the father of Duke Charles who was captured at Agincourt), and then by the Count of Armagnac.

The murder of Duke Louis was what turned a lot of interpersonal unpleasantness into a lot of interpersonal unpleasantness involving soldiers. Civil war in France was pretty good news for the kings of England. While Henry IV just used the time for frighted peace to pant, his son saw it as the perfect context for a new broil. He invaded and, while the Armagnac faction sent an army to face him at Agincourt, the Burgundians remained neutral.

That's pretty extreme, if you think about it. Remaining neutral when your country's being invaded – particularly when the country is France and the invaders are English. But the hatred between the Burgundians and the Armagnacs seemed stronger than the long-running antipathy between England and France.

It reminds me of the left wing of modern British politics. While, in principle, all the various different kinds of lefties claim that their main aim is to keep the Conservatives out of power, in practice many left-wing groupings reserve their greatest animus for each other. In fact, the hard left is inclined to dismiss the centre left as 'Tories', which seems to be missing all kinds of points.

First and foremost, they're not Tories. Demonstrably. It's just a point of fact. The word 'Tory' is not open to interpretation like some words: idiot, hero, coward, hypocrite, statesman, to give a few examples. It just means 'member of the Conservative Party' and none of the adherents of new Labour, so reviled by the Corbynite wing of the party, are even Tory voters let alone members.

The left often uses 'Tory' as a term of abuse, like 'monster'. This is forgetting that it isn't a term of abuse, but a descriptive term that many people are happy to use about themselves. If it's like 'monster', this is a world where monsters both exist and are often in control of the country, happily proclaiming themselves to be monsters. This is an odd context in which to label a non-monster who merely disagrees with you over various points of detail a monster. It's like Churchill calling Attlee a Nazi.

I'm not, let me make clear before any excitement or panic sets in, equating Tories with monsters or Nazis. I am not a Tory myself, but the Conservative Party is a coherent political movement with many decent and sincere adherents. I don't support it, but I don't consider it to be so abominable that its nomenclature should be used as direct synonyms for evil.

That's what the hard left does — but that's not the problem. The problem is that's *all* it does. Otherwise it leaves the Tories alone focusing its ire on people it calls Tories but who are in fact fellow Labour supporters — just ones who are a bit more centrist, a bit more capitalistic, frankly a bit more realistic.

The irony is not lost on me, as a left-leaning centrist, that in this little section I too am reserving my criticism for other people on the left rather than Tories. I've been polite about the Tories, but I'm censuring other left-wingers for dividing the left, which is, in turn, divisive of me. All this lefty mudslinging is a huge help to the right.

In the same way, the English were hugely helped by the conflict between the Burgundians and the Armagnacs. At the start of the civil war, both groups would have said they were pro-French, which meant pro-poor addled Charles VI. By 1418, John 'the Fearless' (if you say so), Duke of Burgundy and leader of the Burgundian faction, was flirting with acknowledging Henry V's claim to the French throne.

It got worse. In 1419, an attempt at rapprochement with the Armagnacs was brokered, at which John was assassinated. This was understandable as Duke John had ordered the murder of Duke Louis twelve years earlier. Sadly this reciprocity didn't lead to the two groups calling it quits. The new Duke of Burgundy, Philip 'the Good' (matter of opinion), signed an all-out alliance with Henry V. The Burgundians were now officially pro-English.

By this stage, the leading Armagnac was the dauphin – that is, the heir to the French throne. He was called Charles and was the fifth dauphin of his father's reign; Charles VI's sons seemed to have a lot of trouble staying alive. So in 1419 the situation for the French royal family was grave. The king was mad and there was a civil war going on in which only one of the two factions acknowledged the king's son as the rightful heir. The other faction wanted the King of England to inherit. On top of this, the King of England had invaded and was assiduously occupying Normandy.

England takes over France forever

That's what Henry had been doing since Agincourt. He went back to England for a bit, to soak up the plaudits and sign a treaty with Holy Roman Emperor Sigismund, no less, in which the empire recognized his claim to the French throne. This must have been exciting. The crazy Plantagenet claim to the French throne, Edward III's chancy punt, was getting endorsed by Europe's biggest-wig. The daft notion that the King of England was also the rightful king of France was becoming mainstream. Think on that when you next assume that all internet conspiracy theories are doomed to be blasted away by the leaf-blower of reason.

In the same month as the treaty, August 1416, Henry's

younger brother John, Duke of Bedford, defeated a Franco-Genoese naval force at the Battle of the Seine. This relieved a siege on Harfleur and gave the English dominance in the Channel. The following year Henry landed in Normandy and started taking it over bit by bit. This was quite different from Edward III's and the Black Prince's technique of *chevauchées* and showy battles: this was about sieges and occupation. Henry meant to take Normandy and keep it. Paralysed by division, the French government did basically nothing so that, by August 1419, Henry's army was at the gates of Paris.

This was the point at which John the Fearless took an Armagnac axe in the face at an emergency summit and the Burgundians signed an alliance with Henry. John's skull was kept by some monks in Dijon for reasons vaguely connected to Catholics being weird, and when, 102 years later, Francis I, the then King of France (who was not, spoiler alert, also the king of England), came to visit, they showed it to him. Whichever monk was doing the tour pointed out the axe hole, saying, 'Sire, this is the hole through which the English entered France.'

He was right. Henry's conquering continued apace and, in 1320, the Treaty of Troyes was signed. This was as close to the absolute jackpot for Henry as could realistically be imagined. He wasn't made king of France but he was made regent and heir to the throne. All he had to do was wait for mad King Charles to finally shatter, or die of eating his own shit, or try to fly from the top of Notre Dame, or something else that reinforces unhelpful stereotypes about mental illness, and he would be king of France as well as England.

Also in the terms of the treaty, it was arranged for him to marry Charles's youngest daughter Catherine de Valois for a nice merging of royal bloods – though the basis for Henry's whole claim to the French throne was that they were already massively merged. So a nice remerging, a non-refreshing of the genetic pot, tainted as it already was by mental illness and a propensity to premature death. I mean, Jesus. Wait till they have a child. The fact that he turned out to be a complete waste of space is not exactly a bolt from the blue.

That's coming up. For now, this is the happy ending of the Hundred Years' War in which England wins, and if that's how you want to remember that war and the whole England vs France aspect of medieval history – and why wouldn't you? – I'd skip on from here to Edward IV and try not to think about why his other kingdom of France isn't getting much of a mention.

History is relentless, like football. I find watching football boring, but I'm not immune to the appeal of institutional triumph. When Liverpool or Manchester United (it usually seems to be one of those two) wins some title, has a great season, breaks some record, I'm drawn to that happy ending. It's joyous and climactic. It often comes with a match referred to as a 'final'.

But it isn't final. They have their triumph but then, next season, they start again and probably do a bit worse. For me, that spoils the narrative. I've often thought that, when a great club wins everything, it should be closed down. Its players and resources could split among other teams. Having achieved its destiny, its greatest triumph, it should be allowed to ascend to sporting heaven rather than continue to scratch around on earth in the hope, at best, of repeating its triumph, but never of bettering it. I accept that this proposal would face opposition from club owners and fans but, had it always been the system, I think it would be great.

In narrative terms, it was a good move of Henry V to die two years after his greatest triumph. He never had to deal with the fallout: the challenges of maintaining and consolidating his position. France wasn't really his: the Armagnacs, led by a dauphin determined to be king of France himself, were still in possession of most of the country and they weren't going anywhere.

After his marriage to Catherine in June 1420, Henry returned triumphantly to England where, in early 1421, Catherine was crowned and impregnated – quickly ticking off quite a lot of a queen consort's to-do list. In June of that year, Henry returned to France to relieve a situation caused by the defeat and death of his brother, the Duke of Clarence, in a battle against an Armagnac army. Henry spent the next year campaigning, chipping away at the dauphin's possessions, before catching dysentery and dying in August 1422. Unlike Edward III, he never had to see himself fail.

Would he have failed? Could he have succeeded in building a long-term cross-Channel Charlemagne-style superstate? Probably not. Edward III couldn't and he was a top-class king. Then again, Henry's approach was different. He was conquering northern France, not just laying waste to it. He had made alliances within the French political milieu. He would *probably* have failed to reign as effective king of France and England but it's far from definite.

It wouldn't necessarily have been good news for England if he'd succeeded, though. France was a far bigger, far richer, far more central state than England. It was cool and fashionable – the popes lived there for a while which was pretty hip at the time. King of France was a promotion from king of England, so France was likely to be any joint king's priority. When the Stuart kings of Scotland inherited the English throne in 1603, they moved straight to the capital of the richer and more central of their two kingdoms. Stuart rule of England did not turn out, in any meaningful sense, to be Scottish rule. A long-term Lancastrian regime based in Paris would have been unlikely to remain Anglocentric for long.

28. King Henry VI

Henry VI never met his father but he wouldn't have remembered if he had. That's not because he was useless, though he was useless, but because he was only eight months old when his father died. This wasn't an ideal situation: the King of England was a baby and the King of France was mentally ill and likely to die quite soon, at which point the baby would take over as king of France as well. Who came up with this system?

Henry V had come up with it and fortunately had enough time, while he knew he was dying, to make some arrangements. And enough energy. I'm not sure, if I were dying of dysentery, I'd be able to summon up the vigour to give a shit about . . . well, anything other than my next agonizing shit. But then I'm fairly agnostic rather than extremely Catholic, so not quite as convinced as Henry was that I'd otherwise turn up in the afterlife and get an immediate rap on the knuckles from St Peter for neglecting my geopolitical admin.

Henry put his eldest surviving brother, John Duke of Bedford, who was a sensible and capable chap, in sole charge of both France and the ongoing war against the Armagnacs. He left his flakier brother, Humphrey Duke of Gloucester, in more equivocal charge of both England and his infant son. So there was a plan, but the situation, like any royal minority, was delicate – and this minority was going to be *long* since the king had acceded at the tender age of nought.

The odd thing about Henry VI's minority, though, was that it was by far the most successful part of his reign. Overall, it didn't go amazingly well but neither was it an unmitigated disaster. The rest of his reign was an unmitigated disaster. At the start, a regency council was appointed to run England and, while there was a certain amount of bickering between Gloucester and the king's great-uncle, Cardinal Beaufort, competent government was for the most part maintained.

What's strange is that no one took the opportunity to call into question the infant king's right to rule. Henry V's charisma seems to have blasted away any question of the Lancastrian dynasty's legitimacy. Henry VI was, in England at least, the unquestioned rightful king. This wasn't due to any strengths on the child's part. It was because there was a lot of loyalty to Henry V and a strong sense that his stellar reign, and therefore his whole dynasty, had been favoured by God.

Later in Henry VI's reign, questions over his legitimacy re-emerged with disastrous consequences, but his remarkably stable minority shows that this wasn't inevitable. Henry IV's usurpation had weakened the monarchy, but Henry V's successes had repaired a lot of that damage. It took rank incompetence from Henry VI to reopen all those cracks. If he'd been a half-decent ruler, the new Lancastrian succession might never have been questioned again.

Obviously England can't be in charge of France

The country of which Henry was not the unquestioned king was France. Charles VI died in October 1422 and Henry was supposedly king of it from then on, though Charles's son Charles, who was previously calling himself the dauphin, now reckoned he was King Charles VII. Events proved him right.

Not immediately, though. The Duke of Bedford was doing a bloody good job of continuing his brother's work, winning a stunning victory in 1424 at the Battle of Verneuil where he defeated a much larger army of French and Scots (who have become almost inseparable from the French by this point — nice work, Edward I) by sheer force of killing them one by one. Events continued to favour the English until early 1429 when Joan of Arc turned up.

It seems to me that Joan of Arc was the quirky personification of an inevitable historical process. It's almost as if God or Fate or Chance – history's great showrunner in the sky – felt the need to jazz up an otherwise predictable narrative. England had neither the united leadership nor the wealth nor the international clout to take over and hold on to France. It would have been not merely like a snake swallowing a basketball but like a fox trying to kill a hippopotamus. The English situation was bound to deteriorate but a young French peasant woman, wearing armour and having holy visions, leading a French army while the dauphin looked on with scepticism turning to amazement, is a much more interesting way for that to happen.

If your awareness of history comes from a primarily English or British perspective, Joan of Arc is an awkward prospect. Her role in the story makes France right and England wrong. She is a rebuke to unworthy and unrealistic ambitions and only really enjoyable from a French perspective. 'This is their bit,' you have to say and let the French have fun.

That wasn't the view of the English at the time. The trouble with personifications of inevitable historical processes is that, unlike the processes themselves, they can be killed. So that's what the English did to her, after their Burgundian allies had captured her and handed her over in exchange for 10,000 *livres tournois*, which is roughly equivalent, in today's money, to a lot.

The English didn't reckon she was a personification of an inevitable historical process at all. They thought she was an annoying piece of shit – otherwise known as a heretic. It was heresy that she was convicted of in a very dodgy trial in front of a lot of pro-English priests. And then she was burned at the stake in 1431. Twenty-five years later, the verdict was overturned and, in 1920, she was made a saint. As a trajectory of posthumous Roman Catholic respectability, this is known as a 'reverse-Savile'.

The reawakening of French national morale and military success was unaffected by Joan's judicial murder. She had already seen the former dauphin crowned King Charles VII at Rheims cathedral in 1429. This had precipitated the crowning of Henry VI as king of England at Westminster later the same year and then, slightly desperately, of France in Paris in December 1431. French kings aren't usually crowned in Paris – Rheims is the place, so it didn't feel proper and it wasn't. The ten-year-old Henry returned to England soon afterwards and never set foot in France again.

English setbacks continued apace. In 1435, the Burgundians swapped sides and the Duke of Bedford died. In 1436 the French reconquered Paris. By 1449, Rouen and most of Normandy were back in French hands and then, in 1453, at the Battle of Castillon, Gascony fell to them. This territory had been in the hands of the kings of England for 299 years. But it was all over. Only Calais remained.

England needs a grown-up

This disaster was Henry VI's cue to lose it. As I've said, the course of his life is eerily similar to that of his maternal grandfather and predecessor as incapable king of France, Charles VI. But Henry's mental health breakdown was considerably lower-energy than his grandad's various collapses, yet somehow weirder. Henry went totally inert. He just froze, stopped, ceased to interact with other humans. He slumped into a catatonic state, brought on by the shock of his final defeat in France. He had to be fed, washed, moved from room to room. He breathed unaided, but that was about it.

It was quite an extreme reaction but, on the plus side, it showed that he got it. Something had gone badly wrong with his reign and his total collapse was at least an acknowledgement of the seriousness of that. It was a catastrophic failure in his kingship but, ironically, his lapse into a state where he didn't seem to know what was going on was one of the few signs he'd ever betrayed of understanding what was going on.

Up to that point, he'd proved to be a terrible king. Ever since the Duke of Bedford died, there'd been a power vacuum. Bedford had been really good. He'd behaved like a king, by which I don't mean that he'd got above himself, but that he'd balanced competing interests, fought bravely and administered with competence. People trusted him and, without him, nobody quite knew what to do. There was no grown-up.

So they looked to the king who, in 1435, was only thirteen. So not a grown-up either. But he was crowned and anointed and so maybe benefited from a bit of magical God-given authority and competence? That was the hope, and indeed the premise of the whole governmental system. 'When can we start pretending little Henry's up to the job?' the magnates wondered.

The answer was 1437. Henry was fifteen. It's a bit young really but, to be honest, that wasn't the main problem. His father had been a capable warrior who had led men at the Battle of Shrewsbury when not much older. Edward III had been a conscious and capable political actor when in his teens. It's possible that, had Henry VI possessed any regal gifts, he might have been able to cope with some aspects of the job at fifteen. But he didn't, so he couldn't. The day when he could never dawned.

Where was this elusive grown-up? Henry, as is typical of weak kings, put all his faith in a favourite, in his case William de la Pole, Earl of Suffolk. This made other major magnates, such as the Duke of Gloucester and Richard Duke of York, resentful and suspicious of him which, in turn, made de la Pole ever more aware of his dependence on the king's favour. This defensiveness made him spiteful and, in 1447, he moved against Gloucester, the next in line to the throne but someone who had largely retired from public life by that point. De la Pole had him brought before parliament and arrested for treason. Gloucester died of a stroke before he could be tried.

De la Pole eventually fell from grace in 1450 when it emerged that, as part of the deal for the king's marriage to Margaret of Anjou (which had happened in 1445), he had agreed that England would cede the county of Maine to Charles VII. This was disastrous news at a time when England was already haemorrhaging continental territory and led to his condemnation by parliament. He was sentenced to execution which, at the order of the king, was commuted to banishment. But then the ship taking him into exile was intercepted by a bunch of lads who executed him anyway.

So Henry had never been much of a king, but his bizarre and rubbery slump of 1453 still presented a problem. The regimes of which he'd been the ponderous and timid centre – de la Pole's and then that of Edmund Beaufort, Duke of Somerset – had relied on the king's conscious assent, if nothing else. Kings were a big deal and without going 'So we'll do this, your majesty, shall we?' and being able to elicit at the very least a tremulous 'Yep,' these ministers' authority lacked legitimacy. They spent ages hoping he'd get better, trying to get some signs of life out of him, to elicit a few decisions on issues like who should be the next archbishop of Canterbury by getting him to wiggle a toe or burp, but to no avail. It was a bit like when they got that octopus to predict results in the football World Cup, except the octopus was considerably more dynamic.

Something had to be done. The king was childless, though the queen was at this point pregnant, and the next in line to the throne was Richard Duke of York. Was he the grown-up? He was forty-one, he'd commanded the English position in France after Bedford's death. Maybe he was. That was the hope anyway. After some umming and ahhing – after the queen had given birth to a healthy baby boy whom the king, in his weird trance, could not be prevailed upon even to acknowledge – the Duke of York was appointed protector of the realm.

A war by any other name . . .

York. Ring any bells? I don't mean Prince Andrew – this is differently grim. This Duke of York is the one I mentioned earlier as having recoined the name Plantagenet to emphasize his royal lineage. He was very royal, directly descended both from the previous Duke of York, a son of Edward III and younger brother of John of Gaunt, and from the Duke of Clarence, another son of Edward III and *elder* brother of John of Gaunt. This complicated, boring and important fact gets a fair few people killed over the next few decades.

The specific thing that will kill them is called the Wars of the Roses and it was between the white rose representing York and the red rose representing Lancaster. If you don't want to know who eventually wins, avoid looking at an England rugby shirt for the next few minutes. The roses couldn't do any of the fighting themselves – they're as inert as floppy King Henry. Still, pricks can draw blood and the aristocracy was full of them.

Historians will tell you that it isn't really called the Wars of the Roses, which is ridiculous because it obviously is. What they mean is that it wasn't called the Wars of the Roses at the time, or for a long while afterwards, and they hugely exaggerate the extent to which this matters. It is not important to refer to things in contemporaneous language. The ancient Egyptians didn't call the pyramids pyramids, but that doesn't mean that they're not really pyramids.

So this war (or wars – it gets pluralized because it happened in fits and starts) was between two royal factions, one led by the Duke of York and the other – well, nominally led by King Henry, who was from the House of Lancaster, but also by Queen Margaret. Plus a whole clutch of vaguely royal people, who wanted to seem more royal than they were, are on that side. All sorts of descendants, of varying levels of legitimacy, of John of Gaunt (who was Duke of Lancaster, remember), most of whose surnames are Beaufort or Tudor.

I bet that last word rang a bell even if York didn't. Yes, the Tudors were shuffling about by this point, waiting for their entrance, which is coming up shortly and will allow me to end this book with their heavily televised section of the past. That should be fun and will give you a chance to join in with the bits you know: 'Divorced, beheaded, died. Divorced, beheaded . . . to see you nice!' But we've got to get the Wars of the Roses out of the way first. They're less heavily tele-vised, possibly because they're so complicated and lack a coherent narrative arc.

Shakespeare plundered them heavily for material and made it work, but he was famously good at writing. Plus he couldn't really do the Tudors because, for the first half of his career, they were in charge and very sensitive unless described in a manner so ludicrously adulatory as to be unwatchable by anyone whose surname wasn't Tudor. At the end of his life, he collaborated on a play about Henry VIII – the Stuarts were reigning by then so he could get away with it – but it's not what you'd call a corker. I suppose it must have been tricky, for the creator of Falstaff, to write about a time when the shouty, boozy fatso was actually king. It unbalances things, like when Del Boy became a millionaire.

The Wars of the Roses as quickly as possible

Okay, here we go. Back to 1454 when Richard Duke of York had just been made protector of the realm: at this point, he showed no signs of trying to become king himself, despite having just been queue-jumped in the line of succession by the new royal baby whom the great big royal baby, Henry, was still too bonkers to notice.

York did a relatively sensible job of running the country, though he couldn't resist putting Edmund Beaufort, Duke of Somerset, in the Tower of London. Somerset had been running the government, ever since de la Pole was shortened at sea, and York thought he was a traitorous dick – letting the king and the kingdom down. The terms of the conflict were still like in the good old days before Henry IV's usurpation: all about the king being 'badly advised' or 'deceived' or 'betrayed' – the notion of just getting rid of him and having a different king had not yet crept back on to the agenda.

Next event: Henry gets better. Hooray? No. He did less harm while he lacked motor function. But, from Christmas 1454 onwards, he was up and about again, getting everything wrong. From this point on, though, he was increasingly managed/dominated/looked after by the queen, who appears to have been genuinely fond of him, but who was also anxious for their son to a) inherit the throne and b) not get killed. She was skilful and determined in this aim, but nevertheless failed on both counts.

As soon as the king was well enough to once again feed himself and obsess over his plans for Eton College (which, let me tell you in case you're looking for another reason to dislike him, he founded), Queen Margaret sacked York and let Somerset out of prison to run things again. Henry's pre-collapse regime was back in business and York stomped off to the north to start plotting with his allies the Nevilles.

The Nevilles were a lovely couple, both called Richard Neville, one father of the other. The father was the earl of Salisbury and the son was the earl of Warwick, which was nice for them. Despite the locations of their earldoms, the north of England was their main power base where they vied with the Percies to be the most important regional aristocrats. York and the Nevilles (sounds like a 1950s band) started raising an army and the government started panicking.

In May 1455, jumpy Somerset announced a big council to be held in Leicester and summoned everyone including York and the Nevilles, who were under strict instructions to behave themselves. But they didn't. They intercepted the king on his way there, at St Albans, where there was a fight – it was somewhere between a small battle and a massive scuffle. Somerset was killed, as was Henry Percy, 2nd Earl of Northumberland (excuse the ordinal number but, of the nine Percies who were earls of Northumberland in the period covered by this book, eight were called Henry – number seven was a Thomas!). So York and the Nevilles were pleased, and the king was captured and taken back to London.

York still said he didn't want to be king and ceremonially handed Henry the crown. The message was: 'You can still be king but please let me run things because you are a massive idiot.' The person who actually started running things, though, was non-idiot but York-hater Queen Margaret, so the York faction were once again gradually sidelined and went off to plot.

We've got to 1459 and a parliament was called in Coventry, without inviting Y and the Ns because no one was in the mood for a disco. No. It was because the purpose of the parliament was to pass 'bills of attainder' against them – a bill of attainder criminalizes you without trial. You can bet Suella

Braverman is trying to bring them back. Y and the Ns fled into exile – York went to Ireland and the Nevilles went to Calais. But in the summer of 1460 the Nevilles were back with an army, defeating the king's troops at the Battle of Northampton and capturing Henry. Queen Margaret escaped.

In September, York came back from Ireland and something had changed. This is when he started calling himself Plantagenet. He arrived bearing the arms of his ancestor the Duke of Clarence, son of Edward III. He'd had enough of trying to work round a fool of a king. At a parliament in October, he basically said: 'Yes, I admit it, I want to be king. So kill me.'

And they did. Two months later. He was giving battle in vain at the time – his last desperate gesture reminding millions of the colours of the rainbow. At the Battle of Wakefield on 30 December, a Lancastrian army led by the Duke of Somerset (son of the one who had died at St Albans) defeated a force led by York and the elder Richard Neville. York was killed in battle and Neville, who had escaped, was discovered later that night and beheaded.

Is it over yet?

No. Not by any means. Richard's forthright claiming of the throne had fundamentally changed Yorkist aims. The political nation had had a good go, in the aftermath of Henry V's glories, at pretending that the office of king was somehow inviolable. Henry VI's legitimacy, the notion of his God-given right to rule, had been respected all the way through his minority, and then into his feeble reign – his failures in France, the collapse of law and order – right through his year and a bit of just being a blob that ate, and then out the other side. But the bill of attainder against York had pushed it too far. No one had forgotten what Henry IV had done. He'd got rid of a king. Ever since 1399, it had been in the back of every magnate's mind: if the worst came to the worst, we can always do that again. For the Yorkists, this was now the plan.

And they had a new candidate: Richard's son Edward, a dashing eighteen-year-old who was bloody good at fighting. On 2 February 1461, at the Battle of Mortimer's Cross in Herefordshire, Edward's army defeated a Lancastrian force led by someone called Owen Tudor and his son Jasper Tudor, Earl of Pembroke.

Who are these guys? Well, Owen was a Welsh nobleman whose claim to fame was that he had secretly married Henry VI's mother Catherine de Valois in 1428. They'd had some kids, Edmund, Jasper who was at the battle, and a couple of less historically significant others, and they were all half-siblings of Henry VI, making them very different from most scions of the Welsh gentry. I imagine Owen as a bit of a charmer, a Richard Burton type. This battle was the end of his chequered career – he was captured and beheaded in Hereford – though not of the Tudors.

Jasper survived. More importantly, Owen's elder son Edmund, Earl of Richmond, had already married and impregnated Lady Margaret Beaufort, daughter and niece of various dukes of Somerset, before dying in 1456. In 1457, she gave birth to a son called Henry, who possessed quite the jazzy cocktail of royal blood: as well as the Tudor stuff from Wales, he descended directly from the French House of Valois through his grandmother the dowager Queen of England, and from the English House of Plantagenet through the Beauforts who descended from John of Gaunt. This might sound like an over-involved episode of *Who Do You Think You Are?* but, unlike Danny Dyer's ancestry, it turned out to be important.

Not yet though. Victorious Edward now headed for London

where he joined forces with the remaining Richard Neville, Earl of Warwick, who had just been beaten at the second Battle of St Albans, losing Henry VI in the process. Henry had spent the whole battle sitting under a tree singing and now he was back with his wife. Undaunted by this setback, on 4 March 1461, Edward was proclaimed king.

Now there were two of them. Shit.

29. King Edward IV

There may have been a new king, but the old king was still very much around, singing and praying and kissing his wife. So the start of Edward's reign wasn't a nice, certain new beginning. Just like when Henry VI was crowned in Paris after Charles VII had also been crowned at Rheims, it was a political assertion, an aspiration more than a fact. Would Edward assert his rule in England more effectively than Henry had in France?

Yes, he would. On 29 March 1461, at Towton in Yorkshire, Edward won the largest and bloodiest battle ever fought on English soil. Henry VI and Queen Margaret were there but managed to escape to Scotland with their young son (also called Edward and who was, in their view, the prince of Wales). That complication aside, it was a decisive triumph for Edward of York which left a very large number of senior Lancastrians dead.

That, you'd think, would be the end of the Wars of the Roses. But I'm sorry to say it isn't. This war is reminiscent of the process of disentangling a very long string of Christmas lights. You sort out one bit and then there are just more twists, more tangles.

Next one: Edward secretly married a woman who was his considerable social inferior. She was still pretty posh, but he was the king and she wasn't posh enough. But she was definitely pretty enough. She was called Elizabeth Grey (née Woodville) and she was the widow of a man who had died fighting on the Lancastrian side at the second Battle of St Albans. So, in every way, extremely unsuitable.

Edward kept the marriage secret because he knew it would go down badly with Richard Neville, Earl of Warwick. Kings weren't supposed to marry their subjects just because they fancied them, or even loved them, or at all. Royal marriage prospects were a major diplomatic resource and Edward had squandered it out of lust. Neville had been trying to cement a treaty with Louis XI, the new King of France, by getting Edward to marry Louis's sister-in-law. When he discovered, in October 1464, that four months earlier the king had married a commoner, he was mightily pissed off.

Edward's marriageable prospects were not the only finite resource that Elizabeth Grey monopolized. She also hugely reduced the amount of titles, honours, jobs and patronage available to Warwick and his cronies because she applied so much pressure on Edward to show favour to her large and impecunious family.

The initial secrecy can only have made the situation even more annoying for Warwick. This was stupid and cowardly of Edward. But he wasn't a stupid and cowardly man in general and this counterproductive subterfuge is a reminder that he was still a kid. That was how Warwick viewed him – the young son of his long-time ally Richard of York whom he had helped to the throne. Warwick has come to be known to posterity as the Kingmaker. He felt he'd made one king, Edward. As the 1460s wore on, it started to occur to him that he could always make another.

This may have been going through Warwick's mind in 1465 as he was escorting Henry VI to the Tower of London. The silly old king had been hanging around the north of England for over a year, sofa-surfing at the castles of various supporters, ever since the Lancastrian defeat at yet another battle, Hexham, the previous May. But the Lancastrian cause wasn't quite finished: Henry's queen and their son were still at large in France, currying favour with the very king with whom Neville had wanted to make a marriage alliance.

Neville has lost the knack

Thanks to Neville, here comes another flurry of Wars of the Roses. He joined forces with George Duke of Clarence, one of Edward's younger brothers who didn't feel enough of a fuss was being made of him compared to Edward's in-laws. In 1469, Clarence married Neville's daughter Isabel and then the two of them rebelled, defeated a royal army at the Battle of Edgcote in July, imprisoned Edward IV in Middleham Castle and executed a brace of Woodvilles.

This would have been a great moment for the Kingmaker to make another king, but he couldn't manage it. He had a go but nothing happened. Let's hope Clarence said, 'That's fine, these things happen – you're probably just tired.' The vibe of the kingdom was that there were still only two possible kings, Henry VI and Edward IV. Unfortunately they were both in prison. That situation was unsustainable so Neville let one of them out – Edward – who then carried on ruling for a bit. As you can imagine, there was a real *atmosphere*.

An uneasy truce continued for a while, but Warwick and Clarence weren't having a very nice time. For example, Edward replaced John Neville, Warwick's younger brother, as earl of Northumberland with Henry Percy. Percy had previously been (4th) earl of Northumberland but the Percies had been stripped of the title for being on the Lancastrian side – Henry Percy the 3rd Earl had been killed fighting for Henry VI at Towton. When the earldom went to John Neville in 1465, that was a big win for the Nevilles in the Neville–Percy struggle to be the biggest northern magnates. Equally,

Edward's reinstatement of Percy in 1470 was a fifteenth-century way of telling Warwick to fuck off.

So Warwick and Clarence rebelled again in March 1470, but it didn't work and the two of them fled to France. There King Louis XI of France, eager for England's paralysis by civil war to continue, introduced them to Queen Margaret of England, who was initially frosty but then spotted an opportunity, so they all teamed up.

In September, Warwick and Clarence landed in Devon, while John Neville marched down from the north. Edward IV was caught in a pincer movement and, along with his other brother Richard Duke of Gloucester, fled to Flanders. Warwick assumed control of England and, since he couldn't seem to make another king, used an extant one. He restored Henry VI to the throne.

I know. I am *so* sorry. It feels like we're getting nowhere.

30. King Henry VI, the Readeption

The word 'set' famously has more different meanings and uses than any other in the English language. It does a hell of a lot of work. The same cannot be said for the word 'readeption'. Readeption just means restoration to the throne and is used exclusively to refer to Henry VI. No one else's restoration – and there have been a fair few over the centuries – is called a readeption. It is the special word just for the time when Henry VI started being king again for a bit, nine and a half years after he'd been deposed.

For most people, this was a depressing development. The Yorkists, obviously. Most of the ordinary people, because they were sick of civil war. Henry VI himself, because it just meant more stress. Most importantly, it's depressing for you and me, because we felt we were getting somewhere, didn't we? Henry had been a terrible king, and there'd been disastrous consequences, and pressure had built up until finally he'd been overthrown. It was dramatic and nasty but, like a violent bout of vomiting after hours and hours of feeling horrendously ill, it was for the best. 'Better out than in' is a fair verdict on Henry VI's relationship with power. And 'better in than out' summarizes his relationship with the Tower of London, if you ask me. This may be unfair on the poor weirdo, but whenever he was wandering freely around the place, he tended, like a bewildered queen bee, to become the focus of lots of dangerous activity – a buzzing of troops and supporters, spoiling for a battle against some Yorkists.

This little coda to Henry VI's calamitous reign reminds me of Napoleon's Hundred Days when, nine months after he'd been defeated, deposed and sent to rule the tiny island of Elba, the disgraced emperor came back to France, took over the place effortlessly and restarted the war. A weary Europe had to get its shit together to defeat him again. It's also like when the last Chinese emperor, who'd been forced to abdicate a couple of decades earlier, was set up as leader of the Japanese puppet state of Manchuria in the 1930s. And, bleakest of all, it's like the last fifteen minutes of the mediocre 1994 Mel Gibson film *Maverick*, the several false endings of which were accompanied for me, when I watched it with friends at university, with the dawning realization that we were all going to miss last orders at the pub.

The new Warwick-led Lancastrian regime didn't last long. Henry was a more pitiful figure than ever, shambling around in dirty old clothes, barely understanding what was going on. Warwick was in charge but most of the Lancastrians who supported the readeption hated him for orchestrating their downfall a decade earlier. The queen and her son didn't even make it to England before the regime started collapsing, hot on the heels of Edward IV returning from Flanders with an army.

He landed in March 1471, defeated and killed Warwick at the Battle of Barnet in April and then defeated the queen and her son, who had just arrived with another army, at the Battle of Tewkesbury in May. The Lancastrian Prince of Wales, another Edward, was killed at this battle and Queen Margaret, broken in spirit by the death of her son, was sent to the Tower where Henry VI had also been reinstalled. She just had time to get reacquainted with him before he was murdered on 21 May, almost certainly by order of Edward IV and very possibly by the hand of his brother Richard Duke of Gloucester.

31. King Edward IV, Alone at Last

Don't think too badly of Edward for killing Henry. By the standards of the time, it was restrained of him not to have topped him much earlier, as soon as he'd been captured. Henry was allowed to last a lot longer than either Edward II or Richard II, the previous deposed medieval rulers – though that was because, while his son and heir was still alive, there wasn't much point in killing him. Margaret's teenage boy was a more dynamic threat to the Yorkist regime than poor Henry.

The big news, though, was that, in Edward IV, England had found the grown-up it had been seeking since the death of the Duke of Bedford nearly four decades earlier. Edward was a capable king and ruled sensibly until his sudden death in 1483. His major achievement was balancing the books, which he managed by various sensible economic measures such as not having a civil war and not trying to conquer France.

For form's sake, he had to have a small go at conquering France, so he landed in Calais in the summer of 1475. But when his ally, the Duke of Burgundy, failed to turn up in support, Louis XI suggested a deal and Edward readily accepted. By the Treaty of Picquigny, Louis paid Edward some money and Edward agreed to go away and shut up about his claim to the French throne for a bit.

Edward was capable, tall, attractive, charismatic and, over matters of state at least, relatively wise. His undoubted military prowess, the strength that had won him the throne, gave him the authority not to turn England into a war state. He allowed some peace and prosperity to creep back. It feels like we should dwell on the many uninteresting things he got right but the trouble is that they don't matter very much because all of his good work got spoiled soon after his death.

If the 1480s had panned out differently, he might have been a Henry II or an Edward I figure, kicking off a whole new phase for his dynasty. He had two healthy, legitimate male heirs and he was in the prime of life. No one had a better dynastic claim to the throne – those who arguably used to have one were now dead. The remnant Lancastrian cause was led by the Tudors, all of whose royal blood came through women and was diluted by that of a sexy Welsh bloke who'd caught the eye of Henry V's widow.

Edward's only major weakness was his weaknesses. His weaknesses for the pleasures of the flesh: food, wine and sex. His desire for Elizabeth Woodville, who refused to have sex with him unless he married her, was what caused the most serious mistake he made in the first part of his reign, which temporarily cost him the throne. In the 1470s, the consequences were more predictable and the strapping warrior of the 1460s morphed gradually, with age and the diminishing requirement to ride into battle, into an obese man who liked taking emetics so that he could throw up and then gorge himself again. It all got a bit flabby and Roman.

It didn't seem to affect his political judgement or diminish his mind, but his health inevitably declined. When a serious illness struck him in his early forties, in March 1483, there was no reason to suspect foul play, though some inevitably did. With modern medicine, it might have been a wake-up call. In the late fifteenth century, it heralded eternal sleep. He had a couple of weeks to put his house in order, and confirm his young son Edward, Prince of Wales, as his heir. Then he died on 9 April.

32. King Edward V

There was no King Edward V. There should have been, but there wasn't. The boy who it should have been was twelve years old when his father, King Edward IV, died. He was proclaimed king, loyalty was sworn to him by many magnates, and then he was taken to the Tower of London.

This wasn't necessarily as sinister as it sounds. The Tower was a royal palace, not just a prison, and a good place for young Edward to prepare for his coronation. Then it turned out it *was* as sinister as it sounds. Edward never left the Tower. He and his younger brother Richard Duke of York were last seen playing there in the summer of 1483, soon after their uncle, another Richard, had been crowned king.

Edward and his brother Richard are known as the Princes in the Tower, and at some point in the second half of 1483 they were murdered, probably by order of their uncle. We will never know exactly what happened, which is why this example of the brutality of the world they were born into has captured the ghoulish side of people's imagination.

One of the reasons for the focus on the Ps in the T is the subsequent Tudor regime. The Tudors needed to demonize the king they overthrew and emphasizing that he had killed his nephews, one of whom was the rightful king, is helpful to that. That's why, when Henry VIII's son Edward became king, he was named the sixth rather than the fifth of that name to have reigned (other than the three Anglo-Saxon Edwards who are conventionally ignored, as I keep saying). They wanted to leave a space for little murdered Edward in order to underline how nasty the pre-Tudor monarchy had been.

Edward V isn't the only ruler who never was. King Louis XVII and Emperor Napoleon II, both of France, spring to mind. Their notional reigns were also part of subsequent regimes' means of self-justification. Louis XVII was the son of Louis XVI, the King of France when the French Revolution happened, who was executed. But when Louis XVI's younger brother, also a Louis, was plonked on the throne after the Napoleonic Wars, he called himself Louis XVIII as a rebuke to the revolutionary republic. He was saying that his little nephew, who had died in prison two years after the king's execution, had, in truth, been a king as well, albeit a maltreated one.

When in 1852 Napoleon's nephew, the all-round chancer Louis Napoleon Bonaparte, decided he'd be emperor instead of president of France, he called himself Napoleon III, not Napoleon II, to acknowledge that there was a time when the original Napoleon's son ought to have been ruling, if France had been doing the emperor thing at the time. Counting a ruler who never ruled in the numbering system is asserting that monarchy is about more than merely who happens to hold power. Like coronation and anointing, it's part of the claim of God-given legitimacy with which rulers in gold hats seek to minimize the extent to which their power is questioned.

33. King Richard III

It is impossible to discuss any aspect of Richard III's reign without mentioning the Tudors. In this, their victory over him is even more complete than at the Battle of Bosworth. That battle, in 1485, marked the end of the Wars of the Roses (hooray!) and, in it, Henry Tudor defeated and killed Richard III and established the Tudor dynasty on the throne where it stayed for 118 years.

That paragraph of spoilers was made inevitable by Tudor propaganda. Our sense of the story of Richard is contaminated by how it ended and what happened next. The Tudors, as we've seen, had a flimsy claim to the throne by blood. The notion of primogeniture, of the reliable passing of the crown from father to son, never felt more distant than when Henry snaffled the throne from his third cousin once removed.

Henry justified his nicking of the crown in several ways and that in itself betrays the dodginess of his claim. As with any excuse for doing something you perhaps shouldn't, it's best to stick to one thing: I was late because the traffic was terrible. I can't come because I've got the shits. These are plausible reasons. But when you say 'I need to cancel the meeting because I've got a bit of a gippy tummy and there's a rail strike and my sister's just about to have a baby,' it starts to sound desperate.

So it was with Henry's complicated justifications for knocking Richard off the throne, which went a bit like this: 1) Richard had usurped his nephew (Henry's fourth cousin) who should have inherited the throne after Edward IV died. 2) Richard was a murderer and had had his nephews killed. 3) And even with them dead, he shouldn't have been king because his elder (though now disgraced and executed) brother Clarence's son Edward Earl of Warwick was further up the line of succession so should have been king first. 4) Except, no, because actually Henry Tudor should be king anyway because he's directly descended from John of Gaunt, just like Henries IV, V and VI were, so he's the Lancastrian claimant. And 5) Henry also maybe should be king because his grandmother was Henry VI's mother – let's factor that in too. Henry Tudor had lots of reasons to be king, none of them quite good enough.

This was why the emphasis on how dastardly the previous regime had been was so important to the Tudors. Richard's having usurped his nephew and then murdered him was vital to assert because it both showed how horrible Richard was and demonstrated a precedent for killing people and nicking the throne. You can spin it either as 'He did that so he shouldn't have been king' or 'The previous king did that so why shouldn't I?'

It's well established, then, that the Tudors worked hard to make Richard III look bad. Too well established. People in modern times got a bit overexcited about it and started to jump to the contrary conclusion that Richard was, in fact, lovely. And that he didn't have a hunchback – the Tudors and Shakespeare made that up. Not that people with hunchbacks can't be lovely, of course – but the Tudors didn't think that they could because they were so nasty themselves. So it was probably them that murdered the Princes in the Tower, not Richard at all.

This is a bit of a leap. The lamentable problem that you can't believe everything you're told is not solved by merely believing the polar opposite. We can't know for sure who killed the princes in the Tower – or if they were murdered at all – but the circumstantial evidence against Richard is far greater than that against Henry Tudor or any Tudor sympathizers.

Plus, even if Richard didn't murder them, he still usurped the throne so he's not exactly Gandhi. He was definitely king instead of his nephew – the Tudors didn't make that up.

If Richard didn't kill them, or order their killing, then what happened? Were they still alive when Henry Tudor took the throne? If so, we have to believe either that Richard kept them locked away – which would have been stupid of him as it meant that everyone unnecessarily assumed he was a murderer – or that the evidence for every occasion when they appeared in public from 1483 to 1485 was subsequently destroyed by the Tudors – an achievement in misinformation that would have wowed the Stasi.

Nevertheless, the notion that Richard was a good man and a fine king, the evidence for whose greatness has been entirely obscured by the horrible Tudors, has proved attractive. It would be brilliant if it were true, of course – if this notorious king turned out to have been the victim of a centuries-long libel and was in fact a sort of statesman-cum-pussycat. But then it would be brilliant if unicorns or dragons or King Arthur turned out to exist. The fact that something would be an amazing narrative twist does not, sadly, make it more likely. Nevertheless the thirst for this to be the case where Richard III is concerned has led to the Ricardian movement – people who are dedicated to redeeming his reputation from the slanders of the Tudors.

The most prominent Ricardian group is the Richard III Society, which helped to get what turned out to be the king's remains exhumed on television from under a car park in Leicester in 2012. The skeleton, DNA analysis of which confirmed was Richard's, caused a sensation and a legal battle between the authorities in Leicester, who wanted to reinter the remains in their cathedral, and another Ricardian organization of descendants from the Yorkist line, called the Plantagenet Alliance, who wanted him to be reburied in

York on the basis that apparently it was what he would have wanted.

I find all this a bit daft. It's nice to take an active interest in history – I've already admitted to supporting Harold of Hastings as if he were a football team. But we don't and can't really know these people. The only meaningful respect we can pay them is to acknowledge that unknowability. The truth is lost under centuries of propaganda and then centuries of contrarian rejection of it. It seems, though, from his skeleton, that Richard suffered from severe scoliosis, so he may have been a hunchback after all.

Richard's nasty little reign

Apart from seizing the throne and having his nephews murdered, Richard seems comparatively nice. I realize that 'apart from' clause is doing a lot of work, but the Ricardians are right that, if they could only pin the whole nephew murder on to someone else, they're a long way towards rehabilitating their hero. The usurpation is vanilla next to child murder. Several English kings started their reigns nicking the throne and yet comfortably evaded pariah status.

Richard still had a fair few other people killed, mind you. But that was mainly for treachery, which is par for the course for a king at the time. They all had traitors killed and you could even argue that, in a medieval context, that sort of firmness in leadership can save lives in the long run. Henry I wasted traitors at the drop of a hat and presided over a nice peaceful reign as a result. Meanwhile King Stephen could be a bit of a soft touch and his reign turned into an absolute car crash.

Before Edward IV died, Richard seemed like a decent, reliable sort. He was devoted to his brother the king and a capable lieutenant. In this he contrasted strongly with his elder (and

Edward's younger) sibling, the truculent Duke of Clarence, who caused so much trouble for Edward that finally the king had him attainted by parliament and discreetly executed in 1478. It's said that this was done by drowning him in 'a butt of Malmsey' (a barrel of sweet wine, a bit like Madeira) but it's probably just a tasty rumour.

Richard, in contrast, was loyal and militarily effective. He might have been the person responsible for murdering Henry VI – he was certainly in the Tower of London at the time – but, that aside, any aura of darkness is retrospectively imposed. He was exactly the kind of dependable member of the family whom Edward would have wanted to hold the fort during his son's minority, just as the Duke of Bedford had done after Henry V shat his last.

Then, when Edward actually died, things changed. The family of Edward's widow, the Woodvilles, had become very influential and her brother, Earl Rivers, was in charge of little Edward V. Richard, along with other influential magnates such as Lord Hastings and the Duke of Buckingham, were worried that the Woodvilles would use their control of the young king to control the government. So, three weeks after Edward IV's death, Richard and Buckingham staged a coup and had Rivers and his nephew Sir Richard Grey, the queen's son by her first marriage, arrested and executed. That's when the young prince/king was taken to the Tower.

It wasn't clear at that stage that Richard meant to make himself king, and maybe he hadn't decided to yet. Moving swiftly against a rival faction was how you survived and succeeded during the Wars of the Roses. But Richard's paranoia grew and, having dealt with the Woodville faction, and with the dowager queen seeking sanctuary in Westminster Abbey in fear of her safety, his allies started to drop away. Hastings was suddenly arrested and executed in June and, by October, even Buckingham had deserted him, joining a rebellion in favour of Henry Tudor. It failed, so Buckingham too was dead by the end of the year.

Richard's initial ruthlessness may have been what he felt was necessary for his own safety. He may have been convinced that, in a Woodville-led government, he would have been an unwelcome overmighty subject whom they would take the first opportunity to dispose of. Hence his pre-emptive strike. Having done that, though, he needed to establish leadership that brought in all the other major factions within the kingdom. But he failed to do this, largely because his regime looked like it was founded on child murder, and probably was. The magnates were reluctant to trust anyone who could do that. Executing someone who betrays you was regal and ruthless and, as long as they weren't minded to be treacherous themselves, could actually make the magnates feel safe. It was harsh but fair. Killing two innocent children in order to steal power was far too harsh and not at all fair. It destroyed trust.

Without trust, powerful people started to defect from the regime, which then became too narrowly centred on old retainers of Richard's from his power base in the north. He couldn't take the whole realm with him. Most of the stalwarts of his brother's government were losing confidence in him. As trust diminished so his paranoia grew, and grew more justified. Gradually Henry Tudor, with his absurd remnant of a Lancastrian claim, a man who had been living in Brittany for years and barely knew England or spoke English, began to pick up support – Yorkish support as well as Lancastrian. Buckingham was an early example, and he failed and got beheaded, but events were moving in Henry's favour.

Meanwhile, for Richard, life got worse and worse. In April 1484 his only legitimate son, Edward Prince of Wales, died at the age of ten. In March 1485 his wife, Anne Neville, died at the age of twenty-eight. Rumours then started to spread that he had poisoned her and was limbering up to marry his niece Elizabeth of York, whom Henry Tudor had already pledged to marry if he became king in order to unite the Yorkist and Lancastrian lines. Even by the standards of medieval royal weddings, Richard marrying his niece was far too incestuous and, to get a dispensation for that, he'd have to catch the pope drunk after a big win on the horses. It was fine for Henry Tudor to marry her though, because he was only marginally more closely related to the royal family than Josh Widdicombe.

The general sense of revulsion was such that Richard ended up publicly denying that he had ever had any intention of marrying his niece. Meanwhile he was making overtures to Francis II, Duke of Brittany, to get Henry turfed out of his long-term place of asylum – but this backfired when Henry fled to Paris and garnered the support of the new French king, Charles VIII.

It was Charles who lent Henry the money to assemble an invasion force in the summer of 1485. Henry and his uncle Jasper set sail from Normandy with a small fleet and 4,000 men and landed near Milford Haven on 7 August. They marched through Wales and into England, picking up some support on the way. The most significant support they picked up, however, was at the actual battle that Henry fought against Richard, at Bosworth in Leicestershire on 22 August. This was from the Stanleys – Sir William Stanley and Lord Stanley, the latter being married to Henry Tudor's mother, Margaret Beaufort.

They had turned up at Bosworth with thousands of troops but undecided as to which side to support. The fact that they plumped for the Tudors at the eleventh hour made all the difference, as did the fact that Henry Percy, (still 4th) Earl of Northumberland, who had arrived with a large force to support Richard, decided not to join in the fighting at all. The confidence in the House of York that Edward IV had earned from the magnates had been wiped out by his brother in little more than two years, so that even those who rode to battle with him were willing to change sides, or abandon him, in the happy event that he looked like losing.

Henry, or rather his general John de Vere, Earl of Oxford, won the day and Richard was killed. The dead king was then stripped naked, his crown plonked on Henry's head, and taken to Leicester where he was buried in the church of Greyfriars which, in 1538, closed down to be replaced by something which was replaced by something which was [insert 500 years of town planning here] replaced by something which was replaced by a car park. He lay there for centuries until he was discovered by Channel 4, only about ten years after I was.

34. King Henry VII

It's the end of the middle ages! I expect you know that that's simplistic. The middle ages aren't something that ended on a specific date. Still, they *have* ended and they *did* happen. So, at some point, the latter state was supplanted by the former. And if you had to pick a year somewhere in that gradual process, 1485 is a reasonable one to go for but for the disadvantage of having been traditionally cited as the end of the middle ages and so attracting a queue of historians keen to say why that's wrong, which isn't the case with other years that might be far less reasonably suggested, such as 112 BC or 1978.

We should enjoy it. Change is in the air – there's a Renaissance already under way down on the Med where it's always nicer, then as now. The paintings are starting to look less wonky. The famous one of Henry VII is quite realistic, though it's strange that he's depicted in a sort of booth with his hands over the edge, rather like a celebrity on *Blankety Blank*. In 1476 William Caxton set up the first printing press in England so more books are becoming available to a more literate populace.

Most of the change, though, is yet to come, which is the problem with declaring the middle ages over. It wouldn't have felt like they were over at the time. The next century would see the growth of towns and huge expansion in trade, industry and population. Items such as glass and chairs, the preserve of the mega-rich up to this point, would become affordable by the merely affluent. Feudalism is fading away and the bourgeoisie is coming. But you couldn't necessarily feel the approach of that change if you were collecting body parts in the aftermath of the Battle of Bosworth.

However, something fundamental had changed about the nature of kingship. That's what gradually became clear once the Wars of the Roses ended. It was weakened. People didn't believe in it in the same way. That has nice long-term consequences like freedom and democracy, but not so great short-term ones.

Emerging as it did from the Dark Ages, the lawless chasm that opened up as the Roman Empire contracted, the concept of kingship turned into something that felt eternal and solid and godly. There simply *was* a king and that was that. For a long time it was his coronation and anointing that mainly made him a king. Then the notion morphed a bit and a man's place in a line of succession based on primogeniture came to feel more significant than an archbishop's deployment of a metal hat and blob of goo. Either way, there was a strong sense that a king wasn't just a normal person. He possessed an ineffable specialness.

But the filthy habit of usurping rightful kings that the English royal family slipped into during the fourteenth century started to erode that sense of specialness. Everyone knew Henry Tudor was a bit of a random king – including Henry himself. He was the least qualified by blood of any ruler since Harold Godwinson, and he didn't have Harold's knowledge or experience to mitigate the flimsiness of his claim. He might do the job of king perfectly well – that was what everyone was hoping after Bosworth – but, if he did, that would weaken the institution further. It would make a mockery of centuries of assumptions about who can rule whom. If Henry Tudor can have a go, anyone can.

A few years ago, in an episode of *QI* that I appeared in, Stephen Fry explained that almost everyone in western Europe is a direct descendant of Charlemagne, and almost everyone in the UK a direct descendant of William the Conqueror. These were facts based on overwhelming statistical likelihood: someone of English ancestry living today will have two parents, four grandparents, eight great-grandparents, etc. Spin this back ten centuries and their number of ancestors hits about eight billion, many times the total number of humans alive on earth at that time, let alone in England and Normandy. So, a person living now must be descended from a person living then by many many different routes, not just one. That makes the chances of any given person with any English ancestry at all *not* descending from William by at least one of those routes so vanishingly small as to be, in practical terms, impossible.

Royal blood gets everywhere, basically. Just ask Richard III after a clean-up at the Tower. As soon as the principle of a line of succession is gone, and kingship is discussed in Henry Tudorish terms of having a bit of royal blood, then the concept of royalty starts to become meaningless. Kings are reduced to what they started out as: dictators. People don't think the kings are legitimate and the kings don't feel legitimate themselves. Governmental self-confidence and confidence in government are both undermined. People are governed not with their consent but through fear. It's not as nice.

It feels strange to be saying this about the beginning of the Tudor age, perhaps the most famous era of English kingship. A lot of that fame, though, is because of the paintings and the palaces they left. The Renaissance blasted the image of Henry VIII and Elizabeth I on to the night sky like the bat signal. But that projection of regal magnificence, of strength, is a technique for concealing weakness. They weren't Plantagenets and they knew it. By reigning as successfully as they did, they proved that being a Plantagenet had never really meant anything anyway.

Anyone can say they're the king

The most interesting consequence of this creeping sense that kingship wasn't really a thing was the advent of a new sort of rival claimant to the throne: normal members of the public. There were two of these in the first half of Henry's reign. They didn't admit they were normal members of the public, they *said* they were members of the House of York. But they were lying.

The first said he was Edward Earl of Warwick, but he couldn't have been because Edward Earl of Warwick was still living in the Tower of London. The second said he was Richard Duke of York, Edward V's younger brother, but he couldn't have been either because Richard was also still in the Tower of London, but not living. Their real names were Lambert Simnel and Perkin Warbeck and they both caused a lot of trouble.

Simnel, who had been schooled in his deception by a priest in Oxford, emerged in Ireland where everyone seemed to believe his story. He was crowned King Edward VI at Christ Church Cathedral, Dublin with a gold headband that they'd pinched off a statue of Mary. His key sponsor/puppet master was John de la Pole, Earl of Lincoln, grandson of the de la Pole who was a favourite of Henry VI but, more relevantly, nephew of both Edward IV and Richard III (his mother was their sister).

They invaded with a reasonable-sized army in June 1487 which Henry VII defeated with a bigger army at the Battle of Stoke Field. Lincoln was killed and the king then pardoned Simnel, giving him a job in the royal kitchens which, at that point, he was very grateful for. What is weird, though, is how the fact that Simnel wasn't really a member of the House of York didn't seem to matter to those supporting him, some of whom were members of that House themselves. They were very happy to have a pop at making him king, even though he had no right to it at all. In practical terms, this didn't disqualify him for the role. They were coming perilously close to concluding that a king is just a guy with a gold hat.

Warbeck's attempts to gain the throne caused even more trouble for Henry, though he didn't have to fight a battle on English soil this time. Throughout the 1490s, Warbeck was pottering round the continent, gaining support at various times from the King of France, Margaret dowager Countess of Burgundy, who was Richard III's sister and the aunt of the person Warbeck was claiming to be, Maximilian, the Habsburg who was soon to be Holy Roman emperor, and James IV of Scotland. A very posh bunch. Henry actually invaded France in 1492 to stop Charles VIII from supporting Warbeck and, much like Edward IV seventeen years earlier, ended up being bought off with a nice treaty and pension.

But still the Warbeck threat persisted – wherever he went people called him Richard IV. Like all conspiracy theories, it started to grow simply because it couldn't be snuffed out. Members of Henry's court, including Sir William Stanley, were revealed as secret Yorkist sympathizers and were beheaded. But Warbeck wasn't a Yorkist really – he was just a guy. Many people must have realized that. Where had this Richard of York been during Richard III's reign if he was still alive? How did he manage to pop up on the international scene eight years after he had disappeared? None of it made sense, except in the context of Henry VII's slender claims to royalty: if Henry Tudor can say he's king, why can't anybody?

Warbeck was finally captured in the autumn of 1497 after trying to start a Cornish uprising. He was taken to the Tower where he was treated reasonably and held alongside the Earl of Warwick, the very person Lambert Simnel had tried to impersonate. Warwick and Warbeck formed a sort of mad bond and resolved to escape together. Their failed attempt to do this in 1499 led to them both being executed. Warwick, as genuine royalty, was beheaded at Tower Hill but Warbeck, who had long since confessed his true identity as a chancer from the Low Countries, had to travel standard class: he was hanged at Tyburn.

A centrist rose

Henry Tudor was crowned in some majesty in October 1485. He did this before he married Elizabeth of York in order to make clear that he had the legitimate Lancastrian claim to the throne and didn't need her permission or bloodline to be king. This was all the more important to emphasize because it wasn't true.

He adopted the red rose to symbolize the House of Lancaster. It's a badge that had hardly been used before, though the white one had become a symbol of the House of York. But Henry adopted it on his accession because he was getting ready to launch a new rose, in the wake of his marriage to Elizabeth of York and her coronation as queen in 1486. This was the Tudor rose and it was red *and* white. That was how Henry intended to spin the House of Tudor: the joining of the two rival sides of the old House of Plantagenet into a new royal dynasty that drew its legitimacy from both of them. By emphasizing this truth, he obscured the fact that it also didn't draw quite enough legitimacy from either of them.

He was no fool. He was cautious and intelligent, but also paranoid and avaricious. In the first half of his reign, he seemed dynamic and strategically astute while dealing with pretenders and putting together diplomatic marriages. He married his eldest son, Arthur, to Catherine of Aragon, daughter of Ferdinand and Isabella, the co-rulers of Spain, and his daughter Margaret to King James IV of Scotland. I am suspicious of the phrase 'it's hard to exaggerate the consequences of . . .' because exaggerating is easy – that's why we have phrases like 'a squillion dollars' and 'totally changed the world for ever'. Nevertheless, if you were to seek to exaggerate the consequences of those two marriages, at the very least you'd need to take a bit of a run-up.

Then, in 1502, things started to go wrong for Henry. In that year Arthur Prince of Wales died, leaving the ten-year-old Henry, Duke of York, as his sole heir. Then, in 1503, the queen died in childbirth. Henry, who showed so few signs of liking anybody, clearly loved his son and wife as these developments devastated him. He retreated into deeper paranoia and meanness.

The thing that's weird about Henry's reign is that he managed to stabilize it despite an almost complete absence of trust between him and his magnates. After decades of civil war, the political community was minded to settle for any regime that wasn't absolutely murderous. Henry's response to nobles who'd aroused his suspicion wasn't usually violent – it was just grasping. He would fine them enormous sums for perceived transgressions but then say they only had to pay some of the fine and could just owe the rest. A lot of the aristocracy were thereby held in a position of perpetual debt to the crown. This made them wary, and it made them poor, but it didn't make many of them fear for their lives.

Henry VII's meanness is reminiscent of Edward II's. In both cases, the treasure the kings stockpiled made them feel safe. In both cases, they were wrong, though Henry VII never had to find that out. Money was important to governments, then as now, but, also then as now, the more important issue was credit, in both the financial and the political sense, and the two went hand in hand.

Monarchs who had trust, who managed parliament well,

also had access to finance. They didn't need to stockpile cash because they could borrow – as stable leaders, they could leverage the enormous wealth of a whole country, not just the resources of the crown and court. Richard I, Edward I and Edward III all spent colossally, but, since they were trusted leaders and generals, their financial position was usually secure. It was only when they faltered as leaders – respectively by being kidnapped, losing magnate support over Gascony and going dribbly and old – that money became a problem.

Conversely, for Henry VII, money wouldn't have been a solution. The problems of loss of trust from the magnates, and therefore credit, were not something he could have bought himself out of, had he needed to. But he didn't. On balance, and in the absence of any easy alternatives presenting themselves, the magnates were willing to go along with Henry's scam – particularly as, by the time he really started to turn the screw, his health was failing. They waited him out and, on 21 April 1509, Henry died as king. He was rich, lonely and unloved.

35. King Henry VIII

When you think of the word 'king', what image springs to mind? This might be a bad time to ask you. You're reading a book all about kings. I've been mentioning them like mad – people in crowns will be buzzing round your head like tweeting birds round a concussed cartoon character. Still, I don't think I've got the rhetorical power to drive out the main kingly picture from your mind. Think of a king and your brain is likely to conjure up a portrait of Henry VIII.

It'll probably be one of the Hans Holbein ones where he's all square: square ends to his feet which are planted wide apart so they're directly underneath his square shoulder pads, framing his big square chest. And plonked on top, his large square head, with beard covering the bottom two corners and hat covering the top two – the slightly jaunty angle of the latter utterly undermined by the extremely unjaunty look on the cruel piggy-eyed face. He looks a right cunt. In summary, that's what he was.

Of course it's more complicated than that and the chances are you already know that. He's such a famous king that almost anyone who would ever buy or read a history book in English knows the main things about him. There are six of them and they're his wives: Divorced, Beheaded, Died, Divorced, Beheaded, Survived. In retrospect we should have given them names. I've stolen that line from the great comedian Rob Brydon who says it after listing his children's ages. It works well for our dismissive relationship with those women. Now, as then, they only seem to matter in terms of their relationship with *him*. We all know men like that – at least Henry had the excuse of being king.

The odd thing about Henry VIII is that we know such a lot about his feelings and desires. He lived his life in public, like a cross between Kerry Katona and Vladimir Putin. We know about his physical vanity, his lusts, his desperation to have a son, the many crises in his love life, his conflicted spirituality, his young athletic sexiness, his embarrassing weight gain and increasing physical decrepitude.

His whole chaotic, bad-tempered personal life is still being played and replayed before us. If you visit the Tower of London, you can see his various suits of armour and how they got larger as he got fatter. How embarrassing for him. He was a very proud and self-important man – the thought of millions of people over hundreds of years knowing all about his ballooning waistline, his festering leg wound and, in later life, his irascible inability to get it up would have made him shudder and shout and have someone executed. In a sense, knowing all that humiliating detail is part of posterity's revenge.

Only part though. The rest of this book is all about how wrong Henry VIII turned out to be about everything. Nothing he tried to put in place really worked out. Power went in very different directions from those he'd planned. His impact on history was not the one he intended, though he did become very very famous.

The sense we get is of an enormous, tyrannical infant, throwing aside chicken bones like toys out of his pram. This vision of the king as child, as spoilt brat, is very influential – it infuses A. A. Milne's poem about King John and also another great one of his, 'The King's Breakfast', in which a monarch goes back to bed in a sulk because someone has suggested he might want to try marmalade: 'Nobody ... could call me a fussy man ...' They certainly couldn't – they wouldn't dare – and they couldn't call Henry VIII a selfish fatso going through a midlife crisis . . . I don't know whether Milne's view of a ruler would make sense without the thought of Henry VIII demanding that his ministers do the impossible and arrange for him to change wives.

For me, this idea that he was spoilt is tied in with the fact that he's got exactly the wrong amount, and type, of entitlement. His father was a self-made man, for all his talk of royal blood. Henry VIII is, in some ways, a typical second-generation waster. Phrases like 'he thinks the world owes him a living' spring to my resentful mind, which is strange because legitimate kings are justified in their sense of entitlement. The idea is that the world *does* owe them a living. They were entitled to be in charge and no one else was. My distaste when Henry VIII exhibits those assumptions is a sign that, heir of his father by primogeniture though he was, he is still tainted by usurpation.

A normal bit

The beginning of Henry's reign was quite nice in a boring sort of way. Everyone thought he was very handsome and clever and he did all the things that were expected of him. He arrested and executed his father's two most unpopular ministers. He married Catherine of Aragon, his brother's widow who'd been hanging around England for seven years waiting for that to happen, thereby cementing an alliance with Spain. He formed another alliance with Maximilian, that Holy Roman Emperor who'd been in Perkin Warbeck's Rolodex a couple of decades earlier.

He even had a little pointless war with France that went perfectly well, although it didn't achieve anything. While he was away doing that, Queen Catherine ran quite a successful war with Scotland, which did achieve something: the death of the King of Scotland. Henry's brother-in-law James IV fell at the Battle of Flodden – so that was nice.

While we're on the positives of killing relatives, he executed the main Yorkish claimant to the throne, Edmund de la Pole (brother of the de la Pole who'd been killed at Stoke Field). Known as the White Rose, he'd been in the Tower of London for some time so he was mainly executed to minimize his chances of escape. There was still another White Rose at large, though. This was Edmund's other brother Richard, who was swanning round Europe enjoying the hospitality of any monarch who liked the idea of annoying the King of England, which was most of them.

This Richard remained a thorn in Henry's at-this-point-still-not-particularly-podgy side until 1525 when he died in the Battle of Pavia, fighting unsuccessfully for Francis I of France against the new Holy-Roman-Emperor-and-King-of-Spain, the greatest Habsburg of them all, Charles V. Charles was very important but, like so many Habsburgs, terribly inbred in a way that affected his jaw and meant that, for everyone's sake, he usually ate privately in rooms soundproofed to conceal the noise of all the weird slurping. (The soundproofing bit is not necessarily true.)

By then Henry had attempted to make friends with Francis I, having had a great big camp international summit with him in 1520. I'm calling it camp both in the theatrical sense and because it was literally a great big camp – an enormous camp camp called the Field of the Cloth of Gold, in which Henry and Francis proclaimed a vacuous bromance that neither of them really felt.

Henry wanted to emulate Henry V, his stellar Lancastrian predecessor, famed for his martial valour and piety. A brilliant but thoughtful prince, always on the right side of history. It was in this virtue-signalling spirit that, in 1521, Henry VIII wrote a treatise condemning Martin Luther, who had nailed his 'Ninety-five theses' to the door of a church in Wittenberg to kick off the Reformation.

Pope Leo X was grateful for the support and awarded Henry the title of 'Defender of the Faith' (Fidei Defensor), an accolade the British monarchy boasts to this day, a cool half-millennium after Henry rejected papal authority. It's still on all the coins – a little 'F.D.' or 'FID. DEF.' – and presumably means that anyone with, say, a CBE who turns republican is welcome to print those letters on their business cards even if they're simultaneously plotting the downfall of the House of Windsor.

Hope for a pope on a rope

'Fair-weather friend of the faith' would have been a more apt title for Henry. In 1534 he rejected papal authority and declared himself the head of the English church. This wasn't quite the same as turning the country Protestant, but the many people in Henry's circle who were in favour of the Reformation delightedly saw it as a step in that direction, even if Henry himself blew hot and cold over ditching tenets of the faith he'd been brought up in.

The only two tenets he was totally comfortable with ditching were 1) his having to obey a man in Italy who didn't seem to understand how sexy Anne Boleyn was and 2) there being monasteries all over the place in possession of lots of land and wealth which Henry couldn't nab even though he could think of thousands of fun ways of spending it. Those couple of tenets could go fuck themselves, he felt. Other tenets like transubstantiation and not letting oiks interpret the scripture for themselves retained his sympathy except when Anne Boleyn was looking particularly alluring.

357

I'm getting ahead of myself, because I reckon you know most of this: Anne Boleyn was the second of Henry's wives, whom he married after Catherine of Aragon had got too old to have any more children. Of the several she'd had, only one had survived infancy and that one, horror of horrors, was a girl. Henry was convinced that he needed a male heir. In this, he wasn't a stand-out sexist – his was the mainstream view at the time, as there was no precedent for a female sovereign successfully ruling England. Empress Matilda had had a go. Enough said.

This crisis was developing in the late 1520s at the same time as Henry was becoming infatuated with the much younger (than either him or Catherine) Anne Boleyn. He'd had an affair with her sister, Mary Boleyn, but Anne was more aspirational than Mary and wouldn't have sex with him unless they were married – a technique known at the time as 'doing an Elizabeth Woodville'. If Woodville's resolve had caused a few problems and a minor civil war, Boleyn's ended up changing the whole nation's belief system as well as doing almost as much long-term damage to the Catholic church as Martin Luther had.

Henry became convinced that the reason he hadn't had a son was that he should never have married his brother's widow so God was cross. He found a passage from Leviticus to back this theory up. He told his chief minister, Cardinal Thomas Wolsey, to persuade the pope to get his marriage to Catherine annulled – so that, in the eyes of God and the church, it had never happened. They'd just been fucking and their little princess, who was called Mary, was a bastard.

Wolsey was an exceptionally capable man. Despite genuinely humble origins, he had risen to become the country's second richest and second most powerful figure. In a hereditary absolute monarchy, that's absolutely as far as merit can take you. He was very bright and very diligent. It is to Henry's credit that he saw this and used it without pausing to consider whether he should have a first minister who was posher. He couldn't have picked a more effective or less troublesome man than Wolsey. He always said yes to the king and then he always made it happen.

Sadly, however, he couldn't achieve the impossible and that's what the papal annulment of Henry and Catherine's marriage turned out to be. On paper, it shouldn't have been that hard. Popes had sorted out divorces for kings many times in the past. Eleanor of Aquitaine's marriage to Louis VII of France is a good example – it was annulled by Pope Eugene III, after fifteen years and two daughters, on the basis of consanguinity. Sounds like a sensible reason, but then loads of royal marriages were a bit too incestuous – that was routinely tolerated. But it could be used as an excuse when the real reasons were less clear-cut. In the case of Louis and Eleanor, it was that they totally hated one another.

Had the pope been amenable to helping the Defender of the Faith's tricky dynastic situation, then the bit of Leviticus would have provided justification enough. Then there wouldn't have been a break with Rome and William Shakespeare would have been a second-rate sculptor. But the pope wasn't amenable and found a bit of Deuteronomy that said the opposite to the bit of Leviticus.

Was that because he preferred Deuteronomy to Leviticus? No, it was because he preferred Charles V, who was at this time pretty much in charge of Italy, hanging around with lots of troops while eating spaghetti in horrendous new ways, to Henry VIII, who had no power south of the Lizard peninsula, and much less than Charles in general. Charles was Catherine of Aragon's nephew and he didn't take kindly to his dear old aunt being cast aside. The pope said no.

Gradually, mind. It wasn't a flat no. There was lots of chat, while Wolsey desperately hoped to get a deal, and Henry desperately hoped to have sex with Anne Boleyn, and managed to convince himself that, in fact, this was a very holy feeling. Henry eventually lost patience with Wolsey, who was disgraced and, in 1530, died of the stress of it all before Henry had even got round to executing him.

Kings of England had fallen out with popes before, and at times had been excommunicated. Henry II and John both had their run-ins. But no English king, however irascible and self-confident, had ever done the full 'Fuck you I won't do what you tell me' to quote from Rage Against the Machine's 1992 protest hit 'Killing in the Name', which, if you ask me, would be a much more appropriate piece of music to be associated with Henry VIII than 'Greensleeves', though neither track reached England until after his death.

Why did Henry do what none of his predecessors had dared to do? Was it because he was angrier, or hornier, or took less shit from foreigners? No, it was just because of the Reformation that was happening in Europe generally. The notion of rejecting the pope was decidedly fashionable. Suddenly, excommunication didn't make you a pariah, it just put you on the other side of a two-sided debate. Henry was kicking the pope while he was down.

Egged on by reformers, those who had rejected Catholicism far more wholeheartedly than Henry ever did, such as Thomas Cromwell, his chief minister from the early 1530s onwards, and Thomas Cranmer, who became archbishop of Canterbury in March 1533 – but opposed by Catholics such as Sir Thomas More (*all* of Henry's ministers seemed to have been Thomases – it must have been very confusing, though useful for pinning blame on colleagues) – Henry married Anne in January 1533.

Then Cranmer, recently installed as archbishop (with full papal approval, the very last of that sentiment to be forthcoming), annulled Henry's marriage to Catherine, declared his marriage to Anne to be valid and, on 1 June, crowned her queen. In the Reformation Parliament, which sat from 1529 to 1536, various statutes made all this official, including the Act of Succession, which had Princess Mary declared illegitimate, the Act of Restraint in Appeals, which said that appeals to the pope in Rome on any matter were now illegal, and, in 1534, the Act of Supremacy, which declared Henry to be the supreme head of the Church of England. He was his own pope, basically.

A lot of this legislation, which was pushed through parliament by Cromwell, was justified by the enjoyable bullshit that England was not a kingdom but an empire, like the Byzantine Empire or the Holy Roman Empire, just smaller. It always had been one, that was the idea. This conforms to the usual pattern of a radical change spun as restoration of something ancient. Henry found some historians who claimed to have traced the English kingdom back to someone called Brutus who'd come to Britain (which was then named after him, albeit approximately) all the way from Troy.

Yes, ancient Troy, as in the stories – the guys that fell for a fake horse and then some of them supposedly went off and founded the Roman Empire. They probably didn't really do either of those things but what they *definitely* didn't do, ever, is go to England at all. If you were looking for a story to make the one about Joseph of Arimathea coming here with the Holy Grail seem comparatively realistic, then Brutus of Troy founding Brutuan is a good choice. But that's what came out of Henry's historians' brainstorm – if it had been raining that day, they'd probably have said the place was founded by Noah, who'd landed at Noahquay in Cornwall.

What this fabricated backstory meant, they said, was that England and Henry, unlike other kings and kingdoms, were not subject to any external European jurisdiction. The idea that someone on the continent could overrule any aspect of

English governance would not be stood for. Sound familiar? The notion of Little Englander exceptionalism was established. This pattern of thinking would develop into a way of bolstering national self-esteem without incurring the expense of attempting to take over France.

Three queens down

Henry and Anne did not have a happy marriage. She kept answering back, which, you'll be amazed to hear, Henry VIII didn't like, and she gave birth to a daughter, which he liked even less. Also, she managed to fall out with Thomas Cromwell despite both of them being Protestants, which fact gave them enemies aplenty without needing each other.

In January 1536, after three years of marriage, the trajectory of Anne and Henry's relationship enjoyed a dead-cat bounce when the news of Catherine of Aragon's death broke. They dressed up in yellow, which was the colour of mourning in Catherine's native Spain, but they didn't mean it respectfully. They did a little celebratory victory dance together. This grubby knees-up may have been the last happy moment in the marriage.

Anne was pregnant again by this point and had a strong sense that it was extremely important that she give birth to a boy. An attractive, quiet, amenable and deferential young woman called Jane Seymour had started hanging round the court and laughing at the king's jokes and this made Anne anxious.

Then, one day, Henry had a jousting accident in which he hurt his leg and, by one account, was unconscious for two hours. The leg injury troubled him for the rest of his life as it developed into a revolting, purulent ulcer which stank and caused him agony. Some reckon that the unconsciousness damaged his brain and caused him to turn into an intolerant, irascible tyrant. I'm not sure about this as he wasn't exactly a pussycat before the accident. Henry post-1536 seems to me entirely consistent with the man he was before – just a bit grumpier because he was old, his leg hurt all the time and he was getting fatter and fatter as a result.

The shock of the jousting accident is said to have been what caused Anne to miscarry a male child a few days later. Henry was not very sympathetic and allowed charges of adultery to be trumped up against her. She was executed in May 1536 and Jane Seymour was betrothed to Henry the next day.

Jane Seymour was Henry's ideal wife: she didn't argue, she gave birth to a boy and then she promptly died without his having to kill her. What a catch. Henry claimed to be heartbroken at her passing, but there's a certain amount of self-pity that has to be waded through before we can properly discern the sincerity of the emotion. I'm sure he thought he was very sad, but he'd known wives die before and bounced back very quickly. On the first occasion he got dressed up in a bright colour and had a party, and on the second, which he had ordered, he was about to get engaged to someone else. So let's keep the size of the violin we play for him under control.

This was 1537 and it's important to note that England had changed hugely in the last few years in a way that was freaking a lot of people out. The European Reformation, this huge schism in the western Christian church, revolutionized the context in which everything was happening. For centuries, there'd been rulers and there'd been the pope – and they argued or got on well, they denounced each other, and made up, and sometimes the one called a crusade and the other trooped off to the eastern Med for some fighting and diarrhoea.

There'd been times when there'd been an antipope – i.e. a rival pope that some people considered to be the real pope.

But the notion that the real pope just didn't matter and was some sort of diabolical impostor, an unwanted intercessor between God and man who obstructed the salvation provided by the scriptures, was a massive shift. If that's what you believed then the pope and all devout Roman Catholics were now heretics. And if you were a Catholic, this new evangelical, reforming, Protestant agenda was itself a worse heresy than Islam.

This complete polarization of views is familiar to us today from social media. Some of the horrendous consequences of the Reformation, such as the Thirty Years' War which raged in Europe during the seventeenth century, and remained unsurpassed in its brutal, martial murderousness until 1914, led to a few centuries in which toleration started to be valued as a mindset, and people in the liberal west could agree to differ. That civilized instinct has no place amid the electric mob rule of a Twitter discussion. The loneliness of pariah status will be familiar to many who have neglected to entirely agree with one or other of two savagely opposed points of view.

Henry VIII was in just such a lonely position, though he probably didn't realize it. His views were unacceptable to both Catholics and Protestants – too keen on transubstantiation for the latter, too down on the pope for the former. The English Reformation is weird: it was shaped by the way different religious groups manipulated Henry's needs, desires and theological musings. The reformers got as much as they could out of him, but were careful not to push their luck. Then the Catholics would try and nudge things back a bit, but were equally careful not to say anything nice about the pope.

One traumatic change that was being implemented by Cromwell was the dissolution of the monasteries. The reformers despised these ancient institutions, and with reason: they were often corrupt and hypocritical. Still, they had been part of the fabric of English life for a lot longer than a sole

English monarchy, let alone a parliament. Getting rid of them was bound to cause trauma.

The reformers dreamed of the monasteries' vast wealth being used to improve the conditions of the people. The Catholics, conversely, considered their ancient role of praying for humanity's salvation, as well as providing vital services such as alms and medicine, to be irreplaceable. The compromise that was reached was to get rid of them but for the crown to keep all their wealth for Henry to build palaces and wage wars. This was how Cromwell got the king onside with the plan.

The process was made all the more sickening for religious conservatives and members of monastic institutions because it happened in two waves. A large number of smaller monasteries were dissolved in 1536 and then the remaining smaller number of large ones got closed down in 1538. In between there were rebellions and, in general, outpourings of national agony, most notably a vast uprising in the north called the Pilgrimage of Grace.

These are a reminder of how quick and radical the changes were – the whole rationale of religious existence was suddenly transformed, and by a diktat from central government rather than through any grass-roots evolution of religious feeling. However flawed many of the monasteries were, this imposition was bound to appal and frighten many. The uprisings caused stress for Henry and Cromwell and, for the rest of the reign, the king was constantly worried that some sort of rebellion would break out and be supported by an invasion from a great Catholic continental ruler, most likely Charles V. It didn't happen, though, because Henry, whatever he thought, was a pretty lucky guy.

Was the dissolution of the monasteries the moment when England started to become accustomed to the unsettling effect of what its authority figures insist is progress? It's often struck me as a lamentable trait in the modern British, and I think it manifests most in England, of glumly accepting change that no one likes or wants. Post office closures, the decline in manufacture, the decimation of shops and pubs in high streets, the requirement to do everything online. These are developments that very few of us like but the consensus seems to be that we need to grow up and take it: things can't be nice, this is the real world. That's life. Shit happens. Nothing pleasant can be made economically viable.

The French don't take the same view. They're much happier using their collective power to sustain a way of life they like. Hence they have a law which prevents people from staying at their desk in an office over lunch. An actual law! I only know about it because, during the Covid lockdown, it was temporarily suspended on the basis that all the restaurants and cafés were closed. Imagine having a law about something like that! Don't work at your desk: get out and have a proper lunch. Go to a brasserie, or go home and cook. The food will be nicer and so will your experience of the day, one of a finite number you will live through.

We'd never vote for a government proposing that sort of law in England. It would get condemned as 'Nanny State'. The notion of freedom, of English exceptionalism, would be deployed by the harsh anti-protectionist right and we'd dutifully carry on eating sandwiches over our keyboards, gradually developing ulcers and then, at the weekend, moaning that there aren't any decent places to eat round here.

Two of these queens actually make it!

Cromwell was riding high in 1539 when he organized the king's next marriage to someone called Anne of Cleves. Her father was the Duke of Cleves and this was part of Cromwell's plan to cement an alliance with the leading Protestant states of western Europe. He dispatched the great painter Hans Holbein the Younger to do a portrait of Anne to show to Henry.

The king responded enthusiastically to the portrait, which is interesting because I wouldn't say it looked exactly sexy. It wouldn't make it into a Pirelli calendar. It's quite a plain picture of a normal-looking woman dressed extremely oddly. The oddness of the dress is to do with it being the sixteenth century so we have to ignore that. Almost everyone I mention in this book dressed very strangely by our standards. All in all, it's not a picture that would make you rule out marrying its subject, but it wouldn't clinch the deal for me.

Nevertheless it clinched the deal for Henry and a marriage was organized. Poor Anne travelled to England, all nervous and excited, and then Henry took one look at her and decided he didn't fancy her at all. But he still married her a few days later, which seems to me to compound the awkwardness. Henry couldn't get it up, and decided that was entirely Anne's fault and not his for being a boozy old fatso with a rotting leg.

By the standards of most relationships, Anne was quite badly treated. By the standards of Henry's wives, she's probably second luckiest. The marriage was swiftly annulled and for the rest of her life she lived in England in quiet retirement, accorded the status of 'the King's Beloved Sister'.

Nevertheless the whole episode was pretty embarrassing for floppy-cocked Henry, so Cromwell's days were numbered. In April 1540, in the wake of the Cleves fiasco, he was made earl of Essex – a meteoric elevation for a man whose background was just as humble as Wolsey's. But it seems Henry was just toying with him. Two months later, he was arrested, attainted and, on 28 July, executed. Henry didn't watch it happen because he was getting married that day.

Henry's fifth queen was Catherine Howard, niece of the

Duke of Norfolk. The Howards are still the dukes of Norfolk today and they're also still Catholics so you won't be surprised to learn that Henry's new marriage, and Cromwell's demise, were signs that a conservative faction was on the rise at court. The king soon regretted this shift. He never had a minister as capable as Cromwell again and Catherine Howard was as unfaithful as Anne Boleyn was accused of being. She was executed in 1542.

But the bloated, wheezing, rotting, increasingly enraged and immobile old romantic hadn't given up on love. The following year he married Catherine Parr. She was a reformer, so marked a turn away from the Howards' religious conservatism and having sex with other men, but Henry's mood continued to oscillate between Catholic and evangelical in a way that made everyone, even his new queen, episodically fear for their lives.

Catherine seems to have been an intelligent, humane woman who managed to make the old wreck of a king feel attractive and loved. She was also instrumental in reconciling him with all his children. His daughter by Anne Boleyn had been removed from the succession and declared a bastard by act of parliament just as her half-sister Princess Mary had been but, under a Third Succession Act in 1543, all of the king's children by his various marriages were legitimized and returned to the line of succession.

One great big, extremely fucked-up family. They would now have the same inheritance rights as if they'd all been born to the same queen. Edward first, because he was a boy, and then the girls starting with Mary and followed by Elizabeth. And that is exactly what happened: they all reigned one after another and died childless. The Tudor line, which Henry had wreaked so much havoc trying to secure, was doomed anyway.

36. King Edward VI

I once saw the diplomatic genius of the Good Friday agreement of 1998 explained as having allowed both sides of the argument over Northern Ireland's sovereignty to exist almost in parallel universes where each had got what it wanted. To Irish republicans, there was now no border so Ireland was united. Practically speaking, that was the reality. Meanwhile, to unionists, Northern Ireland remained part of the United Kingdom – this too was an undeniable fact. Both sides could feel like they'd basically won. Everyone was sick of all the killing and this gave both sides the excuse to give the killing a rest.

In terms of the Reformation, Henry VIII acted almost like a big, terrifying, smelly and angry Good Friday agreement. His muddled and changing conception of the church allowed both sides to think that the national religion was basically what they wanted. At core, Henry remained a Catholic who believed in most of Catholic doctrine and was deeply suspicious of the more egalitarian elements of the reformers' agenda – so the Catholics could feel like the church was still fundamentally theirs. Meanwhile the reformers could rightly reflect on the huge changes that had been made: the break with papal authority and the destruction of all monastic institutions and all the heretical praying for the souls of the dead in non-existent purgatory that that entailed. They must have felt in the ascendant too.

This fudge could not last. It didn't have enough sugar in it. There was no way of bringing up the new king to believe the same jumble of stuff his father had, because it wasn't at all coherent without Henry's presiding personality. Edward had to be brought up either as a Catholic or as a Protestant. Well, it was Protestant and he really took to it.

He was only nine when he became king but he had received a top-class education. He was articulate, pious and he hated the pope. At the start of his reign, his uncle, Jane Seymour's brother Edward, snatched the reins of power from the regency council that Henry VIII had planned and had himself made lord protector of the realm and duke of Somerset. He ran things relatively badly, paying for England's desultory wars against France and Scotland by debasing the coinage.

This led to inflation and exacerbated the agrarian hardship already being caused by the widespread practice among landowners of enclosing common land, preventing the peasantry from using it. Somerset seemed sympathetic to the plight of those affected by this and set up a couple of commissions to look into it. They achieved nothing other than elevating the hopes of the poor, who then rebelled when their circumstances failed to improve. In 1549 there were widespread insurrections on a level not seen since the Peasants' Revolt of 1381.

Weapons of mass destruction

It's not the economy, stupid. It's the church. Of the two major rebellions, the one focused around Norwich was primarily a response to enclosure – and indeed claimed to be acting legally on behalf of Somerset's commissioners. But the other one, down in the West Country, was about the imposition of Protestantism. The Act of Uniformity of 1549 imposed Protestant worship, via Archbishop Cranmer's *Book of Common Prayer*, on the whole kingdom. To most people at the time, this was shocking and ungodly.

Even to some of the ruling class. Despite the overt

Protestantism of the king and his regime, a party of religious conservatives still existed at court and they took the popular rebellions during Somerset's rule as an excuse to remove him, by allying with his Protestant opponents. Most notable among these was John Dudley, Earl of Warwick. He supplanted Somerset, had himself made duke of Northumberland and then sloughed off his Catholic backers by appealing to the dyed-in-the-wool Protestantism of the king. He declared Edward ready for rule and so was made not lord protector but lord president of the Council. Effectively it was Somerset's role, though Northumberland filled it more competently.

So a newly self-created duke of Northumberland was in charge in place of the newly self-created Duke of Somerset. In a way, this unprepossessing wrangle was the inevitable consequence of a minority – the magnates will always squabble for influence. But this was also a Seymour being supplanted by a Dudley. These were not old families; these men are not royal dukes. In the Tudor age, the horizon of ambition is widening and I'm not talking about the rise of the middle class. These families saw what the Tudors had done and didn't see why they couldn't do the same. Now that the bossy fatso had died and his wan orphan was the nominal root of power, it felt like a perfect time to change the royal family's surname.

Throughout this Cranmer was working away making everything Protestant in a steady parliamentary way which appalled Catholics and also appalled some reformers who thought he should be acting more quickly and upsettingly. In 1550 Stephen Gardiner, the staunchly Catholic Bishop of Winchester who was in prison at the time, threw a spanner in Cranmer's reforming works by expressing approval for the *Book of Common Prayer*, basically saying that it could be interpreted in a Catholic way.

This seemed to justify Cranmer's reforming critics who said he hadn't been upsetting enough. It was like he was a teenage girl who had put on a short skirt to go to a party and then her parents had just said, 'Have a nice time, darling.' Nightmare. Cranmer had to stomp back upstairs to look for something so skimpy it showed his religion. (Please enjoy the questions that this metaphor raises.) In 1552, he had another go at upsetting Bishop Gardiner with another Act of Uniformity and a second edition of the *Book of Common Prayer*.

Then it became clear that the king was going to die. He had tuberculosis and gradually weakened from January 1553 onwards. This wasn't just a problem for the poor young king, it was a problem for Protestantism and for the political and literal survival of the reformer aristocracy. The focus of Northumberland's worry was that the next person in the line of succession was Princess Mary, who was very very Roman Catholic. She had seen her mother, Catherine of Aragon, humiliated and sidelined, and herself declared a bastard, in defiance of the pope, whom her father had then renounced and dared to supersede. She'd always been a Catholic but this life experience had only made her more so.

Edward and Northumberland were agreed that they had somehow to stop Mary taking the crown after him. It would be a disaster, they felt – after all, not only was she Catholic, she was a woman. So the young ailing king composed what he called his 'devise for the succession' in which Mary and his other half-sister Elizabeth, who was Protestant but still a woman, were passed over in favour of the male descendants of a group of other Protestant women. These women were Frances Grey, daughter of another Mary Tudor who was Henry VIII's younger sister, and her three daughters, the eldest of whom was called Lady Jane Grey.

This document was questionable to start with – it was an attempt to override Henry VIII's 1543 Act of Succession. But, as Edward's death approached, it became questionabler. It was changed, possibly by Edward but possibly by

Northumberland, and definitely at Northumberland's instigation. The phrase 'L Janes heires masles' became 'L Jane and her heires masles'. I know! The spelling! To be fair, they didn't have standardized spelling back then – the only outlet for their pedantic instincts was religious war.

As you will have spotted, an 'and her' was inserted, so that Lady Jane Grey herself became Edward's chosen heir to the throne. This was weird; suddenly the idea that the ruler shouldn't be a woman was out of the window. Even if you accept that shift of view and move on to Edward's other requirement – that the ruler should be Protestant – it still doesn't make sense. The next in line should have been his sister Elizabeth, and then his first cousin Frances, before his first cousin once removed Lady Jane Grey.

What was it about Lady Jane Grey, who was still in her teens, that had attracted such favour? She had just married Northumberland's son, Lord Guildford Dudley. Yes, the Dudleys were going for it. After sixty-eight years of the House of Tudor, make way for the House of Dudley. On 6 July 1553 Edward died. Northumberland kept this quiet to give himself time to get his ducks in a row. Then, on the 10th, Lady Jane Grey was taken to the Tower of London and proclaimed queen of England.

37. Lady Jane Grey

I didn't know whether to give her a chapter. In the end I did, because I felt sorry for her. She didn't want to be queen and responded to the news with trepidation and then a nervous sense of religious duty. She was a devout Protestant and, like the late king, thought it vital that England's monarch should continue the reforming agenda and not revert to Catholicism, which she considered to be heresy. But she was being used by her father-in-law in his attempt to retain power, and to become part of the royal family himself.

Despite being only fifteen years old, she didn't lack gumption and, for example, refused to allow her husband, Northumberland's son, to be proclaimed king. He had no royal blood and she determined that it would be her, not him, who would be the ruler.

But there her power ended. It was up to Northumberland to consolidate the attempted usurpation of which she was the figurehead. This he couldn't do. Before Edward died, Princess Mary had left London for her castle at Kenninghall in Norfolk. Northumberland's failure to prevent this was a big mistake from which he never recovered. Mary made it clear that she considered herself the rightful queen and popular support swiftly gathered around her in East Anglia.

Catholics rallied to her, of course, but so did many Protestants, who saw the absurdity of Lady Jane Grey's sketchy claim. Mary was a daughter of Henry VIII, a princess of the blood, royal through and through. Lady Jane Grey, despite her tenuous blood claim, felt like a random member of the aristocracy.

On 14 July, Northumberland rode out of London at the head of a small force to try and arrest Princess Mary, but it became clear that he would be met by an overwhelmingly larger force. On 20 July, when he was at Cambridge, a letter arrived from the Privy Council in London saying that they had proclaimed Mary queen. He went quietly and was executed on 22 August.

Lady Jane Grey was executed too, though not until the following year. She'd been convicted of treason, but Queen Mary was inclined to mercy because she knew how blameless Jane was. Nonetheless when Jane's father and two brothers joined a rebellion against the new queen, Mary concluded that she couldn't risk letting the girl live. On 12 February 1554 Jane was beheaded. Like Edward V, she never really ruled and was killed because of other people's political ambitions. Unlike Edward V, at the moment of her death, she was also denounced as a traitor. What a bitter insult to add to mortal injury.

38. Queen Mary I

Queen Mary was known as Bloody Mary because of the large number of people she killed. And also because of misogyny. She was the first properly crowned woman to rule as queen regnant, not just queen consort. You weren't supposed to be able to do this job if you were a woman, so a lot of people didn't like it. That may be why she gets the soubriquet 'bloody' when many of her male predecessors were responsible for more deaths – in battles as well as executions.

That said, if you're going by executions alone, Queen Mary was right up there on the leader board. She had almost 300 Protestants killed, mostly by burning – something else that undermines the 'bloody' thing. Beheadings feel bloody, burnings are more ashy. Or smoky. Smoky Mary would sound quite sexy, like a jazz singer, but, from the sound of her, that too would have been inappropriate. Still, considering the form of execution that she favoured, it seems odd to associate her with a non-flammable liquid.

The image of her that comes down to us is of a dour figure, usually depicted wearing black. At first glance, she looks a lot more puritanical than her Protestant would-be nemesis Lady Jane Grey. That's not a mistake you'd survive making to her face: she was Catholic to the core and had lived a life of suffering because of it, sidelined and reduced to bastardy by her father's epoch-making midlife crisis.

In 1536, after her mother's death, she had written a humiliating letter of apology and supplication to her father, which resulted in her return to court and, ultimately, to the line of succession. But she obviously felt very guilty and bitter about it. In 1557, the Venetian ambassador to her court, Giovanni Michieli, described her as 'very grave. Her eyes are so piercing that they inspire not only respect, but fear in those on whom she fixes them ... besides the facility and quickness of her understanding, which comprehends whatever is intelligible to others ... she is skilled in five languages, not merely understanding, but speaking four of them fluently.' So: sad, harsh and clever.

The main thing about Mary was that she turned the whole country Roman Catholic again. Frankly, the idea is exhausting. Impatient though I am with those of my fellow opponents of Brexit who now say that we have to accept it and move on, when I think about England going Catholic again I get a sense of where they're coming from. Sometimes nothing matters more than the avoidance of more hassle.

Not much fun

My feelings about this are informed by the fact that I know, which Mary and co. did not, that England broke with Rome again after her reign and never returned to the papal aegis. If Mary's had been the final move, it would be Henry's and Edward's rejection of the pope that would feel like the waste of energy. Mary thought, or hoped, that she was setting right a brief aberration.

Key to keeping the aberration brief was preventing a Protestant inheriting the throne after her so she needed to produce some heirs who'd then be higher in the line of succession than her Protestant half-sister Elizabeth. She was thirty-seven at the time of her accession which, to this day, the NHS startlingly classifies as a 'geriatric mother'. It's unnecessarily extremist terminology today but, in the sixteenth century when no one had a clue about germs, it really was a grand old age for popping one out.

In order to have a probably fatal pregnancy, Mary needed first to have sex with a man and in order to have sex with a man, she needed to get married. That was her strong feeling. You can't go burning hundreds of Protestants over what a wafer is made of if you've got a racy sideline in extramarital sex. Smoky Mary might get away with it, but not her buttoned-up namesake Bloody.

Mary's magnates (led by Bishop Gardiner, who'd been let out of prison the moment she took the throne) wanted her to marry someone English such as Edward Courtenay, son of the Marquess of Exeter, who'd been in the Tower for ever such a long time for being Catholic and deserved a treat. But Mary wasn't having it – she wanted a big international dynastic marriage, even though this made the English fear that the kingdom would then be dominated by a foreign power. They were already worried about that sort of thing, what with Mary's keenness to do whatever the pope wanted.

If Mary's aim had been to allay their fears, her choice of husband was idiotic. If her aim was to give birth to a healthy child, it was idiotic too – though I suppose we can't expect her to understand genetics. She chose Prince Philip, son of Charles V, the Holy Roman Emperor, Mary's mother's nephew and, as discussed, a man already suffering severe effects of inbreeding. Philip was marrying his cousin, but then his mother, Isabella of Portugal, was his father's cousin, so it was a family tradition. He and Mary never had a child – Mary thought she was pregnant a couple of times but she was probably wrong, which was probably for the best.

The prospect of the eldest son of the great Habsburg imperial potentate becoming Mary's husband and therefore, *jure uxoris* (by right of his wife), king of England sounded nightmarish to lots of English people. The Protestants hated the idea because the Habsburgs were extremely Catholic. So did anyone at all xenophobic and that was most people. In January 1554, this sparked Wyatt's Rebellion led by Sir Thomas Wyatt (son of another Sir Thomas Wyatt, the famous poet). This was the uprising that Lady Jane Grey's family joined in with and that led to her execution.

The leaders of the rebellion wanted to restore Protestantism, but many of the people who followed it favoured the old faith – the strength of pro-Catholic feeling among ordinary people had become clear the previous summer when Mary swept aside Lady Jane Grey. It was only anti-Spanish sentiment that united it – a fear that, since at the time husbands were masters of their wives, Philip would be master of Mary and therefore of England.

It caused an anxious moment for the new regime, particularly when the Duke of Norfolk led a force out of London to take on the rebels which then defected en masse to Wyatt's side, leaving the duke scurrying back to town. The queen's fortitude in addressing her own troops at London's Guildhall on 2 February was crucial to turning the momentum of events against the rebels. They were defeated. Any spirit of optimism that accompanied the new reign had also been snuffed out.

No fun at all

There were a couple of positives: in 1554, the Queen Regent's Prerogative Act was passed which made explicit, for the first time, that when a woman inherited the throne – became the sovereign, queen regnant rather than consort – she enjoyed the same powers as a king. Or had them, anyway. It really doesn't seem like she enjoyed them. In the same spirit, the Queen's Marriage Act of the same year made it clear that, while Philip, once they were married, would be accorded the same honour and respect as a king, the power lay with her and, as soon as their marriage ended, so did his rights as a ruler.

This was a forthright response to people's fears about Philip – and treated him with a humiliating level of suspicion. But he took it on his weird Habsburg chin – those guys played a long game. Emperor Maximilian's deft and lucky playing of the royal marriage market meant that his grandson, Charles V, ruled most of Germany, Italy, Spain and the Netherlands as well as, thanks to Christopher Columbus, an increasing chunk of South America. The strategy was clear: why conquer when you can just inherit? Had Mary and Philip been blessed with a son, he would have been a Habsburg and a Catholic king of England by right.

In general, it was a miserable reign. Apart from anything else, it rained a hell of a lot. It gets us down today – back then it made thousands of people die. Crops failed, so there was famine and then disease. The sense of God's favour, that everyone at the time looked for, seemed entirely lacking, as it poured and people starved or died of disease, warming themselves on the burning Protestant martyrs.

Religious divisions got so nasty. Wyatt's Rebellion had straightforwardly sought to kill Mary and put Elizabeth on the throne. The ringleaders weren't really pretending otherwise. There was no talk of 'bad counsellors' that they wanted to remove, as there usually had been when people rose against rulers in the past. Similarly, no one questioned Mary's dynastic right to rule, other than to assert her bastardy because of the annulment of her mother's marriage to Henry VIII. All that bloodline stuff was old hat: now it was all about religion. Her legitimacy or otherwise lay in the fact that she was a Catholic.

There is an irony that the key figure who helped her turn England Catholic again, Cardinal Pole, the papal legate who became archbishop of Canterbury when Cranmer was sacked, was actually another White Rose, a direct descendant of Edward IV's younger brother the Duke of Clarence. By the terms of the previous century, he had a better claim to the throne than Mary. But this old rivalry seemed quaint by the 1550s when the two of them, Yorkist and Tudor, were united by religious zeal.

They set about reversing all the changes that had been made since the break with Rome: in October 1553 all the religious laws of Edward VI's reign were repealed. In November 1554, the heresy laws of the fourteenth and fifteenth centuries were reintroduced and in January 1555 the royal supremacy over the Church of England was repealed. The only thing that wasn't put back was the monasteries – this was deemed unworkable as the aristocracy, Catholic and Protestant alike, had bought those lands from the crown, were really enjoying them and, if it came down to it, gave much more of a shit about their vast new properties than they did about the difference between the mass and holy communion.

Weird, isn't it? People were willing to die for these religious differences, but they wouldn't sacrifice real estate. The English obsession with property came early. In the sixteenth century, religion was worth being burned to death for, but not worth losing land over. Then, in the twenty-first, when practically the entire economy was closed down because of Covid, estate agents were still allowed to do viewings and there was a stamp duty holiday to stimulate the market. We're fucking nuts.

Poor old Cranmer really didn't want to be burned to death and signed several recantations of his Protestant beliefs, and then recanted those recantations, finally being burned at the stake in 1556. I have a strong feeling that I'm supposed to be inspired by his integrity and heroism, and that of all the other martyrs. But empathy fails me: I think they all needed to get a sense of perspective and say what they needed to say to avoid being burned. But that's just me: I avoid discussing trans issues on social media.

The bleakness of the reign did not abate. Mary's unequal relationship with her husband who, from 1556, was also King Philip II of Spain, resulted in her agreeing that England should join Spain in a war against France in 1557. This was something that her miserable, starving and diseased realm could ill afford and its only tangible consequence came the following January when the French took Calais.

The last English outpost in France was gone. That fig leaf which had, throughout the fourteenth century, concealed the ridiculousness of the English monarchy's claims on France had been torn aside. Mary may have been the wife of a great king, and the daughter-in-law of an emperor, but, with that loss, the parochial mediocrity of her own kingdom was laid bare.

Mary is supposed to have said of the disaster: 'When I am dead and opened, you shall find Calais engraved on my heart.' She wasn't great at human anatomy. She was always getting things wrong about her innards. At the same time that she said this, she had once again convinced herself that she was pregnant. She wasn't. It was probably cancer. She died on 17 November 1558. Philip couldn't spare the time to visit his wife in her last weeks, but when the news of her death reached him he did propose marriage to her successor Elizabeth, so that was nice.

39. Queen Elizabeth I

Elizabeth rejected the proposal. She and Philip II didn't get on. The trademark Habsburg technique for taking places over having failed in this instance, Philip tried to do it the old-fashioned way by sending the Spanish Armada. This was much later, in 1588, by which point all of Catholic Europe was on a mission to destroy Elizabeth at the instigation of Pope Pius V, who had practically declared a crusade against her.

In his papal bull of 1570 (a bull is an edict but only one made by the pope, in much the same way that a readeption is a restoration but only one happening to Henry VI), Pius declared Elizabeth illegitimate, excommunicated her, absolved all Catholics from obedience to her even if they'd sworn oaths to the contrary and, for good measure, excommunicated anyone who obeyed her. Now a Catholic couldn't even bring her the drink she'd ordered without going to hell. 'What is this papal bull?' Elizabeth must have exclaimed.

By 1588, England having been at war with Spain for three years already and the English having harassed a lot of Spanish shipping, Philip thought he'd do the holy thing and seize the chilly little half-island and kill its queen. It just felt right. So he sent an absolutely enormous fleet of . . . 130 ships (apologies if that's fewer than you were expecting) towards England which was only defended by its tiny, plucky fleet of . . . 200 ships (go with it), so that it could pick up the Duke of Parma's army (the most feared of all fighting forces with internal rhyme) from Flanders and drop it off in England to then conquer the place. It's quite an involved plan featuring not enough ships and involving coordinating lots of people to meet up,

400 years before anyone had the technology to text anyone else with an ETA. Unsurprisingly it fucked up.

That's not how it was spun, though. Elizabeth preferred 'amazingly it fucked up' or better still 'amazingly it was defeated'. Defeated by English resolve, courage, righteousness and naval valour plus the all-important help of God, who we now definitely know was *never* a Catholic despite going along with a millennium and a half of popes and saintly images and everyone claiming to be solemnly eating bits of his son.

Harassed by the English fleet as it sailed east up the Channel, dispersed by fireships while at anchor outside Calais and then blown up the North Sea by the wind, the Armada didn't manage to pick up any troops, which was probably for the best since most of it was smashed to bits by bad weather as it tried to find a way home round the north of Scotland and west of Ireland.

This victory was the high point of Elizabeth's reign. She had withstood many attempts on her life, the sabre-rattling hostility of the head of international Catholicism and now a full-on attack by the closest the sixteenth century had to a global superpower, apart from the Ottoman Empire and China. She was allowed to enjoy it and she did. Philip II didn't propose marriage again, however. He obviously didn't find it sexy.

Marriage

Like her father's reign, Elizabeth's was dominated by thoughts of marriage. On average, they got married three times each. Poor Elizabeth had zero spouses. It looks as if she went to her grave straight from the shelf, where she'd been desperately hoping for a guy.

That's not how it was. She didn't want to get married but felt it impolitic to say so. She played along, apparently entertaining the notion of several suitors, including King Eric XIV of Sweden (wow – fourteen Erics! The Louis-loving French were only on twelve at this point). He sounds fun. And he was fun – he conquered Estonia, went insane and was deposed. In general, Elizabeth used her eligibility on the international marriage scene to short-term diplomatic advantage, but never let it get too serious.

She had her crushes, mind you. Most notably, she was very keen on her childhood friend Robert Dudley, another son of the Duke of Northumberland who had tried to put Lady Jane Grey on the throne. Small world. Dudley was Elizabeth's favourite for much of her reign and she might have thought about marrying him, but he was already married. And then, in 1560, his wife died in suspicious circumstances – which made people suspect that he or Elizabeth had had her killed so that they could get married. But that very suspicion then meant they certainly *couldn't* get married so, if that was their plan, it was a bad one. They didn't marry but, in 1564, she made him earl of Leicester instead.

The reason for the pressure on Elizabeth to marry was the need to sort out the succession. She was the last of Henry VIII's children and the other two hadn't lived very long. If Elizabeth died without issue, it wasn't clear who the next ruler would be and fifteenth-century history suggested that the clarification process would be bloody – plus the Reformation had now given everyone an extra reason to hate everyone else. When Elizabeth nearly died of smallpox in 1563, her ministers panicked, started making speculative lists, and questions were asked in parliament afterwards.

So why didn't she marry? We must resist the answers that conform to the value system of the many screen depictions of her: that she never fell in love. Or, she did fall in love with someone, but the match was forbidden by the mores of the time. And she could never bear to marry another. Fuck all that. The fact that she wasn't in love with anyone, or was in love with someone else, didn't get in the way of royal marriages in the sixteenth century – it didn't get in the way of Prince Charles's in the twentieth century. Those royals weren't looking for love in a marriage and, for a monarch, a loveless marriage didn't preclude finding love elsewhere, unless you ran into someone unusually stubborn like Anne Boleyn.

Elizabeth was Anne Boleyn's daughter so maybe she had inherited some of that stubbornness – or, to put a more positive spin on it, sense of self-worth. Her other parent also had abnormal levels of self-esteem. Was it in that spirit, of stubborn tyranny, contrarianism, that Elizabeth resisted the enormous pressure to marry?

I don't think so. She was well educated and very clever. Also she'd had a traumatic life. Her mother had been executed when she was two, she had endured the slur of bastardy, restoration to legitimacy and bastardy again. Her brother's will had passed her over in the line of succession in favour of random cousins, and then her Catholic sister had suspected her of disloyalty for her whole reign, even briefly putting her in the Tower in the aftermath of Wyatt's Rebellion. She acceded at a perilous time, with everyone wishing she were a man and half of everyone wishing she were a Catholic. The tenor of international relations having darkened somewhat in the previous half-century, the latter group was not above trying to murder her. How does an intelligent person react to all this? With caution.

The hallmark of Elizabeth's reign was caution. She didn't marry because to marry anyone was a risk. It would have weakened her position. It was also weakened by there being no clear succession, but either by calculation or by default she took that long-term risk instead of the sharper immediate existential risk of being married to, and so owing obedience to, the wrong man: an English nobleman with a thirst for power or a foreign prince with mental health issues. As time went on and she didn't die, there were fewer short-term nerves among the magnates, and then it gradually became clear that she had become too old to have children. The pressure to marry was off because it was too late for it to help with succession planning.

Taking care of business

She showed similar caution in her religious policy. She was a Protestant and so had to reverse Mary's changes and turn England Protestant again. Her religious conscience aside, she would have been toast if she hadn't done that as Protestants formed her entire support base.

However, she was bitterly aware that this would alienate the Catholics. Unfortunately it was a binary issue. There was no compromise third position that wouldn't have had both sides calling her a heretic. Centrism was even more intellectually unrespectable than it is now.

So she turned the country Protestant again but tried to soften the blow. She didn't like Catholicism but she didn't tolerate Puritans either. The version of the *Book of Common Prayer* she introduced was milder, less alienating to Catholic sympathizers. She brought back Protestant forms of worship but kept significant and mollifying Catholic elements such as vestments. She repealed the heresy legislation and kept the penalties for recusancy (i.e. remaining Catholic) relatively mild. And in her Act of Supremacy of 1559 she made herself supreme governor, not supreme head, of the Church of England.

These compromises of principle in order not to upset people set the Church of England on its path. It is despised by many for this. It is deemed to be soft, lacking in intellectual and theological rigour, trying to please everyone. Proper convinced Christians, and indeed ethical people of any belief system, should, it is often proclaimed, be fearless about upsetting people in order to uphold their values. Maybe. But I reckon most of the people who genuinely have no fear of upsetting others don't just have no fear of it, they actively enjoy it.

Elizabeth didn't mind upsetting people, but she knew it was stupid and risky to do it unnecessarily, so her Protestantism was mild. She would not, as Francis Bacon apparently put it, 'make windows into men's souls'. Don't ask, don't tell. It was a vital part of the process of England finding some sort of religious peace: you think what you like, just don't make a big fuss and we can all rub along okay.

This caution was also on display in her foreign policy where it caused some frustration. As a leading Protestant monarch, she was supposed to get behind that cause across Europe, but her support for Protestants in the Dutch Netherlands and France was half-hearted and expense-averse. She provided too few troops too poorly supplied and preferred them not to get involved in fighting if possible. She was keener on naval actions where Drake could whizz in, do some damage, steal some stuff and whizz out.

This approach may not have garnered much international success, but it protected her precarious position at home. Unlike her father she had no interest in emulating Henry V and she lacked the resources and opportunity to do so anyway (so did her father, but he was too vain to realize). She wanted to survive and prioritized that above glory.

This wasn't, however, how she presented herself. Projecting caution would have been incautious. Outwardly, it was all grandeur and entitlement. She styled herself 'Gloriana' and used her imposing image and beauty to dazzle. She emphasized feminine and masculine qualities and used their juxtaposition to entice – it was the PR equivalent of what salted caramel tastes like.

She could turn on the Henry V act when she needed it. Her speech to the troops at Tilbury, preparing for the Duke of Parma's expected invasion, is spine-chilling, and delivered over a decade before Shakespeare put similarly stirring words in the mouth of her Lancastrian predecessor:

> I know I have the body but of a weak and feeble woman; but I have the heart and stomach of a king, and of a king of England too, and think foul scorn that Parma or Spain, or any prince of Europe, should dare to invade the borders of my realm.

Mary Queen of Scots

Female rulers were suddenly all the rage. England was on its third in a row, if you count Lady Jane Grey. So Scotland had to have one too. This was Mary Queen of Scots who, to be fair, had acceded before any of the English queens, in 1542 at the tender age of six days. That's even younger than Henry VI had been and, like that Henry, the most successful section of her reign was the bit she played no conscious part in.

In 1558 she married the Dauphin of France and, in 1559, he became King Francis II of France, and in 1560 he died, so that was a bit of a rollercoaster. In 1561, still not twenty but already dowager queen of France, she returned to the other place she was queen of, Scotland, and had a bash at ruling it.

She took a very different approach to Elizabeth's: she kept marrying terrible men. But she was unlucky too: she was Catholic and so had Scotland been when she left. Unfortunately, in her absence it had gone Protestant – quite firmly. Mary tried to go along that, which disappointed the Catholics but didn't allay the suspicions of the Protestants. Her position was weak and she decided she needed a big, strong man to help her. So in 1565 she married a psycho called Lord Darnley. He promptly knocked her up and murdered a man called David Rizzio, who was Mary's secretary, friend and possibly lover, right in front of her while she was pregnant. All very Jeremy Kyle.

The marriage didn't bounce back from there. Luckily, in 1567, Darnley was murdered, probably by someone called Lord Bothwell who then abducted Mary, may have raped her, but definitely married her. She and Bothwell were not a popular couple to be running Scotland and soon they weren't. In July 1567, she was forced to abdicate in favour of her infant son, who was called James and who was taken off to be brought up as a Protestant. Mary was imprisoned but escaped the following year and fled to England where she threw herself on the mercy of Elizabeth, who, you will be unamazed to hear, was also her cousin.

Remember how one of Henry VII's daughters, Margaret Tudor, married King James IV of Scotland? This is where it becomes relevant. That branch of the family had been excluded from the line of succession by the terms of Henry VIII's will but, by blood, were major claimants to the throne. Mary was Margaret and James's granddaughter and a lovely Catholic option for queen of England if anything should happen to Elizabeth. And a lot of people were working on that.

So Elizabeth behaved cautiously as usual and put Mary in prison – nice prison, but she wasn't allowed out. And that's where she stayed for nineteen years. Was this a good sort of caution or would it have been safer to kill her? She immediately became the focus of plots and rebellions. In 1569, there was a major Catholic rising in the north which aimed to free Mary, marry her to the Duke of Norfolk, and put her on the throne. When it was defeated, Elizabeth had 600 rebels executed (so it wasn't just her sister who could be bloody).

When the papal bull came out the following year, everything got more fraught. Still Elizabeth resisted killing her cousin, but Sir Francis Walsingham, England's notorious spymaster, was piecing together a case against Mary. Not all the papist plotting, it seemed, was happening outside of Mary's ken. By late 1586, with England now at war with Spain, Elizabeth was willing to countenance putting Mary on trial.

As a queen of another country, Mary refused to acknowledge the court's jurisdiction. Her view was that, since she was a foreign head of state, she wasn't subject to English law. Also she wasn't being tried by her peers – that would have involved assembling a jury of monarchs. Nevertheless she was convicted of treason and sentenced to be executed. Elizabeth stalled over signing the death warrant, and claimed, when she did sign it, that she hadn't meant it to be dispatched. Was this remorse, a sense of mercy, or just the ultra-cautious ruler's reluctance, as with marriage, to do anything irreversible?

The last act

The defeat of the Armada in 1588 was Elizabeth's high point. Things went downhill after that. Militarily the triumph against Spain was rather undermined the following year when Elizabeth sent her own massive Armada, commanded by Sir Francis Drake, to Spain and Portugal. This was annihilated too. So maybe God was neutral. Or Muslim.

The queen was ageing and her core team of ministers was dying. Dudley in 1588, Walsingham in 1590, her lord chancellor Sir Christopher Hatton in 1591 and finally William Cecil, Lord Burghley, her most trusted minister and councillor who had supported her for the entire reign, in 1598. The new generation of help was less reliable and less united – there was a power struggle between Robert Cecil, Burghley's son, and

Elizabeth's late-reign favourite, the Earl of Essex. The old queen found it hard to restrain them. Caution and vigilance require energy and hers was running out.

She had no heir but, once Essex had disgraced himself by getting involved in a doomed and joyless rebellion, the younger Cecil was able to address that. Not in the obvious way – she was far too old. Mary Queen of Scots' infant son was now in his thirties and settled as the Protestant King James VI of Scotland. He was also Elizabeth's first cousin twice removed. Cecil encouraged a warm correspondence between the two sovereigns and, to the extent that the old queen felt it safe to acknowledge her own mortality at all, she tipped James the wink. When she died, in 1603, he inherited the throne without incident.

Something else was happening while the queen and her government withered. A flowering of words. Amid Protestant suspicion of imagery, creativity was finding other paths. The English language, the heir to the Anglo-Saxon tongue, rejected by the ruling class for centuries after the Conquest and then readopted and celebrated in the reigns of Edward III and Henry V, was coming into its own. It had been lurking in the background throughout English history and its time had come. This was happening in the printed books that were increasingly available, but most startlingly on stage.

The golden age of Elizabethan drama defined the civilization that England was and went on to be. For the first time, the nation had the means to reflect upon itself. So much of this book is about that reflection. The kings that lived before the Elizabethan era were like the tree in the forest, their noise was irrelevant until they were observed. England started to look at itself, and see itself, as Elizabeth faded away. Her self-consciousness as a sovereign was part of a broader trend that mattered more than any ruler or dynasty.

Before Shakespeare the Renaissance didn't hugely affect

England. It was like a copy of French *Vogue* in a Guildford hairdressers — just something people who wanted to be aware of things were aware of. It didn't touch many. When Shakespeare wrote *Hamlet* and it played to packed theatres, something new had begun. Renaissance is underplaying it. It was a birth, not a rebirth — but novelty is more approachable when spun as restoration.

Bookend

My wife gives the best explanation of why William Shakespeare is brilliant. With most writers, she says, you know where they're coming from. Their prejudices, their upbringing, their milieu seep out of what they write. You can ignore it, or you can factor it in, but it's there. With Shakespeare, it isn't. He's too good at writing.

She cites the phrase from *Macbeth*, 'boneless gums', as an example – as in the boneless gums of a baby that Lady M says she'd pluck her nipple from. My wife says it shows an instinctive understanding of what it's like to suckle an infant. 'If you say so,' is all I can reply. 'How did a man write that?' is her question. And, not being a moron, her answer isn't something like 'Aah, maybe he didn't – maybe Shakespeare is really Mary Queen of Scots?!' Her answer is 'Because he's the best.' There had to be a best and it happens to be him.

I think he's the best too. I was lucky enough to portray him on television as an irascible, fearful, careerist sitcom character. I feel oddly close to him as a result, and very protective when people claim he doesn't exist. Historically speaking, there is no justification for the claim. Those who say 'we know so little about him' seem to be unaware of how little we know about *anybody* from late sixteenth-century England. Compared to most, William Shakespeare is documented in enormous detail. Why claim that he didn't exist, or rather that the person of that name didn't write all those plays and poems, and assert that it was someone posher and therefore supposedly more plausible? The evidence doesn't support it – so, to believe that nonsense, you really have to *want* it to be true.

Who would want *that* to be true? Rather than the actual

truth? Here's the actual truth: a man with a normal background and education, an impecunious member of the provincial bourgeoisie in a backward kingdom on a war-racked island at the edge of civilization, turned out to be the greatest writer, and possibly the greatest artist of any kind, who ever lived. So far. That might be the most life-affirming fact in the entire history of humanity. Sometimes it makes me want to cry with joy. It's such a celebration of what humans can be. To want the truth to be otherwise is an act of spite against the very sanctity of our species.

He's where this book has been heading, it turns out. From King Arthur to William Shakespeare – a literary character to a literary genius. From someone everyone wishes existed to someone that some people, inexplicably, wish didn't.

Shakespeare is a good reason to stop writing about kings because his brilliance makes them seem silly. And when they don't seem silly, it's just because he has put words into their mouths that they could never have thought of themselves.

Richard II, for example, was a colossal twat. And yet Shakespeare has him say this:

> For God's sake let us sit upon the ground
> And tell sad stories of the death of kings:
> How some have been depos'd, some slain in war,
> Some haunted by the ghosts they have deposed,
> Some poisoned by their wives, some sleeping kill'd,
> All murdered – for within the hollow crown
> That rounds the mortal temples of a king
> Keeps Death his court, and there the antic sits,
> Scoffing his state and grinning at his pomp,
> Allowing him a breath, a little scene,
> To monarchize, be fear'd, and kill with looks;
> Infusing him with self and vain conceit,
> As if this flesh which walls about our life

Were brass impregnable; and, humour'd thus,
Comes at the last, and with a little pin
Bores through his castle wall, and farewell king!
Cover your heads, and mock not flesh and blood
With solemn reverence; throw away respect,
Tradition, form, and ceremonious duty;
For you have but mistook me all this while.
I live with bread like you, feel want,
Taste grief, need friends – subjected thus,
How can you say to me, I am a king?

It's poor characterization, isn't it? Richard didn't get within a million miles of that level of self-knowledge. Perhaps Shakespeare should have cut the speech. Although, in under 200 words, it says as much about the nature of kingship as I've managed in the rest of this book. To be fair to myself, I've put in more details, but still . . .

'Mock not flesh and blood with solemn reverence.' Ultimately, the reverence shown to monarchs is a mockery, a joke. It's pretending they're something they're not. This is a bitter and clear reduction of kingship to its essentials: an office accepted only because an unjust hierarchy is preferable to anarchy. Out of the gangsterism of the lawless post-Roman land of Britannia, a few local big shots emerged, their power gradually coalescing into kingship.

Mortal temples

It wouldn't have lasted if everyone had seen it as clearly as Shakespeare. The reverence for kings and queens had to be sincere and, over time, the revered had to come to believe they deserved it. It had to feel natural. To this day, the instinctive assumption that it is natural for a country to have a king and queen is deeply ingrained. Republics see themselves as a step forward from monarchy – something more advanced and fair – but, even in that, there is an implication that countries start off as kingdoms. That is our original state.

But it isn't. They don't. England didn't. It was a Roman province, part of an empire that was nominally a republic, though effectively a military dictatorship. Crowns, like Christianity, had to be introduced. The notion of royalty, of royal blood, hadn't always been – it had to be invented. In England the more successful Anglo-Saxon tribal bullies turned themselves into kings. Following continental trends, they started adding ceremonial and religious elements – giving kingship an aura of legitimacy and sanctity. But it was just made up. At some point someone with a sociopathic dislocation from the truth had to start asserting it, like the first conspiracy theorist who said that 5G masts spread Covid or that the current royals are lizards. (Though there's a certain poetic justice to that last lie – that's where centuries of asserting that there is something holy and superhuman about a crowned royal will get you.)

When the Vikings started invading, a sense of English unity developed in opposition to the raiders. English national identity was first defined merely as *not* being Scandinavian or Celtic – negativity can give you a strong sense of belonging, as Twitter shows. The most powerful of the families ruling the various Anglo-Saxon kingdoms, the House of Cerdic, gradually assumed leadership, not only of the West Saxons, but all the Anglo-Saxons, and finally the *Angli*. As a result, microscopic quantities of Cerdic blood still flow in the veins of Britain's current king.

The English monarchy's close association with France began with William of Normandy's dazzling smash and grab. For all the Conqueror's talk of his right, it was a chancy piece of entrepreneurialism that spectacularly came off – a huge, surprising event that led to England being ruled by a French-speaking monarchy and aristocracy for centuries. The Houses of Normandy and then Plantagenet were very proud to have their own kingdom but, in their hearts, those families were France-based – that was their centre of gravity. They would have jumped at the chance to trade England in for France.

This gradually created tensions with the aristocracy in England. Those barons may have been totally Norman in 1066, but a hundred years later they were decidedly Anglo-Norman, and when King John lost Normandy they became English by default. They didn't share their monarchs' France-owning ambitions and this motivated them to find a way to limit their kings' campaigning and spending. This imperative eventually led to parliament.

The randomness of it is wonderful to behold. Parliament came about as an indirect result of King Harold taking an arrow to the eye. It was the post-Conquest kings' split focus that caused the most significant English constitutional developments, not the deliberate policy of England's greatest kings.

In fact, generally speaking, when the kings were any good – when they had the skill to balance competing interests, deploy brutality in a timely but predictable way, create stability through even-handedness and the judicious use of fear – their powers and prerogatives didn't change much and the constitution remained the same. It was under the capricious or vacillating rulers, like John and Henry III, that the desperate barony reached for ways of limiting royal power.

For all the regal professionalism of the likes of Henry II, Edward III and Henry V, their triumphs were fleeting and soon reversed – if not in their own lifetimes, then shortly afterwards. It was all pointless in the end (one of the many suggested titles for this book). The constitutional advances during the reigns of terrible kings, on the other hand, have lasted to this day. Magna Carta and parliament are held up proudly as national achievements. I've got no problem with that, but the 'principles' that were supposedly asserted through them – notions of representative government and the rule of law – weren't in the forefront of the minds of those who devised them.

These nascent principles were straws the barons clutched at in the face of the huge principle they were ignoring, the doctrine at the core of medieval government: that everyone owed obedience, loyalty and homage to their anointed king. To us today the idea of a king's God-given right seems like obvious bullshit. Back in the middle ages, what smelled of excrement (apart from *everything*) was the proposition that it was lawful to defy a figure of such sanctified authority as a king. The fine constitutional principles we have inherited from Magna Carta and parliament started off as the mere rhetorical perfume the barons doused themselves in to cover the stench of their own treachery.

It is vital to bear this in mind because those surviving medieval institutions, and the high ideas we tell ourselves underlie them, are the main source of English, and British, national pride. Our sense of identity derives more from that feeling of continuity than from anything we think about ourselves now.

The UK's crown and parliament, and the judicial system of England and Wales, are nominally the same entities that operated during the period covered by this book – they have merely undergone adaptation and reform. That's okay – in fact it's pleasing, like an old house that still has Bakelite light switches. It's harmless as long as they've been properly rewired. But the story behind these constitutional artefacts is confused, contradictory, messy. Parliament, like the monarchy itself, was a random product of circumstance. Magna Carta was a failed attempt to prevent civil war. These developments were not driven by anyone's progressive conscience. Fondness may be a more appropriate thing to feel about them than pride.

The death of kings

The words of kingly self-knowledge that Shakespeare gave to Richard II are not just insightful about the nature of kingship – they're also an astute reflection on how views about it were changing at the time of that king's fall. It was a hugely significant turning point. After centuries of unchallenged Plantagenet succession, an unquestionably legitimate ruler had been usurped. The loss of confidence in the notion of kingship expressed by Richard in the speech may not have been a realistic idea to put in the head of that particular crowned narcissist, but others were definitely thinking it.

The idea of reining in difficult monarchs with things like Magna Carta and parliament was based on the premise that the king was the king and that was that. Legitimate and anointed rulers were immovable, however incompetent. But, when Bolingbroke stole the throne from Richard II by the simple use of military force – something that hadn't happened since the days of Henry I and Stephen, back when primogeniture was not yet established and the line of succession was consequently much fuzzier – that all changed. No need to focus on imposing financial or legislative encumbrances on bad kings – you can just overthrow them and bring in someone more conscientious.

There's a weird paradox here. In a way, a less well-defined order of succession – a milieu where the next king can emerge from a wider group of leading magnates with royal blood – allows a greater element of meritocracy to enter the process. Back in Anglo-Saxon days, this meant Alfred could rule instead of his infant nephews. It made Henry I king instead of his feckless elder brother Robert. And it ushered in the capable and pious Henry IV instead of the vain idiot Richard II.

But the positive consequences of this very limited meritoc-racy are totally outweighed by the loss of stability it causes. You may get better kings but the transfer of power from one to the next is likely to be an absolute shitstorm. Plus, as Henry IV showed, the potentially capable king you then get isn't all he might be because a) he's terrified and watching his back and b) people are less inclined to obey him because he's a usurper. They figure why should they? He's just some guy. Maybe someone's going to usurp *him* in a minute. So the sta-bility of the crown is undermined.

This was a bit of a shame and made rather a mockery of the centuries that had been spent developing institutions to mitigate poor kingship. During the Wars of the Roses, parlia-ment sat there pointlessly, like a fax machine in the corner of an office with wifi. Meanwhile the exchanging of the throne between Lancastrians and Yorkists, both with imperfect claims to rule, permanently weakened people's belief in the monarch's divine legitimacy. Also it killed loads of people.

By the time Henry Tudor took over, the deep Plantagenet belief in 'God and their right' was a distant memory. Tudor was just a bloke, quite distantly related to the royal family. I mean, he had a surname for God's sake! The Tudors did their best to project royalty and prestige – Henry VIII and Eliza-beth I were particularly good at that. But the truth of royal power had been exposed for the first time since the Anglo-Saxon gang leaders put on airs and graces.

That feels like a good place for this book to end. The great era of English kingship is over. That may feel like a grandiose assertion, with 420-years-and-counting more English mon-archy between then and now, and millions tuning in so recently to watch the latest incumbent process to the abbey for his hat and a splat. So let me explain the various ways in which it's true.

First, after 1603, the kings and queens of England are also

kings and queens of Scotland. Or rather the other way round – James Stuart, already King of Scots, inherits England and Ireland too. It's another century before the Kingdom of Great Britain is officially ushered into existence but that's the way things are heading and that's a different story from that of medieval England and a more complex one.

Second, kings and queens become less dominant after 1603 – not immediately but relatively swiftly. This book is about rulers and, by covering them, the political story of the age is more or less told. That's not the case from the seventeenth century onwards. Other people are more central – prime ministers, foreign ministers, chancellors of the exchequer . . . Telling that history through the lives and doings of kings starts to feel antiquarian. The kings and queens are often interesting and remain major figures, but they don't matter so much. All of the monarchs I've talked about were at the epicentre of politics in a totally different way from, say, George II, let alone Edward VII. Much of the story around the crown descends to the level of golfing anecdotes – plus obviously a shitload of hunting.

The third big sign that kingship as a concept is irrevocably on the slide is an event that happened less than half a century after Elizabeth's death: the execution of an English king by order of parliament. By the mores of the centuries covered by this book, the judicial beheading of Charles I on a scaffold in Whitehall was as shocking as a public blowjob being administered on an altar.

I feel sorry for Charles I, as I do for Richard II and Edward II and Robert Curthose. They were victims of the system as surely as all the millions of peasants whose existence is forgotten. But they were not, despite what they had been told about themselves, touched by the divine – or no more than all humans. They were not amazing people. Neither, really, were the supposedly great rulers of this time. They were capable, but they were also brutal, flawed and fundamentally limited. Personally, I wouldn't rank Henry II, Edward III, Henry V or Elizabeth I alongside Franklin D. Roosevelt, Nelson Mandela or even Angela Merkel, let alone Jane Austen, Alfred Hitchcock or Marie Curie.

There must have been amazing people, but we don't hear about them because most of them couldn't write. They left no mark. But the flowering of Elizabethan drama, and Shakespeare in particular, is a reminder that they existed. Amazing people existed but they did not seem to matter. That is probably the most far-reaching conclusion we can draw from centuries of violent kingship.

These rulers are fun to remember. They are interesting, and it is weird, almost surreal, that such people were so powerful. There are still tyrants in the world today and the strangeness of their power is something we must hold in mind. It's extremely odd. That fact can get lost in our anger at the injustice of what they do. The anger dignifies them, it makes them important. But they're not important, they're random.

They're a product of a flawed system, like litter or traffic jams. The people themselves are as inconsequential as the biographical specifics of a burglar who has been enabled to take all your stuff by lax security, poor law enforcement and a grim socio-economic environment. The rulers in this book inherited or acquired a lot of power. They did things that affected millions of people's lives. But, if they hadn't, someone else would have done. Unlike Shakespeare, they were not important. We had but mistook them all this while.

Further Reading

At this point, I'd probably recommend a thriller, really. Or a whodunnit. Maybe even a graphic novel. You know, for a bit of variety. You must feel up to your ears in history. But that's not the form in these sections. They tend to work more like Amazon algorithms: 'Seeing as you just bought gardening gloves, perhaps you'd be interested in these gardening gloves?'

So, if you would like to continue reading on a similar theme, here are some books that were helpful and enjoyable to me and that you would probably enjoy too, even if they contain some of the same information as the book you've just read.

Marc Morris, *The Anglo-Saxons: A History of the Beginnings of England* (London, 2021)

Norman Davies, *The Isles: A History* (London, 2000)

Tom Holland, *Athelstan: The Making of England* (London, 2016)

Hugh M. Thomas, *The Norman Conquest: England After William the Conqueror* (Plymouth, 2008)

Dan Jones, *The Plantagenets: The Kings Who Made England* (London, 2012)

Charles Spencer, *The White Ship: Conquest, Anarchy and the Wrecking of Henry I's Dream* (London, 2020)

Catherine Hanley, *Matilda: Empress, Queen, Warrior* (London, 2019)

Ian Mortimer, 'The Reputation and Legacy of Henry IV' (Cross Tree Press Audio, 2022)

Ian Mortimer, *A Time Traveller's Guide to Medieval England: A Handbook for Visitors to the Fourteenth Century* (London, 2008)

Miri Rubin, *The Hollow Crown: A History of Britain in the Late Middle Ages* (London, 2005)

Thomas Penn, *Winter King: The Dawn of Tudor England* (London, 2011)

Susan Brigden, *New Worlds, Lost Worlds: The Rule of the Tudors 1485 – 1603* (London, 2001)

Tracy Borman, *Crown & Sceptre: A New History of the British Monarchy from William the Conqueror to Charles III* (London, 2021)

Acknowledgements

This is quite a long list of names for which I make no apology. It wouldn't surprise you at the end of a TV show or film and, like those other media, books require the hard work and talent of a large group of people to make the thousands and thousands of words the author reckons the world can't do without palatable to the wider public. You may notice that, in place of the apology I said I wouldn't give, I've wasted an equivalent amount of your lives with this slightly petulant explanation. For which I am also making no apology. I'm clearly unbearable so, if you've enjoyed this book at all, my thanks must go to (in no particular order . . .) (I'm trying to make this exciting):

Stephan Biddle, Jennifer Breslin, Colin Brush, Ellie Hughes, Sriya Varadharajan, Beatrix McIntyre, Peter James, Jon Kennedy, Alice Mottram, James Keyte, Stella Newing, Christopher Thompson, Helena Sheffield, Christina Ellicott, Tineke Mollemans, Kelly Mason, Laura Garrod, Sophie Marston, Allison Pearce, Hannah Padgham, Louise Moore, Tara Lynch and Michele Milburn. Plus, if you bought this book because someone working in a book shop suggested it, I'd love to give them a mention. If you know their name you could write it here: . . . .

Extra special thanks to: the editor of this book, Jillian Taylor, who has been extremely hard-working, supportive, communicative, cheerful and clever throughout the publication process and has, as far as I can remember, made no suggestions for changes that I didn't like; my book agent, Ivan Mulcahy, who lightly nudged me towards a history book while we both came to the realization that I was never going to write a novel; my wife, Victoria Coren Mitchell, for most of the good things in my life but, specifically here, for saying that I should just write a book about kings and queens because that's what people want to read; and finally to a man I have never met: Henry VIII. No, not him, he was awful. The person is Simon Winder whose book *Germania* I found so enjoyable – funny and fascinating – that it made me want to try to write something in a similar tone: a history book that aims to be funny but not spoof, irreverent but not trivial. If you hated this book, do still give his a go, because that's what I was aiming for. And if you hate his book too, you can blame him for both.

List of Illustrations

1. Anonymous illustration of King Arthur, British Library Royal MS 20 a ii, f. 4r. © British Library Board. All Rights Reserved / Bridgeman Images

2. Illustration by Richard Rowlands, 1605. © GL Archive / Alamy Stock Photo

3. From *Life and Miracles of St Cuthbert*, British Library MS Yates Thompson 26. © British Library Board. All Rights Reserved / Bridgeman Images

4. Burial mound at Sutton Hoo. © geogphotos / Alamy Stock Photo

5. Anglo-Saxon helmet. © David Lyons / Alamy Stock Photo

6. From *De Similitudinibus*, British Library MS Cotton Cleopatra C.XI. © British Library Board. All Rights Reserved / Bridgeman Images

7. *Anglo-Saxon Chronicle*, British Library Cotton MS Tiberius B.i, f.128. © Bridgeman Images

8. Offa's Dyke on Llanfair Hill, Shropshire. © ricky leaver / Alamy Stock Photo

9. Anglo-Saxon coin. © fotolincs / Alamy Stock Photo

10. Reconstructed Viking longboat, 'Hugin'. © PA Images / Alamy Stock Photo

11. Mezzotint by John Faber, 1712. National Portrait Gallery. © National Portrait Gallery, London

12. From *Abingdon Chronicle*, British Library MS Cott. Claude B.VI folio 87v. © CBW / Alamy Stock Photo

13. Alfred Jewel. Ashmolean Museum. © Ashmolean Museum / Bridgeman Images

14. Odda's Chapel in Deerhurst, Gloucestershire. © Stephen Dorey – Gloucestershire / Alamy Stock Photo

15. From *Life of St Edward the Confessor*, Cambridge University Library MS Ee.3.59. © Cambridge University Library

16. Bayeux Tapestry opening scene. Bayeux Museum. © GL Archive / Alamy Stock Photo

17. Bayeux Tapestry. Bayeux Museum. © NMUIM / Alamy Stock Photo

18. Bayeux Tapestry. Bayeux Museum. © NMUIM / Alamy Stock Photo

19. William the Conqueror by an unknown artist, *c.*1597 – 1618. National Portrait Gallery. © GL Archive / Alamy Stock Photo

20. Domesday Book. The National Archives. © The National Archives, ref. E31/2/2

21. From Peter of Langtoft's *Chronicle of England*, British Library Royal 20 A. II f.6v. © Bridgeman Images.

22. From *The Golden Book of St Albans*, British Library Cotton MS Nero D VII. © Art Collection 3 / Alamy Stock Photo

23. Copper plaque. St Julien's Cathedral in Le Mans, France. © Yogi Black / Alamy Stock Photo

24. Illustration from Cassell's *History of England* (1903). © Bridgeman Images

25. From Matthew Paris's *Historia Anglorum*, British Library Royal 14 C VII f.9. © British Library Board. All Rights Reserved / Bridgeman Images

26. From Henry of Huntingdon's *Historia Anglorum*, British Library Arundel 48 f. 168v. © British Library Board. All Rights Reserved / Bridgeman Images

27. From *St Alban's Chronicle*, MS. 6, fol.136v. Lambeth Palace Library. © Lambeth Palace Library / Bridgeman Images

28. From *Chroniques de France ou de Saint Denis*, British Library Ms. Royal 16 G VI, fol. 352v. © British Library Board. All Rights Reserved / Bridgeman Images

29. From the *Wriothesley Garter Book*, British Library Add MS 45132. © The Picture Art Collection / Alamy Stock Photo

30. Conwy Castle, Wales. © Realimage / Alamy Stock Photo

31. Sedilia, *c*.1300. Westminster Abbey. © Angelo Hornak / Alamy Stock Photo

32. From *Chronica Roffense*, British Library Cotton Nero D. II, f.182. © British Library Board. All Rights Reserved / Bridgeman Images

33. Tomb of Edward II. Gloucester Cathedral. © Angelo Hornak / Alamy Stock Photo

34. From Froissart's *Chronicles*, Bibliotheque Nationale MS Fr. 2643. © incamerastock / Alamy Stock Photo

35. From Froissart's *Chronicles*, Bibliotheque Nationale Ms Fr 2643. © Chronicle / Alamy Stock Photo

36. Engraving from *With the World's People* by John Clark Ridpath (1912). © 19th era / Alamy Stock Photo

37. Statue designed by George Cruikshank and made by Scottish sculptor Andrew Currie. Stirling. © Dorling Kindersley ltd / Alamy Stock Photo

38. From Froissart's *Chronicles*, Bibliothèque de l'Arsenal. Ms 5188. © Photo Josse / Bridgeman Images

Index